Ruins of Identity

Ruins of Identity

Ethnogenesis in the Japanese Islands

Mark J. Hudson

UNIVERSITY OF HAWAI'I PRESS
HONOLULU

Printed in the United States of America

04 03 02 01 00 99 5 4 3 2 1

Library of Congress Cataloging-in-Publication Data

Hudson, Mark, 1963-
Ruins of identity : ethnogenesis in the Japanese Islands / Mark J. Hudson.
p. cm.
Includes bibliographical references and index.
ISBN 0-8248-1930-6 (cloth : alk. paper). — ISBN 0-8248-2156-4 (paper : alk. paper)
1. Ethnology—Japan. 2. Japanese—Origin. 3. Japan—Civilization—To 1600. I. Title.
DS830.H83 1999
952—dc21 99-11829
CIP

University of Hawai'i Press books are printed on acid-free paper and meet the guidelines for permanence and durability of the Council on Library Resources.

Designed by inari

Printed by The Maple-Vail Manufacturing Group

Contents

Preface vii

1 Introduction 1

PART I *Japanese Ethnicity: Histories of a Concept*

2 Tales Told in a Dream 23

PART II *The Yayoi and the Formation of the Japanese*

3 Biological Anthropology and the Dual-Structure Hypothesis 59

4 The Linguistic Archaeology of the Japanese Islands 82

5 From Jōmon to Yayoi: The Archaeology of the First Japanese 103

6 An Emerging Synthesis? 146

PART III *Post-Yayoi Interaction and Ethnogenesis*

7 Ethnicity and the Ancient State: A Core/Periphery Approach 175

8 The Unbroken Forest?: Ainu Ethnogenesis and the East Asian World-System 206

9 Japanese Ethnicity: Some Final Thoughts 233

Postscript 245

Notes 249

Bibliography 255

Index 319

Preface

The subject of this book is the origins of the peoples of the Japanese Islands. I have, however, for the most part avoided the word "origins," since it implies a much too static concept of ethnic formation. Human populations can only be said to have origins in a very broad spatial and temporal sense. To quote Sir John Myres' conclusion to his book *Who Were the Greeks?*, ethnic groups are "ever in the process of becoming" (Myres 1930: 538). The present volume, therefore, deals with one phase in the becoming of the peoples of Japan.

Chronologically the book covers a span of over 1,500 years from about 400 BC to AD 1200. This time frame may seem somewhat idiosyncratic to anyone brought up on European history, but it reflects the integral position of the Japanese Islands in cultural developments on the Eurasian mainland. The period begins with the spread of rice farming to the Islands in the fifth to the fourth century BC, a process that was probably in turn related to the diffusion of ironworking through East Asia. The end of the period corresponds with the East Asian medieval economic revolution. By the twelfth century AD, trading contacts with China and her satellite states led to major social and ethnic changes at both the northern and the southern ends of the Japanese archipelago, in Hokkaido and Okinawa. It would be wrong to propose that 1492 is a date unimportant to East Asian history, since the arrival of the Europeans in Far Eastern waters in the early sixteenth century led to the establishment of a new, *global* trading system. As recent historical research has made abundantly clear, however, for the most part European merchants used existing Asian trade networks. No better example of this process exists than the kingdom of the Ryukyus, which became an important trading state in the early 1400s, before Columbus had even been born.

Like the ethnic groups it analyzes, this book often seemed to be "ever in the process of becoming." Its final completion gives me a chance to thank many of the people without whom it would never have been accomplished. My most heartfelt thanks must go to my parents and sister Sue and, above all, to my wife Hiroko, for their patience in the face of what must often have seemed like a strange obsession with ancient Japan. At the School of Oriental and African Studies, Professor K. N. Chaudhuri taught me that history and archaeology not only can but should mix. At Cambridge, Gina Barnes encouraged me to work on the Yayoi and has provided considerable support over the past decade. This book derives from a doctoral dissertation submitted to the Australian National University in September 1995, and a special debt of gratitude must go to my supervisors, Peter Bellwood and Ian Farrington. In Japan, invaluable assistance was provided by the staff and students of the Department of Archaeology of the University of Tokyo. Professor Okita Masa'aki and the rest of the Tenri crowd were an unfailing source of help in the Kansai. Professor Inada Takashi and the staff and students of the Department of Archaeology at Okayama University provided a friendly atmosphere in which to conduct revisions to the book in 1996–1997.

This book was kindly read in part or in whole by a number of people: Akazawa Takeru, Atholl Anderson, Robert Attenborough, Ruth Barzel, Peter Bellwood, Peter Bleed, John Caiger, Walter Edwards, Ian Farrington, Roger Green, Colin Groves, Ishida Hajime, Koizumi Junko, John Maher, Gavan McCormack, Tessa Morris-Suzuki, Richard Pearson, Igor de Rachewiltz, and Tokunaga Katsushi. None of these people should be held responsible for the often rather controversial views contained in this book. In fact, several readers disagreed with some of my conclusions, but their comments were always much appreciated.

I must also acknowledge the help of the following individuals and institutions: Bruce Batten, Chiyonobu Yoshimasa, Doi Naomi, Stuart Fiedel, Hara Kimie, Hayashi Kensaku, Simon Holledge, Ikehata Kōichi, Inoue Masataka, Simon Kaner, Katayama Kazumichi, C. T. Keally, J. E. Kidder, Kōmoto Masayuki, Josef Kreiner, Merritt Ruhlen, Nakayama Seiji, Shichida Tada'aki, Takamiya Hiroto, Toyama Shūichi, Tsude Hiroshi, Yogi Keiko, Yoshizaki Masakazu, Historical Museum of Hokkaido, Menda Board of Education, Nabunken, Department of Anatomy, Sapporo Medical University, and Department of Anatomy, Tohoku University. Yogi Keiko was not able to see this book completed, but I feel sure that no one would have been more critical of its weaknesses—not least its superficial treatment of Okinawa. Her memory is an inspiration for research still to come.

Financial support toward the revision of the manuscript in 1997 was provided by a grant from the Japanese Ministry of Education as part of a project titled "Interdisciplinary Study on the Origins of Japanese Peoples and Cultures" headed by Professor Omoto Keiichi.

NOTE ON CONVENTIONS

Japanese personal names are given in their traditional order of family name followed by given name (e.g. Akazawa Takeru). The Japanese convention of referring to premodern historical figures by their given name is also used here (e.g. Arai Hakuseki becomes Hakuseki).

1

Introduction

Summer grass:
the remains of
warriors' dreams

Matsuo Bashō (1644–1694)

In the early summer of 1689, the poet Matsuo Bashō visited the town of Hiraizumi in northern Japan during his journey up *The Narrow Road to the Deep North.* Five hundred years previously, Hiraizumi had been the capital of the powerful Northern Fujiwara clan and one of the largest cities in Japan, but now its former splendor had gone, overgrown by the summer grass of Bashō's famous poem.

The impermanence of existence is a central theme in Bashō's work. Yet within that impermanence there is also continuity, symbolized by the material traces of the past, the *ato*—the ruins or sites of history. Earlier in his journey, Bashō had come across an ancient inscribed stele at Taga castle, leading him to reflect on its historical significance: "Time passes and the world changes. The remains of the past are shrouded in uncertainty. And yet, here before my eyes was a monument which none would deny had lasted a thousand years. I felt as if I were looking into the minds of the men of old. . . . I forgot the weariness of my journey, and was moved to tears for my joy" (Keene 1955, 366). Bashō's choice of *ato* was itself derived from the medieval Japanese tradition of travel diaries, wherein the significance of a place was determined by its history—its location in time, rather than by geography. In other words, consciousness of a place was brought forth by *antecedence*

(Plutschow 1981, 22), lending in turn a sense of continuity to historical change.

Bashō's writings exemplify a number of themes dealt with in this book. In trying to grapple with the problems of ethnicity and ethnogenesis in the Japanese Islands, I am constantly confronted with the relationship between permanence and impermanence, continuity and change, reality and dreams. In adopting a primarily archaeological framework, I am particularly faced with the problem of Bashō's *ato,* the physical sites and artifacts of history and how they relate to human identities. At times, all seems like a dream. As Oscar Wilde remarked, "The actual people who live in Japan are not unlike the general run of English people; that is to say, they are extremely commonplace, and have nothing curious or extraordinary about them. In fact the whole of Japan is a pure invention. There is no such country, there are no such people" (Wilde 1911, 45). It will be argued here, however, that the imagined identities of the Japanese Islands are to some extent based on antecedence, the remains of the past. Even at Hiraizumi, excavations have uncovered remains of the Northern Fujiwara beneath Bashō's summer grass. Like Bashō, I cannot fail to be awed by the sacred sites of Japanese history that have accumulated still further layers of antecedence since the seventeenth century. Perhaps unlike Bashō, I feel no need to adhere to all the traditions surrounding these "ruins of identity"—but whether I shall succeed in breaking those bonds is for others to judge.

The focus of this book is the origins of the peoples of Japan. More precisely, the book looks at the processes of ethnogenesis—the formation of ethnic groups—in the Japanese Islands from the early agricultural Yayoi period until the beginning of the Middle Ages. The book begins in Part I with a discussion of previous theories on the formation of the Japanese people. It is argued that nationalistic ideologies have profoundly affected the course of research on this topic. The major assumptions of these ideologies are: (1) the biological, linguistic, and cultural aspects of Japanese identity overlap almost completely with each other; (2) culture and ethnos are closed, bounded units; and (3) Japanese culture is derived from several such units, but there is an essential Japanese psychic unity that permeates these various cultural building blocks right down to the concrete *kiso bunka* (basic culture) below. These are, of course, quite astonishing assumptions, but they can be found at all levels of Japanese society.[1] For example, it is accepted by many people in contemporary Japan that only ethnic Japanese can speak Japanese fluently; foreigners who become highly proficient in the language are usually seen as somehow threatening exceptions to this rule (Miller 1982, 147). There is a similar widespread assumption that people who do not *look* Japanese cannot be Japanese citizens (Yoshino 1992, 117–118). While such beliefs are naturally much less common among professional anthropologists than among the general population, their influence is still visible. Sasaki Kōmei, one of Japan's leading anthropologists, defines the Japanese as those people "who speak the Japanese language as their mother tongue, who possess traditional Japanese culture, and who think themselves to be Japanese" (Sasaki 1991b, 12). Though Sasaki admits this is a "loose" definition, in my view it is highly problematical. Today most Ainu, Okinawans, and Korean and Chinese minorities in Japan speak Japanese as their mother tongue, yet few would probably see themselves as embracing "traditional" Japanese culture, however that is defined. Many of these minorities may think of themselves as Japanese *citizens,* yet they are essentially viewed as foreigners by most "ethnic" Japanese. Sasaki's definition is essentially little changed from the more obviously nationalistic interpretation of historian Kita Sadakichi, who defined *Yamato minzoku* (the Japanese race) as "a general term for the whole populace which has lived in our island country for many years, spoken the same national language *(kokugo),* possessed the same customs, considered themselves as a single people, and also reverently accepted the unbroken imperial lineage of the emperor" (Kita 1978, [1929]: 211).

After discussing the historical development of these nationalistic views of Japanese ethnogenesis, Part II goes on to present a model for the formation of a Japanese core population in the early agricultural Yayoi period (ca. 400 BC–AD 300). The outline of this model can be summarized in a few paragraphs. As its basis, it takes the so-called dual-structure hypothesis of population history now supported by a majority of Japanese anthropologists. According to this model, the Japanese Islands were settled by populations from Southeast Asia and/or south China sometime during the Pleistocene. These peoples were the ancestors of the Jōmon people who occupied the Islands from the beginning of the Holocene until the late first millennium BC. In the Yayoi period there was an influx of Northeast Asian groups who spread rapidly through the Islands, reaching the Tohoku region by the Kofun period. The modern inhabitants of the central islands of Kyushu, Shikoku, and Honshu derive primarily from these Yayoi immigrants, although the genetic contribution of the indigenous Jōmon people is thought to increase with distance from north Kyushu—the original port of entry of the migrants. Aspects of this population model, including the concept of Yayoi immigration, have been debated in the literature for a long time. Over the past few years, however, scholars have arrived at a remarkable consensus that large-scale immigration really did occur in the Yayoi. This consensus is based on a wide range of new cranial, dental, and genetic studies that are summarized in chapter 3.

From the starting point of this hypothesis that large-scale immigration into western Japan occurred in the Yayoi, I go on to consider the linguistic and cultural aspects of that population movement. I argue that both the linguistic and the archaeological records support the two-stage biological scheme. My approach to the linguistic side is two-pronged. First, several archaeologists have recently tried to develop explicit theories for the relationship between language dispersals and human populations. Bellwood (1991, 1993a, 1993b, 1994), Renfrew (1987, 1989, 1991, 1992a, 1992b) and others have argued, I believe convincingly, that following initial human dispersal in the Pleistocene, colonization resulting from agricultural expansion was the major factor in the spread of the world's languages before AD 1500. Theoretically, therefore, initial dispersal in the Pleistocene and agricultural expansion in the Holocene should be able to explain the distribution of most languages in prehistory, at least in agricultural latitudes. With these theoretical expectations in mind, my next step is to look at the language patterning of the Japanese Islands. The presence of only three languages in the archipelago—Japanese, Ryukyuan, and Ainu—suggests that language replacement has occurred at some quite recent time in the past. If such replacement had not happened, then we would expect the language(s) of the initial Pleistocene settlers of Japan to have split into hundreds of surviving local languages. Linguists agree that modern Japanese and Ryukyuan are derived from a single parent language (Proto-Japanese) that existed sometime before the texts of the eighth century AD. Various linguistic estimates, including those from glottochronology, suggest that Proto-Japanese was spoken in or around the time of the Yayoi. It thus seems highly parsimonious to link the spread of the Japanese language through the Islands with agricultural colonization in the Yayoi. For reasons discussed in chapter 4, I argue that Ainu may be derived from a Jōmon language.

While it is important to bear in mind that the transition from Jōmon to Yayoi was a complex phenomenon that cannot be explained *solely* by migration, chapter 5 and chapter 6 argue that the archaeological record of the transition contains evidence of immigration from the Korean Peninsula, of population expansion within the Japanese Islands, and of hybridization with indigenous Jōmon peoples. The identification of population movements in prehistory is one of the hardest tasks faced by the archaeologist. In order to gain a deeper understanding of the Yayoi case, I make use of comparative analyses of migration in the Pacific, northeastern America, and Anglo-Saxon England. I believe this comparative approach to be invaluable in assessing the inevitable obscurities of the archaeological record and in judging the relationships between the biological, linguistic, and cultural data.

In Part III of the book, the emphasis shifts toward the cultural construction of ethnicity out of the basic core population that was established in the Yayoi. I argue that the cultural aspects of ethnicity should be seen as cumulative negotiation rather than as something "born" in a pristine, fully formed state. Such a view necessitates an approach to culture change that takes into account complex interactions within the larger system. Part III, therefore, adopts a world-systems approach to the problem of post-Yayoi ethnogenesis in the Japanese Islands. While world-systems theory has been widely used by archaeologists in recent years, many theoretical problems with it remain, not the least of which is the question of how it may be applied to understanding ethnogenesis. The starting point for the model developed here is Hechter's (1975) internal colonialism theory, whereby ethnic differentiation is attributed to uneven economic and political interactions between core and periphery rather than to the social isolation of the periphery.

The Ainu, who form the subject of chapter 8, provide an excellent example of the approach used in Part III. For a long time, the Ainu have been seen as pristine primitives and hunter-gatherers. As recently as 1993, Umehara wrote, "thinking I wanted to know the essence of Jōmon culture, I naturally couldn't help but pay attention to Ainu culture because the Ainu are a people who have lived in the Japanese archipelago and maintained a hunter-gatherer culture from a timeless past right until recently" (Umehara 1993, i). Similar comments are common in the literature. Watanabe Hitoshi, the late doyen of Ainu ethnography, concludes that "it seems quite reasonable to state that until 1867, the Japanese had relatively little effect upon the life of the Ainu" after himself describing the encroachment of Japanese trading posts in Hokkaido from the sixteenth century and the virtual enslavement of some Ainu in *basho* (fishing stations) in the early nineteenth century (Watanabe 1972a, 451). In contrast to such statements, chapter 8 argues that the very defining elements of the Ainu period and culture (which began around AD 1200) can be linked with a dramatic increase in Japanese trade goods flowing north as Hokkaido was exploited more and more by core regions to the south. Biologically, and probably linguistically, the Ainu appear to be descended from a Jōmon core population, but culturally we can distinguish a transition to the pattern of Ainu culture known ethnographically at the end of the Satsumon era around 1200. In others words, around 1200 the Jōmon/Ainu core population reformed itself for the first time into an etic ethnos that can be termed culturally Ainu.

PERILOUS IDEAS: JAPAN, ETHNICITY, ETHNOGENESIS

An outline of the arguments regarding Japanese ethnogenesis made in this book has been presented above, but so far the terms "Japanese" and "ethnogenesis" have not been defined in any rigorous way. Nash (1989, 1) calls "ethnicity" and "ethnic group" "among the most complicated, volatile, and emotionally charged words and ideas in the lexicon of social science." Together with "race" and "culture" they are indeed "perilous ideas" (Wolf 1994). The term ethnogenesis is equally problematical, implying an almost Biblical creation of ethnic groups that, once formed, remain forever unchanged. Needless to say, in this book ethnogenesis will be used to refer to a process rather than to an event; nevertheless, the concept of ethnogenesis remains plagued by misunderstandings, and we must begin by clarifying my use of this term.

Two recent papers by anthropologist John Moore exemplify current difficulties with the concept of ethnogenesis. Central to the whole debate is the relationship between the biological, linguistic, and cultural components of human communities. Earlier anthropology assumed that these components overlapped, archaeologists proposing that the distribution of material remains such as pottery and axes could be directly linked with past peoples. Despite a long critical tradition (e.g. Boas 1940; Leach 1954; Mongait 1968; Trigger 1968), this set of assumptions has proven remarkably persistent, not least in Japan, where it still underlies most research on Japanese origins. However, the fact that the coevolution of human biology, language, and culture can be disproved on empirical grounds means that the study of ethnic history becomes enormously complex.

Moore argues that there are two types of theories that account for the historical formation of ethnic groups: cladistic and rhizotic. Cladistic theory uses the classic family-tree model of divergence to "emphasize the significance of a historical process by which daughter populations, languages or cultures are derived from a parent group" whereas rhizotic theory uses a "river channel" model to "emphasize the extent to which each human language, culture, or population is considered to be derived from . . . several different antecedent groups" (Moore 1994b, 925). Moore himself favors the rhizotic model, arguing that the term ethnogenesis should be limited to this approach.

Moore suggests not only that most recent synthetic studies that attempt to link biology, language, and culture in prehistory rely on cladistic taxonomies, but that "Such attempts require the premise, usually implicit, that human societies have always been bounded or discrete to some extent, so that each society's language, physical type, and culture have coevolved" (Moore 1994b, 925). Moore (1994a, 14–15) notes that in some situations a cladistic model may be used effectively, but his otherwise polemical binary division is contradictory and too simplistic. In reality, cladistic and rhizotic processes are both at work in any given population. To give a linguistic example, the English language is derived from an earlier Germanic subgroup, a genetic relationship that is best illustrated using a cladistic model; at the same time, however, a rhizotic model would be more appropriate to diagram the influence of borrowing from Norman French. Similarly, ethnic groups as a whole undergo processes of both divergence and integration (Bromley 1983, 11–12; Horowitz 1975, 115). The European colonization of Australia, for instance, can be seen as, on the one hand, the process of divergence from parent European societies, and, *at the same time*, of integration into a new ethnic identity (Table 1.1).

TABLE 1.1

PROCESSES OF ETHNIC FUSION AND FISSION

ASSIMILATION		DIFFERENTIATION	
Amalgamation	*Incorporation*	*Division*	*Proliferation*
A+B→C	A+B→A	A→BC	A→A+B
			(A+B→A+B+C)
Two or more groups unite to form a new, larger group.	One group assumes the identity of another.	One group divides into two or more component parts.	One or more groups (often two) produce an additional group from within their ranks.

Source: Horowitz (1975, 116).

That Moore has not understood these basic processes is implied by his contrast between linguistic differentiation due to "slow cladistic" rather than "dramatic ethnogenetic" developments (Moore 1994a, 18). Nothing in cladistics says that change has to be slow. Linguistic change is, of course, the result of human behavior, *but both cladistic and rhizotic models of linguistic relationships diagram the history of languages rather than the underlying behavior*. The task facing the anthropologist is that of how to relate the history of biological, linguistic, and cultural relationships to past human behavior. As noted, Moore reserves the term ethnogenesis for his favored rhizotic approach. Since I argue that rhizotic taxonomies are not better but are rather simply different models of the past, I cannot accept this usage, and consequently in this book ethnogenesis refers to the process of ethnic formation in its broad sense. A more precise definition is hindered by debate over the meaning of the term "ethnic group" or *ethnos* (plural *ethnoi*).

Within Western social science, reaction to earlier views of the coevolution of biology, language, and culture has led to a recent shift toward emic rather than etic categorization, toward "identification itself rather than the content of identity" (Friedman 1994, 174). This change in emphasis is reflected by the neologism "ethnicity," which began attaining popularity only in the 1960s but which is now a central theme of social science research. Unlike earlier concepts such as those of "race" and "tribe," an ethnicity is held to be determined much more by the *belief* in a common heritage than in actual lines of descent. An ethnos can thus be defined as "a collectivity within a larger society having real or putative common ancestry, memories of a shared historical past, and a cultural focus on one or more symbolic elements defined as the epitome of their peoplehood" (Schermerhorn 1970, 12). Theoretically, ethnic community in a shared historical descent can exist without actual genetic continuity. In such cases the presence or absence of population continuity is irrelevant, since ethnicities "are constituted, not by lines of physical descent, but by the sense of continuity, shared memory and collective destiny, i.e. by lines of cultural affinity embodied in distinctive myths, memories, symbols and values retained by a given cultural unit of population" (Smith 1991, 29).

This approach to ethnicity leads to all sorts of problems for the study of ethnogenesis. To begin with, it is clear that prehistoric emic identities are completely beyond reach. Even premodern societies lack sufficient documentary records to enable us to reconstruct ethnic self-identities—except perhaps for a very limited sector of society. Moore (1994b, 939) writes that, "The basic problem for all of us, cladists or ethnogeneticists, is determining the relationship between Ethnos A, observed somewhere in time and space, and Ethnos B, observed perhaps at a different location and later in time." If an ethnos is defined as an emic collectivity, however, we have no way of even identifying such units outside the ethnographic record. Moore himself ignores this problem, barely pausing to define the ethnos as "an idealized (and perhaps nonexistent) unit of human society, the irreducible social species" (Moore 1994a, 13). It seems to me that the only way to resolve this dilemma is to somehow incorporate the objective, etic elements—what Nash (1989, 5) calls the "building blocks"—of ethnicity into our analysis.

There are several theoretical reasons accounting for the necessity of a shift away from a predominantly emic view of ethnicity. First, an emic perspective is unable to explain the historical causes behind the formation of ethnic groups. Typically, ethnicity is seen either as resulting from a priori, "primordial" attachments or else is reduced to the false ideology of "instrumentalism" (cf. McKay 1982; Yoshino 1992, 70–74). Bentley (1987) has tried to explain ethnic identity through Bourdieu's concept of the *habitus*, but as Shennan (1989, 16) notes, "having provided a basis for the generation of ethnic sentiment, Bentley still has to deal with the question of why and how an ethnic sentiment comes into existence." The answer, as Shennan (1989, 16) realizes, is a historical perspective, but most discussions of ethnicity in recent Euro-American anthropology ignore this historical aspect and concentrate on the synchronic construction of identity in relation to other groups. The irony here is that anthropologists and historians recognize the importance of history in legitimizing the ethnos (e.g. Alonso 1988; Foster 1991, 240–242; Hobsbawm and Ranger 1983) and archaeology, with its apparently scientific basis, has a particularly central role to play in such imaginings (e.g. Dietler 1994; Edwards 1991; Anderson 1991, 178–184; Fawcett 1996). An historical dimension to the study of ethnogenesis was central to Soviet anthropology (Libby 1962; Dragadze 1980; Petrova-Averkieva 1980).[2] In the Soviet tradition, emic self-awareness was important, but it was not the central defining feature of an ethnos. Instead, the ethnos was thought to possess a nucleus of a stable common culture that reproduced itself through endogamy in the sense of preferential marriage within a community (Bromley 1974a). Although the long tradition of Soviet and Russian research on ethnicity and ethnogenesis has much to recommend it, the whole idea of the common culture of an ethnos remains rather vague and depends upon a priori assumptions about its stability. Bromley (1974b, 66), for example, writes that "no ethnos is either eternal or immutable, but this does not contradict the fact that stability is a characteristic feature of [an] ethnos. . . ." In reality, of course, the stability or otherwise of an ethnos is one of the very variables that we hope to discover.

As we are all too aware these days, a group's *perceived* identity is often of great significance and may even be sufficient cause for genocide. Nevertheless, ethnicity probably always involves some objective elements. The Jewish nationalist Ahad Ha'am (1856–1927) claimed that national identity depends "on no external or objective actuality. If I feel the spirit of Jewish nationality in my heart so that it stamps all my inward life with its seal, then the spirit of Jewish nationality exists in me; and its existence is not at an end even if all my Jewish contemporaries should cease to feel it in their hearts" (cited in Kedourie 1960, 81). Of course, anyone can convert to Judaism as a religion, and the example may not be a good one; nevertheless a white Anglo-Saxon or a black American cannot currently become fully Japanese or Korean however much he or she might identify with those groups. In other words, the subjective elements of ethnicity are mediated, to a degree that is itself culturally determined, by reference to more objective biological, linguistic, and cultural markers.

As mentioned, with the shift of focus to the practice rather than the content of ethnicity, there have been calls to study the social processes of the construction and naming of ethnic groups. Johnson (1994) does this effectively for modern Taiwan, discussing Taiwanese nationalism as a fiction, an impossible contradiction between claims of an ancient autochthonous community and the reality of a particular political origin in the late 1940s. Yet the construction of Taiwanese identity only becomes a possible focus of research because the recent history of that island is well known. To take another example (discussed in more detail in Part III), the Northern Fujiwara appear to have identified themselves with the Emishi "barbarians" of eastern Japan rather than with the ethnic Japanese, but research on the mummified remains of the family has shown that a Kyoto Japanese origin is probable. The point is not whether the Northern Fujiwara were or were not Japanese, but rather that the practice of ethnicity only makes sense in terms of social action. In this case, for example, an Emishi self-identification may have been used to oppose Japanese power. In analyzing the relationship between image and reality, many recent scholars have concentrated on the construction of the former, but such analysis is not possible without a detailed knowledge of the underlying reality.

A final reason for my belief that we should move away from a strictly emic view of ethnicity relates to the contemporary political usages of identity. Friedman (1994, 174) writes that "One cannot make headway in ethnic conflict by trying to convince the adversaries that the contents of their identities are quite mixed up." This is rather like the debate over the historicity of the Holocaust: in the end some people will believe what they want to regardless of the facts—but that should not stop the study and broadcast of those facts. A long-term, etic view of ethnicity, with its inescapable conclusion that ethnic groups change quite profoundly over time, is surely the most effective theoretical deconstruction of ethnic factionalism that there is. Furthermore, the emic ethnicities of powerful nations can easily become hegemonic ideologies when applied to their weaker neighbors. The current Japanese assumption that the Ainu and their prehistoric Jōmon ancestors are ethnically Japanese (discussed in Part I) is an excellent example. At present there is a conceptual break between Jōmon and Ainu. This break is well illustrated in the display of the Historical Museum of Hokkaido in Sapporo, where the Ainu exhibit appears suddenly, without clear precedent, in the stone tools and pottery of the previous display cases. If the Ainu were linked to the Jōmon—one of the most affluent foraging societies known to prehistory—then contemporary views of their status would be transformed. Because the Ainu are a small, disadvantaged minority, however, their emic protestations that they are *not* Japanese fall largely on deaf ears. Selective and selected memories are a sine qua non of modern nationalism, making the historian's task of remembrance more essential than ever.

CORE POPULATIONS AND ETHNOI

Rather than concentrating on ethnicity in terms of its now-common use to mean a self-identity, therefore, much of this book will focus on the formation and development of core biological and linguistic *populations*. Several explanatory points need to be made in this respect. The population concept is used in the human sciences in a number of ways, ranging from the purely arbitrary to the strictly genetic and ecological. In most cases, however, such populations involve a hierarchical classification. For example, genetic, or Mendelian, populations are defined by the extent to which individuals share common genes, but within this general definition there exists a hierarchy of populations ranging from the nuclear family to the human species as a whole (Harrison and Boyce 1972, 3). The same sort of hierarchy also exists for social or ethnic groups, with age, class, gender, and occupation serving as some of the subsets (e.g. Barth 1984). *There is no question, therefore, of there ever having been a single, homogeneous Japanese or Jōmon population.* The concept of a "Japanese population" is used heuristically to refer to a hierarchy of groups that were the biological, linguistic, and cultural ancestors of the modern Japanese in a way that the Jōmon and Palaeolithic inhabitants of the Islands were not.

A summary of the three levels of ethnicity discussed in this book is shown in Table 1.2. In using the concept of "core populations" I am not arguing for any sort of biological reductionism. The concept is simply a practical, preliminary

TABLE 1.2

A THREE-TIERED HIERARCHY OF ETHNIC CONCEPTS

JAPANESE	THEORETICAL CONCEPTS	AINU
Japanese-speaking Yayoi immigrants (some Jōmon intermarriage)	CORE POPULATION (Biological and often linguistic continuity)	Jōmon population (Proto-Ainu and other languagues)
Japanese cultures (regional and temporal variations on basis of agrarian civilization in the Chinese sphere)	ETIC ETHNOS (Cultural patterns: punctuated evolution within the world-system; in prehistory usually conforms to an archaeological culture)	Ainu culture (from ca. 1200)
"Original Palaeolithic inhabitants of the Islands"	EMIC ETHNOS ("Imagined" self-identity)	"Indigenous people of Hokkaido"

step toward a fuller analysis of ethnogenesis. It will be argued that the more "objective" aspects of ethnic identity are part of the same overall phenomenon as are the subjective, socially constructed ones. For want of a better term, I call this phenomenon "ethnicity," but I am not suggesting that these aspects must necessarily overlap. Rather, since ethnicity is always undergoing processes of negotiation and reconstruction, I argue that both approaches are important. Even though there is a basic biological and linguistic continuity, for example, the emic ethnicity of a fifth-century Saxon, an Elizabethan Englishman, and a Briton in the 1990s would be quite different. Williams (1985) makes this point effectively for Wales, discussing the various types of historical Welshness. In both the English and Welsh cases there is a *core* of biological and linguistic continuity, although these have also been subject to quite major modifications, for instance through Viking and Norman settlement. The medieval incursions of Vikings and Normans are arguably not perceived as significant to *contemporary* English ethnicity, but we cannot understand the historical formation of English identity without taking those incursions into account.

While establishing the concept of core populations may be a useful preliminary step, at some stage we need to consider the question of how a certain core population may relate to an ethnos as it is usually defined. The levels of ethnicity shown in Table 1.2 must be perceived as shifting sets rather than as fixed types. Within the framework, the individual constructs identities through contextual reference to each level. The analogy of a painting may be useful here: if the landscape being painted corresponds to the "core population," then the emotions and perceptions of the painter are the emic ethnicity and the style of the finished work the etic ethnicity. The major problem with this analogy, of course, is that in reality emic ethnicity occurs at a group rather than—or as well as—an individual level. That is, an emic ethnos is an imagined *community* in Anderson's (1991, 6) sense of the term. In the last chapter of this book I attempt a few speculations regarding the possible nature of Japanese emic ethnicity in the premodern era. I conclude that the core population here termed "Japanese" almost certainly did not see itself as a single ethnos until the twentieth century, and furthermore that it is impossible to assign any distinctive cultural criteria that might give a unity to this population throughout the whole of its history. This book thus takes the basic stance that, although the historical context of a particular culture is important, no society has an immutable cultural essence. Instead, ethnicity (both etic and emic) is discussed here in terms of cumulative definition through interaction. Ethnic identity is continually recreated through interaction within and without the society concerned. In other words, I focus on sociocultural processes *between* rather than simply within ethnic groups, on complex ethnic formations in a multiethnic society rather than on isolated "tribes"(cf. Cohen 1978, 383-384). As Lockwood (1984, 4) writes, "Ethnicity is peoples in contact. No ethnic group, by definition, can exist in isolation." This is hardly a new idea—in fact it can be said to mark the central difference between studies of ethnicity before and after Barth's (1969) pathbreaking work (Lockwood 1984, 1). Rather than focusing on bilateral relations between two groups, however, I extend this approach to consider ethnogenesis within the larger world-system, looking at the role of interaction between core and periphery in the formation of new ethnic identities.

The approach to ethnicity espoused here differs quite fundamentally from that used in most Japanese scholarship and popular discourse. As noted above, many Japanese people continue to believe themselves to be an essentially unchanging, bounded unit, with near total overlap between biological population, language, culture, nation, and ethnos. In other words, and here the Japanese differ from many Third-World scholars who see the tribal concept as a colonial imposition, the Japanese have tended to exalt a view of their culture that emphasizes those features listed in the tribal column in Table 1.3. Although the role of outside influences in the origins of the Japanese is widely accepted, the idea that, once formed, the Japanese were an isolated, bounded, and traditional nation is widespread. While acknowledging it as a norm that

TABLE 1.3

THE ANTHROPOLOGICAL SHIFT FROM "TRIBE" TO "ETHNICITY": SOME BASIC EPISTEMOLOGICAL FEATURES

"TRIBE"	"ETHNIC"
isolated	non-isolated
primitive-atavistic	contemporary
non-Western	universally applicable
objective emphasis	subjectivist emphasis or both objectivist and subjectivist
bounded units	a unit only in relation to others; boundaries shift
systemic	degree of systemic quality varies

Source: Cohen (1978, 384).

is not shared by all members of the society, the Japanese ideal of their ethnicity can thus be described as tribal. Rather than referring merely to an isolated ethnos however, the Japanese tribe takes on the more specialized meaning of the word in its Middle Eastern context, that is, as a large, bounded political community based on descent from a common ancestor (cf. Crone 1986, 51; 1993, 356). Of course, I am not suggesting that the Japanese were really organized along the lines of Middle Eastern tribes, but rather that the tribal metaphor best encapsulates a certain view of an unambiguous nation of people related by blood to the emperor, who was in turn descended from the gods through the first emperor Jimmu. The various forms of this tribal view of Japaneseness are discussed at some length in Part I.

THE JAPANESE AND THE JŌMON

The major focus of this book is the formation of a Japanese core population in the Yayoi period and the influence of that population on other ethnic groups in the Japanese Islands. It is argued that, as a result of basic biological and linguistic continuities, "Japanese" is the most appropriate designation for the core population formed in the Yayoi. This use of "Japanese" is similar to the use of "English" in the example given above. Today both English and Japanese are controversial terms when applied to all the inhabitants of Britain and of Japan, respectively. Although they are all citizens of the modern Japanese nation-state, the Ainu and the Okinawans, like the Welsh, the Irish, and the Scots in Britain, differentiate themselves ethnically from the so-called mainland Japanese *(Wajin)*.[3] Just as the term English can be used to refer to a specific ethnic group in the past, that is, the Anglo-Saxon invaders of the British Isles, however, so too is Japanese used here to refer to a specific population that spoke an earlier form of the Japanese language and is biologically closely related to the present mainland Japanese. Of course, both English and Japanese are really only convenient labels with which to refer to what were internally heterogenous and changing groups. Nevertheless, these terms can be assigned a certain historical utility.

The word "Japan" and its European variants are derived from Marco Polo's corruption of a Southern Chinese pronunciation of the characters 日本 that are now read *Nihon* or *Nippon* in Japanese (Miller 1967, 11). These characters were first used by the rulers of the Yamato state in the late seventh century AD, but there is controversy over their meaning and pronunciation in antiquity (Amino 1992a, 124–132). Perhaps the most likely scenario is that 日本 (meaning "sun root") was adopted by the Yamato state to replace the earlier characters 大倭, which were felt to be unflattering. At first, 日本 like 大倭 was probably read as "Yamato," although by the Heian era the Sino-Japanese reading *Nihon* was also common. However it was read, the name 日本 does not seem to have become a fixed or widely accepted term outside the Japanese court until at least the medieval era. As late as the fourteenth century, for example, raiders from the Japanese Islands were called Wakō (Wa pirates) using the old name Wa 倭 instead of *Nihon:*

> Neither the people of the Korean Peninsula nor the Koryŏ government, the Chinese people nor the Ming government called the Wakō "Nihon pirates." Six or seven hundred years after the court of the Yamato/Ritsuryō state had established the name "Nihon" and used it in diplomatic relations, the people of medieval East Asia called the attacking Japanese pirates, "Wa pirates" (Kadowaki 1992, 1).

Traditional views of what is commonly known as Japan have emphasized a homogenous nation centered around a unified Japanese state. The concept of the Japanese people has become almost inseparable from the political state of Japan. This (mis)use of the term "Japan" has served to mask the ethnic and cultural diversity of the premodern Islands and to legitimize the ideology of the emperor. A number of Japanese scholars, most eloquently Amino Yoshihiko, now argue that Japan should only be used to refer to the state of that name—or should even be rejected entirely (see Amino 1992a, 132). Amino's comments gain extra pertinence in the light of a recent trend toward using

Japan and Japanese in a more inclusive sense than ever before. As discussed in Part I, until the 1930s Japanese anthropologists differentiated strictly between Japanese and non-Japanese peoples and cultures in the Islands. In reaction to the then-dominant imperialist view of Japanese history, however, Yamanouchi Sugao and other archaeologists made a conscious break from such ethnic interpretations of prehistory. After World War II, it became common to use the term Japanese to mean *all* the inhabitants of the Islands, past and present. In his 1951 book *Nihon Minzoku no Keisei (The Formation of the Japanese People),* Tōma Seita takes the basic approach that "The Japanese have inhabited this Japanese archipelago from the beginning" (Tōma 1951, 1). Historian Inoue Kiyoshi (1963, 1) writes, "From as far back in our history as it is possible to go through until the present, we Japanese have lived as the same race *(shuzoku)* in the same region—the present Japanese archipelago." The influence of this view in contemporary Japan is shown by Bornoff's (1991, 25) description of a small boy's visit to the 1988 Tokyo National Science Museum exhibition on Japanese origins:

> "Although we are Jōmon people," [the boy] read aloud from a notice flanking the exhibit, "we can speak Japanese." When [one of the female attendants pretending to be a Jōmonette] congratulated him effusively on his reading abilities, the little boy cried out "*Yappari, Nihonjin-da!*" with a mixture of surprise and relief: "I thought so—she's Japanese!" The thought that Jōmon people might have been otherwise, even to a small boy, is disturbing.

The antiscientific tautology inherent in this use of "Japanese" seems lost on most users. Sahara (1993, 48), for instance, includes a footnote in a general history of Japan to explain that the term Japanese means a specific ethnic group with a shared culture and language, but that in his chapter Japanese will simply be used to mean the ancient humans who lived in the Islands. The implication, from this one of Japan's leading archaeologists, is that these definitions amount to the same thing.

My use of the word "Japanese" in this book avoids both the exclusive and the inclusive trends of the recent literature. The inclusive approach of Sahara and others hides the ethnic diversity and conflict that is an important part of the history of the Islands. As employed by Sahara, the term seems to be more liberal than the meaning implied by its traditional use; however, because it incorporates the primitive Other into the Japanese Self, it is one of the best indicators of the success of the agricultural mainland Japanese who, having almost totally replaced the biological, linguistic, and cultural identities of the other Islanders, have now begun to incorporate them into a monolithic history to an extent never before achieved. The exclusivist position of Amino, on the other hand, places too much emphasis on the ideologies of Nihon by linking the Japanese people to the Japanese state (see also Kikuchi 1994, 33–34). In Amino's writings, "Japan" is rejected because of its powerful connotations, but, while the Japanese state (i.e., Nihon) did not exist before about AD 700, the people who formed that state did.

In this book the Japanese are defined as the population that was formed in the Yayoi period through the immigration of Peninsular farmers and their subsequent mixing with indigenous Jōmon people. The contribution of the Jōmon people to the Japanese varied by region, but in much of the western archipelago was probably less than one quarter (see chapter 3). It is important to stress that over much of the past 2,000 years this Japanese *population* has probably not seen itself as a single ethnic group (see chapter 9). Even as regards biology and language, I am not suggesting that the Japanese were ever completely differentiated from their neighbors or that the biological and linguistic criteria coincide completely. As well as genetic influence from the Jōmon people on the Yayoi/Japanese core population, some linguistic borrowing from the Jōmon languages cannot be ruled out.

The cultural manifestations of the Japanese are irrelevant to the definition of that population used here. The association of the Japanese with rice has long been a potent one. In his *Kokyō Nanajūnen,* folklorist Yanagita Kunio (1875–1962) writes, "I am convinced that the Japanese are a people indivisible from that thing called rice" (cited in Sasaki 1993, 225). By my definition, they would still be Japanese even if they had subsisted entirely on pineapples and pistachio nuts. Of course, rice cultivation and other aspects of Japanese culture have influenced the ways in which the Japanese people view their identity and, in turn, the ways in which they are viewed by others. These cultural traits, however, have always been in a process of flux and negotiation, and to *define* the Japanese by such traits is a form of circular reasoning that only serves to support the myths of Japanese uniqueness.

There is, however, one cultural trait that we are justified in including in any definition of the Japanese agriculture. The *type* of agriculture is irrelevant; what is of primary significance is the presence of an expanding, predatory farming *system*. The history of the world since the Neolithic has been one of the expansion of farmers at the expense of nonfarming peoples. There are now no hunter-gathering peoples unaffected by farmers, and during the next century the world's few remaining hunter-gatherers may totally disappear.

Many of these farmers have, of course, reached an industrial level and live in a world where their influence on nonfarmers has increased phenomenally. For example, Japanese and other companies exploit Southeast Asian rainforests, forcing foragers off their land thousands of kilometers from the companies' home countries. Despite such complexities, however, the basic process of expansion is the same, and in this respect industrial cultures can be considered advanced agricultural ones.

The Japanese Islands have been no exception to this worldwide phenomenon. Full-scale food production began in the Islands in the Yayoi period (Hudson 1990a). As well as being the basic cause of the expansion of the Japanese population, agriculture provided the basis for the growth of social complexity that culminated in the Ritsuryō state of the eighth century AD. This social complexity in turn brought about the conditions for the complex processes of ethnogenesis that occurred in the Islands after the Yayoi. This is not to say, however, that the *form* of these cultural developments has any sort of inherent link with agriculture. As Gellner (1988, 19) notes, agriculture establishes the essential conditions, but it does not predetermine the forms that culture will take. To some historians of Japan my emphasis on agriculture may seem to contradict the recent stress given to nonagricultural peoples by Amino (1984, 1994, 1995, 1996) and others. Umehara (1991, 163) writes, "Hitherto, understanding of Japan and Japanese culture has assumed that Japanese culture is unitary and above all based on agriculture." But to say that Japanese culture was based *above all* on agriculture is a truism that should not excuse our ignoring the nonfarming peoples of the Islands. Fishermen, nuns, and actors all lived in an archipelago where food production was the basis of political power and were all part of what was *above all* an agricultural society.

Apart from the Japanese, the other core population discussed in this book is the Jōmon. My use of these terms may appear contradictory: if there is a core of biological and linguistic continuity between Jōmon and Ainu, should not the Jōmon people be designated as an "Ainu population"? In view of the biological evidence for Jōmon-Ainu affinity discussed in chapter 3, it may indeed be appropriate to refer to the Jōmon people as Ainu. That this has not yet happened is almost certainly due more to the ideological factors discussed in Part I than to any scientific reasons. There are several problems, however, with a too-hasty Jōmon=Ainu identification. To begin with, Hokkaido was essentially prehistoric until the nineteenth century, and the exact degree of continuity between, say, the Epi-Jōmon and Satsumon periods relies on still-debated archaeological and anthropological interpretations. Second, and more important, we do not know when the hypothetical Jōmon/Ainu population was first formed or when the Ainu language was first spoken. For these reasons, it may presently be best to limit the term "Ainu" to the period and culture of that name in order to test more synthetic hypotheses about Ainu origins.

PART I

Japanese Ethnicity

Histories of a Concept

2

Tales Told in a Dream

[Arai] Hakuseki set out to demonstrate that the "deities" of [the Age of the Gods] were neither divine entities operating outside the scope of the will of heaven nor cosmological or metaphysical elements belonging to the realm of heaven itself. The former notion—that of the original Kojiki *and* Nihon shoki *accounts—he termed the products of the "naive and credulous" people of antiquity, who, in transmitting the events of the past, had turned history into a "tale told in a dream."*

Kate Wildman Nakai, "The naturalization of Confucianism in Tokugawa Japan: The problem of Sinocentrism"

This chapter argues that the course of research on ethnogenesis in the Japanese Islands has been strongly influenced by nationalististic discourses in Japanese society. It is not suggested that Japanese archaeologists and anthropologists as a whole have consciously supported the emperor-centered nationalism of the Japanese state. As a generalization, the opposite is true, but nationalism has always provided a context for debates on prehistory. In particular, a primordialist view of ethnicity, the view that the Japanese *Volk* was created at a single time in antiquity and has continued to be a bounded and essentially unchanging essence ever since, will be shown to have very deep roots in the Japanese tradition and to have played an important role in debates on ethnogenesis.

A three-stage chronological division is a useful way of ordering the material discussed here. The rise of the nativist Kokugaku (National Learning) movement and the growing significance of the Ainu are the major themes of the first stage, which spans the period from about 1600 until the eve of the introduction of scientific archaeology into Japan. The second stage lasts from 1877 to 1935 and marks a new intensity in the debate over Japanese origins that arose as a result of the influence of the new fields of archaeology and anthropology. Stage 2 was the time of transition between a textual and a truly archaeological approach to the past. Stage 3, which began with the Minerva Debate of 1936 and continues today, is the era of scientific archaeology on an increasingly elaborate scale, but it is also a stage of complex discourse between nationalism and identity. Of these three stages, only the second saw a firm conception of a non-Japanese people inhabiting the Islands before the arrival of the Japanese themselves. For most Japanese scholars of the first and third stages, all ancient inhabitants of the Islands are ethnic Japanese.

STAGE 1: JIMMU, WU TAIBO, AND NATIVIST DISCOURSE, 1600–1876

Before the introduction of archaeology and anthropology, ancient Japanese and Chinese texts were the main source of information about the origins of the Japanese people. The early chapters of the *Kojiki* (AD 712) and the *Nihon Shoki* (720) describe the creation of the Islands in the Age of the Gods, followed by the eastward advance of the first human emperor Jimmu from Kyushu into the Kinai region and his subjugation of the primitive tribes he found along the way (cf. Aston 1972, 1: 1–137; Philippi 1968, 47–182). Traditionally, Jimmu's conquest has been seen as marking the beginning of the Japanese people in the Islands. While interpretations of this myth have changed over the centuries, its significance remains unchallenged with, for example, Umehara (1990, 14) arguing that it reflects Yayoi colonization at the expense of the Jōmon people. National Foundation Day, a national holiday celebrated on February 11 to commemorate Jimmu's ascension in 660 BC, was revived by the Japanese government as recently as 1966 (Yoshino 1992, 207).

An understanding of the two major philosophical schools of the Tokugawa period (1600–1867) is essential if one is to comprehend Japanese views of their origins and of antiquity during Stage 1. Confucianism was the first of these schools; the second was the Kokugaku movement. For present purposes, the most important difference between the two schools was the degree of emphasis given to continental influences on Japanese history. Both the tradition and the actual texts of Chinese historical writing were central to the Confucianist approach, whereas Kokugaku nativists did their best to play down the influence of China on Japanese history.

An excellent example of differing Tokugawa approaches to Japanese origins is provided by the debate over Wu Taibo (Brownlee 1988, 41; Kracht 1986, 140–141; Miyazaki 1988, 38–41; Nakai 1980, 188–195; Webb 1958, 20–21). Taibo is mentioned in several early Chinese texts as an ancestor of the Zhou royal lineage who gave up his legitimate rights of succession in deference to his father, who wanted his second son to succeed. The official histories of the Jin and Liang dynasties follow the now lost *Wei Lue* in noting that the Japanese saw themselves as descendants of Taibo. Similar stories describe the exploits of a son of Shaokang of the legendary Xia dynasty and the Qin Daoist exile Xufu.

The Taibo story was openly criticized as early as the fourteenth century by Kitabatake Chikafusa (1293–1354) in his *Jinnō Shōtoki (Chronicle of the Direct Descent of Gods and Sovereigns):*

> One Chinese source states: "The Japanese are descended from . . . [Taibo] . . . of Wu," but this assertion has absolutely no basis in fact. It was also claimed in ancient times that the Japanese were of the same stock as the people of Korea. . . . After the separation of heaven and earth, [the god] Susanoo-no-mikoto did in fact go to Korea. Hence the assertion that the Korean people are also descended from [the gods] is not really so incredible. Yet however plausible, even this assertion was rejected long ago. *Since the Japanese are descendants of the* [gods], . . . *how could they possibly derive from* [*Taibo*] *of Wu, who lived in a much later age* (Varley 1980, 104, emphasis added)?

However, a hypothetical reconstruction by Confucianist Hayashi Razan (1583–1657) of the views of a medieval monk who had reputedly written a book arguing that Taibo could be identified with the *Kojiki/Nihon Shoki* god Ninigi-no-mikoto, led to the story becoming a subject of controversy in the seventeenth and eighteenth centuries (Nakai 1980, 189). Although he stressed that it was no more than a private opinion, Razan argued that Ninigi and Jimmu may have been derived from Taibo (Tsunoda et al. 1958, 358–360). In his *Shōkōhatsu* (*A Blunt Discharge of Words;* 1781), Tō Teikan (1732–1797) was less circumspect than Razan, proposing that Jimmu was related to Taibo, whose descendants had reached Kyushu from China by way of the Ryukyus. Teikan derived various aspects of Japanese culture from Korea as well as from China and proposed that the date ascribed to the ascension of Jimmu in the Nara texts was 600 years too early and should really be 60 BC (see Hoshino 1980, 18–19; Torii 1926, 60–76).

Razan and other Confucianists' use of the Taibo myth can be seen as an attempt to bolster Japanese imperial prestige through an appeal to Confucian values (Nakai 1980, 189–190; Webb 1958, 21). In the *Analects,* Confucius himself describes Taibo as a paragon of virtue: "The Master said, Of [Taibo] it may indeed be said that he attained to the very highest pitch of moral power. No less than three times he renounced the sovereignty of all things under Heaven, without the people getting a chance to praise him for it" (Waley 1938, 132). A number of Confucian scholars, most notably Arai Hakuseki (1657–1725), however, did not accept a Chinese origin for the Japanese people (Miyazaki 1988, 41). Hakuseki specifically rejected the Chinese accounts of Taibo, Shaokang, and Xufu as progenitors of the Japanese imperial family, but in his *Koshitsū Wakumon* (1716) he suggests that certain Kyushu chieftains may have been descended from Taibo or Shaokang (Arai 1906, 390). Tokugawa Mitsukuni (1628–1701), patron of the Confucian history the *Dai Nihonshi,* was astounded by support for the Taibo story. "What sort of nonsense is this?" he asked in 1670. "This is like some foreign book calling the Heavenly (i.e., Japanese) Dynasty an offshoot of the [Zhou] line. This idea comes from a mistaken tradition entirely unworthy of credence" (Webb 1958, 21).

Kokugaku scholars did not look very favorably on the legends of Wu Taibo and the other proposed Chinese "ancestors," either. For nativists such as Moto'ori Norinaga, it was the very fact that the Japanese emperors could boast an unbroken line of descent back to the sun goddess Amaterasu that gave Japan her innate superiority. Norinaga was so outraged by Teikan's *Shōkōhatsu* that he wrote a detailed attack on the book entitled *Kenkyō jin* or *Silencing a Lunatic* (1785) (see Moto'ori 1972, 273–303). The nativist agenda, however, went much further than mere name calling. It aimed at the removal of the Japanese "from the Other [mainly China] and from both history and culture" by emphasizing "those aspects that made all Japanese irreducibly Japanese—the same and thereby different from the Other" (Harootunian 1988, 409). Even the most superficial knowledge of Japanese history made it clear that Japan's debt to China and Korea was enormous. In denying these influences, the nativists also had to deny the real complexities of Japanese history in order to construct a new, purely "Japanese" culture. Though it harkened back to the Age of the Gods before Chinese influences, this new identity was pure only in the way it was imagined. Norinaga "often likened the *Kojiki* to the 'clear mirror' in which the image of the age of [the gods] is reflected. The task to which Norinaga dedicated most of his life was to clarify and disclose the 'image' as it is, by wiping the 'dust' or 'veil' of the 'Chinese spirit' from the 'mirror'" (Matsumoto 1970, 80). In reality, the nativists saw only their own nostalgic reflection, yet in their remarkably successful construction of Japanese identity they created a powerful, imperialist myth of common descent and superiority.

The following passage from the *Kodō Taii (Summary of the Ancient Way)* by Hirata Atsutane (1776–1843) leaves no doubt as to the nationalistic appeal of Tokugawa nativism:

> People all over the world refer to Japan as the Land of the Gods, and call us the descendants of the gods. Indeed, it is exactly as they say: our country, as a special mark of favor from the heavenly gods, was begotten by them, and there is thus so immense a difference between Japan and all the other countries as to defy comparison. Ours is a splendid and blessed country, . . . and we, down to the most humble man and woman, are the descendants of the gods (Tsunoda et al. 1958, 544).

Similar ideologies have been used in many parts of the world through history, but few have been as successful as the Japanese "myth of uniqueness." As we shall see later in this chapter, even after the diverse roots of Japanese culture became widely accepted, the idea that a "pure," unitary culture was formed out of those roots remained—and continues to remain—a powerful one.

European Perspectives

Works by early European visitors to Japan reflect various influences on their interpretations of Japanese origins. The Portuguese Jesuit João Rodrigues concluded that Japan was settled by different continental peoples at different times in the past. He argued that in addition to the Chinese and Koreans who settled in the western archipelago, Tartars from "the Tartar island called Ezo [i.e., Hokkaido]" settled north Honshu (Cooper 1973, 45), an idea that probably reflected contemporary Japanese beliefs that Ezo was linked to the mainland (cf. Kamiya 1994):

> It is true that the Japanese have been subject to one leader or king above all the rest, with the same language and general customs

> throughout all the kingdom; nevertheless it is well known to anybody who has seen all of Japan that *each region has many special things similar to those parts whence they were peopled*, and that there are differences between some regions and others (João Rodrigues, 1561?–1633; Cooper 1973, 46, emphasis added).

Although Rodrigues supported the legends of Wu Taibo and Xufu (cf. Cooper 1973, 39–43), German physician Engelbert Kaempfer (1651–1716) argued against a Chinese origin for the Japanese because of what he saw as irreconcilable differences in language, religion, and "civil customs and way of life" (Kaempfer 1906, 133–138). Instead, Kaempfer proposed a Babylonian origin:

> In the first Ages of the World, not long after the Deluge, when the . . . Babylonians [were] dispers'd all over the World, . . . then the Japanese also set out on their Journey. . . . after many years travelling, . . . they alighted at this remote part of the World [and] being well pleas'd with its situation and fruitfulness, they resolv'd to chuse it for the place of their abode; . . . consequently they are an original Nation, no ways indebted to the Chinese for their descent and existence. . . (Kaempfer 1906, 151–152).

What is interesting here is the way Kaempfer attempted to explain what he saw as the linguistic and cultural uniqueness of the Japanese by deriving them from a single source. That his Christian background led him to propose Babylon as the ultimate origin of the Japanese is perhaps less important than the fact that he saw fit to propose the same sort of primordialist theory of Japanese ethnicity that was espoused by many of his Japanese contemporaries. Kaempfer admitted that "from time to time new Colonies were sent over [to Japan], chiefly from China and Corea," but "their number must have been very inconsiderable with regard to the bulk of the Japanese Nation" (1906, 146–147). In other words, despite these minor incursions, in Kaempfer's view the essence of the Japanese people was formed at a specific but undated time in antiquity.

Kaempfer (1906, 158) makes the interesting comment that the Japanese "have . . . little to say concerning the state of their Country, and the history of their ancestors before the time of Sinmu [Jimmu] their first Monarch. For this reason several of their own Writers have ventur'd to call Japan Atarasikoks, and Sinkokf, that is, New Country, as if it had been newly found out and peopled under the reign of their first Emperor." Although he simply placed the creation of the Japanese farther back in time, Kaempfer was critical of this native view of history, arguing that "the Japanese Nation must needs have existed, and liv'd in the Country, a considerable time before their first . . . Emperor, since when he was rais'd to the throne, they were then already grown very numerous" (Kaempfer 1906, 159). This question of who inhabited the archipelago before Jimmu is a crucial one. Kaempfer believed that the Japanese people had settled the Islands long before Jimmu and had "led for many ages a wandring life, erring from place to place" and "living on their Cattle, on what the earth produced of plants, roots and fruits, and the Sea afforded of fish and crabs" (1906, 159 and 146). Few Japanese scholars of the Tokugawa period, however, seem to have shared such a prosaic view of their origins, seeing instead an essential continuity from the Age of the Gods through Jimmu into the present era. Yamaga Sokō (1622–1685), a pupil of Razan, wrote "In *Chūgoku* [i.e., Japan] alone, although from the time of creation until the first human Emperor, some two million years . . . have elapsed, the Imperial line of the heavenly gods has never changed" (Earl 1964, 48). Norinaga expressed similar thoughts in a more poetic fashion:

> Yononaka no
> aru omobuki wa
> nanigoto mo
> kamiyo no ato o
> tazunete shirayu

> ["What ever exists in the world can be understood by tracing it back to the age of the deities"] (Yoshikawa 1983, 262).

Norinaga did not argue that the Japanese were created ex nihilo, but that they developed from *kami* (the gods) in a smooth process: he saw "no distinct dividing line between the age of kami and [the] human age" (Matsumoto 1970, 178).

Understandably, a number of Tokugawa scholars found the Age of the Gods rather hard to weave into a historical narrative. Few would have agreed with Asaka Tampaku (1654–1737), who called the Age of the Gods "far-fetched and insignificant" (cited in Brownlee 1988, 42), but Tokugawa Mitsunori wrote that, "The matters of the Age of the Gods are all strange, and hard to include in the chronicle of Emperor Jimmu"; for this reason his *Dai Nihonshi* "did not begin with the founding of Japan by the gods, but with the inauguration of imperial rule by Jimmu" (Brownlee 1988, 42). Arai Hakuseki attempted to place the Age of the Gods into an explicitly *historical,* Sinocentric view of the past (Nakai 1988, 242–264). He argued that the "gods were men" (Arai 1906, 219) and that Takamagahara, the High Plain of Heaven, could be identified with a real place in Hitachi province. Hakuseki saw the submission of the local Yamato chiefs to Jimmu as an example of the transfer of the mandate of power rather than as an ethnic Japanese/barbarian conflict (see Nakai 1988, 242–264). After the ascension of Jimmu, almost all Tokugawa observers agreed on the unbroken line of imperial descent. If a few shadowy barbarians *had* lived in the Islands before Jimmu, they were of no real significance in seventeenth- and eighteenth-century historical discourse. Indeed, for Confucianists, the presence of barbarians surrounding the central kingdom was the natural order and not something that required detailed explanation.

A fundamental shift in this view of ancient Japan occurred in the nineteenth century, when increased Japanese encroachment on the Ainu led to their appropriation as a primitive people who could be associated with barbarians living in Japan before Jimmu. This idea was not a totally new one. The Kamakura-era *Soga Monogatari* had proposed that the Ezo (Ainu) were descendants of the demon king Abi, who had been banished to Sotogahama (Aomori) by Jimmu (Kikuchi 1994, 48). Medieval perceptions of the impurity of the regions beyond the state boundaries were, however, clearly at work in this predominantly *spatial* model. The addition of a *historical* perspective was the crucial development of the nineteenth century.

The appropriation of the Ainu into Japanese (pre)history has many facets and requires location in the complex discourses of colonialism and exploration. From early European writers we know that the seventeenth-century metropolitan Japanese knew very little about the native inhabitants of Hokkaido, or Ezo as it was then called (see e.g. Caron and Schouten 1935, 13). Most eighteenth-century Japanese writings on Ezo origins were based primarily on ancient Chinese accounts of northern barbarians. Arai Hakuseki, in his influential *Ezo-shi* (1720), uses these accounts to argue that the Ezo were "northern Wa" and thus basically Japanese (Arai 1906, 681; Miyazaki 1988, 245). Matsumae Hironaga's *Matsumae-shi* (1781) takes the same basic approach (Matsumae 1979, 102–104). Hayashi Shihei's *Sangoku Tsūran Zusetsu* (1786) argues that the Ezo were human beings like the Japanese but that they had not yet been civilized like the inhabitants of Japan, China, Korea, and Holland had been (Hayashi 1979, 41).

Changing Japanese views of the Ainu were deeply intertwined with Japanese colonial concerns in the north. The potential economic benefits to be gained from the colonization of Hokkaido and the other islands were stressed by several writers, most notably Honda Toshiaki (1744–1821). Yet despite these perceived advantages, and despite the strategic threat from the Russians who had established several small colonies on Kamchatka and the Kuril Islands in the eighteenth century, actual colonization of Hokkaido by the Japanese did not occur until the late nineteenth century. In the late eighteenth and early nineteenth centuries, the proposed common ancestry of the Ainu and Japanese was used to support colonization of the north (Keene 1969, 117; Kikuchi 1994, 227–230). Honda Toshiaki's comment that, "Since [the Ainu] are all the descendants of the Emperor Jimmu, they are of the same race as ourselves" (Honda 1935, 209; Keene 1969) echoes the sympathetic attitude to the Ainu held by explorer Mogami Tokunai: "This year [1784] I encountered many Ainu, and I realized what a great mistake it is to think of them as belonging basically to the species of dogs; in fact, they are of the same Japanese stock as ourselves. They have only to adopt the teachings of the Imperial Land for them to become Japanese" (quoted in Keene 1969, 134). Keene (1969, 134) suggests that Mogami may have been the first Japanese to believe that the Ainu, though barbarians, were of the same race as the Japanese. As Ezo was argued to be an integral part of Japanese territory, it was natural for its inhabitants to be Japanese.

By the nineteenth century, however, as the Japanese came more and more into direct contact with the Ainu, views of the Ezo began to change. In the eyes of the Japanese, the Ainu became more primitive and less Japanese. The old idea that the Ainu were in part descended from a dog gained a new popularity at this time. Lt. S. W. Holland of the Royal Navy found it "curious that all Japanese books give [this] account of the *origin* of the Ainos, and all exactly agree" (Holland 1874, 236, original emphasis). A popular *Volksetymologie* of the late nineteenth century even derived Ainu from *inu* (dog), though few Western observers seem to have been convinced by this.

What we are in effect seeing in late nineteenth-century Japan is the development of ideas of *racial* inferiority with respect to the Ainu. Such ideas did not appear in a vacuum: "the half century or more during which the Japanese initially turned to the West for education coincided almost exactly with the period when scientific racism dominated the natural and social sciences in Europe and the United States" (Dower 1986, 204). A racist view of the Ainu thus became intertwined with an image of them as the primitive aborigines of the Islands who had been driven north by Jimmu and the (racially superior)

Japanese. As noted by Fawcett (1986, 51), in the context of the late-nineteenth century colonization of Hokkaido, this ethnic interpretation of prehistory could be used as justification for continued Japanese expansion at the expense of what were considered non-Yamato peoples.

By the time of the Meiji Restoration, therefore, American Albert Bickmore could write that "the Japanese all believe that [the] aborigines [encountered by Jimmu] were the ancestors of the present Ainos" (Bickmore 1868, 359-360). Little more than a decade earlier, Klaproth had been less sure of the connection, proposing only that the aborigines "resembled" the Ainu:

> ce pays, originairement habité par des autochthones, a été civilisé par des colonies chinoises, arrivées à différentes époques dans les provinces occidentales du Japon. On verra plus bas que le théâtre de l'histoire mythologique qui précède l'époque de *Zin mou ten o* [emperor Jinmu], est placé dans le *Fiougo*, province de l'île de Kiouziou [Kyushu], qui est la plus occidentale du Japon, et que ce conquérant partit de là pour aller soumettre la partie orientale de cet empire, habitée par un peuple qui ressemblait aux Aïnos du Yéso, du Taraïkaï [Sakhalin], des îles Kouriles et du Kamtchatka (Kalproth 1854, x).

It is widely argued that Philipp Franz von Siebold (1796–1866), a German medical doctor stationed at Dejima in the 1820s, was the first to link the Ainu with the aboriginal, pre-Jimmu inhabitants of Japan (e.g. Kreiner 1993, 30). Siebold did indeed propose that an aboriginal, hunter-fisher Ainu population, originating in the north, had been pushed back to Ezo under Japanese expansion (Siebold 1930, 732–734 and 1261), but the question of whether or not this conclusion is original is a difficult one. Certainly, Siebold—who admitted "Je n'ai jamais vu des Aïnos" (1831, 79)—was strongly influenced by Japanese writers. He used "dissertations" written by his Japanese students in the compilation of his work, *Nippon* (Vos 1983). In his famous chapter on *magatama* (comma-shaped jewels), Siebold (1930, 731) quotes a Japanese writer as proposing that the ancient Japanese lived in caves like the contemporary inhabitants of Hokkaido and Sakhalin. The idea of comparing the Ainu with the pre-Jimmu "Japanese," therefore, may have been a borrowed one, but Siebold gave it a scientific basis, arguing that the primitive Islanders had been "Fischern und Jägern" and that the material evidence of *magatama* from both Hokkaido and the Ryukyus supported Japanese expansion through the central islands (Siebold 1930, 729–735).

Both Japanese and Western thinking on Japanese origins on the eve of the first archaeological excavations in Japan are well summarized in an 1876 pamphlet by William Borlase entitled *Niphon and its Antiquities*. Following Siebold, Borlase derived the Ainu from the north, arguing that they must have occupied all of Honshu before the arrival of Jimmu. Borlase was less certain, however, of the origin of the Japanese "invaders," apparently agreeing with Klaproth that they were autochthonous in Kyushu (Borlase 1876, 35). Again largely through Siebold, Borlase (1876, 25) was aware of the many stone artifacts that had been found in Japan and "which Japanese authors themselves agree in attributing to the Yebisu [=Emishi/Ezo]." During the Tokugawa era, a number of scholars had linked the ancient stone points and pottery that were occasionally unearthed in various parts of Japan with the people of Ezo (Bleed 1986, 60–63). Matsuoka Gentatsu (1669–1746) thought the points were carried south by birds that had been shot but not killed by Ezo arrows. Kiuchi Sekitei (1724–1808) argued that, since stone points were common in north and east Japan but rare in the west, the Ainu had preceded the Japanese in the former regions. None of these scholars, nor indeed William Borlase, however, can be said to have possessed what Daniel (1963) termed the "idea of prehistory," that is, the concept of a period before written history that could be investigated using the archaeological record. Kiuchi Sekitei, for example, called the stone artifacts he described "Things from the Age of the Gods" even though he knew they were man-made (Bleed 1986, 63). In 1876, in the first Western general history of Japan written in the Meiji era, William Griffis wrote:

> The evidences of an aboriginal race are still to be found in the relics of the Stone Age in Japan. Flint, arrow and spear heads, hammers, chisels, scrapers, kitchen refuse, and various other trophies, are frequently excavated, or may be found in the museum or in houses of private persons. *Though covered with soil for centuries, they seem as though freshly brought from an Aino hut in Yezo* (Griffis 1886 [1876], 29, emphasis added).

It was in this intellectual atmosphere that on June 20, 1877, American zoologist Edward Morse, having arrived at Yokohama a few days earlier, made his first journey into Tokyo. From his railway carriage, Morse saw shell middens beside the tracks at Ōmori and in the autumn of that year conducted Japan's first scientific archaeological excavation.

STAGE 2: THE OTHER WITHIN—FROM TEXTS TO ARCHAEOLOGY, 1877–1935

The period 1877–1935 was pivotal in the study of the origins of the Japanese people. Following the Meiji Restoration of 1868, Japan transformed herself into an industrial nation-state. Nationalist sentiment, the seeds of which had been present in Stage 1, was no longer limited to the elite but was manipulated to become the ideological basis of the Meiji state. The Western disciplines of archaeology and anthropology were introduced to Japan, and the preexisting trend to see the Ainu as the pre-Japanese aboriginal inhabitants of the Islands was now given a "scientific" basis and linked with the newly discovered Stone Age (Jōmon) remains and a growing sample of prehistoric skeletons. The first Yayoi pottery was found in 1884, but the concept of a Yayoi *culture* was not developed until the very end of this stage.

The influence of Edward Morse (1838–1925) on Japanese archaeology is undeniable, but his excavation at Ōmori did not represent a complete break with previous approaches to the past:

> Morse stated firmly that the Omori site was "prehistoric" and that it must predate the earliest available historical sources. . . .
>
> A closer look at Morse's work strongly suggests, however, that he did not grasp the significance of "prehistory" and could not have led Japanese scholars away from a text-oriented approach. . . . In an article in *Popular Science Monthly* (1879b) Morse described not only his work at Omori but also Japan's mythical history. The early chronicles were not critically evaluated, and written records were apparently presented as the context within which Japanese archaeology should be undertaken and understood (Bleed 1986, 66).

Though less well known than Morse, Heinrich Philipp von Siebold (a son of Philipp Franz) excavated as many as seven shell middens in Japan in the late 1870s (Kreiner 1980). Siebold's approach to interpreting the past was similar to Morse's in that he argued that archaeology was a new, scientific way of proving the authenticity of historical records:

> Japanese history records that [the "tribes of savages with whom Jimmu Tenno met when he advanced northwards"] did not know the use of metals, that they lived in caves, and awaited the attacks of the Japanese on the heights of the mountains. But even if we do not believe in these old historical records, yet more trustworthy

> ones consist in the implements etc. which they left behind, and [which] give sufficient proof that the earliest inhabitants were none other than the present inhabitants of Yezo (Siebold 1879, ii).

During Stage 2, the desire of the Meiji oligarchy to unify Japan in the face of the threat of European colonialism was a crucial stimulus to the new nationalism. A statist nationalism developed in which the state was seen as an organic, natural extension of the Japanese people (Weiner 1995, 444–449). The Japanese state, it came to be believed, was a unique polity centered around an unbroken imperial line that headed a *family* of subjects. In the 1875 words of Fukuzawa Yukichi, the *kokutai* (national polity) was the "grouping together of people of one race" (quoted in Healey 1983, 263). The attempted erosion of Tokugawa-period class divisions was an important part of the country's modernization, and the general who headed the new conscript army that put down the 1877 revolt by ex-samurai Saigō Takamori announced his victory by noting that, "The Japanese, whether of the military class or not, *originally sprang from the same blood,* and, when subjected to regular discipline, could scarcely fail to make soldiers worthy of the renowned bravery of their ancestors" (quoted in Crump 1991, 68, emphasis added).

In this nationalistic climate, the "superiority of the Japanese people was naturally emphasized and the identification of the savage Stone Age producers of the pottery and lithics found in shell middens as the ancestors of the Japanese was rejected. Instead, the Stone Age people were regarded as aborigines who were driven out by the settlement of the superior descendants of the gods who formed the ancestors of the Japanese" (Saitō 1974, 135). Ethnic substitution theories thus provided the main interpretive framework for Japanese prehistory during Stage 2. Though some scholars began to question the historicity of Jimmu (cf. Hoshino 1980, 98–125), the assumption that the Japanese were a separate race of divine origin remained widely accepted. For this reason, the origins of the Japanese never really became a problem at this time (Kudō 1989b, 56). The real question that occupied anthropological minds was, Who had been in Japan *before* the Japanese? The Ainu were the main candidates, but so-called pre-Ainu theories also gained wide currency.

As noted already, the concept of racial determinism, which was prevalent in both academic and popular circles in Europe and America in the late nineteenth century, had a pervasive influence on early Japanese anthropology. "Race is the key to history" announces the title page of W. E. Griffis' 1907 book *The Japanese Nation in Evolution.* At that time this was no idle motto, and Griffis (1907, 10) could seriously propose that "Ainu intelligence is limited, but it seems to be of the same kind as our own and not of the Asiatic order." Yet Japanese and Western concepts of race were subtly different. Generally speaking, in Japan the biological component of race has been less important than the cultural aspects. The Japanese model of divinely ordained supremacy has carried greater weight than mere skin color. This has enabled the Japanese to avoid confronting their own status in the eyes of Western racists, who overwhelmingly tend to view white skin as superior to all other colors, including yellow. As a result, "whereas racism in the West was markedly characterized by denigration of others, the Japanese were preoccupied far more exclusively with elevating themselves" (Dower 1986, 204).

The complex discourse in Stage 2 between Japanese concepts of divine superiority based on the traditional texts, Western anthropology and its racial determinism, and the new hard "facts" of the archaeological record is well illustrated by the Korpokunkur (or Koropok-guru) theory. The Ainu legend that a race of dwarflike pit dwellers had inhabited Hokkaido before them is recorded in Japanese sources as early as 1660 (Kudo 1979, 25). These were the Korpokunkur (see Koganei 1896, 22–27). The archaeological appropriation of the Korpokunkur was stimulated by the presence in Hokkaido of overgrown but still distinguishable ancient dwelling pits, together with the fact that late-nineteenth-century Kuril Ainu still used that type of building (Fig. 2.1). According to Milne (1882, 188), T. Blakiston had drawn attention to the pit dwellers of Ezo as early as 1872 (they had also been noticed by Japanese explorer Matsu'ura Takeshirō in the 1850s [see Matsu'ura 1982: 212]). It was John Milne, however, who was primarily responsible for the development of the Korpokunkur theory in the Western literature. Milne (1880, 1881) argued that although the shell middens found across Japan had probably been made by the Ainu, the pit dwellings of the far north were the remains of a non-Ainu people such as the "Kamschadales or Alutes." By 1882, Milne had heard the Ainu legend of the Korpokunkur from missionary John Batchelor and had made the obvious link between that story and his own field observations.

Tsuboi Shōgorō (1863–1913), the most important Japanese anthropologist of the early Meiji era, became the main supporter of the Korpokunkur thesis after Milne. In contrast to Milne, however, Tsuboi argued that the Korpokunkur had produced *all* the Stone Age remains from across Japan, citing various differences between Stone Age and Ainu cultures (absence of pottery in the latter, lack of beards and clear Ainu features on Stone Age figurines, etc.) to support his theory that the Ainu were unrelated to the Stone Age people. Instead, Tsuboi proposed that the Stone Age relics

FIG. 2.1. Korpokunkur women making pottery. The clothes and hair designs are based on Jōmon figurines. From Tsuboi's "Customs of the *Koropok-guru*" (Tsuboi 1971b[1885]: 85).

had been made by a people who resembled the Eskimos, a conclusion based on the presence of ceramics in both cultures, similarities in clothing, and proposed "snow goggles" on some Stone Age figurines (Tsuboi 1887). Tsuboi became the first professor of anthropology at Tokyo University in 1893, but after his death in St. Petersburg in 1913, the Korpokunkur theory was more or less laid to rest with him. The Ainu theory then became the dominant interpretation of the Stone Age remains, supported by Aston (1972[1896], I: 109–110, 1905), Chamberlain (1905), Torii (1920), Matsumoto (1920), Buxton (1925, 208–209), and others. Munro (1911, 661) saw the Ainu as the "sole survivors of the primitive inhabitants" of the archipelago; other primitive peoples had included the Hayato and Tsuchigumo mentioned in the *Nihon Shoki* and the *Kojiki*.

Central to archaeological interpretation at this time was the perceived primitiveness of late-nineteenth-century Ainu culture: "The reluctance of Tsuboi and Morse to acknowledge that the Ainu were capable of manufacturing the relatively sophisticated artefacts found on prehistoric sites may reflect general Japanese attitudes toward the Ainu people at this time when Hokkaido was undergoing massive colonisation" (Fawcett 1986, 51). In the second half of the nineteenth century, similar concerns were being debated in North America as to the identity of the builders of the earthen mounds of the Midwest. It was widely believed that these mounds were too complex to have been built by the "primitive" Indians who then occupied the region. A pre-Indian "lost race" of Moundbuilders was proposed and variously identified as Tartars, Malays, Welsh, Phoenicians, and others (see Silverberg 1968). In America, as well as in Hokkaido, this debate was more than just academic: "The Native Americans of North America were in the process of being exterminated as the United States spread westward, and the more primitive the Indians were thought to be, the easier it apparently was to justify their destruction or displacement" (Willey and Sabloff 1980, 40; see also McGuire 1992b, 820–821; Kotani 1994).

The scholar who was most critical of this sort of approach in Japan was John Milne. As he (1881, 409–410) notes, in the late nineteenth century the two main objections to the Ainu=Stone Age Man theory were (1) that "the Ainos are not essentially pot-makers, and the art of pot-making when once acquired is never lost," and (2) that the shell middens "show evidence of cannibalism, and that there is no record of such a habit amongst the Ainos." Milne efficiently disposed of these objections, using documentary sources and travelers' accounts to show not only that the Ainu still made pottery to a limited extent but also that they "have daily become more and more connected with the Japanese, from whom they could obtain better and cheaper utensils than those they could manufacture themselves" (Milne 1881, 410). Stone Age cannibalism had been first suggested by Morse (1879a), based on the scattered human remains at Ōmori. Morse emphasized the mild and gentle nature of the contemporary Ainu, but Milne, while not ruling out the possibility of further archaeological proof of cannibalism, argued that there was no reason that the Ainu should not in the past have lived in "a state of savagery, from which even the early inhabitants of Britain do not seem to have been exempt" (Milne 1881, 412).

The Ainu/Korpokunkur debate occupies much of the early literature from Stage 2, but as Teshigawara (1988, 4) reminds us, "within the framework of the 'aboriginal people' concept—which regarded the legends of the *Kojiki* and *Nihon Shoki* as truths and proposed that the superior descendants of the gods [i.e., the Japanese] had repelled the inferior Stone Age people—both the Ainu theory and the [Korpokunkur] theory were no more than empty hypotheses with little scientific basis." Despite a growing number of archaeological excavations, in this period the texts still provided the dominant context for the interpretation of Japan's prehistoric past. This was as true for Western scholars as for Japanese. Both cause and effect of this text-based approach were the interpretive assumptions held by the majority of Japanese anthropologists during this stage. A direct link was assumed between types of excavated pottery and peoples known from the historical record or from Japan's colonial advances on the Asian mainland. There was as yet little conception of the *chronological* relationships between these groups or of prehistoric peoples who were not mentioned in the texts (Barnes 1990a, 936). Torii (1920), for example, argues that, though both were made by the Ainu, the Stone Age pottery of the Kanto could be divided into two types—thick and thin. Instead of positing a chronological relationship, Torii suggests that they could be linked with contemporaneous tribes *(buzoku):* a coastal group associated with shell middens that used thin-walled pottery and an inland hunting group that used thick-walled wares.[1]

Many factors combined to bring about the demise of this type of ethnic prehistory by the mid-1930s. One such factor was opposition to the growing extremism of nationalist ideology. Another was the more refined use of excavation techniques, particularly stratigraphic analysis. A third was the increased prevalence of the concept of human cultures introduced from Western anthropology. The interplay of these and other factors is clear in changing interpretations of the Yayoi.

The Problem of the Yayoi

In his Ōmori report, Morse refers to the decorative technique found on the ceramics from that site as "cord marked" *(jōmon)*. Following Morse, *jōmon* began to be applied to a distinctive ceramic tradition present at many sites. Gradually the term also began to be used to refer to a period and culture within the archipelago, now argued to have begun with the first appearance of pottery at about 10,500 BC. In 1884, a few years after Morse did his work at Ōmori, a pot missing its rim was found in another part of Tokyo. This vessel also displayed cord-marked decoration and differences between it and other Jōmon wares were not immediately remarked upon. Other finds followed, however, and in 1896 the pottery was given the name Yayoi, since it had first been found in the Yayoi district, which now forms part of the Hongō Campus of the University of Tokyo (Tsuboi 1971a[1889]; Makita 1896).

In the early days of Japanese archaeology the Yayoi period posed a considerable problem of interpretation because of its initially uncertain position between the Stone Age or Jōmon period and the Yamato or Kofun period. If Stone Age remains had been made by the Ainu or by some other "pre-Japanese" people, and the "Japanese proper" were responsible for the *kofun* (tomb mounds) of the protohistoric Yamato era, then who had made Yayoi pottery? Yagi (1898) first argued that Yayoi pottery was made by a Malay-type population and then later by the Tsuchigumo. He saw the pottery as an "intermediate" type (Yagi 1906), an idea taken up by Munro. Munro (1911, 294) regarded Yayoi pottery as a type of ceramics made by low-class people of the early Yamato era—a people akin to the outcaste *eta*. He concluded that the Yayoi was "a domestic pottery of the early Japanese and that, during the era following the primitive culture, it may have been made by native artizans, to supply the wants of the Yamato conquerors" (Munro 1911, 307). Before long, however, the Yayoi became linked with the Japanese people. Torii (1918) argued that two types of people had lived in Stone Age Japan: in addition to the aboriginal Ainu who made and used Jōmon pottery, the "Japanese proper" had arrived from the continent and used Yayoi pottery. These Yayoi Japanese were linked with the mythological accounts of Japanese origins and posited to be the direct ancestors of the modern Japanese people. Kita Sadakichi (1871–1939) also proposed that the Yayoi people were the ancestors, or at least formed the main component, of the Japanese (Kita 1978[1929]: 261).

Within the context of the Yayoi, both Torii and Kita emphasized the assimilative aspects of Japan's prehistory (Kita 1978, [1929]: 213–214; Ōbayashi 1991, 2–3). At this time the so-called *senjūmin setsu* (aboriginal theory) still dominated the literature. A basic assumption of this theory was that if the prehistoric inhabitants of Japan were not the Korpokunkur, then they were the Ainu (Nishioka and Schrenk 1937, 25). In the early decades of the twentieth century, however, so many Stone Age sites were being found all over the country that it became increasingly difficult to argue that the Stone Age people bore little or no relation to the Japanese. This was an extremely significant trend since, for the first time, the Japanese or Yamato "race" was incorporated into the *prehistory* of the Islands through so-called "Proto-Japanese" or hybridization theories. To put this another way, the Stone Age and Ainu people ceased to be viewed as the primitive Other within Japan's history and became reconstructed as part of a uniform *Japanese* heritage.

Early examples of hybridization theories can be found in the writings of Miyake (1886), Dönitz (1887), and von Baelz (1908), but it was the growth of anatomical comparisons of Jōmon and Ainu skeletons that provided the real stimulus to this approach. Following on the work of Koganei (e.g. 1896) and others, Kiyono Kenji (1885–1955) is regarded as the foremost progenitor of the Proto-Japanese hybridization theory. Based on studies of Jōmon skeletal remains, Kiyono concluded that modern Japanese and Ainu populations had evolved gradually from a Proto-Japanese base through admixture with surrounding groups as well as through secular variation (Kiyono 1938, 1949; Mizoguchi 1986, 109). Though his work was increasingly based on scientific data, Kiyono still relied on the mythological texts for part of the context of his interpretations (Harunari 1984a, 85–86). As the following quotation makes clear, the nationalistic appeal of his Proto-Japanese theory was exploited by Kiyono, who served as an advisor to the 731 medical experimentation unit: "*The Japanese Islands have been the homeland of the Japanese since the Islands were settled by humans. The Japanese were first formed in Japan. . . . Since humans have lived in Japan, the motherland of the Japanese race, the homeland* (furusato) *of the Japanese has been Japan* (Nihon koku)" (Kiyono 1938, 2, quoted in Harunari 1984a, 85, Kiyono's emphasis).

During the early decades of this century, the Yayoi became increasingly better understood as a result of archaeological excavations that took place all over Japan. A major turning point was the discovery of stone tools associated with Yayoi pottery in Nagoya in 1908. Similarities between these tools and lithics found on the continent led Torii Ryūzō to propose a mainland origin for his Yayoi immigration of the Japanese proper (Mori 1988, 49). Yayoi ceramics were also being found with bronzes at several sites in western Japan. The existence of a Japanese Bronze Age had already been anticipated by Milne (1882, 420) and proposed by von Baelz (1908, 535–537). By about 1915 it was clear that both bronze and stone tools had in fact coexisted during the Yayoi, and the term *kinseki heiyō jidai* (Aeneolithic) was coined by both Nakayama Heijirō and Hamada Kōsaku in 1917 (Oda 1988, 57–58).[2]

The most important figure in early Yayoi archaeology was Morimoto Rokuji (1903–1936). Morimoto's contribution to the Yayoi was the concept of *culture*. According to Nishikawa (1992, 195–196), the word *bunka* (culture) was first used in Japan in its anthropological sense by a journalist in 1887, but from Table 2.1 it can be seen that it was not until the 1930s that this usage became common in archaeological writings. Nishikawa (1996, 246) writes that he "cannot say exactly when the translated term *minzoku* (nation or *Volk*) came into general use [in Japan], but it was certainly part of the diffusion of the concept of culture." While the word *minzoku* was not commonly used by Japanese archaeologists until the 1920s, however, the concept of ethnic groups (most commonly termed *shuzoku*) was widespread, and the real importance of the culture concept lies in the fact that it *replaced* the earlier interpretation of archaeological variation as mainly resulting from racial or ethnic differences.

TABLE 2.1

PRE-1940 USES OF THE WORD *BUNKA*

AUTHOR AND YEAR OF PUBLICATION		TITLE
1913	Gotō Shūichi	*Connections between Chinese culture and Japanese culture as seen from craftwork*
1917	Hamada Kōsaku	*Etruscan sites and their culture*
1922	Takahashi Kenji	*Kofun and ancient culture*
1923	Takahashi Kenji	*The transmission of Chinese culture in Japan's antiquity; The origins of Japan's Bronze Culture*
	Gotō Shūichi	*Regional variation in our ancient culture; The transmigration of culture*
1924	Takahashi Kenji	*The importation of continental culture as seen from ancient artifacts*
1925	Torii Ryūzō	*Our ancient culture as seen from anthropology; On the megalithic culture(s) of the Pacific Islands*
	Gotō Shūichi	*The ancient culture of Gunma as seen from ancient mirrors*
1927	Hasebe Kotondo	*Ento pottery culture*
	Morimoto Rokuji and Nakayama Kyūshirō	*A consideration of Japan's ancient culture*
	Takahashi Kenji	*Bronze culture in Japan's antiquity; Our [Japanese] ancient culture seen from archaeology*
1930	Morimoto Rokuji	*The Bronze Age culture Aki Fukuda site*
	Torii Ryūzō	*Fossil Man and his culture*
1932	Torii Ryūzō	*Lifestyles and culture of our prehistoric (ancient) age; Connections between our country and Qidan culture*
	Shibata Tsuneyoshi	*The chlorite schist culture area of the Kanto*
	Kita Sadakichi	*On the development of ancient Japanese culture as seen from sea routes*
1932–1933	Yamanouchi Sugao	*Japan's most ancient culture*

AUTHOR AND YEAR OF PUBLICATION		TITLE
1933	Gotō Shūichi	*The influence of Tang culture on medieval (Japan)*
	Morimoto Rokuji	*The southern and northern spread of Ou culture*
1934	Fujita Ryōsaku	*The ancient culture of Korea*
	Nakaya Jūjirō	*The influence of continental culture on Japan's Stone Age*
1935	Yamanouchi Sugao	*Jōmon-type culture*
	Morimoto Rokuji	*Yayoi-type culture—in the Pensées style*
	Gotō Shūichi	*A consideration of the development of ancient culture*
	Hamada Kōsaku	*Japan's protohistoric culture; The origins of Japanese culture*
1936	Torii Ryūzō	*Qidan culture as seen from archaeology*
	Kōno Isamu	*On the roots and lower limit of Japan's Stone Age culture; An investigation of the ancient cultures of Hokkaido, the Kurils, and Sakhalin*
	Nakaya Jūjirō	*A consideration of Japan's stone age culture—with special reference to distribution zones and culture areas*
1937	Fujita Ryōsaku	*Cultural connections between Japan, Korea, and Manchuria as seen from archaeology*
1938	Sakazume Nakao	*On the cultural artifacts found at the Aratachi midden [Yokohama]*
	Gotō Shūichi	*Kofun culture*
1939	Torii Ryūzō	*In search of Liao culture*

Titles in the table are of publications of twenty-three archaeologists in the *Nihon Kōkogaku Senshū (Selected Works of Japanese Archaeology)* series, Tsukiji Shokan, 1971–1986. All works are in Japanese.

From the 1930s, the idea that the archaeological record could be explained through the presence of different cultures became increasingly common.

While Morimoto was not the first Japanese scholar to use the concept of prehistoric cultures, his work stands apart as the most explicit discussion of the overall implications of this concept. For most anthropologists before Morimoto, even if they used the terms "Jōmon culture" and "Yayoi culture," it was the proposed ethnic differences that really separated the two. In contrast, Morimoto developed the idea of a Yayoi culture based on behavioral criteria—primarily rice agriculture and bronze (see e.g. Morimoto 1933a, 1933b). In his use of the concept of "culture complexes," Morimoto seems to have been influenced by Wissler's 1923 *Man and Culture* (Tsude 1988, 138). Morimoto argues that the Yayoi shared the same cultural complex or pattern as traditional Japan, an assumption that still dominates debate on Japanese culture. Despite Morimoto's use of the culture-complex concept, however, Okamoto (1991, 57) notes that Morimoto still saw a certain degree of overlap between Jōmon and Yayoi in eastern Japan (e.g. Morimoto 1933c). It was the young Yamanouchi Sugao (1902–1970) who took the culture concept to its logical extreme by arguing in the so-called Minerva Debate that Jōmon culture had come to an end more or less simultaneously right across Japan.

STAGE 3: ARCHAEOLOGY, NATIONALISM, AND THE RETREAT FROM ETHNICITY, 1936–1997

The concept of culture that developed in Japanese archaeology by the 1930s provided a means of breaking away from the simplistic ethnic interpretations that dominated Stage 2. The Minerva Debate symbolizes this paradigm shift in Japanese archaeological theory. February 1936, the month during which the first round-table discussion of the debate took place, saw an attempted military coup that, although it was put down after a few days, had the actual effect of increasing the power of the army and of antidemocratic forces in Japan (see Shillony 1973). Full-scale war with China began in 1937, and hostilities continued thereafter until the end of the Pacific War in August 1945. During these years, Japan was a strictly regimented fascist state dominated by ultranationalist ideologies (Brown 1955, 200–237). This political background is crucial, since it is widely accepted in Japan that the culture-based approach to prehistory advocated by Yamanouchi Sugao in the Minerva Debate was a conscious reaction to the emperor-centered view of Japanese history, which emphasized ethnic interpretations (Teshigawara 1988, 12–13; Anazawa 1990, 75; Nakamura 1990, 58).

The Minerva Debate is named after the short-lived journal *Minerva,* in which a series of articles and a round-table discussion appeared in 1936 (Kōno et al. 1971[1936], Kita 1972[1936], 1936; Yamanouchi 1936a, 1936b; cf. Barnes 1990a, 935–937; Hudson and Yamagata 1992: 84–85). An important focus of the debate was the date of the end of the Jōmon. Kita (1972[1936]) argued that the Ainu continued to use Jōmon pottery until the medieval era. Gotō Shūichi proposed that Jōmon pottery had been used in some regions until at least the end of the Kofun period (Kōno et al. 1971[1936], 86). In contrast, Yamanouchi argued that since Tohoku Final Jōmon Kamegaoka pottery influenced Final-phase ceramics in the Kanto, Chūbu, and Kinai regions, those phases must all have been contemporary, and thus the Jōmon period must have ended more or less simultaneously throughout Japan (Kōno et al. 1971[1936], 86).

In complete contrast to earlier aboriginal substitution theories, most participants in the Minerva Debate espoused hybridization-type explanations for the formation of the Japanese. According to Egami Namio, whatever the ultimate origin(s) of the Japanese, after they settled in the Islands they "adapted to the natural environment of Japan and became Japanized—particularized (to Japan) . . ." (Kōno et al. 1971, 95). This last phrase—*koyū-ka shita*—is almost impossible to translate but means "became peculiar, characteristic, proper to." Torii used the same word to refer to his "*koyū Nihonjin*" (Japanese proper). What Egami appears to be arguing here is that the prehistoric inhabitants of the Islands *consciously* evolved to conform to a set pattern of Japaneseness. Egami's approach is remarkably similar to biologist Imanishi Kinji's (1976) Lamarckian concept of group evolution, whereby "when environmental change presents a species with a challenge, then the species . . . throws out the appropriate genetic trump card enabling it to adapt precisely to these new conditions" (Dale 1986, 195).

Similar views of Japanese ethnogenesis seem to have been widespread at this time. The work of Kiyono Kenji has been mentioned already. A Ministry of Health and Welfare wartime policy document discussed by Dower (1986, 262–290) is also highly illuminating in this respect. The document is titled "An Investigation of Global Policy with the Yamato Race as Nucleus." The authors of this report

> endorsed the thesis of certain Western scholars that no modern races were pure. Elsewhere they explicitly acknowledged that this was true of the Yamato race itself. Concerning the racial origins of the Japanese, they cited with approval the speculations of Erwin

> Baelz . . . to the effect that the modern Japanese probably represented the intermingling of three racial strains: Ainu, Malay, and Mongoloid.
>
> Despite these diverse origins, it was still possible to speak of the Japanese (and other races as well) as being "pure" in all practical senses. . . .
>
> . . . the researchers cited with approval Hitler's concern with identifying the "Germanness" of his own people, and rested content with arguing that even in ancient times there had been a "main line" or "main race" among the peoples who came together to form the Japanese race. This main line could be called the original Japanese, and by a process of natural selection and assimilation it gradually absorbed the other racial strains into a single "enduring structure" (Dower 1986, 268–269).

This view that the Japanese were "made in Japan" became extremely influential in the 1930s. Although he emphasizes the external connections of the Japanese (in contrast to Yamanouchi, who saw the Jōmon as a "cultural island" [Kōno et al. 1971, 96]), ethnologist Oka Masao (1898–1982) also proposes the assimilation of various diverse elements into a single Japanese culture. Oka studied in Vienna before the war and was strongly influenced by the Vienna-based *Kulturkreis* (culture circle) school of anthropology, which emphasized the diffusion of culture complexes or *Kreise*. Oka proposed five "ethnic culture complexes" in the makeup of the Japanese (Oka 1994[1956]; cf. Ōbayashi 1991, 4–5): (1) Matrilineal taro-growing culture from the Middle Jōmon; (2) Matrilineal dry-rice cultivating people who reached Japan from south China at the end of the Jōmon and probably spoke an Austroasiatic language; (3) Patrilineal swidden-farming and stock-raising people of northern origin who introduced an Altaic languge in the Yayoi; (4) Wet-rice growing people of Austronesian type from southern China; and (5) Patriarchal Peninsular culture of people speaking an Altaic language in the Kofun period. Though many of the details of Oka's scheme have since been supplanted, his influence has been enormous, and Japanese ethnologists of the generation following Oka continued to use the same basic approach of distinguishing groups of associated cultural traits that are argued to have diffused *in association* into Japan. The work of Ōbayashi Taryō and Sasaki Kōmei—arguably the two most senior cultural anthropologists in Japan today—clearly falls into this category (e.g. Ōbayashi 1990b, 1991; Sasaki 1971, 1991a, 1991b).

Postwar Cultural Nationalism

Following Japan's surrender in 1945, the emperor-based ultranationalism of the preceding fifteen years was brought to a sudden end. Emperor Hirohito renounced his divinity, and wide-ranging democratic reforms were instituted by the Allied Occupation forces. Nationalism, however, was far from dead; in the postwar years it simply moved down from the level of the state to the people as a whole (Brown 1955, 252). Notions of the *cultural* unity of the Japanese people began to replace the concept of a divine familial state (Edwards 1991, 20). The term "cultural nationalism" thus best describes Japanese nationalism since 1945 (Yoshino 1992). In many ways, postwar Japanese cultural nationalism is a continuation of pre-1945 nationalist ideology (McCormack 1996; Seifert 1977; von Wolferen 1989, 245–272).

Yoshino (1992, 50) argues that, in contrast to the Kokugaku movement, postwar cultural nationalism has given less emphasis to historical concerns, but I believe this view is mistaken. Right from the late 1940s, prehistory has been used to renegotiate Japanese ethnic and cultural identities (see Edwards 1997; Ōbayashi 1995; Oblas 1995). Edwards (1991) has analyzed the formative stage of postwar cultural nationalism through a discussion of the excavation of the Toro site in Shizuoka. The remains of Yayoi paddy fields were discovered at Toro in 1943, but full-scale excavation did not begin until 1947. Archaeologically, the excellent preservation of wooden agricultural tools and actual bunded rice paddies made Toro extremely significant (Nihon Kōkogaku Kyōkai 1978[1954]; Barnes 1982). In the postwar context, however, Toro took on much more than academic importance. One of the student volunteers at Toro later recounted that "We had accepted as natural that the emperor was a god and we were the descendants of gods, but with the war that belief crumbled completely. Here [at Toro] were the remains of our ancestors as proof that he [the emperor] was an ordinary mortal. *For the first time I began to wonder what our ancestors had really been like*" (cited in Edwards 1991, 2, emphasis added). The ease with which the view of the emperor's divinity was abandoned after the war suggests that many Japanese had accepted that divinity through habit rather than out of firm conviction. Nevertheless, a sense of ideological and historical bewilderment was very real at war's end. The question of how Japan should reconstitute her national identity between the twin poles of traditional values and modernization was a similar one to that faced at the time of the Meiji Restoration. In the late 1940s, this problem was approached through an increasing emphasis on rebuilding Japan as a "cultural nation" *(bunka kokka)*. In this context the finds at Toro were interpreted as evidence for the existence of peaceful, harmonious, rice-growing farmers from the very dawn of Japanese history:

> To the extent that the postwar Japanese could see their ancestors in such peaceful, and industrious, terms, they were able to reclaim a positive sense of national identity using the very logic of the prewar ideology they sought to deny: by virtue of their continuity with an immutable essence handed down from the past. This logic moreover allowed, and in a manner again resembling the prewar ideology, beliefs that this essence was uniquely indigenous and, in many regards, superior among nations of the modern world (Edwards 1991, 21).

In the late 1980s, the early postwar view of peace-loving Yayoi farmers was replaced by an emphasis on conflict, warfare, and the international relations of the Yayoi (cf. Hudson 1990a). In the late 1940s, however, Japan's indigenous cultural developments were stressed at the expense of connections with the mainland:

> The Marxist historiography that—in reaction to the imperial mythological history—had secretly influenced the study of Japanese history and archaeology from before the war, stressed social "evolution" through dominant internal causes within the society of the archipelago and had a strong tendency to ignore the contribution of immigration and the adoption of foreign cultures in sociocultural development. Particularly within Japanese archaeology, works published in the period around the war . . . had shown that the ancient culture of Japan had developed without interruption from Jōmon to Yayoi to Kofun. Most archaeologists accepted that there was little possibility that large immigrations or invasions from outside the archipelago had made a significant contribution to the cultural development [of Japan](Anazawa 1990, 75).

A complementary approach was espoused by many physical anthropologists at this time. Kanaseki Takeo (1897–1983) developed Kiyono's hybridization theory, arguing for the mixing of Yayoi-period immigrants with local Jōmon populations (Kanaseki 1976). In his support for group migration into western Japan in the Yayoi, however, Kanaseki's thesis differed from Kiyono's in a quite substantial way (Harunari 1988, 96). Hasebe Kotondo

(1882–1969) argues that a late Pleistocene or early Holocene population evolved in isolation within the Islands into the modern Japanese and that "the geographical variation in physical characters within the modern Japanese population was primarily a reflection of the variation that originally existed in the ancestral population, and was not caused by admixture with other races" (Mizoguchi 1986, 111; see Hasebe 1949, 1975[1954]). Hasebe (1975[1954], 14) attacked earlier Japanese scholars for their uncritical acceptance of the "inadvertent proposals of foreigners" (meaning Morse, and others) that a non-Japanese aboriginal people had lived in Japan. Among physical anthropologists, the endogenous approach was given its extreme expression by Suzuki Hisashi, who studied skeletons from both prehistoric and historic sites in Japan and argues that two major periods of physical change could be seen: the first was during the transition from foraging to farming, and the second occurred during the switch from a "feudal" to an industrial society in the late nineteenth/early twentieth centuries. Since the second change had occurred without substantial genetic input from outside Japan, Suzuki concludes that the first transition could also be explained through in situ microevolution (Suzuki 1960, 1963, 1969, 1981).

An alternative to the endogenous development approach did, however, exist quite early in the work of scholars who emphasized Japan's position in East Asia as a whole. Anazawa (1990, 75) sees this scholarship as specifically anti-Marxist in intent. Important figures in this category are Oka Masao and Egami Namio. Egami's Horseriders theory of Japanese state formation has been very influential (Egami 1964; cf. Ledyard 1975; Edwards 1983; Anazawa 1990). Egami's (1964, 37–38) comments on the Jōmon-Yayoi transition stand in contrast to the evolutionism of many scholars of the early postwar years. Egami is unusual among Japanese archaeologists in arguing that there must have been good reasons for the Jōmon people to adopt rice agriculture: "We cannot assume that hunters, fishers or food-gatherers will invariably adopt rice as their staple food after having been served with rice on one or two occasions" (Egami 1964, 41). Based on the fact that a whole rice-farming *complex* was established in Japan in the Yayoi, Egami proposed that the transition must have been caused by immigration.

Yayoi Archaeology Comes of Age

While the outline of Japanese prehistory, and the division into Jōmon, Yayoi, and Kofun, had been known since the 1930s, the period after the war saw a phenomenal increase in archaeological knowledge, including the discovery of

Palaeolithic remains in 1949. Postwar economic growth led to a huge program of rescue excavation as new roads, factories, and apartment blocks were constructed throughout the country. Until the 1970s, the Yayoi had been defined by pottery, but by that time new discoveries had made it impossible to draw a clear dividing line between Jōmon and Yayoi on ceramic criteria alone. In 1975, Sahara redefined the Yayoi as "the period in which food production first formed the basis of life in Japan" (Sahara 1975, 114), but despite this important shift in emphasis, the transition from Jōmon to Yayoi still tends to be seen as an event rather than a process. The question of *causality* is rarely a topic of debate in the Japanese literature on the formation of the Yayoi. Since rice is widely seen as so central to traditional Japanese culture (Rabbitt 1940; Ohnuki-Tierney 1993), there is no conception of farming as a lifestyle inferior to foraging. In the West, it has been accepted since the 1960s that foraging can make for an extremely affluent lifestyle and that consequently hunter-gatherers will usually only take up intensive cultivation when they are forced to do so by outside pressure of some sort, but for most Japanese archaeologists the step from foraging to farming appears natural and in need of no specific explanation. In their view, therefore, explaining the Jōmon-Yayoi transition merely involves identifying the temporal and spatial diffusion of Yayoi culture traits.

Exceptions to this rule are Watanabe Hitoshi (1986, 1989) and Akazawa Takeru (1981, 1982, 1986a) who were influenced by the rise of ecological-evolutionary paradigms in Western anthropology in the 1960s. The work of these scholars has, however, had little effect on the overall development of Japanese archaeology, which continues to be focused around a culture-historical framework.[3] The processual archaeology of the 1960s never caught on in Japan, but many Western archaeologists specializing in the country took on a processual slant, particularly in their "retreat from migrationism" (cf. Adams et al. 1978). This Western reluctance to emphasize population movements as a causal factor in culture change came at a time when the Japanese were stressing endogenous developments as a reaction to the racial anthropology of Stage 2. Thus, Western and Japanese explanations tended to reinforce each other in a closed circle.

Few Western archaeologists have specialized in the Yayoi, and there are no extended discussions of the Jōmon-Yayoi transition in Western languages (except for Akazawa's articles mentioned above). Kidder (1959, 89 and 91) posits a "large migration" in the Yayoi but also notes that the earliest Yayoi assemblages in Kyushu are not easily distinguishable from those of the Jōmon. By the early 1970s, Bleed was less sure of the degree of immigration and saw admixture with indigenous Jōmon groups as likely (Bleed 1972, 1974). Aikens (1981) argues for a social interpretation of the transition whereby "the primary incentive for the changeover from a broad-spectrum forest economy to an agricultural one was an increasingly enforceable demand by an increasingly organized and powerful elite upper stratum of society for energy inputs beyond those which an unspecialized forest economy could provide" (Aikens 1981, 272). This important suggestion was unfortunately not developed in detail by Aikens himself, although it can be seen as a forerunner to Watanabe's (1986, 1989) social elites theory, wherein influential males who were too old to hunt turned to farming. Pearson (1992) combines a social approach with the new biological data, writing that, "The decision to adopt a new subsistence pattern requiring intensive labor may have been motivated by a desire to emulate the customs of new groups of rice farmers who had access to superior technology. Such social factors must have been preeminent, since there seems to be no indication of food shortage or population pressure" (Pearson 1992, 86). Finally, Barnes (1993b) provides a useful comparison of theories applied to the Jōmon-Yayoi transition with those developed to study the spread of farming in Neolithic Europe. She suggests that Dennell's (1985) "imitation" model fits well with the transition in Kyushu. This model assumes somewhat "distant contact between hunter-gatherer populations and foreign agricultural societies, resulting in the active importation, adoption, and reproductive imitation of technological and cultural elements—but no genetic contribution—from a range of agricultural societies contacted. Important assumptions in the imitation model are that the Mesolithic populations had already begun their control over food resources, and that the major reason for contacting the foreign agricultural communities was to co-opt the technology to increase their own production" (Barnes 1993b, 182). Barnes attributes most of the responsibility for the Jōmon-Yayoi transition to indigenous foragers, stating plainly that "In northern Kyushu, the local Jōmon people adopted rice farming" (Bellwood and Barnes 1993, 142).

The Japanization of the Jōmon

Since 1945, the dominant approach in Japanese archaeology has been an endogenous one that has played down influences from outside Japan while assuming that the people known as the prehistoric Japanese were particularly good at adopting aspects of foreign culture that they perceived to be of use. Anthropologists have usually supported various outside influences on

Japanese ethnogenesis but have also typically argued that those foreign elements coalesced at an early stage to form a monolithic Japanese *Volk*. Over the past few decades, Western scholars have tended to propose similar theories to their Japanese colleagues. Sometimes this has been due to uncritical acceptance of the Japanese literature, but more important has been a move within Anglophone anthropology toward evolutionary explanations and away from questions of migration and ethnicity. European scholars have to some extent maintained a traditionally wide interest in Japanese ethnogenesis (e.g. Arutjunov 1962; Haguenauer 1956; Levin 1961, 1963; Slawik 1955; Tamburello 1969, 1970), but here the emphasis has been ethnological rather than archaeological. Despite a trend, that began in the 1980s and has since been growing, toward looking at the international context of Japanese prehistory (Kaner 1993), the endogenous approach of Yamanouchi and others remains extremely influential in Japan, so much so that Ikawa-Smith (1990, 68) argues that Japanese archaeologists' "répugnance pour les interprétations racistes de la préhistoire japonaise qui caractérisaient le XIXe siècle les empêche de percevoir les interactions ethniques." Nakamura (1990, 57–58), for example, attacks Sahara's (1987c) proposal that the spread of Early Yayoi ceramics up the Japan Sea coast reflects population movement. While elsewhere he puts forward some archaeological evidence for this view (Nakamura 1988, 180–184), his real objection seems to be political, seeing the association (*any* association) of people and pottery as a return to Nazi theories of Aryan supremacy. Jansen's (1985, xii) comment that "Postwar Marxist scholarship [is] a history without people, whereas prewar scholarship had been a history of the wrong people" is as relevant to prehistory as to any other period of Japan's past.

Okamoto (1991) presents a rare critical analysis of Yamanouchi's work and a reappraisal of Sugihara Sōsuke's idea of a steplike transition from Jōmon to Yayoi. Okamoto argues for a return to a consideration of the ethnic aspects of the transition, pointing out that even Yamanouchi posits a major "step" in Hokkaido with his concept of an Epi-Jōmon parallel with the Yayoi in the rest of Japan (Okamoto 1991, 58). However, the ways in which Japanese scholars have constructed Japanese and aboriginal identities in prehistory requires a more rigorous reflexive analysis than that provided by Okamoto. Avoidance of the questions of ethnicity, ethnic conflict, and Japanese colonialism within the Islands leads to a harmonious and homogenous view of the past that effectively silences other historical voices such as those of the Ainu and Okinawans. The work of Umehara Takeshi provides an excellent example of this problem.

A specialist in philosophy and religion and one of Japan's best-known intellectuals, from the early 1980s Umehara began to expound a vision of Japaneseness that emphasizes the preagricultural, Jōmon roots of Japanese culture. Umehara uses the image of the Japanese as a modern people with prehistoric tails: though superficially Westernized on the outside, close inspection reveals the retention of a host of traditional traits from the Jōmon (Umehara 1985, 156). Not only does Umehara argue that the Japanese need to rediscover their Jōmon roots, he also proposes that the values inherent in the ecological harmony of the Jōmon are a solution to the impending collapse of ego-centered Western civilization (Umehara 1985, 155–158, 1991, 186–190), a theme also taken up by politician Ozawa Ichirō (1993, 175).

Umehara's work is an excellent place to conclude this chapter, since it shows so clearly the differences between the typical Japanese approach to their ethnogenesis and the approach followed in this book. Both Umehara and I support the dual-structure hypothesis of Japan's population history discussed here in chapter 3. Umehara, however, argues that Jōmon and Yayoi populations became "more or less integrated and formed a homogenous people" (Umehara 1990, 15). No archaeological evidence in support of this conclusion is presented. Instead, Umehara (1990, 15) asks us to accept that "The principle behind this integration and homogenization of the Japanese people was harmony *(wa)*." On the one hand, in bringing the Ainu and Okinawans into the debate on Japanese origins, Umehara (1987, 1991, 163–164) can argue that he does not support a unitary "Yamatoist" view of the Japanese, but on the other hand, in denying those peoples the right to their own, *non-Japanese* histories he "submerges their identity in the national identity, and undermines their status as "nations within," entitled to their own culture and destiny."[4] Like many before him, Umehara faces a "fundamental contradiction between the impossibility and the necessity of creating the other as the other—the different, the alien—and incorporating the other within a single system of domination" (Sider 1987, 7).

We began this chapter with Arai Hakuseki's criticisms of the "naive and credulous" people of antiquity who turned history into a "tale told in a dream." Though Umehara's Jōmon tales require more credulity than do some other stories about Japanese origins, it is we who are naive if we believe that archaeological remains are not malleable into ever-changing tales of identity and difference. Several commentators have argued that Umehara's "Jōmonology" was in part a response to calls for a new Japanese identity in the face of growing internationalization in the early 1980s (Tsude 1986; Buruma 1987; Kaner 1993). What is interesting is the way that Umehara and others of the so-called New Kyoto School drew upon prewar nationalist precedents (Ajisaka 1986; Iwai 1986; McCormack 1996). The roots of Umehara's approach in the Proto-Japanese theories of Kiyono and others is clear from the discussion in this chapter. The wider implications of Umehara's work relate to the debate between so-called primordialists and instrumentalists in the construction of ethnicity. The Japanese case discussed in this chapter shows that ethnic identities are both born *and* created, inherent *and* imagined. Specific political conditions may influence the intensity of ethnic behavior, but ethnic (re)constructions are always within a specific cultural tradition. Sahlins (1985, 155) writes that culture is "the organization of the current situation in the terms of a past." Jōmon culture was as foreign to Tokugawa nativist Moto'ori Norinaga as was that of the Sioux or Berbers, yet his call for a return to an age of the gods pure from foreign influence—and therefore superior—is remarkably similar to Umehara's Jōmon "relief measures" for the collapse of Western civilization. Both juxtapose patriotism and nostalgia for a pristine past in the same way (cf. Nosco 1990, ix–x), even though one uses eighth-century mythological histories and the other the archaeological record. For Umehara, the Ainu have retained Jōmon (for him, Japanese) culture in its purest form, whereas the Wajin Japanese have been corrupted by all sorts of unpleasant foreign influences from China, Korea, and Europe (Umehara and Nakagami 1984, 78). Norinaga might have expressed it as, "Whatever exists in the world can be understood by tracing it back to the Jōmon period."

CONCLUSIONS

To anyone unfamiliar with the scholarship on Japanese ethnogenesis, this chapter will give the impression that Japanese scholars are conservative in the extreme in their theoretical approaches to that subject. In many respects, such a conclusion is justified. The development of the discipline of archaeology in Japan led to a distrust of ethnic interpretations of prehistory, which were thought to support the emperor-centered view of Japanese history. As a result, Japanese archaeologists continue to use a 1930s-type model of archaeological cultures, with only a few dissenting voices such as Niiro (1991) beginning to introduce critical perspectives on the concept. Cultural anthropologists working on Japanese origins also typically retain earlier culture-complex and diffusionary approaches. Since the war, many younger cultural anthropologists have avoided the contested field of Japanese ethnogenesis and turned their attention to countries other than Japan. These younger researchers tend to have a far more critical view of culture and ethnicity than the (now comparatively few) older scholars who work on Japanese origins.

Perhaps the most searching recent criticism of Japanese culture has come from Nishikawa Nagao (1996), who argues that the whole concept of human "cultures" is inextricably bound up with nationalist ideology. Nishikawa, however, is very much the exception rather than the rule: as Morris-Suzuki (1993b, 17) notes, "Even Aoki Tamotsu [1988], in calling for the dissolution of Japanese culture, does not seem to doubt that such an integrated cultural essence exists. Indeed, he likens the process of cultural borrowing in Japanese history to the way in which a soft-bodied mollusc creeps into borrowed shells: the outer covering changes, but the inner being stays the same." Most Japanese scholars working on the problem of Japanese ethnogenesis continue to take for granted that culture and ethnicity are unitary, bounded entities that have changed very little over the centuries. In the terminology of Blacker (1988, 65), they tend to assume that the Japanese are a chosen people whose essential qualities can be traced back to a golden age at the beginning of time. While many Japanese archaeologists and anthropologists may be described as liberal by personal conviction, these assumptions must be seen as part of wider discourses in Japanese society about the nature of Japaneseness. A survey conducted by Nishikawa (1993) provides a useful illustration of this discourse:

> I gave a questionnaire about Tennoism [Japanese imperial ideology] to five hundred students who were attending my lectures. Almost 80 percent of the students said they were against Tennoism. Then two weeks later, I asked them to write a report on "Japanese culture and Tennoism." Most of the students were earnest protectors of Japanese culture and recognized the important role of the Emperor in Japanese culture. In other words, once they started to argue about the Emperor from [the] viewpoint of Japanese culture, they turned into supporters of Tennoism.

The attitudes of Japanese anthropologists and archaeologists toward Japanese culture tend to be similarly ambivalent, and in this sense their work on Japanese ethnogenesis should probably be termed "culturalist" rather than "nationalist."

PART II

The Yayoi and the Formation of the Japanese

3

Biological Anthropology and the Dual-Structure Hypothesis

Upon the whole, the wide difference which is still observ'd between the Japanese Inhabitants of several Provinces, as to their shape, seems to argue strongly, that from time to time, different and new branches were grafted into the original Tree of this Nation.

Engelbert Kaempfer, *The History of Japan Together with a Description of the Kingdom of Siam, 1690–92,* Vol. 1

This and the two following chapters discuss three types of evidence pertaining to the Jōmon-Yayoi transition and thus to the initial formation of the Japanese people. This evidence is the result of biological anthropology, historical linguistics, and archaeology. It will quickly become clear that these are academic fields with very different histories and characteristics. Biological anthropology is the most international field. Not only do Japanese scholars publish prolifically in English, but foreign anthropologists are also widely involved in the analysis of Japanese material. The Euro-American contribution to Japanese historical linguistics has similarly been of great importance. Here, however, the field is more fragmented, with Japanese and foreign scholars often differing on questions of methodology. Japanese archaeology, in turn, provides considerable contrast with the other two subjects, since it is highly insular and introverted, both in theoretical orientations and in publishing practice. Because of the differences between these three subjects, the multidisciplinary approach adopted in this book is rare in Japanese scholarship, but the argument advanced here is that such an approach is essential to any real understanding of ethnogenesis.

IMMIGRATION VERSUS TRANSFORMATION: THE NEW CONSENSUS

In 1991, Japanese anthropologist Hanihara Kazurō published his so-called dual-structure hypothesis on the population history of the Japanese Islands. This model has been extremely influential, and a majority of scholars working on Japanese origins now support at least its main elements. Within what is generally a highly contested field of scholarship, such consensus is a rare and quite recent phenomenon. My own 1990 review of the Yayoi period demonstrates that even by the late 1980s there was little agreement on the role and extent of immigration in the Yayoi (Hudson 1990a, 66–69). Ten years ago, many scholars still supported transformation theories whereby Jōmon populations evolved into the modern Japanese with little or no immigration, physical differences being attributed to environmental and cultural factors associated with the transition to farming (Hasebe 1949, 1975; Suzuki 1960, 1963, 1969, 1981; Kouchi 1983, 1986; Aikens and Akazawa 1988; Akazawa 1986b, 75). As a result of research over the past decade, however, a majority of anthropologists now see immigration as having played the major role in the formation of the Yayoi people. While there is little agreement on the *number* of immigrants—either absolute or relative to the indigenous Jōmon people—few, if any, anthropologists now attribute the observed physical changes from Jōmon to Yayoi purely to environmental factors.

The dual-structure hypothesis can be summarized as follows (Fig. 3.1). Sometime during the Pleistocene the archipelago was settled by "proto-Mongoloid" populations from the south. These were the ancestors of the Jōmon people, and their morphological characteristics are still visible in Ainu and Okinawan populations. From the Yayoi period, populations with a quite different Northeast Asian or "Neo-Mongoloid" morphology began to arrive in the Islands. Although many local Yayoi-period populations still retained Jōmon characteristics, by the following Kofun period there was much greater mixing of indigenous and immigrant groups as far as the southern Tohoku. Genetically, the modern Japanese are primarily derived from the Yayoi-period immigrants, with some uncertain but regionally variable degree of Jōmon admixture (Hanihara 1991, 1992).

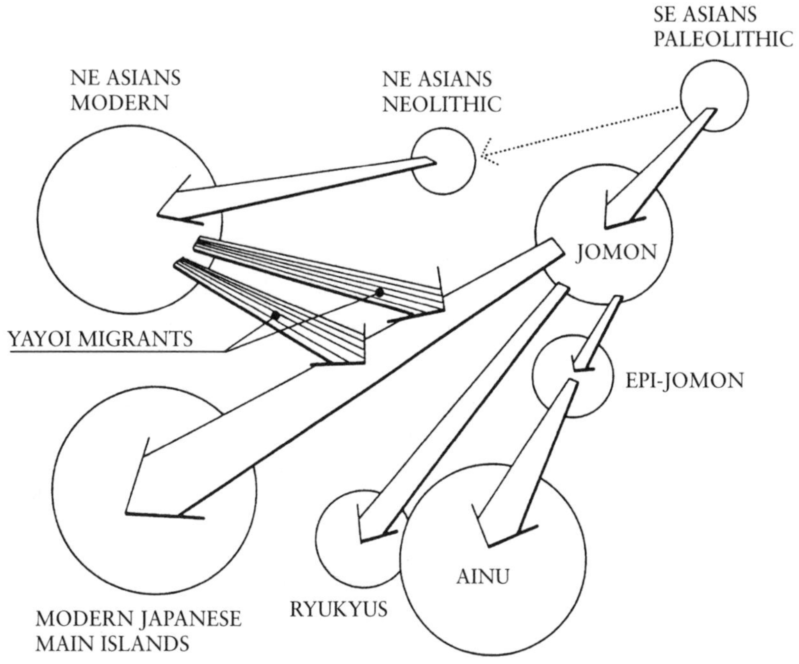

FIG. 3.1. Schematic representation of the dual-structure model of the population history of the Japanese Islands. From Hanihara (1991).

Although, as noted already, the dual-structure hypothesis has met with wide support, as research progresses certain aspects of the model have been subject to criticism. In particular, a number of recent genetic studies have failed to find the close links between the Ainu and Southeast Asian populations proposed by Hanihara (Nei 1995; Omoto 1995; Omoto and Saitou 1997). This problem is one of great significance for an overall understanding of the population history of the Japanese Islands, but it is not of direct relevance to the question of Yayoi immigration. In this chapter, the evidence for Yayoi immigration will be argued in some detail before we return to a consideration of some of the problems associated with the dual-structure hypothesis.

Cranial Analyses

One reason for the dual-structure hypothesis' widespread acceptance is a growing agreement that nonmetric cranial features are particularly suited for the study of genetic inheritance (Dodo 1974, 1987; Dodo and Ishida 1992; Dodo et al. 1992; Ossenberg 1992b, 65; but cf. Saunders 1989). Systematic nonmetric analyses of Japanese skulls using multivariate statistics began to be performed only quite recently, but a number of such studies have been completed. Two basic results are common to these studies, as they are also to most recent metric analyses (Brace et al. 1989, 1991; Dodo 1974, 1986, 1987; Dodo and Ishida 1990, 1992; Dodo et al. 1992; Hanihara K. 1985; Hanihara T. 1992; Howells 1986; Ishida and Dodo 1992; Kozintsev 1990, 1992; Mouri 1988; Ossenberg 1986; Yamaguchi 1987). First, Jōmon and Ainu populations invariably cluster together, and second, Yayoi populations cluster with historic and modern Japanese rather than with the Jōmon and Ainu (Fig. 3.3). This implies that the Japanese are genetically primarily derived from Yayoi rather than from Jōmon populations, suggesting considerable gene flow into the Islands during the Yayoi period.

Two basic types of skeletal population are known to have existed in the Islands in the Yayoi period. One type shows a continuation of typical Jōmon features, whereas the other is clearly different from preexisting Jōmon people. The non-Jōmon type, long assumed to be an immigrant population, is known primarily from the plains of northern Kyushu and from western Yamaguchi Prefecture. Within this group, average height (estimated by Pearson's method) is about 162–163 cm for adult males and 151 cm for females, the facial skeleton is high and narrow with a shallow nasal root and a very flat interorbital region, and dental occlusion is overbite (Naitō 1992; Nakahashi and Nagai 1989; Yamaguchi 1987). In contrast, the Jōmon-type skeletons known from northwest Kyushu have an average height of around 158–159 cm for adult males and 148 cm for females; the facial skeleton is low and wide, giving it a squarer appearance than the more rectangular face of the north Kyushu/Yamaguchi Yayoi specimens; the interorbital region is deep-set; and dental occlusion is edge-to-edge (Naitō 1992; Yamaguchi 1992).

The north Kyushu/Yamaguchi-type Yayoi population is known at a number of sites including Kanenokuma, Mitsu, Yoshinogari, Tateiwa, Asahi-kita, Nakanohama, and Doigahama (Kanaseki H. 1986; Kanaseki T. 1976; Ma-tsushita 1994; Matsushita and Naitō 1989; Naitō 1971; Saiki et al. 1994; Wakebe et al. 1994). Matsushita (1994, 93) divides Yayoi skeletons from this area into two subgroups that he terms the "Doigahama" and "Yoshinogari" types; of these the former has a narrower, more "delicate" face than the latter (Matsushita 1994). As we shall see below, Matsushita argues that these two subgroups may have different origins on the mainland.

FIG. 3.2. Major sites mentioned in chapter 3. 1, Hirota; 2, Yoshinogari; 3, Shinmachi; 4, Kaneno kuma; 5, Mitsu; 6, Tateiwa; 7, Doigahama; 8, Koura; 9, Karako; 10, Bishamon and Ōurayama; 11, Awa Shrine and Sano; 12, Tenjinmae; 13, Iwatsubo; 14, Shinonoi and Shiozaki; 15, Hinata I; 16, Goshōzan; 17, Usu 10.

Owing to preservation factors, almost all Yayoi-period skeletal remains have come from jar-burial and sand-dune sites in north Kyushu and western Yamaguchi, respectively. A few north Kyushu/Yamaguchi-type skeletons are, however, known from other Yayoi sites in western Japan, including Karako-Kagi in Nara (Matsushita 1994, 97) and Koura in Shimane (Kanaseki 1976, 12). As already noted, elsewhere in the Islands unadmixed Jōmon-type skeletal morphologies continued into the Yayoi period and beyond. One such region was northwest Kyushu, that is, the area corresponding to west Saga Prefecture, Nagasaki, and the Gotō Islands. Most sites in this area are coastal, and it has been argued that the region was the home of Jōmon populations who continued a predominantly fishing subsistence in contrast to the immigrant rice farmers who occupied the plains to the east (Matsushita 1994, 72; Matsushita and Naitō 1989; Naitō 1992).

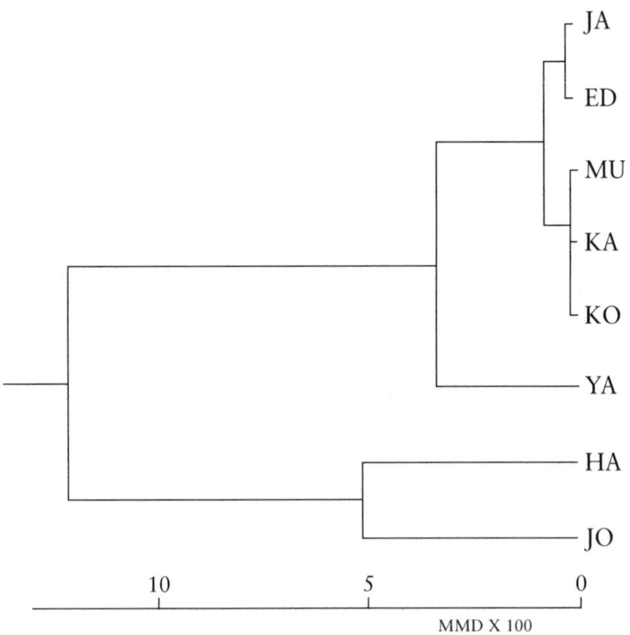

FIG. 3.3. Dendrograph of eight population samples from Japan based on cluster analysis of MMDs. JA, modern Japanese; ED, Edo; MU, Muromachi; KA, Kamakura; KO, Kofun; YA, Yayoi; HA, early modern Hokkaido Ainu; JO, Jōmon. From Dodo and Ishida (1990, 275).

In southern Kyushu, a third Yayoi-period population known from south Kagoshima and the Tanegashima and Amami islands is characterized by short skulls; low, wide facial skeletons; and an even shorter stature than that of the northwest Kyushu group (155–157 cm for males) (Matsushita and Naitō 1989). This population is usually also considered to be of Jōmon derivation (Naitō 1989, 149), but is somewhat different from other known Jōmon groups. Recent finds of sixty skeletons dating from the Final Jōmon to the Middle Yayoi from the Mashiki Azamabaru site in Ginowan, Okinawa have shown that this south Kyushu type was also found in the Ryukyu Islands. Matsushita (1994, 136–137), however, notes that the Mashiki Azamabaru population is different in certain respects from Jōmon groups in the region, and he raises the possibility that it may represent another immigrant group of different origin from that of the tall north Kyushu/Yamaguchi people. Matsushita (1994) goes on to suggest that this possible southern immigrant group may have arrived in Okinawa in the Final Jōmon before moving north to south Kyushu in the Middle Yayoi. At present, this suggestion remains largely unsubstantiated and is highly controversial.

Outside of Kyushu and Yamaguchi, Yayoi skeletal morphology is poorly known owing to the scarcity of human remains. A study of nonmetric dental features on poorly preserved Middle Yayoi remains from the Shinonoi and Shiozaki sites in Nagano City found some degree of immigrant influence (Shigehara et al. 1995). In the Kanto region, only five Yayoi sites or groups of sites have produced nonfragmentary skeletal remains. Early Middle Yayoi specimens from Iwatsubo in Gunma and from Sano Cave and Tenjinmae in Chiba have been described as very similar to typical Jōmon skeletons (Kaifu 1992; Suzuki 1963, 110; 1964; 1969). In contrast, Late Yayoi remains from Awa Shrine Cave in Chiba are seen as intermediate between Jōmon and Kofun period specimens (Koike and Suzuki 1955): "Facial conformation among these specimens is more variable. Some skulls show the same kind of prominent Jōmon-like glabello-nasal region seen at Sano cave and Tenjinmae, while others show a pronounced flatness of the same region that is characteristic not of Jōmon period skulls, but of later Kofun period facial skeletons" (Aikens and Akazawa 1992, 78). Late Middle Yayoi specimens from Bishamon and Ōurayama Caves (two of a group of cave sites on the Miura Peninsula in Kanagawa) are the most similar to the north Kyushu/Yamaguchi Yayoi population: "these skulls are more long-headed and have flatter faces [than the above specimens], poorly developed glabella, and a wide, low nasal root" (Aikens and Akazawa 1992).

An early Middle Yayoi female cranium from Hinata I Cave in Yamagata is reported as being closer to modern Japanese and Doigahama Yayoi than to Tsukumo Jōmon, despite the presence of some Jōmon characteristics (Katō and Ishida 1991). Though a full analysis has not yet been published, a three- to four-year-old child recently excavated from Yayoi-period deposits at Abakuchi Cave in Iwate Prefecture is thought to be of immigrant Yayoi type (Dodo Yukio, personal communication). In Hokkaido, skulls of the Epi-Jōmon period (ca. 100 BC–AD 700) are considered intermediate between Jōmon and Ainu populations though slightly closer to the latter (Ōba et al. 1978; Yamaguchi 1981; Dodo 1983). Matsushita (1994, 99) notes similarities between Epi-Jōmon skulls from the Usu 10 site and the Doigahama specimens and raises the possibility that immigrant genes may have reached Hokkaido by that stage.

The lack of good Yayoi-period cranial material from Shikoku and western Honshu represents an unfortunate gap in our present knowledge, but by the following Kofun era (ca. 300–700) there is no doubt that the north Kyushu/Yamaguchi morphology was widely distributed through the Islands. Studies of both metric and nonmetric cranial characteristics have shown that by the Kofun period, the population of the Kanto region was close to the "immigrant" Yayoi types of western Japan and remote from Jōmon populations. Yamaguchi (1987) studied metrical criteria from 100 adult skulls from Kofun- and Nara-period sites in the Kanto and southern Tohoku.[1] He found these crania to be most similar to the Yayoi series from Doigahama and concluded, "It is thus highly probable that a population which is considerably different morphologically from the indigenous Jōmon people . . . [had] spread into the eastern part of Honshu by around the 8th century" (Yamaguchi 1987, 7). Dodo's (1987) nonmetric cranial analysis produced similar results, with Kofun-era east Honshu populations clustering very closely with immigrant Yayoi and western Kofun, but being very distant from Jōmon specimens of both the east and west archipelago. A female skull (No. 1) from the Goshōzan cave, Miyagi (ca. AD 600) is typical of Kofun-era specimens from western Japan, but a male (No. 5) from the same site is morphologically close to the Hokkaido Ainu (Yamaguchi 1994, 114–118). All these results suggest that the genetic influence of the Yayoi immigrant people had already advanced to a high level by the seventh century even in eastern Honshu.

Matsushita (1994, 215–216) distinguishes two Kofun-period populations in southern Kyushu. The first, found in the mountainous regions of Kumamoto and Kagoshima, is basically of Jōmon type; the second, located in the plains, is similar to north Kyushu Yayoi and Kinai Kofun populations. It is not clear what might have happened to Matsushita's south Kyushu Yayoi group mentioned above. A recent dental study also found significant immigrant influence on Kofun-era populations in south Kyushu (Oyamada et al. 1995). In August 1997 the author participated in excavations at the Obama site on Tanegashima with a team from Kumamoto University. Skeletal remains of a male, a female, and an infant were discovered. Although the site produced only a few sherds of pottery, the burials are thought to date to the fourth to sixth centuries. Osteological analysis is currently being conducted by Doi Naomi of the University of the Ryukyus, but provisional observations suggest that the Obama population is quite different from the remains found at the Yayoi-period Hirota and Torinomine sites on Tanegashima and is similar to the people found on the plains of southern Kyushu.

In Hokkaido, skeletal remains of the Satsumon period (ca. 700–1300) are rare, but known examples are close to the recent Hokkaido Ainu (Dodo et al. 1991). Remains associated with the Okhotsk culture, which was found in northeast Hokkaido at about the same time as was the Satsumon, are morphologically quite different and share closest relations with northern Mongoloid populations such as the Nanai, Ulchi, Nivkh, and Sakhalin Okhotsk people (Ishida 1988, 1990, 1994; Hanihara T. 1991a). The physical anthropological evidence thus seems to confirm archaeological theories that the Okhotsk people were migrants from the north.

Within the wider context of East Asia as a whole, Jōmon and Ainu crania are thought to be closer to Southeast Asian and southern Chinese populations than to specimens from north China. *Homo sapiens* skulls from Minatogawa in Okinawa (ca. 18,000 BP), Liujiang in Guangxi Province, China (ca. 67,000 BP?), and Niah Cave, Sarawak (ca. 40,000 BP) are regarded as being closer to Jōmon people than to Pleistocene or Neolithic north Chinese (Wu 1992a, 1992b). Beginning with the Yayoi, though, there was a dramatic increase in cranial traits that cluster with the Mongoloid populations of Northeast Asia (Dodo and Ishida 1987; Hanihara K. 1985, 1991, 1992; Hanihara T. 1992; Ishida and Dodo 1992; Kozintsev 1990, 1992). An apparent exception to this model of Northeast Asian links from the Yayoi is provided by a metrical analysis by Pietrusewsky et al. (1992), who conclude that the modern Japanese are much closer to Southeast than to Northeast Asians. No Yayoi sample was, however, included in their analysis.

Very few skeletal remains from the period corresponding to the Yayoi are known on the adjacent Asian mainland (Matsushita 1994, 101). Furthermore, Matsushita (1994) notes that Chinese anthropologists are rarely interested in studying such "late" skeletal material and tend to focus their attention more on Pleistocene remains. On the Korean Peninsula, over 200 skeletons dating back to the fourth to the seventh century AD were excavated from the Yeanni site. Though poorly preserved (Nakahashi 1990a, 156), these specimens are said to have an average stature of 164.7 cm for males and 150.8 cm for females; with their high facial skeleton and flat naso-frontal region they also show a close affinity with Yayoi and Kofun populations in north Kyushu and Yamaguchi (Mine et al. 1994).

As mentioned above, Matsushita (1994, 135) suggests that his Yoshinogari and Doigahama skeletal types may have different geographical origins on the continent. He proposes possible source areas, with the former stretching from the mouth of the Yangzi up to the northern Korean Peninsula and the latter extending from the Shandong Peninsula up to the Maritime Provinces, the two zones thus overlapping on the Shandong and Korean peninsulas. In our present state of knowledge, such proposals remain very hypothetical, but recently Matsushita has conducted preliminary analyses on a large collection of Western Han-period skeletal remains from Linzi County in Shandong. These remains are reported to be similar to the north Kyushu/Yamaguchi Yayoi people, although it is not yet clear if they are closer to one or the other of Matsushita's subgroups.[2]

TEETH

Dental evidence played a major role in Hanihara's original formulation of the dual-structure hypothesis. Secondary dental traits in human populations from Asia and the Pacific have been divided into two types by American anthropologist Christy Turner (1987, 1989, 1990, 1992a, 1992b). Turner terms these two types "Sundadonty" and "Sinodonty," the latter characterized by "significantly higher frequencies of incisor shoveling and double shoveling, 1-rooted upper first premolars, upper first molar enamel extensions, missing-pegged-reduced upper third molars, lower first molar deflecting wrinkles, and 3-rooted lower first molars, as well as a lower frequency of 4-cusped lower second molars" (Scott and Turner 1997, 270). Sundadonty is the older pattern, developing out of an even older, more generalized dental pattern represented by Niah Cave and by Tabon in the Philippines (ca. 20,000 BP) and includes Southeast Asians, Polynesians, the Jōmon, and the Ainu. According to Turner, the original center of this dental type was the now-submerged Sundaland, a continental shelf that linked island and mainland Southeast Asia when sea levels were lower during the Pleistocene. From here, Sundadonty spread east to Polynesia and north to Japan. Although the sample is very small, the 18,000-year-old Minatogawa people on Okinawa were probably Sundadont, and such populations may have reached the main islands of Japan by around the same time (Turner 1987).

According to Turner, Sinodonty developed out of Sundadonty in northeast Asia as the latter population moved northwards. The Sinodont pattern is found at the Upper Cave of Zhoukoudian and in Chinese, Japanese, Mongols, northeast Siberians, and Native Americans. Sinodonty is first found in Japan in the Yayoi period: "Yayoi teeth closely resemble those of the modern Japanese, but they differ markedly from the Jōmonese (the Sundadonts who had migrated along the coast to Japan ten millenniums before) or the Ainu, their probable descendants" (Turner 1989, 73). In contrast to most cranial analyses that suggest a Northeast Asian link, Turner (1992b, 103–104) argues that the Yayoi people originated in south China. No details of his small Yayoi sample are given, however, and the sample is noticeably absent from his table of Mean Measures of Divergence (Turner 1992b, 101–102).

Turner's proposal of substantial differences between Jōmon and Yayoi teeth is matched by other researchers using both metric and nonmetric crown characteristics (Brace and Nagai 1982; Matsumura 1990; Matsumura et al. 1992, 1996; Oyamada 1992). The fact that Yayoi teeth are larger than Jōmon ones in itself suggests immigration, since such increases through secular causes are rare (Brace and Nagai 1982).[3] Hanihara Tsunehiko (1989a, 1989b, 1990a, 1990b, 1991a, 1991b) has conducted a series of both metric and nonmetric analyses of dental characteristics throughout East and Southeast Asia and Oceania. He concludes that the teeth of modern Japanese are "closely related to the Yayoi samples and [to] Chinese from the northeastern part of China (Manchuria). Jōmon, Ainu and [Ryukyu] islanders including Okinawa form another group, showing close affinities to Micronesians, Polynesians, and Negritos but not to the Australian Aborigines. [These] findings . . . support the dual structure model for the population history of [the] Japanese proposed by K. Hanihara (1991)" (Hanihara T. 1992, 126).

GENETIC DATA

Japan can boast a higher density of genetic data than can any other country in Asia (Cavalli-Sforza et al. 1994, 249). Within the Islands, many genetic traits show a *cline,* a gradual increase or decrease in frequency, from west to east. In many cases, the Ainu are closer to populations in northeast Honshu, whereas Koreans are often closer to southwestern Japanese. For example, within the ABO blood-group system, there are weak but well-defined clines, particularly for the A allele, from west to east (Tanaka 1959; Nei and Imaizumi 1966a, 1966b; Fujita et al. 1978). A statistically significant cline was observed between Aomori and Nagasaki in two alleles of the serum protein system Gc (Gc*1F and Gc*2) (Omoto 1986; Yuasa et al. 1983). Omoto (1992, 143) notes that "this cline can be extended to the Ainu in the north and to the Koreans in Seoul in the west." Similar clines are known from another serum protein, haptoglobin (Hp), and the Gpt1 allele of the red-cell enzyme glutamate-pyruvate transaminase (Ishimoto and Kuwata 1973; Omoto 1992, 143).

Evidence for the separate origins of Ainu-Okinawan and Japanese populations includes the distribution of human serum orosomucoid (ORM) and Alpha-2-HS-glycoprotein (AHSG) polymorphisms (Umetsu and Yuasa 1990, 19; see also Umetsu et al. 1989). A high percentage of AHSG*5 in parts of the Ryukyu Islands, however, may suggest a separate migration from the Asian mainland at some time in prehistory (Umetsu and Yuasa 1990, 18). According to Omoto (1992, 142), the strongest evidence for the common origin of Ainu and Okinawans comes from the frequency of the r" or cdE haplotype of the Rh blood group. Though extremely rare throughout the world, high frequencies have been reported amongst both the Ainu (12.4 percent) and Ryukyu Islanders (7 percent on Okinawa Island); on Honshu, in contrast, the frequency is only about 3 percent (Nakajima et al. 1967).

These genetic data have often been explained by the variable mixing of native and immigrant populations from the Yayoi period onward, but little theoretical modeling of the processes involved has been attempted. Yuasa et al. (1983) argue that their observed Gc*2 cline reflects migration, since the frequency of that allele usually decreases with sunshine, whereas in Japan it increases from north to south. Aoki and Omoto (1980) developed a migration model based on ABO blood-group frequencies. Although they concluded that Jōmon/Yayoi admixture was a likely explanation for the observed cline, a more recent study by one of the authors notes that "their claim, lacking a statistical test for goodness-of-fit, was premature" (Aoki 1994, 292). Aoki's (1994) admixture model gives an acceptable fit to clines in Gc*2 and Hp*1 alleles but not to allele A of the ABO blood-group locus. Aoki (1994, 285) reports that "the maximum likelihood estimates of the elapsed time since [the] beginning of admixture are compatible with the proposal that the immigrants arrived at the end of the Jōmon period." Maximum likelihood estimates for eastern Japan, however, suggest that the immigrants reached the north Kanto in the first stage of colonization, a quicker rate of expansion than that accepted by most archaeologists (Aoki 1994, 292–293).

In recent years, new developments within genetic anthropology have stimulated much research on the wider genetic relationships of the Japanese, expanding on the basis of earlier work on genetic variability within the archipelago. Due to its role in the control of immune response, the HLA (human leucocyte antigen) system has been well studied in the medical field. The high degree of polymorphism of HLA means it is also important to anthropology as a genetic marker (e.g. Serjeantson 1985). Groups (or haplotypes) of HLA genes belonging to the major histocompatibility complex (MHC) have recently been studied in East Asian populations, and a variety of migration routes into Japan have been proposed. The most common haplotype in the Japanese was absent in south China but found at a frequency of 2 to 4 percent in Beijing and Seoul. In Japan this haplotype was particularly common, reaching frequencies as high as 13 percent in Kyushu and western Honshu. This pattern suggests a dispersal from north China through the Korean Peninsula to Kyushu and western Japan (Tokunaga and Juji 1992). In a nearest-neighbor analysis of HLA data from thirty populations worldwide, Saitō (1994, 18–19) found Japanese and Koreans to be very close to each other along an otherwise Chinese branch. An HLA study of the Ainu by Bannai et al. (1996) found that population to be distinct from the mainland Japanese. These authors conclude that their "observations may support the hypothesis that the Ainu people are the descendants of some Upper Paleolithic populations of northeast Asia from which Native Americans are also descended" (Bannai et al. 1996, 1).

Work on the distribution of the Adult T-cell leukemia virus (known as HTLV-I) has shown a high proportion of carriers among Ainu and Ryukyuan populations, which is in contrast to populations in central Japan, where carriers are rare (Table 3.1). Carriers are almost nonexistent on continental Asia, but are found in West Africa, New Guinea and northern Australia, and the Caribbean and northern South America (Ishida 1993, 366). Farris (1993, 384) quotes American AIDS expert Robert Gallo, who argues that HTLV-I was transmitted to Japan by sixteenth-century Portuguese sailors who brought infected slaves and monkeys from Africa. Japanese researchers, however, propose a quite different scenario: populations containing a high percentage of HTLV-I carriers occupied the Japanese Islands in the Palaeolithic or Jōmon period; they were followed in the Yayoi by immigrants from China and Korea who did not carry the virus. The Yayoi people then expanded through the Islands, leaving the indigenous carriers at the northern and southern peripheries (Hinuma 1986, 1993; Ishida 1993; Tajima 1994;

Tajima et al. 1992). This scenario seems a far more likely explanation for the present distribution of HTLV-I than does Gallo's theory.

A similar pattern to HTLV-I is shown by the distribution of Hepatitis B viruses. The type common in Hokkaido, the Tohoku, and the Ryukyus was also found to be common in Taiwan, the Philippines, and south China; conversely, that type was rare in western Japan, north China, Manchuria, and Korea (Sasaki 1991b, 291). Again, this study can be interpreted as providing support for the theory of Yayoi immigration. It must be stressed, however, that in all cases this support comes from the fit with other evidence rather than from the intrinsic nature of the genetic data. There is no reason why one type of hepatitis should necessarily be linked with the Yayoi; theoretically it could have arrived in the middle of the Jōmon, but consideration of all the relevant evidence makes association with a Yayoi migration most likely. Hōrai et al. (1996) analyzed nucleotide sequences from the D-loop region of mitochondrial (mt) DNA from mainland Japanese, Ainu, Okinawans, Koreans, and Chinese. They found that the largest number of shared types were possessed by the mainland Japanese and Koreans. In this study, Hōrai's team found no shared types between the Ainu and Okinawans, an absence that they explain as a result of the time since separation of the two populations (Hōrai et al. 1996, 586). Hammer and Hōrai's (1995) work on Y chromo-

TABLE 3.1

HTLV-I CARRIERS IN EAST ASIAN POPULATIONS

POPULATION	%TESTED POSITIVE FOR HTLV-I
Hokkaido Japanese	1.0–1.1
Honshu Japanese	0.3–1.2
South Kyushu Japanese	7.8
Korean	0.0
Mongolian	0.0
Chinese	0.0
Hokkaido Ainu (1960s)	45.2
Hokkaido Ainu (1980s)	40.0
Okinawans (1980s)	33.9

From data in Ishida (1993, 368).

some variation appears to lend further support to a genetic division between Okinawans and mainland Japanese. They found the Y *Alu* polymorphic (YAP) element to be absent in surveyed individuals from Korea and Taiwan but present in Japan at frequencies varying from 33 percent in Shizuoka to 56 percent in Okinawa. Based on its absence on the East Asian mainland and on its higher frequency in Okinawa than in Honshu, Hammer and Hōrai (1995, 958) argue that the YAP element may trace Jōmon male lineages. Frequencies of the DXYS5 Y2 allele appear to mark continental immigrants who arrived during the Yayoi period (Hammer and Hōrai 1995, 958–959).

Not all genetic research on East Asia has been as consistent with the dual-structure hypothesis as have the studies mentioned so far. Variations of the gamma globulin type *ab3st* in East Asia were plotted by Matsumoto (1984, 1988; Matsumoto et al. 1982) who found the following results: (1) there is a major split between north China/Manchuria and south China/Southeast Asia; (2) the Okinawans and the Ainu are slightly different from the mainland Japanese, but there is no noticeable cline within the latter population; (3) the Ainu and the Okinawans are closer to the northern continental group than to the southern one. Of these results, (3) is the opposite of what we might expect based on the other genetic markers considered above.

Another apparently unique result has recently been obtained by Cavalli-Sforza and his associates using classic genetic polymorphisms such as blood groups, other immunological polymorphisms including HLA, and electrophoretic variation of proteins and enzymes (Cavalli-Sforza et al. 1994). In this work, a technique for deriving distribution maps of genetic variability known as "synthetic maps" was used to great effect. In East Asia a number of patterns were visible. Some 35 percent of the genetic variation could be explained by an east-west gradient across Asia, which appears to represent the division between Caucasoids and Mongoloids. A north-south division, accounting for 18 percent of variation, probably represents the boundary between northern and southern Mongoloids and is similar to the classic split between north and south China. Most interesting of all, however, is the map that shows a circular gradient of genetic variability around central Japan. This pattern accounts for 8 percent of variation and is marked by progressively decreasing values as one moves west across Asia. According to Cavalli-Sforza and his colleagues, this genetic gradient around Japan would be most easily explained by a population expansion from central Japan. Unfortunately, there is little archaeological or historical evidence that could support such a hypothesis. Cavalli-Sforza et al. suggest high population levels in the Chūbu Middle Jōmon may have "fixed" a genetic pattern that was numerically too strong to have been much diluted by later immigration. Although this might possibly explain variation within the archipelago, without regular Jōmon interbreeding with continental populations, it is not clear how this could have led to an Asiawide gradient visible as far as Tibet (cf. Cavalli-Sforza et al. 1994, 248–252).

Cavalli-Sforza et al.'s (1994, 230–232) results from within the Japanese Islands also present some problems of interpretation. Although the Ryukyuans are second closest to the Ainu, it is the Hokkaido Japanese who are the least distant. For their part, the Ryukyuans are closest to the Hokkaido Japanese, but the Hokkaido Japanese are most similar to the Koreans. While intermarriage between the Ainu and the Hokkaido Japanese is known to have occurred since Japanese colonization, it is not clear how the close relationship with the Ryukyuans on the one hand and the Koreans on the other can be reconciled.

An obvious drawback to all the genetic research described so far is that it is based upon modern humans. Recently, however, it has become possible to extract and analyze ancient DNA from skeletal remains, and such work is quite advanced in Japan (Ōta and Hudson 1998). In 1989, mitochondrial DNA was successfully amplified from a 6,000-year-old Jōmon skeleton. The amplified nucleotide sequence was found to be nearly identical with that of two contemporary Southeast Asians; no identical match was found with living Japanese. This suggested to the authors of the study that "the ancestor of [the] Japanese who presumably lived in the central part of Japan about 6000 years ago had [a] common origin with . . . some contemporary Southeast Asians" (Hōrai et al. 1989, 232). This result has been confirmed by further research. Mitochondrial DNA extracted from four Jōmon and two late historic Ainu skeletons was found to cluster in the same group as that extracted from four Malaysians and Indonesians as well as from fourteen contemporary Japanese. In another study, DNA extracted from immigrant-type Yayoi skeletons in Saga Prefecture, Kyushu, was found to be close to that of modern Japanese (Ōta 1994; Ōta et al. 1995). These results are seen as support for the two-stage model of the peopling of Japan (Hōrai 1990, 1992, 1993, 1994; Nakahashi 1993).

ANTHROPOMETRIC OBSERVATIONS

As suggested by the quote at the beginning of this chapter, there is a long tradition of research on the phenotypic aspects of the Japanese people. As early as the 1880s, German physician Erwin von Baelz had classified the Japanese into two physical types that he termed "Satsuma" and "Chōshū." The Satsuma type was shorter and more stockily built; the face was broad with a wide nose, thick lips, and large eye openings with double eyelids. The Chōshū type was taller and more slender, with a long face, narrow eye openings and nose, thinner lips, and single eyelids (von Baelz 1885). Satsuma and Chōshū are the old names for Kagoshima and Yamaguchi, and the physical types described by von Baelz bear similarities to the two skeletal types known from the same parts of Japan during the Yayoi period some 2,000 years earlier. This suggests that mixing of Jōmon and immigrant populations was still occurring as late as the Meiji era, a conclusion supported by later anthropometric and genetic research.

Building on the early work of von Baelz and others, there is a growing literature that attempts to discern Yayoi and Jōmon types in the contemporary Japanese. A sensationalist element is common in some of these writings. In the work of Umehara Takeshi, for example his *Kimi wa Yayoijin ka Jōmonjin ka? (Are You a Yayoi or a Jōmon Person?)* (Umehara and Nakagami 1984), the Jōmon and Yayoi types take on *psychological* as well as physical characteristics. Despite such trends, however, this approach does have a serious side, and it is probable that some of the observed physiognomic variation in modern Japanese can be attributed to Jōmon/Yayoi admixture (see Matsushita 1994, 185–251). Physical differences in modern Japanese have a wider distribution than von Baelz's names suggest. Like many of the genetic markers discussed above, the anthropometric data often show a cline from western to eastern Japan. A wide variety of anthropometric data has been collected for Japanese populations (see Kohama 1968; Watanabe et al. 1975; Omoto 1978; Yamaguchi 1990, 44–94; Aikens and Higuchi 1982, 3–7). These data include the frequency of detached earlobes and eyelids with double folds, traits that are both high in the Ainu and low in southwestern Japan (Kohama 1968; Watanabe and Nakagawa 1975). Based on the ratio of whorls to arches and loops, a fingerprint index can be derived, and the following values were observed: Ainu, fifty-one; eastern Japanese, eighty-nine; western Japanese, ninety-seven; south Koreans, ninety-nine (Aikens and Higuchi 1982, 7). Data collected in the 1940s on head shape show a similar cephalic index (the ratio of head length and breadth) between Korea and many parts of western Japan. Stature can also be seen to increase as one progresses eastwards through the archipelago. Taste sensitivity of the chemical phenylthiocarbamide (PTC) was found to have a clinal distribution, with low sensitivity among the Ainu contrasting with higher values for southwest Japanese (Kohama 1968). Of the two phenotypes of earwax—wet and dry—the latter is characteristic of Mongoloid populations. Over 80 percent of mainland Japanese have the dry type, compared with less than 40 percent among the Ainu and less than 60 percent in Okinawans (Omoto 1992, 140). Research by Kohara Shisei has demonstrated an interesting pattern in the ability to wink, that is to completely close one eye while keeping the other open. In Kohara's study, the proportion of mainland Japanese able to wink was as low as 43.1 percent for women and 45.5 percent for men; among the Okinawans and Ainu it was much higher: 60.0 percent and 68.8 percent, respectively, for the former and 69.0 percent and 71.6 percent, respectively, for the latter (see Yamaguchi 1990, 68–71). To what extent ear-wax types and winking ability are actually under genetic control, however, has yet to be proven.

Although it seems easy to explain much of the anthropometric data by the admixture of Jōmon and Yayoi/Japanese populations, we should not forget that some anthropometric variation may have environmental causes. Research conducted by Kouchi (1986) has demonstrated that increasing stature along the archipelago is significantly correlated with temperature. Her work has also shown that the cephalic index distribution observed on data collected in the 1940s had changed dramatically by the 1980s, an instability that she sees as "not compatible with the hypothesis which explains the geographic distribution of cephalic index by the effects of migrations from Korea in prehistoric times" (Kouchi 1986, 99). Kondo and Kobayashi (1975, 10) report an average increase in stature of Japanese seventeen-year olds between 1900 and 1970 of 8.7 cm for males and 9.6 cm for females. As possible causes of this increase they suggest better nutrition and health care, a breakdown in previous geographic/genetic regionalism, and the increased practice of sports. Matsushita (1994, 231–237) discusses what he sees as quite major changes in the Japanese physique over the past fifteen years, changes that are of course due to cultural factors, not to genetic inflow.

DOGS AND MICE

Evidence from two other, rather unexpected sources may also support the dual-structure hypothesis. The oldest domesticated dogs known in Japan are from the Kamikuroiwa and Natsushima sites dating to between 9,000 and 10,000 years ago. Wolves existed in Japan until the Meiji era, but because Japanese dog breeds are so small and because no transitional skeletal remains have been uncovered, it is believed that dogs were introduced rather than domesticated in the Islands (Sahara 1987b, 81–86). Tanabe (1992) studied protein polymorphisms in blood samples taken from 3,445 individual dogs from across Eurasia. Tanabe's work shows close relationships between dogs from Taiwan, south China, the Ryukyus, Hokkaido, and some Japanese breeds, and between Korean and most native Japanese breeds in Honshu and Shikoku. This suggests that there were two dispersals of dogs into Japan, the first from Southeast Asia and the second from the Korean Peninsula: "It is assumed that the Hokkaido (Ainu) dog breed is a descendant of an old type of Japanese dog which was brought 10,000–12,000 years ago by Jōmon [people] who came from southeast Asia. Most of the other Japanese native dog breeds or populations, except [one] breed (the Ryukyu) and some populations in [the Ryukyu] islands, are descendants of the hybrid between the old type of Japanese dogs and Korean origin dogs which were brought 1,700–2,300 years ago by the Yayoi migrants who came through the Korean peninsula" (Tanabe 1992, 161, 1993; Tanabe et al. 1991).

A similar pattern was found in studies of the mtDNA of Japanese house mice *(Mus musculus molossinus)*. The mtDNA sequence of mice in Hokkaido and northeast Honshu was found to be the same as that of those in south China and southeast Asia; conversely the sequence of mice from southwest Japan is the same as that of mice distributed in a wide area through northeast Asia, north China, south Siberia, and east Europe. As mice, like dogs, are commensal with humans, it is believed these genetic differences reflect an early, Pleistocene human migration from the south followed by a later dispersal from northeast Asia (Moriwaki 1989; Moriwaki and Yonekawa 1993; Yonekawa et al. 1980, 1981, 1988).

Taken by itself, the evidence of differing abilities to wink or genetic polymorphisms in mice has limited value; what is important is the *combination* of the cranial, dental, anthropometric, and genetic data summarized above. Together these data are convincing support for the dual-structure model of Japanese population history in which an early arrival of a proto-Mongoloid population was followed by a neo-Mongoloid population in the Yayoi. Of course, a number of controversial areas remain. One of these is the timing of the arrival of the first population or whether we are indeed dealing with one or more episodes of colonization. This problem is intimately related to the overall population history of East Asia and to the origin of the Mongoloids. As mentioned above, recent genetic work concluding that the Ainu are much closer to Northeast Asian than to Southeast Asian populations has further complicated this issue. As Omoto and Saitou (1997) take pains to point out, however, debate over the ultimate origins of the Jōmon people does not alter the fact that most of the biological evidence still supports a large-scale migration into the Islands in the Yayoi period. Two other problems with the dual-structure hypothesis—the status of the Okinawan islanders and the degree of admixture between Jōmon and Yayoi groups—will be discussed briefly below.

THE RYUKYU ISLANDERS: JŌMON OR JAPANESE?

Phenotypical similarities between the Okinawans and the Ainu were noticed by von Baelz as early as 1911. Compared to the mainland Japanese, both groups tend to be shorter in stature and to have thicker body hair. Some genetic studies mentioned earlier in this chapter have also supported a close relationship between Ainu and Okinawans. Skeletal analyses by Ikeda (1974), Yamaguchi (1982), Hanihara (1985), and others found further similarities between modern/historic Ainu and Okinawans and prehistoric Jōmon populations, leading to the hypothesis that the Jōmon people were ancestral to both the Ainu and Okinawans. While, as we have seen, this hypothesis now seems correct as regards the Ainu, controversy still marks the literature on the Okinawans.

Miyake (1940) and Suda (1950) argue that the Okinawans should be seen as a regional Japanese population. Kanaseki (1976, 8) notes that the short-headed Okinawans contrast with long-headed Ainu. An anthropometric study by Tagaya and Ikeda (1976) argues that the Ainu and Okinawans were very distant from each other. Nonmetric cranial studies by Mouri (1986) and Dodo (1987) find that the Okinawans show closer affinities to modern Japanese than to the Jōmon or the Ainu. Based on his data, Kozintsev (1990, 26) concludes that "in the Ryukyu people, contrary to the Ainu, the Mongoloid component predominates over the Jōmon component." Recent work by Doi Naomi and her colleagues has tended to confirm this conclusion, showing that a major change had occurred in the cranial morphology of Okinawans by the modern era (Doi 1997a, 1997b, personal communication; Dodo et al. 1998).

In a number of papers, Hanihara Tsunehiko (1989a, 1989b, 1990a, 1990b) has proposed that dentally the Okinawan, Ainu, and Jōmon populations are quite similar, as are Tokushima and Aogashima islanders, also. The case of Aogashima is particularly interesting, since no prehistoric sites are known there (Hudson 1988). If, based on present evidence, the modern Aogashima islanders cannot possibly be derived from an in situ Jōmon population, could their dental characteristics be explained by geographical isolation rather than by a Jōmon inheritance? Might the same explanation be applicable to the Okinawans or Ainu? Hanihara concludes that there is some conservatism as a result of isolation in these populations, but he also sees a Jōmon inheritance as likely (Hanihara T. 1989a, 1989b). He does not attempt to explain, however, why Aogashima islanders should have teeth that are closer to those of the Okinawa-Ainu-Jōmon group than to those of modern Japanese-Yayoi. Results of metrical dental analyses conducted by Suzuki and Takahama (1992) and Suzuki et al. (1994) were slightly different from those of Hanihara in that in the two former studies, populations from Okinawa clustered with Doigahama Yayoi and with modern teeth from Pusan, Tsushima, and Akita rather than with Jōmon specimens, which clustered with modern teeth from Taiwan and Tanegashima.

The population history of Okinawa thus remains problematical. As will be discussed in more detail in the following three chapters, the lack of any real consensus on the biological history of the Ryukyu islanders currently makes it extremely difficult to incorporate Okinawa into the overall model proposed in this book.

JŌMON-YAYOI ADMIXTURE

Another major problem regarding the population history of the Japanese Islands is the precise relationship between the Jōmon and the Yayoi/Japanese populations. The presence of genetic clines suggests that the first population was not totally replaced by the second, but the dental and cranial nonmetric results imply that the immigrant Yayoi people have made a much greater genetic contribution to the modern Japanese than have the native Jōmon people. On dental traits, Matsumura et al. (1992) suggest that the Yayoi genetic contribution to the modern Japanese could be as high as 70–90 percent. Brace et al. (1989) even appear to argue for the *replacement* of the Jōmon by Yayoi people, although they also propose some Jōmon-Ainu genetic contribution through the samurai class.

The only scientific simulation of the number of migrants into the Islands is that of Hanihara (1987). Hanihara used two models to estimate immigration during the Yayoi and Kofun periods. The first used Koyama's (1976, 1984) population estimates for the beginning and end of the period to derive figures for the number of migrants and the proportion of Jōmon/migrant lineages in the final stage. Hanihara's second model used changes in cranial morphology to estimate rates of admixture. Both models supported a large influx of migrants. At a population growth rate of 0.2 percent per year, for example, the proportion of Jōmon to migrant populations was estimated to be almost 1:9 or 2:8 by AD 700, ratios consistent with the results of the morphological change model (Hanihara 1987, 400). Even at this relatively high rate of 0.2 percent, the total number of Yayoi and Kofun migrants was estimated to be between 1.3 and 1.5 million (Table 3.2).

TABLE 3.2

HANIHARA KAZURŌ'S DEMOGRAPHIC SIMULATION FOR JŌMON AND MIGRANT POPULATIONS BETWEEN 300 BC AND AD 700

POPULATION SIZE		ANNUAL GROWTH RATE (%)	NUMBER OF JŌMON DESCEN-DANTS	NUMBER OF MIGRANTS		JŌMON/ MIGRANT RATIO IN AD 700
300 BC	AD 700			PER YEAR	TOTAL	
75,800	5,399,800	0.1	206,046	3,024	3,024,156	1 : 26
		0.2	560,000	1,517	1,516,516	1 : 9.6
		0.3	1,522,485	610	610,379	1 : 3.5
		0.4	4,138,540	94	94,316	1 : 1.3
160,300	5,399,800	0.1	435,741	2,890	2,890,412	1 : 12.3
		0.2	1,184,466	1,321	1,320,869	1 : 4.6
		0.3	3,219,712	343	343,196	1 : 1.7

From Hanihara (1987, 396).

Imamura (1996, 155–160) has criticized Hanihara's estimates, which he sees as inflated. Imamura's main focus is on Jōmon population dynamics, and he does not attempt a new estimate for the number of Yayoi migrants. Instead he suggests that "groups of immigrants, or local communities with a high proportion of immigrants and their descendants, which by comparison with other indigenous group[s] held more advanced agricultural techniques, realized and maintained higher rates of population growth over a considerable period of time, resulting in the increase and spread of the mainland gene" (Imamura 1996, 160). I am in full agreement with Imamura here. Although this book adopts an immigration model for the Jōmon-Yayoi transition, the type of agricultural colonization proposed here does not necessarily require a massive number of migrants. What is important is the number of immigrants and their descendants *relative to* the number of indigenous Jōmon people. Agricultural colonization could have been accomplished by an initially quite small population—perhaps of no more than a few hundred—if the immigrant lineages had a high rate of population growth. In this respect, it may be appropriate to consider annual growth rates much higher than those used by Hanihara, possibly even approaching 1 percent for short periods in the early Yayoi.

In concluding this section, brief mention must be made of recent attempts to model the proportion of immigrant versus native genes from genetic data. Hōrai et al. (1996, 585) calculated that in modern Japanese the proportion of mtDNA derived from Yayoi immigrants is 65 percent, whereas only 35 percent is derived from the Jōmon. Since mtDNA is inherited maternally, these figures could be seen as being minimum estimates, as male farmers often marry hunter-gatherer females, whereas the reverse is rare (see Spielmann and Eder 1994, 308). Such an interpretation is apparently contradicted by Hammer and Hōrai's (1995, 959) estimate, based on paternally inherited Y chromosomes, that in modern Japanese 39 percent of mtDNA is derived from the Yayoi and 61 percent from the Jōmon. However, both of these estimates rely on the unproven assumption that the present-day gene frequencies in Ainu/Okinawan and in Korean/Chinese populations are similar to those that existed in the Jōmon and Yayoi periods, respectively (Hammer and Hōrai 1995, 959; Hōrai et al. 1996, 585).

Many problems thus remain in attempts to estimate the number and proportion of Yayoi immigrants, but the following provisional conclusion seems warranted: although the Jōmon people were not totally replaced by the incoming Yayoi migrants, their genetic contribution to the later Japanese was small, perhaps less than one quarter. We need now to see how the linguistic and archaeological records match such biological expectations.

4
The Linguistic Archaeology of the Japanese Islands

[F]or modern Japan, any acknowledgment of far-reaching linguistic relationships has seemed a surrender of identity for which the culture is still unprepared.

Roy Andrew Miller, "New Light on Old Korean"

In this chapter I argue that the Japanese language first spread through the Japanese Islands with agricultural colonization from the Yayoi period, replacing the previous Jōmon language(s) except for Ainu in the north. This hypothesis is based on recent theoretical work on the relationship between languages and population movements and on linguistic research on the historical development of Japanese dialects. The model proposed here provides linguistic support for the expansion of Yayoi/Japanese populations out of Kyushu and is thus consistent with the biological evidence presented in the previous chapter. The model does not directly support immigration from the continent, but circumstantial evidence makes it probable that the Japanese language did in fact arrive in the Islands from the Korean Peninsula at the end of the Jōmon.

GENETIC AFFILIATIONS

There are three main types of theories with regard to the genealogy of Japanese, proposing genetic links with (1) the Altaic family, (2) proposing links with South/Southeast Asian or Pacific languages (mainly Austronesian), or

(3) viewing Japanese as some sort of mixed language (mainly Austronesian-Altaic). In practice, these theories may be further condensed to two, as most linguists who argue for an Austronesian link also support a relationship with Altaic, leading to the concept of a mixed language.

Of the three theories, the first has the longest and most respectable pedigree. Boller (1857) began comparative work on Japanese with the proposition that it is related to Altaic, a widely dispersed family with around sixty languages spoken by some 250 million people (Ruhlen 1987, 127).[1] Korean had been linked with Altaic in the early nineteenth century, and this link was later supported by the research of Aston (1879), Ramstedt (1949), Poppe (1960), Lee (1964), and others (see Lewin 1976). In 1966, Martin published a body of more than 300 etymologies connecting Korean and Japanese. A few years later, Miller (1971) attempted to show that Japanese also belongs within the Altaic group, a conclusion further supported by Menges (1975), Whitman (1985), and Starostin (1986, 1991). Despite this work, classification of the Altaic family remains controversial. The position considered to be the orthodox one supports a Proto-Altaic unity as reconstructed by Ramstedt and Poppe; this original language then split into Turkic, Mongolian, and Tungusic subdivisions. Japanese and Korean are believed to have branched from an early eastern division of this family. A contrasting view, however, sees the traditional Altaic classification as premature. Central to this criticism is the validity of a genetic relationship between Turkic, Mongolian, and Tungusic and thus the whole concept of an original Proto-Altaic unity. Summarizing a recent conference discussion, Unger (1990a, 479) writes that, "Indeed, as far as Japanese and Korean are concerned, we are not even sure that bringing Mongolian into consideration, let alone Turkic, is worthwhile given the present state of knowledge." With regard to Japanese, Unger proposes that work should be directed to the reconstruction of what has been termed the Macro-Tungusic group of Northeast Asia, but his suggested approach, whereby we work outward from a small "kernel" of secure genetic relationships, may be the wrong way of dealing with the problem. There is widespread agreement that the Altaic languages and Japanese and Korean are related at some level; what is unclear is the *overall* pattern of the relationship and how these languages in turn relate to Indo-European, Uralic, and larger groupings such as Eurasiatic.

In Japan itself the perceived scarcity of convincing cognates between Japanese and the Altaic languages, and the phonological simplicity of Japanese, have led many linguists to look to the south rather than the north. In particular, phonological similarities with the Austronesian languages have determined the main source of comparisons, although Matsumoto (1928) and others have also proposed Austro-Asiatic links. This "southern hypothesis" cannot be understood based on linguistic criteria alone: it derives in part from a wider debate on Japanese cultural origins, wherein the apparent opposition of tropical and temperate cultural traits is interpreted as the result of the mixing of various waves of migration from the north and south (see Pauly 1980). It is not surprising, therefore, that most linguistic theories in this category also postulate a mixing of Austronesian and Altaic languages in the formation of Japanese. Building on earlier work by Shinmura (1980[1911]), Polivanov (1924), and Izui (1952), Ōno Susumu appears to have been the first linguist to propose an Austronesian "substratum" in the sense that an Austronesian language had once been spoken in the Japanese Islands (see Shibatani 1990, 103–107). In the late 1950s, Ōno proposed a two-stage model of an original Austronesian language followed by an Altaic language in the Yayoi (Ōno 1970). By 1980, he had inserted a third language (Tamil, a Dravidian language of south India) into his scheme (Ōno 1980, 1987, 1989). At first Ōno (1980) argued that Tamil arrived in the middle of the Jōmon but has since changed this to the Yayoi period (Ōno 1990, 1994).

Unlike Ōno, Murayama Shichirō (e.g. 1976) supports the view of Japanese as a "mixed language" with an earlier Austronesian element influenced by Altaic forms. Although this idea of Japanese as a mixed language was first proposed by the Soviet scholar E. D. Polivanov (1890–1938), it has found most support among Japanese linguists. In Japan one often comes across the opinion that Japanese is such a unique language that its historical development must have also followed uniquely complex processes. Theoretically, of course, this is nonsense. There is absolutely no reason to assume that Japanese has had a developmental history totally unlike that of any other language (Miller 1976). Even if it were some sort of mixed language, it would still have to be possible to study Japanese according to general theoretical principles equally applicable to other languages. Although a mixed language involves a unique type of structural borrowing, this cannot invalidate an underlying genetic relationship. A genetic relationship with one language family necessarily rules out a similar relationship with another. Japanese is *either* an Altaic *or* an Austronesian language; it cannot be genetically derived from both, unless those families are both in turn derived from an even more remote common ancestor. As a result of such theoretical problems associated with the concept of mixed languages, many Western linguists have dismissed the concept. This may have blinded us to the importance of considering what happens in language-contact situations, an oversight Maher (1991, 1996) has recently tried to remedy with an explicit consideration of the sociolinguistic aspects of Yayoi language change. Maher's "North Kyushu Creole" hypothesis will be discussed in more detail below.

The theory of a genetic relationship between Japanese and Austronesian has not been supported by Japanese scholars alone. In addition to several early works (e.g. Whymant 1926), particular mention should be made of Paul Benedict's 1990 book *Japanese/Austro-Tai*. Through a series of proposed phonological correspondences, Benedict attempts to show that Japanese and Austronesian share a common ancestor ("Austro-Japanese"). He ignores the competing Altaic hypothesis and describes Japanese solely in terms of his Austro-Tai link. In a review of the book, Austronesian linguist David Solnit tabulates Benedict's Austronesian cognates with Altaic cognates proposed by Starostin (1986), concluding that the results "seem to mirror the notion of co-existing Austronesian and Altaic strata in the Japanese lexicon" (Solnit 1992, 194). Japanese specialist Alexander Vovin (1994a, 1994b), however, has been highly critical of Benedict's proposed Austronesian etymologies and continues to support an Altaic affiliation for Japanese.

LANGUAGE AND ARCHAEOLOGY: EXPLAINING THE LINKS

Given the lack of any real consensus on the genetic affiliations of Japanese, how can we use linguistic information to understand the prehistoric settlement of the Islands? The first scholar to systematically propose direct links between linguistic and archaeological data was the German Gustav Kossina (Renfrew 1987, 15). Kossina's theory (later used to support the racist designs of the National Socialist movement) was that the spread of the pottery known as Corded Ware was the result of the expansion of Indo-European speakers from their north German homeland (Kossina 1902). Kossina was thus "effectively the first to equate prehistoric peoples (and hence languages) with pottery types, and he founded thereby a school of thought which survives to this day" (Renfrew 1987, 15).

This type of approach, whereby the spread of a specific artifact type is held to reflect the spread of a language or language family, relies heavily on migration as a major stimulus for culture change. It is an approach that has been central to the study of the Indo-European languages, and also of the Altaic family. The current standard interpretation of Altaic origins as developed by Menges (1968, 1975, 1977) and Miller (1980, 1989, 1990) is clearly influenced by the traditional view of Indo-European expansions. An original Altaic homeland is posited in the Transcaspian steppe area at around 6000–

7000 BC. Some time around 2000 BC, these Altaic speakers then moved to a second homeland in the south Altai Mountains. This migration is believed to have been the direct result of the expansion of Indo-European speakers who "at about this time, began a vigorous series of migrations and travels of conquest" (Miller 1989, 14). Although they arrived in the second homeland more or less as a linguistic unity, from here it has been posited that they began to split into the three separate subgroups of Altaic. Migration from this second homeland is argued to have been caused by the expansion of the Huns in the eastern steppes from about the third century BC (Miller 1989, 15).

Of course, this model is based on the premise that Altaic is a valid linguistic taxon. The positioning of the original homeland in the far west of Central Asia is determined solely by the assumption of ancient links with the Uralic and Indo-European families. The position of Japanese in this scheme is extremely problematical. Menges (1968, 55–58) wisely leaves both Korean and Japanese out of his original formulation, and it is Miller who developed this end of the model. The most obvious discrepancy in Miller's hypothesis is chronological. Although he proposes an Altaic migration to the second homeland just before 2000 BC (slightly earlier than Menges' first half of the second millennium BC), he also suggests that a Tungusic subgroup moved down into Japan "probably sometime between 3000 and 2000 BC" (Miller 1990, 14). Even if we reverse these dates and accept that the migration from the Transcaspian steppe occurred before the movement into Japan, this still represents a phenomenal rate of linguistic change—implying that what was a Proto-Altaic unity became Proto-Korean-Japanese in a few centuries! Miller (1980) links the arrival of the Japanese language in the Islands with the appearance of a comb-incised ceramic ware in Early Jōmon Kyushu. While Miller (1990, 16) himself notes that this pottery dates to well before 3000 BC, he does not appear to accept the implications of this for his overall model. A further contradiction within Miller's view is in his suggestion that the presence in Japanese of Turkic, Mongolian, *and* Tungusic elements is "best explained by a hypothesis of multiple, successive invasions by Altaic speakers coming over from Eurasia more than once in prehistoric time" (Miller 1986, 110).

Miller's Early Jōmon theory has been discussed elsewhere (Hudson 1994a, 236–237). Even if a new style of pottery had spread from the Peninsula at this time, it would not necessarily prove a population movement of any sort. In this case, recent research has tended to stress local developments over outside influences. There is no evidence of major cultural discontinuities or population influx, and there is, therefore, little reason to support language replacement, though it is a possibility we cannot disprove. Though it is impossible to prove that a new language did *not* arrive in Kyushu in the Early Jōmon, Miller's explanation for the spread of that language to the rest of the archipelago is particularly unconvincing. From Kyushu, Miller (1980, 125–130) argues that comb-pattern pottery spread slowly east, reaching the Kinai in the Middle Yayoi. This interpretation is based on the presence of comb decoration on ceramics in the Kinai region from this time. Like many early archaeologists, Miller makes the easy mistake of equating a decorative technique with a culture and thus with a people and a language, talking about a "comb-pattern population and its culture" (Miller 1990, 20). The proposed comb-pattern culture is defined on the basis of a single decorative technique, but comb decoration would not have been difficult to reinvent many times, and there is no reason to assume that the two occurrences have any sort of ethnic significance.

A fault common to both Japanese and Western scholarship has been the lack of serious research on the sociolinguistic aspects of Japanese origins. Since most Westerners tend to use a cladistic, family-tree model of language change and to link Proto-Japanese with a single population, they look for archaeological evidence of a migration into the Islands that may have been linked with the arrival of the language. While, as we have just seen, it is by no means problem-free, because this approach does at least have some theoretical basis, it is preferable to the typical Japanese approach, which starts from the linguistic assumption that many languages "coalesced" to form Japanese but does not seriously consider how that might have come about in social terms. Rather than a single genetic lineage with various borrowings, Japanese scholars often appear to give equal significance to all linguistic "influences" on Japanese. This is perhaps best explained by using English as an example: if they applied the same criteria to English as they do to their own language, many Japanese linguists would be forced to argue that instead of being a Germanic language with borrowings from Norman French, English is in fact a unique "mixed language" comprising German, Latin, French, and Sanskrit strata. Of course, in the Japanese case we are uncertain as to the primary genetic relationship; nevertheless, the difference in theoretical approach is marked. In many Japanese works there is simply no explict discussion of how prehistoric language change occurred. In others, languages as diverse as Indonesian, Khmer, Burmese, Chinese, and Palaeo-Siberian flow like tributaries into a single river to form Japanese (e.g. Yasumoto 1991, 135). Elsewhere, Yasumoto (1990, 152–153) argues that Japanese spread east from Kyushu in the third century with the (hypothetical) conquest of the Kinai by the Kyushu kingdom of Yamatai. Nakamoto (1990, 144) proposes that the transition from nomadic hunting to sedentary farming led to the formation of "strong culture areas"; languages such as Japanese then moved from strong to weak culture areas (Nakamoto 1990, 119), but the role of the actual people involved remains unclear. In an excellent example of circular reasoning between archaeology and linguistics, Shibatani (1990, 117) argues that one reason that the comparative method is not effective in Japan is that "*due to several successive landings of different cultural groups in the Japanese archipelago,* Japanese in origins may well have been a mixed language in the Polivanov-Murayama sense" (emphasis added). Within the Japanese linguistic community, the work of Ōno Susumu is unusual in that he proposes a quite explicit mechanism for the arrival of at least one component of the Japanese language in the Islands. Unfortunately, Ōno's (1990, 1994) suggestion that Tamil rice farmers migrated by boat from southern India to Korea and Kyushu can easily be dismissed on archaeological grounds (Hudson 1992b).

Among Japanese linguists, it is the work of Hattori Shirō that comes closest to the model proposed in this chapter. For reasons that are discussed in more detail below, Hattori (e.g. 1959, 1961) argues that Proto-Japanese was spoken in northern Kyushu in the Yayoi period, from there spreading to the rest of the archipelago. However, Hattori (e.g. 1959, 88) places too much emphasis on the then-prevailing assumption that there was no substantial immigration at the start of the Yayoi and thus that the Jōmon and Yayoi cultures were produced by the "same Japanese people." This leads him to rely on rather complex elite-dominance models for the spread of the Japanese language based on the expansion of Yamatai (cf. Hattori 1959, 85–87).

I have already mentioned that interest in language strata and mixing derives partly from anthropological theories on Japanese origins in general. Oka Masao has suggested that Japan had been settled by successive waves of migratory peoples who brought with them the various cultural traits that made up Japanese civilization (see Part I). While Oka offers explicit linguistic hypotheses about these peoples, these are based not on linguistic data but on a priori assumptions about the origins of cultural traits such as rice farming. The continuing influence of this type of approach can be seen in a recent paper by cultural anthropologist Ōbayashi Taryō (1990b, 40–41):

> Considering the fact that the basic characteristics of Jōmon culture were of northern type, there is a possibility that the language of the Jōmon period was also northern—probably not Altaic but Palaeo-Asiatic in the loose sense. It is thought that an Austronesian language,

> or more precisely a language of the Hesperonesian branch, played a part in the formation of Japanese but it is still not well understood when and with what culture it entered Japan. The Hesperonesian languages, however, can be connected with slash-and-burn cultivation and with Wa culture, and also influenced the languages of the Kumaso and Hayato. Although the Wu and Yue were culturally similar to the Wa, I believe they were probably linguistically different.
>
> An Altaic, or specifically a Tungusic or similar language, was probably brought to Japan with an elite culture, absorbing the Austronesian and other elements to form Japanese. Such a model fits well with ethnological theories on the formation of Japanese culture. Rather than the Kofun period, however, this elite culture seems to have already entered in the Yayoi and to have formed the ruling stratum of Wa society.

While Ōbayashi's scheme is more sophisticated than Oka's in that Ōbayashi admits the possibility of cultural influence without language replacement, the overall approach has changed little. The diverse cultural roots of Japan are undeniable, but these cannot be mapped directly onto languages, and more consideration needs to be given to how cultural and linguistic influences interacted in the prehistoric archipelago.

Several linguists have proposed that Japanese is best explained as a pidgin or creole. This has usually led to sociolinguistic analyses of the formation of the language, although Chew's (1976, 1989) suggestion of a Yayoi *lingua franca* is only superficially related to the archaeological record. Perhaps the most sophisticated attempt to relate archaeology and linguistics is Maher's (1991, 1996) "North Kyushu Creole" hypothesis. Maher starts from the assumption that substantial migration into the Islands occurred in the Yayoi and considers how the language(s) of the immigrants interacted with the language(s) of the Jōmon people, suggesting that a creole developed in north Kyushu and then spread through the Islands. A number of comments can be made about Maher's hypothesis. I find unconvincing his suggestion that the Jōmon people spoke languages "from the north (Palaeo-Siberian), the south (Malayo-Polynesian) and the west from China and Korea (Proto-Altaic)" (Maher 1991, 15). Of course, this is not something about which one can be certain, but Maher's (1991, 29) mention of cultural influences from the south, for instance, in no way represents evidence of a *linguistic* relationship with Malayo-Polynesian. It seems unlikely that the Japanese Islands were ever either a center of language-family diversification or the destination of migrants from so many families. Another problem is the relationship with Ainu. Both Maher and I see Ainu as a descendant of a Jōmon language (see below), but Maher's scheme lacks an explanation of why the other Jōmon languages became creolized so easily (or else died out), whereas Ainu alone remained separate. Lastly, I fail to be convinced that Yayoi language contact led to a creole rather than to language replacement, perhaps with a limited amount of borrowing. Linguists continue to debate whether or not creoles are recent phenomena, the products of complex colonial societies (cf. Bynon 1983, 259–261). To an outsider in this debate it seems that a distinction must be maintained between some degree of "substratum" influence (which may quite possibly have occurred in the case of Japanese and would in no way invalidate the model proposed here) and true pidgins and creoles, which are above all trade languages. In the Yayoi, there is little to suggest the type of intensive trading activities that might have led to the need for a creole. As argued below, language replacement through the expansion of farmers appears a much more likely scenario for Yayoi language change.

THE SUBSISTENCE/DEMOGRAPHY MODEL

Recent years have seen growing interest in how linguistic data may be used to understand prehistoric population movements. Of course, linguists and some archaeologists have long been publishing their views on this subject, particularly within the field of Indo-European studies. The active participation of archaeologists in such debates, however, is increasing—a development that can be attributed to a variety of causes. A return to the consideration of the question of human migration in prehistory is one reason for the increase. Another is recent work by certain linguists on large-scale language classifications—work that may be able to shed light on very early dispersals. A third reason is the growing potential for the integration of linguistic, biological, and archaeological data for understanding the spread of human populations. In the past few years, a number of books and articles have appeared that are written in whole or in part by prehistorians and that deal with the "linguistic archaeology" of Europe (Mallory 1989; Renfrew 1987; Sherratt and Sherratt 1988; Zvelebil and Zvelebil 1988), Southeast Asia and the Pacific (Bellwood 1991, 1992, 1993a; McConvell and Evans 1997), and North America (Fiedel 1987, 1990, 1991; Moratto 1984, 529–574; Palmer 1994), as well as with more general, pan-regional concerns (Bellwood 1993b, 1994, 1996, 1997; Mallory 1992; Renfrew 1989, 1991, 1992a, 1992b).

Renfrew has proposed the following four categories of language replacement:

(a) *Subsistence/demography model,* where large numbers of people speaking the new language move into the territory. They do not conquer by force of arms but are able to settle because they are possessed of a subsistence adaptation which either occupies a different ecological niche from that of the earlier population, or is significantly more effective and productive within the same niche through the possession of some technological advantage.

(b) *Elite dominance,* where an incoming, minority elite is able, usually by military means, to seize power within the territory. This implies that the incoming group will have some centralised organisation (that is, a stratified or highly ranked structure), and often that the group conquered will have some ranking also.

(c) *System collapse,* where the collapse of a highly centralised (state) society leads to instability on its perimeter and to significant local movements of people and of power. Such was the position in the late days of the Roman Empire and their aftermath, the so-called "migration period." Here again the pre-existence of a stratified or state society is a precondition.

(d) *Lingua franca,* where a trading language (pidgin) develops within the territory as the result of intense trading or other activity by outsiders. The pidgin is usually a simplified version of the outsider language, and a creole may develop, spoken by many of the inhabitants as their natal tongue (Renfrew 1992a, 15–16).

In the next section, I suggest that the first of these categories—the subsistence/demography model—may help us explain language replacement with agricultural colonization in Japan during the Yayoi period. Of the other three categories, the concept of a lingua franca played an important part in previous thinking about the history of Japanese. As Renfrew points out, however, such pidgins and creoles are not formed easily and are the result of particular circumstances: "It is doubtful if any long-lasting creole languages came into existence before the formation of major imperial powers" (Renfrew 1992a, 22). It is for this reason that I remain skeptical of the *Mischsprache* so favored by Japanese scholars. It is not that mixed languages never occur; it is just unlikely that they became widespread in prehistoric Japan. Renfrew's second category—elite dominance—is also relevant to the Japanese case. Egami's thesis that a group of horse-riding nobles, ultimately of north Korean (Puyŏ) origin, came to dominate Japan in the fifth century AD still holds a fascination for some linguists (e.g. Kazar 1980, 1989; Unger 1990b). Linguistically, it does represent a possible scenario for language replacement and has the added advantage of explaining links—to be discussed below—between Japanese and the north Korean languages. Archaeologically, however, the Horserider theory has little or no supporting evidence and must therefore be discounted as a case of language replacement through elite dominance.

LANGUAGE CLASSIFICATION WITHIN THE JAPANESE ISLANDS

Most studies attempting to provide cultural explanations for observed linguistic patterns have revolved around the possible relationships of Japanese with larger language families such as Altaic and Austronesian. In this section, I want to take a slightly different approach and look at language and dialect divergence *within* the Japanese Islands. For me, the most noticeable thing about the archipelago is the comparative *lack* of linguistic variation. Of course, there are many dialects of Japanese (some of which are said to be mutually unintelligible), yet basically there are only three languages: Ainu, Japanese, and Ryukyuan. Many Japanese linguists assume that Japanese has a long history stretching back into the Jōmon period for 10,000 years or more (e.g. Sakiyama 1989, 169). The present linguistic conformity of the Islands, however, does not seem easily reconciled with such a time depth. If there had been no language replacement in the Islands since the first Palaeolithic occupation, then we might expect a situation rather like that in New Guinea, where there are over 600 languages. If the Japanese archipelago had a similar number of languages per square kilometer as New Guinea does, then there would be about 300 separate "Japanese" languages instead of only three.

Few if any linguists would deny that there is a rough correlation between language diversity and time depth (see Nichols 1992). Putting a scale to that diversity is difficult, but once we propose that language replacement has probably taken place in the Japanese Islands since the Pleistocene, then, following Renfrew's (1992a) principles, agricultural colonization becomes the most likely sociolinguistic explanation for that replacement. This explanation in turn supports the biological evidence for Yayoi immigration, since, as Bellwood (1993b, 51) points out, "if agriculture spread mainly by diffusion through existing hunter gatherer communities without the adoption of new languages . . . we would not expect much change in preexisting Palaeolithic language distributions." It is important to emphasize that this is *not* circular reasoning, since the biological evidence for immigration stands on its own.

Of the three Insular languages, Ryukyuan clearly holds a very close genetic relationship with Japanese. In fact, most Japanese linguists regard Ryukyuan as a dialect of Japanese (Shibatani 1990, 191).[2] Ryukyuan and Japanese are thought to have split from a common ancestor as recently as the early centuries AD. The earliest Ryukyuan texts date to the late fifteenth/early sixteenth centuries, and little is known for certain about the earlier history of the language (Hokama 1981, 266). For Miller (1980), Ryukyuan, Old Japanese, and Middle Korean are separate offshoots from a Proto-Korean-Japanese stock. Since Japanese and Ryukyuan are clearly much closer to each other than they are to Korean, however, Japanese linguists such as Hattori (1976) prefer a later branching from a separate Proto-Japanese group. Hattori (1954) proposes a glottochronological date for the separation of the Kyoto and Shuri dialects of Japanese and Ryukyuan at between about 1,450 and 1,700 years ago (cf. Lees 1956). He later revises this to between 1,500 and 2,000 years ago (Hattori 1976). Discounting a move in the opposite direction, Hattori argues that the split between the two languages was caused by a population movement from mainland Japan (Hattori 1976, 43–45). Hokama (1977, 192–194) agrees with Hattori's basic conclusions, noting that Ryukyuan has attributes of eighth-century or even earlier Japanese, implying a date of separation similar to that of the glottochronological estimates, that is, between the second and seventh centuries AD (Hokama 1981, 266–267, 1986, 94–96). Hattori (1976, 21) in fact argues that Ryukyuan and mainland Japanese cannot be derived from the eighth-century Nara dialects of the early historical records: their common parent language must have existed *before* the Nara period. On cultural grounds, it is thought unlikely that the split could have occurred before the Yayoi (Kamimura 1965, 58).

Nakamoto has argued that the spread of Proto-Ryukyuan through the Okinawan chain can be linked with the spread of rice farming (Table 4.1), although the actual cultural mechanisms of the language diffusion are not discussed in his scheme. As will be seen in the next chapter, however, archaeological evidence for both the introduction of agriculture and the population movement into the Ryukyu Islands remains poorly understood, and thus it is at present difficult to reconcile the linguistic expectation of the spread of a new language in the late Yayoi or thereabouts with the archaeological record. Hattori (1959, 83) notes that it is unlikely that the split between Ryukyuan and the mainland dialects can be attributed to a movement of people from the Kinai region and proposes northern Kyushu as the most probable home of Proto-Japanese.

It is widely accepted that Ryukyuan and the dialects of mainland Japan are all derived from a common source, namely Proto-Japanese (Chamberlain

TABLE 4.1

THE LINGUISTIC DEVELOPMENT OF THE RYUKYU ISLANDS

I.	Prehistoric Ryukyuan *pre-Ryukyuan languages spoken*	?–300 BC
II.	Proto-Ryukyuan *spread of rice farming and Proto-Ryukyuan*	300 BC–AD 500
III.	Village Stage *dialectical differentiation on village and island level*	AD 500–1186
IV.	Regional Stage *dialect units evolve around small regional polities and chiefs*	1187–1476
V.	The Shuri Kingdom *Shuri dialect forms spread in wave pattern from Okinawa Island*	1477–1608
VI.	Spread of Kyushu Influence *following invasion by Shimazu clan*	1609–1878
VII.	Spread of "Standard" Japanese *spread of Tokyo speech following incorporation in the Meiji state*	1879–present

Translated from Nakamoto (1981, 212–222, 12–19). At present no archaeological evidence exists for Nakamoto's Stage II.

1895; Grootaers 1983; Hattori 1961). On glottochronological estimates and rough comparisons with the rates of divergence of the Romance languages, it is thought that Proto-Japanese was spoken about 2,000 years ago (Hattori 1961, 25–26), although bringing this date back to the start of the Yayoi should present few problems. In the main islands, a tripartite division of dialects into Kyushu, western Japan, and eastern Japan is usually recognized, although as a whole Kyushu falls into the western Japan branch (Miller 1967, 141–171; Shibatani 1990, 185–214). The eastern dialects are known to be at least as old as the Nara period, since the *Man'yōshū* of 759 includes poems known as the *Aduma uta* and the *Sakimori uta,* which contain dialectical forms quite different from those of the capital.

An historical understanding of Japanese dialects is complicated by later developments. After the country became centralized in the eighth century, the speech of the capital (Kyoto after 794) was the most prestigious, and elements of Kyoto dialect spread both east and west. The presence of certain eastern dialectical traits in western Japan, however, suggests that the eastern dialect may have originally been used throughout the archipelago (cf. Shibatani 1990, 200). The speech of the capital then spread out in a wavelike pattern; regions that retain historically older dialectical forms (Tohoku, San'in, Hachijōjima, Kyushu, and the Ryukyus) are those that have traditionally been least influenced by the capital (Shibatani 1990, 207). For our present purposes, however, this late spread of Kyoto speech is quite irrelevant. Taking a different approach, Inoue (1992) compares the amount of independent dialectical forms with the degree of usage of "standard" Japanese for each prefecture. Within mainland Japan, he found that Kyushu and the Tohoku both made the least use of standard speech. Of these two, however, the Tohoku also had a low level of divergent dialectical forms. Ruling out geographical and social factors, Inoue convincingly explains this situation as a result of the comparatively late settlement of the Tohoku by Japanese speakers associated with the expansion of the Yamato state in the Kofun, Nara, and Heian periods.

If the Yayoi expansion model were correct, then we would expect Proto-Japanese speakers to have spread from northern Kyushu during the Early Yayoi (ca. 300–100 BC) and to have reached the Nagoya area very quickly. Until recently, archaeologists thought that Yayoi expansion farther east occurred at a much slower rate. We now know that Yayoi *culture* spread to parts of eastern Honshu almost immediately, but the role of population movement in the east remains controversial. A more gradual spread of the Japanese language into the Chūbu, the Kanto, and especially the Tohoku regions would, of course, be consistent with Inoue's findings. According to this scenario, Ryukyuan would have split from the Kyushu dialect in the Yayoi period.

In general, the Japanese dialectical evidence appears to support this model. One expectation for which I have not found support is that the north Kyushu dialect should be the oldest form of Japanese. Particularly if, following Miller's theory, Japanese arrived in Kyushu in the Early Jōmon but only spread to the rest of Japan in the Yayoi, we would expect quite noticeable variations between Kyushu and other dialects. The apparent lack of such major variations may imply that Japanese arrived in Kyushu at the very end of the Jōmon and then spread almost immediately to the other islands. This would agree with the biological evidence for immigration at that time. The alternative scenario espoused by Hattori (1961, 27–28), that Proto-Japanese was spoken in north Kyushu for millennia but later became somehow fused with Yayoi people and culture involves all sorts of complex conjectures and premises such that Hattori (1961, 27–28) himself ends up by concluding that "'Proto-Japanese' is but a hypothetical concept . . . which does not accord with the historical facts."

The arrival of Proto-Japanese in Kyushu in the Yayoi thus seems the most natural explanation for the relative uniformity of Japanese dialects. The problem here, of course, is the *source* of the new language, since modern Japanese and Korean are considered too different to have split from a common ancestor only 2,000 years ago. A possible way around this problem may be the fact that Old Japanese is believed to have been closer to the language of Koguryŏ than to that of Silla, from which modern Korean is derived. Most of our knowledge of the Koguryŏ language derives from place-names preserved in the twelfth-century *Samguk sagi*. Lewin (1973, 23) cautions that "many of the reconstructed Koguryŏ words are hypothetical, and the reconstructions given by Korean and Japanese scholars differ in their sound shape. Moreover the probability of false identifications is relatively high, for a good many correspondences are supported by only one example." Nevertheless, some eighty Koguryŏ words have been reconstructed, and of these as many as thirty-four can be compared with Old Japanese (Lewin 1976, 408). Lewin (1973, 1976) provides useful summaries of the Koguryŏ connection, but much of the original work was done by Yi Kimun (Lee Ki-moon) and Murayama Shichirō. A sample of the correspondences is given in Table 4.2.

TABLE 4.2

KOGURYŎ AND OLD JAPANESE COMPARISONS

KOGURYŎ	OLD JAPANESE
*mil "three"	mi "three"
*uc "five"	i-tu "five"
*nanïn "seven"	nana "seven"
*tök "ten"	tōwō "ten"
*papa "mother"	FaFa [< *papa] "mother"
*kus "child, boy"	ko "child"
*tan "valley"	tani "valley"
*wus "cow"	usi "cow"
*i "enter"	ir- "enter"
*kap(pi) "gorge, hole"	kaFi [< *kapi] "gorge, mountain cleft"

From Lewin (1973, 24–25).

The agreement of four numerals here is particularly remarkable; the others have not been preserved, but may also have been closely related. Of course, it is not impossible that some of these words are borrowings. Koguryŏ immigration to Japan is attested to by archaeological, textual, and place-name evidence, particularly in the central mountains in the late Kofun and early historic eras (e.g. Kirihara 1989). The ancient name of Yamanashi, that is, OJ Kapï, is thought to mean "gap in the mountains" and is probably related to the Koguryŏ word **kap(pi)* of the same meaning. The similarity of so many basic words, however, makes a genetic relationship more likely than borrowing, and Lewin (1976, 408) concludes that "it can be assumed that Japanese was closely related to the Koguryŏ language and that in its core it belonged to the Puyŏ group, or was at least close to it."

While this Koguryŏ theory is attractive, it contains a number of obvious problems. First, since modern Korean and Japanese, the only existing representatives of the Puyŏ-Han group, are so different, a considerable history of separation on the Peninsula is implied after the original split of the two groups. More difficult to explain is their geographical inversion. The Han languages were spoken in the south and the Puyŏ languages in the north of the Peninsula. Although some Paekche aristocracy may have come from Puyŏ (cf. Lewin 1980), Yayoi-period archaeological links were mainly with the south. Ro's (1992) recent suggestion that bronze-using people from the northern Peninsula moved south during the Korean Bronze Age (ca. 500–200 BC) is relevant here, but more work is needed on the archaeological manifestations of that proposed migration.

AINU AS A JŌMON LANGUAGE

What is the position of the third Insular language, Ainu, in the scheme proposed here? Over the years, Ainu has been linked with many languages and families, including Hebrew, Assyrian, and Indo-European. Although Chamberlain (1887) and later Kindaichi (1960) argue that Ainu is not related to Japanese, Hattori (1959, 1964) and others have maintained the possibility of a distant genetic link. A number of scholars have suggested a link with Austronesian (e.g. Gjerdman 1926; Murayama 1992, 1993). Patrie (1982) concludes that Ainu, Japanese, and Korean form a subgroup within Altaic but that Ainu is closer to Korean than to Japanese.

The genetic relationships of Ainu can only be approached through linguistic evidence; we can, however, use cultural data to test the hypothesis that

Ainu, or an earlier form of Ainu, was used in the Jōmon period. I believe there is a good possibility that this was the case for the following reasons. Historical records imply that the language spoken by the so-called Emishi of northeast Honshu was not Japanese. Several early texts mention the presence of *osa* (interpreters) used by the central government, which was engaged in military conflicts with the Emishi (Fukuda 1965, 5–8 and 34–37). From these records, we know that the language of the Emishi was clearly different from the Japanese then spoken in the rest of the archipelago. Exactly how different is unclear from the texts themselves. Fukuda (1965, 34–35) argues that textual references to languages with a geographical prefix (e.g. "Azuma," "Hida") were dialects of Japanese, whereas the ethnic prefix "Emishi" denoted a separate language.

Toponymic research may enable us to link the Emishi language with Ainu. It has long been suggested that many Tohoku place-names are derived from Ainu. In Hokkaido, a large number of place-names are corrupted Japanese versions of Ainu words (Yamada 1982–1983). Names ending in *-nai* and *-betsu* (e.g. Wakkanai, Noboribetsu) are especially common and are derived from two Ainu words for "river," *nai* and *pet*. Place-names with these endings are also widely distributed through north Tohoku, with around 400 examples of the *-nai* form appearing in the Aomori, Akita, and Iwate prefectures (Imaizumi 1992, 167). Other Ainu derivative forms are also known, but, because we only have detailed knowledge of the Ainu language from the nineteenth century, there are probably many more such names in the Tohoku (and possibly in the rest of Japan) whose origins have been lost. A further link here is through the so-called *matagi* hunters of the Tohoku, who still use several Ainu words in their specialist vocabulary (Kudō 1989a, 134).[3]

Kudō (1989a, 135) writes that there is no possibility that Tohoku Ainu place-names were formed in the medieval or later periods. It seems safe to assume, therefore, that a language spoken in Tohoku from at least the eighth century was an earlier form of Ainu. Bearing in mind the cultural continuities visible over this general time period (see chapter 8), it does not seem too much of a shot in the dark to suggest that this ancestor of Ainu may have been spoken in the Jōmon period. As Wright (1984, 286) puts it in the Iroquoian context, "Although the association of a language with any prehistoric culture can never be proven, the assumption of a language association with an unbroken archaeological sequence that terminates with a historic language group would appear to be a more valid option than the possible alternatives." Naturally, this does not rule out the possibility that other languages were also spoken in the Jōmon. If Ainu were descended from a Jōmon language, then the replacement of similar (or quite different) Jōmon languages in the western and central archipelago in the Yayoi would seem a very parsimonious way of linking the biological evidence for Yayoi immigration with the linguistic data for northern Japan. The spread of the Japanese language into Hokkaido only occurred on any substantial scale with the agricultural colonization of that island by the mainland Japanese in the nineteenth century.

If Ainu is descended from a Jōmon language, then it most probably has very ancient roots in the Japanese Islands, perhaps stretching back into the Palaeolithic. Such a time-depth might appear inconsistent with the relative lack of dialectical variation in modern Ainu. Asai (1974) and others have proposed three main dialect groups within Ainu: Hokkaido, Sakhalin, and the Kurils. Although further subdivisions exist within Hokkaido and Sakhalin, and despite the fact that the Hokkaido and Sakhalin groups are said to be mutually unintelligible (Refsing 1986, 53), this basic threefold division most likely derives from Ainu expansion from Hokkaido to Sakhalin and the Kuril Islands in the early medieval era. At the risk of playing down evidence that contradicts my own model, however, we should be wary of overly hasty conclusions regarding Ainu dialects. First of all, studies such as Asai's were conducted at a time when native speakers of Ainu were already rare, and some dialects are represented by single speakers. Second, the major social changes that have occurred in Hokkaido over the past two millennia mean that some degree of language replacement or "standardization" within Ainu dialects may have taken place. For instance, it is not inconceivable—though it is impossible to prove—that the Satsumon expansion of late Antiquity may have resulted in the spread of a southern Hokkaido dialect across the rest of that island.

CONCLUSIONS

Recent work by a number of archaeologists has suggested that population expansion following the development of agriculture may have been the primary cause of the dispersal of human languages in the Holocene. Following Renfrew's (1992a) minimalist principles, language distributions that cannot be attributed to agricultural expansion are very likely the result of much earlier, Pleistocene dispersals. There may only have been one such Pleistocene dispersal: "The principle of parsimony invoked here suggests that we should prefer one wave to several, unless we can see clearly how—that is, by what ecological factors—second and successive 'waves' might be propagated" (Renfrew 1992a, 17). These principles of language dispersal are a powerful analytical tool for hypothesizing about prehistory. When applied to Japan, they suggest a number of interesting possibilities. If the Japanese dialects, including Ryukyuan, can be derived from a common language of the last few centuries BC or the early centuries AD, then it seems highly probable that their spread through the archipelago was accomplished by the expansion of Yayoi agriculturalists. This "subsistence/demography" model also, to my mind, rules out creolization between existing Jōmon hunter-gatherer languages and the incoming agricultural one.

The status of Ryukyuan is somewhat problematical with regard to this Yayoi replacement model, since evidence for large-scale immigration from Kyushu during the Late Shellmound period is ambiguous. The source of the new Yayoi language (Proto-Japanese) is a further problem. Theoretically, it could be a language that had existed in north Kyushu for some time, and for this reason we cannot totally dismiss Miller's Early Jōmon theory in its broad outlines. Another possibility is a link with the north Korean Puyŏ-Koguryŏ languages. Here, while the linguistic relationship with Japanese is undoubtedly close, the main difficulty is cultural, since Yayoi Japan was mainly influenced by the southern Peninsula.

Japanese is widely thought to be an Altaic language, or to be at least closely related to the Altaic family, and a full understanding of the origins of Japanese needs to take into account the linguistic prehistory of East Asia as a whole. This is a complex problem with a large, though uneven, literature, and only a few comments are possible here:

(1) *Homelands*. The location of the original Altaic homeland has never been the same subject of debate as has its Indo-European counterpart, but many Altaicists accept two basic premises. The first of these is that because of ancient contacts with Uralic, Indo-European, and Dravidian (in that order of acceptability), the Altaic family originated to the west of its present distribution (Menges 1968, 1977; Miller 1980, 1989, 1990). The second point is that the original Altaic expansions were linked with the rise of nomadic pastoralism on the steppes and thus were quite late. Following Menges, Miller (1989, 14) argues that Altaic speakers moved east to a second homeland around the Altai mountains at about 2000 BC, yet he continues to link the arrival of Altaic speakers in Japan with Early Jōmon comb-incised ceramics. While Miller (1990, 16) himself notes

that this pottery dates to well before 3000 BC, he does not appear to accept the implications for his overall Altaic model.

(2) *Divergence.* Could Japanese have diverged from Proto-Altaic in 2,000 to 3,000 years? This is a question that needs to be tackled by qualified linguists, but such a short time-depth seems incompatible with the general confusion over the genetic relationship of Japanese. If the answer to the previous question is no, then two possibilities present themselves. The first is that the Altaic hypothesis is incorrect. Many linguists, of course, do not support the classic view of a Proto-Altaic unity (cf. Poppe 1965, 148–154). We are reminded of Unger's statement (quoted above) that connections between Japanese, Korean, and Tungusic are of a different order than are those between the other Altaic branches. It is not impossible, therefore, that this "Macro-Tungusic" subgroup represents an early dispersal that was followed much later by the expansion of a Turkic and Mongolian branch from the western steppes. What we need in order to test this hypothesis is a workable classification of the languages concerned.

A second possible way of getting around the apparently short divergence time for Altaic would be to argue that its real time-depth is much longer. Following Renfrew's principles, however, we would need to tie in any earlier Altaic dispersal with a suitable ecological explanation for human migration. Could Altaic (or a Tungusic-Korean-Japanese branch of Altaic) have been a Pleistocene dispersal into East Asia? Again, a more complete understanding of the wider linguistic relations across Eurasia, perhaps within the concept of macro-families such as Nostratic and Eurasiatic, seems essential.

(3) *Ainu.* Based on the Tohoku place-name evidence and on general cultural continuities, Ainu seems to be descended from an ancient language in the Islands and is unlikely to have arrived after the Yayoi. In this case, the chances are good that it is descended from a language of the initial Pleistocene colonization of the region. If Ainu is related to Korean and/or to Japanese, then those languages could also belong to a Pleistocene eastern branch of "Altaic"—or Eurasiatic, if that term is more appropriate. The status of the so-called Palaeo-Siberian languages is obviously relevant here, as is the work of linguists who see an Austronesian derivation for Ainu. The Austronesian hypothesis has the advantage of appearing to fit with the biological evidence for a southern origin for the Jōmon populations, but

even if Ainu spread to the Japanese Islands as late as the beginning of the Jōmon, then Austronesian and Ainu would share only a very distant relationship: that is, the Austronesian family and Ainu would both be derived from a common ancestor of the late Pleistocene. Since Ainu seems to be a very ancient language in the region, an understanding of its development and linguistic relationships is crucial to a full picture of early human dispersals in East Asia.

5

From Jōmon to Yayoi

The Archaeology of the First Japanese

In important respects [the Yayoi] people were Japanese, whereas the people of the Jōmon culture merely happened to live in Japan.

Richard K. Beardsley, "Japan Before History: A Survey of the Archaelogical Record"

In the previous two chapters, I argue that the biological and linguistic records support the model of Yayoi immigration and population expansion outlined in the introduction to this book. It is now time to see whether this model is also supported by archaeology. This chapter discusses the archaeological evidence relating to three major topics. The first is the development of food production in the Islands. Since my model of Japanese ethnogenesis is based on agricultural colonization by Yayoi farmers, we need to see to what extent the Yayoi period marked an economic transition. Are we correct in describing the Yayoi as Japan's first full-scale agricultural society, or was Jōmon cultivation more important than has hitherto been realized? The second topic is the formation of Yayoi culture in Kyushu. The focus here is on relations with the continent and evidence for immigration into the Islands during the Initial Yayoi (ca. 400–300 BC). The final section considers the expansion of Yayoi culture out of Kyushu in the Early Yayoi (ca. 300–100 BC). Did this expansion involve the actual movement of people, as my model suggests, or did the Jōmon people adopt rice cultivation themselves, with minimal contact with immigrant groups? This chapter is essentially descriptive:

an extended analysis of the implications of the archaeological data presented here is held over until chapter 6.

REVOLUTION OR TRANSFORMATION?: AGRICULTURAL TRANSITIONS IN THE ISLANDS

The Yayoi is usually described as marking the beginning of full-scale food production in the Japanese Islands (e.g. Sahara 1975, 114), yet claims for pre-Yayoi cultivation go back as early as 6000 BP. There have been two main foci for such claims: the Chūbu highlands in the Middle Jōmon and western Japan in the Late and Final phases. For over seventy years, the high site density and complex material culture of the Chūbu Middle Jōmon have been linked with agriculture on the assumption that hunter-gatherers could not have produced such remains (Torii 1974a[1924]; Ōyama 1927; Fujimori 1970). The exact nature of the proposed agriculture has always been problematical, however, and no plant remains have been identified to support the hypothesis of Middle Jōmon agriculture (Crawford 1992b, 17). Theories of cultivation in western Japan have stressed the cultural simplicity and resource scarcity of the western broadleaf evergreen zone. West Japan is regarded as the poor man's Jōmon. Population levels were very much lower than they were in the east. Based on Koyama's (1984) figures, for example, the population of the regions from the Kinki west was 3.63 percent of that of eastern Honshu in the Middle Jōmon phase (Fig. 5.1). Jōmon ritual artifacts such as clay figurines come mostly from the east, and Jōmon pottery also reaches its aesthetic heights in that half of the archipelago. Differences between the western and eastern Jōmon are usually explained by ecological factors, the broadleaf evergreen forest of the west being thought to have been far less productive than were the deciduous forests of the east. As a result of the low productivity of the western forests, Jōmon cultivation there is usually argued to have developed through outside contacts. The influential "broadleaf evergreen forest culture hypothesis" of Nakao Sasuke (1966) and Sasaki Kōmei (1971, 1982, 1987, 1991a, 1991b, 1993) proposes that a variety of cultural traits, including the swidden cultivation of millet and rice, were shared across the broadleaf evergreen forests of East Asia. Other scholars have stressed the role of influences from eastern Honshu (Watanabe 1975, 170–172; Yamazaki 1978). Watanabe (1975, 170–172) proposes that cooler conditions in central Honshu after the late Middle Jōmon led to the westward spread of Jōmon groups, as is evidenced by the appearance of various items of eastern Jōmon culture in the west. The spread of leaching technology

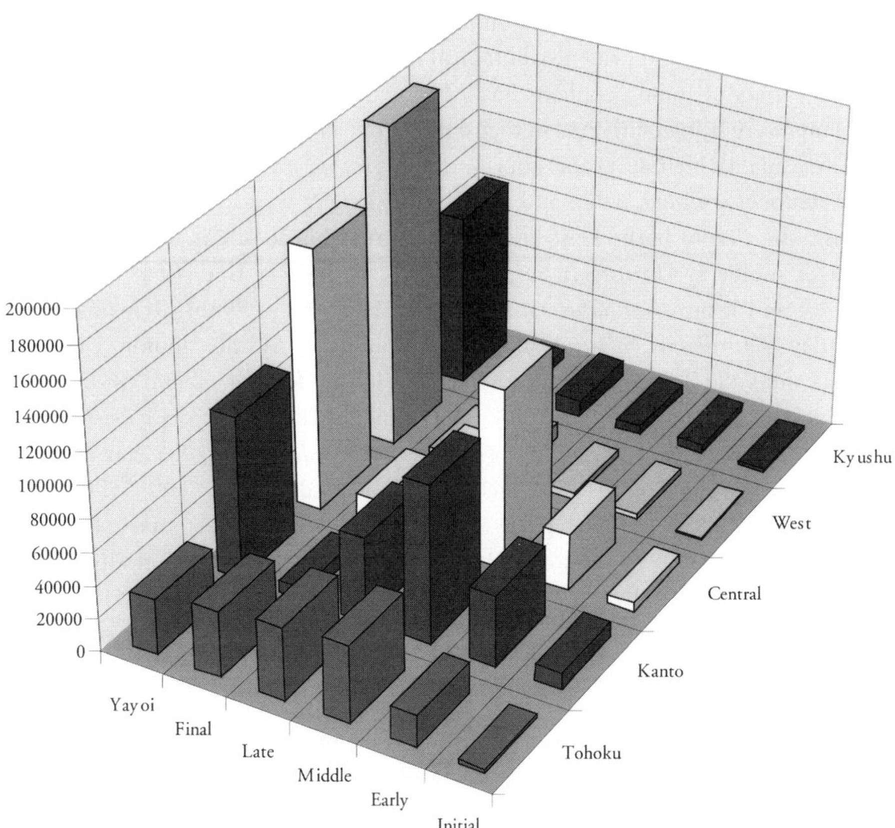

FIG. 5.1. Regional population levels in Japan from the Initial Jōmon to the Yayoi. "Central"=Hokuriku, Chūbu, and Tōkai; "West"=Kinki, Chūgoku, and Shikoku. From data in Koyama (1984, 31).

is thought to have been particularly important: "the diffusion of the east Japan Jōmon culture complex around the middle of the Late Jōmon phase brought about an abrupt change in the subsistence activity of Kyushu. The exploitation of previously unused tubers and nuts was made possible by . . . chipped stone axes, shallow bowls, and tannin-removal technology" (Fujio 1993, 50). Although certain "east Japan" artifacts spread west before the Late Jōmon, that phase still saw a noticeable increase in horse-chestnut finds in the west, suggesting subsistence stress and intensification, since this nut needs leaching before it is consumed.

While much previous work on Jōmon cultivation has been based on circumstantial cultural evidence, botanical remains do exist, and their presence in a variety of Jōmon contexts has led to wide agreement that a number of plants were being cultivated in the Islands from as early as the Early Jōmon. These plants include bottle gourds *(Lagenaria siceraria),* barnyard millet *(Echinochloa utilis),* azuki and mung beans *(Vigna angularis* and *V. radiatus),* the *Perilla* herbs *shiso* and *egoma,* great burdock *(Arctium lappa),* paper mulberry *(Broussonetia papyrifera),* the lacquer tree *(Rhus vernicifera)* and hemp *(Cannabis sativa)* (Crawford 1992a, 1992b). Remains of barley *(Hordeum vulgare)* have been found at Middle Jōmon Ueno (Saitama) and Tsurune (Gifu), and at Late Jōmon Kuwagaishimo (Kyoto), Uenoharu (Kumamoto), and Shika A (Fukuoka) (Fujio 1993, 53; Nishida 1975; Sasaki 1987). Buckwheat *(Fagopyrum esculentum)* pollen has been found at Ubuka Bog in Yamaguchi in sediments dating to 6600–4500 BP (Tsukada 1986), from Ishigake (Aomori) and Higashikazetomari (Hokkaido) at ca. 3000 BP (Fujio 1993, 53), from burnt clay at the Late Jōmon Kyūnenbashi site in Iwate (Yamada 1980), and also from Torihama (Fukui), Kamegaoka (Aomori), and Naemisaku (Chiba) (Nasu 1981, 53). However, only one carbonized buckwheat seed (from an Early-phase pit house at Hamanasuno, Hokkaido) has been discovered from Jōmon deposits (Crawford 1983, 1992b, 28).[1] Other finds of possible pre-Yayoi cultigens include (1) peach seeds from Ikiriki near Nagasaki (Early Jōmon; Minamiki et al. 1986; Crawford 1992b, 19), (2) broomcorn millet *(Panicum miliaceum)* from Kazahari, Aomori (Late Jōmon; D'Andrea 1992; D'Andrea et al. 1995), (3) foxtail millet *(Setaria italica),* also from Kazahari (D'Andrea 1992; D'Andrea et al. 1995) and possibly from Middle Jōmon Usujiri B in Hokkaido (Crawford 1992b, 24), and (4) a melon seed (possibly *Cucumis melo*) from the Initial Jōmon level at Torihama (Crawford 1992b, 18 and 27–28, with references). Crawford (1992b, 28) also mentions Chinese cabbage *(Brassica campestris)* from Jōmon sites but gives no details. A number of other plants may have been husbanded to a greater or lesser extent in the disturbed habitats around Jōmon settlements (cf. Crawford [1983] on southwest Hokkaido). The possible cultivation of nuts, roots, and tubers is discussed below.

Finds of rice first appeared in the Islands at the end of the Late Jōmon. Rice is thought not to be native to Japan and to have been introduced from outside (Satō 1992, 18; but cf. Watabe 1993, 156–163). Rice farming began in the Yangzi valley perhaps as early as 7000 BC (Yan 1992), but did not spread to Korea and Japan until much later. The origins of agriculture in

FIG. 5.2. Major sites mentioned in chapter 5: 1, Sakushu-Kotoni River; 2, Hamanasuno; 3, Kamegaoka; 4, Sunazawa; 5, Tareyanagi; 6, Kazahari; 7, Jizōden B; 8, Ikegami; 9, Arami; 10, Saihiro; 11, Bishamon and Ōurayama; 12, Shimotakabora D; 13, Tabara; 14, Toro; 15, Asahi; 16, Torihama; 17, Kuwagaishimo; 18, Karako-Kagi; 19, Miwa; 20, Tamura; 21, Hayashi-Bōjiro; 22, Mure; 23, Tsushima-Edō; 24, Minami-Mizote; 25, Ubuka; 26, Doigahama; 27, Shimogōri-Kuwanae; 28, Itazuke; 29, Magarita; 30, Shinmachi; 31, Nabatake; 32, Yoshinogari; 33, Yamanotera; 34, Higashinabeda; 35, Uenoharu.

Korea are still poorly understood, and controversy marks the literature (Choe 1990; Nelson 1992). It is not known whether rice spread to Korea directly from China across the Yellow Sea or came overland via Manchuria. Although early dates for rice in west Korea at 2400 and 2100 BC have been reported (Choe 1991, 37), more secure dates are about 1200 BC at Hunamni (Kim W-Y 1982, 515). The relationship between the beginning of rice farming and possible population movements into Korea is hotly debated, as is the relationship between rice, bronze, and Plain pottery. Nelson (1993, 162) writes that "the earliest sites with [Plain] ceramics [radiocarbon dated to ca. 2000 BC] also contain semi-lunar reaping knives, making it not unreasonable to believe they represent the beginnings of rice cultivation in Korea, even though C14 dates do not confirm rice before 1500 BC or so." The slow spread of rice north and south from the Yangzi basin probably relates to the time needed to develop new varities of the plant, which were adapted to quite different growing seasons (cf. Diamond 1997, 183–191).

Five main types of evidence can be used to understand the beginnings of rice agriculture in Japan: carbonized rice grains, impressions on pottery, pollen, phytoliths, and actual paddy-field remains. The following summary is based on Toyama and Nakayama (1992); where separate references are not given, the data are from that article or from earlier works by the same authors (Toyama and Nakayama 1990; Nakayama and Toyama 1991).

(i) Carbonized Rice Grains. One carbonized rice grain and an unspecified quantity of rice husks have been reported from Late Jōmon deposits at Kuwagaishimo in Kyoto Prefecture (Nishida 1975). At least four northern Kyushu sites from the first half of the Final Jōmon have produced carbonized rice. Another recently reported example is from the Kazahari site in Aomori Prefecture: both broomcorn and foxtail millet as well as rice were present; the rice came from within 5 cm of the floor of a Late Jōmon house (D'Andrea 1992; D'Andrea et al. 1995). Calibrated AMS dates on rice from the site are 925 BC (2810±270 BP; TO-4086) and 787 BC (2540±240 BP; TO-2202) (D'Andrea et al. 1995). Im Hyo-Jai (personal communication) has argued that the Kazahari rice may have been brought to the Aomori region directly from the Korean Peninsula rather than moving northeast up the archipelago from Kyushu.

In the second half of the Final Jōmon, most carbonized rice is still from Kyushu, although two sites are known in Hyōgo Prefecture. This stage corresponds to the Initial Yayoi, when we know wet rice cultivation had begun in

Kyushu. By the first third of the Early Yayoi, carbonized rice is found as far north as Aomori.

(ii) Rice Impressions on Pottery. A late Late Jōmon sherd with a rice impression was reported from Minami-mizote in Okayama Prefecture in 1992, but most early Final Jōmon examples are from Kyushu; a site in Osaka is the only exception listed by Toyama and Nakayama. The later eastward expansion of pottery with rice impressions seems to follow a quite regular pattern, reaching Kyoto by the Initial Yayoi, Yamanashi by the beginning of the Early Yayoi, and Aomori by the middle of that phase. Finds correlate well with the spread of paddy-field remains.

(iii) Pollen. Nakamura (1981, 45) quotes dates of before 3400 BP for rice pollen at Itazuke and another locality along the Ongagawa River, arguing that paddy fields were present before that. Elsewhere, he writes that rice first appears at Itazuke at about 3700 BP but that he cannot be sure that pollen from upper layers has not moved down in the sequence (Nakamura 1982, 74) (Fig. 5.3). Toyama and Nakayama (1992, 17, Note 4) only list sites where rice pollen is at least 30 percent of the total *Gramineae* pollen count; percentages greater than this are thought to be clear evidence for paddy-field cultivation (Nakamura 1981, 45). This proportion was reached at Itazuke by 2900 BP (Nakamura 1981). Tsukada (1986, 48) reports rice pollen at about 2900 BP from the Nakamura site in southern Kyushu. This site is not listed by Toyama and Nakayama, possibly because the percentage was too low. At the Jōtō site in Okayama Prefecture, rice pollen first appears below a level radiocarbon dated to 2880±95 BP (N-2599), but does not exceed 18 percent until the topsoil level of the core (Miyoshi and Usui 1976, 32–33).

(iv) Phytoliths. Phytolith work in Japan is very advanced, and the analysis of phytoliths from pottery fabric as well as from soils has contributed to our understanding of the beginning of rice cultivation there (Fujiwara 1987, 1993; Sahara 1987a, 46–48; Toyama 1992).

Tsukada (1986, 50) lists two Late Jōmon sites in Fukuoka Prefecture where phytoliths have been reported from artifact-bearing strata. One of these (Higashi-nabeda) is actually in Kumamoto Prefecture, and Tsukada quotes only a 1977 newspaper report for this site. The other site (Shika-higashi) is reported as producing rice phytoliths from early Final Jōmon deposits by Fujiwara (1990, 94; 1993, 152). According to recent newspaper

TABLE 5.1

PLANT NAMES MENTIONED IN TEXT

ENGLISH NAME	JAPANESE NAME	SCIENTIFIC NAME
Cereals:		
Rice	*ine*	Oryza sativa
Broomcorn millet	*kibi*	Panicum miliaceum
Foxtail millet	*awa*	Setaria italica
Buckwheat	*soba*	Fagopyrum esculentum
Barnyard millet	*hie*	Echinochloa utilis
Barnyard grass	*inubie*	Echinochloa crusgalli
Barley	*ōmugi*	Hordeum vulgare
Wheat	*komugi*	Triticum aestivum
Sorghum	*morokoshi*	Sorghum bicolor
Roots and tubers:		
Taro	*sato-imo*	Colocasia esculenta
Yam	*yama-no-imo; jinenjo*	Dioscorea japonica
Arrowroot	*kuzu*	Pueraria thunbergiana
Adder's tongue lily	*katakuri*	Erythronium japonicum
Cluster amaryllis	*higanbana*	Lycoris radiata

reports, Fujiwara has also identified rice phytoliths in a Late Jōmon sherd from the Minami-mizote site in Okayama.[2]

Tsukada (1986, 50) lists two Late Jōmon sites in Fukuoka Prefecture where phytoliths have been reported from artifact-bearing strata. One of these (Higashi-nabeda) is actually in Kumamoto Prefecture, and Tsukada quotes only a 1977 newspaper report for this site. The other site (Shika-higashi) is reported as producing rice phytoliths from early Final Jōmon deposits by Fujiwara (1990, 94; 1993, 152). According to recent newspaper reports, Fujiwara has also identified rice phytoliths in a Late Jōmon sherd from the Minami-mizote site in Okayama.[2]

All four early Final Jōmon rice phytolith sites given by Toyama and Nakayama (1992, 17) are in Kumamoto Prefecture.

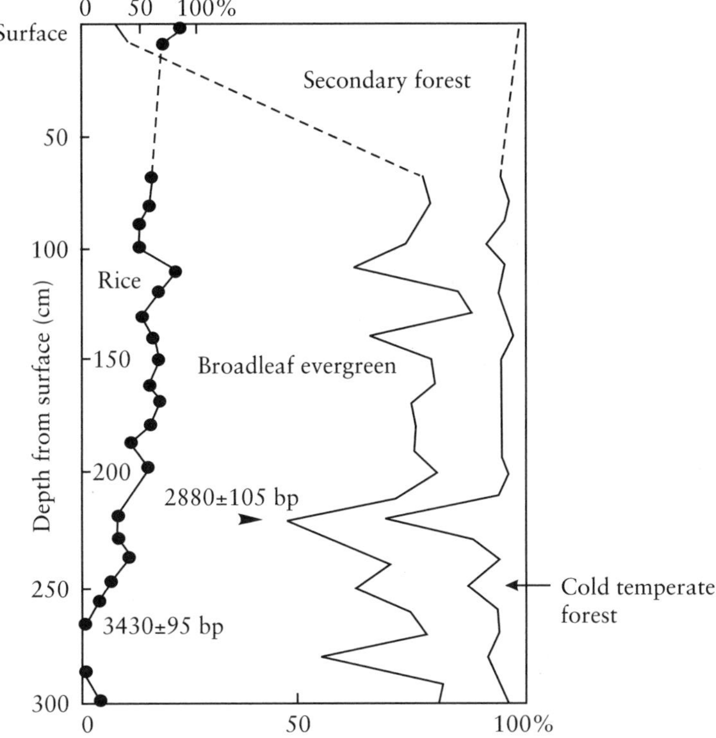

FIG. 5.3. Pollen sequence at Location J-23, Itazuke site, Fukuoka. Redrawn from Nakamura (1981, 46).

(v) Paddy Fields. At least 500 paddy-field sites have been excavated in Japan (Kuraku 1991a, 13); of these, about one-fifth date to the Yayoi period (Kuraku 1991b, 15). The earliest paddy field remains in Japan are from Nabatake in Saga. Several paddy levels were identified, but the earliest dates from the Yamanotera phase of the Initial Yayoi. This paddy field was associated with various continental stone tools and a wooden agricultural implement (Nakajima and Tajima 1982; Sahara 1987a, 41–42). A radiocarbon date from the Yamanotera stratum at Nabatake gave a result of 2680±80 BP; the Yu'usu level immediately above (which also produced paddy fields) has a date of 2620±60 BP. Yamazaki (e.g. 1991, 21) has argued on stratigraphic

grounds that the earliest paddy-field level at Nabatake dates to the Yu'usu rather than to the Yamanotera stage. This controversy is unresolved, and Yamazaki (e.g. 1991, 21) himself accepts that because carbonized rice has come from the Yamanotera levels at the site, paddy fields may have existed nearby. Other Initial Yayoi paddy fields are known at Itazuke and Notame in Fukuoka and Tsushima-Edō in Okayama. A water channel from this stage at Mure in Osaka was possibly also part of a paddy-field system. In addition, wooden agricultural tools were discovered from the Sasai site, Fukuoka, and from a water channel at Hayashi-Bōjiro in Takamatsu, Shikoku, and stone reaping knives have been found at Kigawa, Fukuoka, and at Kuchisakai, Hyōgo (for summaries of Initial Yayoi finds, see Harunari [1990] and [Hudson 1990a]).

What conclusions can be reached based on the five categories of evidence just summarized? There are a number of reported Late and early Final Jōmon sites with remains of rice (Table 5.2), but there is debate over the status of several. Toyama and Nakayama (1990, 1992) do not include any of the Late Jōmon sites. Out of the fourteen early Final sites that they list, only one (Osayuki) is found in a compendium of early rice-cultivation sites made for a 1991 conference (Maizō Bunkazai Kenkyūkai 1991). Toyama and Nakayama (1990, 32; Note 65) mention that doubts have been raised over the pottery used for the phytolith analysis from the Kaminanbu site: they give no details, but presumably this means that there is debate over which type the sherds belong to. The examples from Uenoharu and Amagi seem better substantiated (Fujiwara 1976, 59; 1982). Kazahari is the only site where rice remains have been dated directly.

There have recently been a number of early rice finds in Japan. While many of these remain problematical and/or as yet poorly published, it is unlikely that they can all be discounted as the result of stratigraphic disturbance. The next few years, therefore, may see significant changes in our understanding of the introduction of rice into the Islands. On present evidence, however, a date of about 1000 BC is probably a reasonable estimate for the first arrival of rice in Japan. Evidence for rice over the following 500 years gradually increases, but it was still mainly limited to north Kyushu. Then, from the Yamanotera phase of the fifth or fourth century BC, rice suddenly became more common; wet-rice paddies appeared together with wooden and stone agricultural tools and a variety of other continental influences.

Of course, the mere presence of rice in Jōmon contexts does not necessarily mean it was cultivated in situ. Direct evidence of cultivation (i.e., associated field systems) is not found until the Initial Yayoi, but it has been widely

TABLE 5.2

EVIDENCE FOR RICE FROM LATE AND EARLY FINAL JŌMON SITES

SITE	PREFECTURE	EVIDENCE	DATE	REFERENCE
Itazuke	Fukuoka	pollen	before 3400 BP	(Nakamura 1981)
Kurade	Fukuoka	pollen	before 3400 BP	(Nakamura 1981)
Higashi-nabeda	Kumamoto	soil phytoliths	Late Jōmon?	(Tsukada 1986)
Minami-mizote	Okayama	pottery impression and phytoliths	late Late Jōmon	(newspaper reports)
Kuwagai-shimo	Kyoto	carbonized grain	Late Jōmon	(Nishida 1975)
Kazahari	Aomori	carbonized grains	925 and 787 Cal BC	(D'Andrea et al. 1995)
Itazuke	Fukuoka	pollen	early Final	(Nakamura 1981)
Osayuki	Fukuoka	pottery impression	early Final	(Yamaguchi and Uno 1983)
Shika-higashi	Fukuoka	phytoliths (soil)	ca. 1000 BC	(Fujiwara 1993)
Kureishiba ru	Nagasaki	pottery impression, carbonized rice	early Final	(Furuta 1977)
Oharushita	Nagasaki	pottery impression	early Final	(Furuta 1968)
Ikada	Nagasaki	pottery impression	early Final	(Terasawa and Terasawa 1981)
Hyakuhana-dai	Nagasaki	pottery impression	early Final	(Suzuki 1974)
Wakudoishi	Kumamoto	pottery impression	early Final	(Tomita 1993)
Uenoharu	Kumamoto	carbonized seeds, phytoliths (pottery and soil)	ca. 1000 BC	(Kotani 1972)
Kaminanbu	Kumamoto	phytoliths (pottery)	ca. 800 BC	(Fujiwara 1993)
Kokai	Kumamoto	phytoliths (pottery)	early Final	(Esaka et al. 1978)
Amagi	Kumamoto	phytoliths (soil)	Goryo/ Kurokawa	(Fujiwara 1976)
Eryōharu	Ōita	carbonized seeds	early Final	(Kagawa 1971)
Ōishi	Ōita	pottery impression, carbonized seed(s)	early Final	(Kagawa 1972)
Goryōgun jōri	Osaka	pottery impression	early Final	(Toyama and Nakayama 1992)

Early Final Jōmon (= before Yamanotera-type pottery)

argued that upland, dry-field rice cultivation existed in parts of Kyushu in the Late-Final Jōmon (e.g. Fujiwara 1988, 120–121; Sasaki 1991b, 242–243). A number of scholars have proposed that Late- and Final-phase cultivation of rice and other crops was of the slash-and-burn or swidden type. Swidden cultivation was common in the mountainous parts of Japan until recently and still continues in some remote areas (e.g. Hashiguchi 1987), although according to Fujiwara (1993, 158) swidden cultivation of rice is not found in Japan today. Sasaki strongly emphasizes the supposed antiquity of swidden farming:

> Swidden cultivation is . . . a form of agriculture antedating the cultivation of padi-rice. Countless examples of a shift from swiddens to paddies may be observed in Southeast Asia and India, but apart from some singular exceptions, there are no instances of the reverse process from paddies to swiddens. In view of this fact, the swidden cultivation that was so widespread throughout the mountain regions of Japan and other parts of the laurilignosa [broadleaf evergreen] region is considered to represent a form of agriculture that antedates wet-rice cultivation (Sasaki 1991a, 30–31).

It is doubtful, however, whether ethnographic examples of a move from dry to wet rice can be used to argue that such a developmental sequence always occurred in prehistory. White (1995) has proposed that in Southeast Asia both upland and wet rice developed from simple, opportunistic forms of wetland cultivation (see also Helliwell 1991). Archaeologically, Sasaki (1991b, 240–241) sees the population trends of late Jōmon west Japan as demonstrating low growth with stability, factors that he sees as consistent with the practice of incipient agriculture. Work by archaeobotanist Kasahara Yasuo has shown a transition in north-central Okayama Prefecture from a large quantity of typical swidden weeds including *Oxalis corniculata, Solanum nigrum, Capsella bursapastoris,* and *Stellaria media* in the Final Jōmon to paddy-field weeds including *Sagittaria trifolia, Commelina communis,* and *Monochoria vaginalis* in the Middle Yayoi (Sasaki 1991b, 243). A similar sequence is known at Nabatake (Sasaki 1991b, 242–243; cf. Kasahara 1982). Sasaki (1991a, 34) concludes that it is "beyond question that a laurilignosa-type culture based on swidden cultivation developed in western Japan in the [L]ate and [F]inal Jōmon periods." My own view is that, while some limited cultivation of rice may be an increasingly likely scenario for parts of western Japan in the later Jōmon, conclusive evidence is still lacking. Since pre-Yamanotera sites with rice remains are particularly common on upland volcanic soils in Kumamoto and Nagasaki Prefectures, dry-field cultivation is a distinct possibility, but the idea of a broadleaf evergreen "culture complex" has clearly had its day.

Animals and Other Plants

Having engaged in a detailed discussion of rice, we must now look briefly at debates over the domestication of nuts, roots and tubers, and animals. The importance of nuts to Jōmon subsistence is well known. Nishida (1983) argues that, as sun-loving plants, chestnuts *(Castanea crenata)* and walnuts *(Juglans ailanthifolia)* tended to concentrate around clearings made for settlements, becoming symbiotic with Jōmon populations in the Chūbu highlands from the late Early phase. The long reproductive cycle of most trees makes "full" domestication an unlikely proposition (Nishida 1983, 318; cf. Harris 1977, 206–208), but some human intervention in the forest ecosystem is likely. Matsui (1992, 7) notes that chestnuts from the Awazu site in Shiga are more than 2 cm in size and are sometimes as large as 3 cm—significantly larger than wild species, which are about 1.5 cm. Yamanaka (1997) reports a significant decrease in the genetic diversity of DNA extracted from chestnuts from Sannai Maruyama in Aomori between 5500 and 5000 BP.

It has been widely argued that roots and tubers played an important role in Jōmon subsistence, but the lack of any direct botanical evidence has hampered research. *Colocasia esculenta* var. *aquatilis,* a wild taro and possible progenitor for cultivated taros (Matthews 1991), is known in the Ryukyu Islands, but Matthews et al. (1992) argue that it was probably introduced there by humans at some unknown but ancient date. Based on a possible association with pigs, Matthews et al. (1992, 31) suggest that the introduction of taro may even date to as early as the late Pleistocene in the Ryukyus. Proposed early dates for the arrival of taro in mainland Japan are common: Sasaki (1991b, 148) suggests it spread to the Islands from China in the Early Jōmon during the Holocene climatic optimum (see also Tanaka M. 1986). A first-century BC Chinese agricultural work, the *Fan Shengzhi Shu,* describes the cultivation of taro in northern China (see Shih 1958)—from which fact several authors, including Matthews et al. (1992, 28), assume taro would also have been present in Japan by that time.

Turner (1979) reports a high level of crown caries and other oral pathologies in Middle to Late Jōmon crania from central Japan. The 8.6-percent caries rate in his Jōmon sample is more similar to averages for caries in agricultural (10.43 percent) and mixed forager-farmer groups (4.37 percent) than to those among hunter-gatherers (1.3 percent) (Turner 1979, 622). Turner suggests that consumption of cultivated taro may have been responsible, but he provides no corroborating evidence, and Spriggs (1982, 8) finds his argument unconvincing. Other than the vague "central Japan," Turner provides no details as to the location of his samples. Certainly, taro consumption is not specifically linked with the Middle Jōmon of the Chūbu highlands, and a recent study by Fujita (1995) has shown a high caries rate among some coastal Jōmon populations.

Claims for Jōmon yam cultivation are also common (e.g. Kidder 1993, 65), but again direct evidence is absent. The yam *Dioscorea japonica* is thought to be native to the Islands, but Fujio (1993, 21) notes that there are no ethnographic examples of its husbandry in Japan. The plant is not gregarious and does not seem to respond easily to selective pressures. Fujio (1993, 21) concludes that it is an unlikely candidate for a Jōmon cultigen.

It is noted in chapter 3 that domesticated dogs are known in Japan from the beginning of the Jōmon period, but that these animals are believed to have been introduced rather than to have been domesticated in situ. Jōmon people also appear to have had a close relationship with the boar, probably transporting it to regions such as Hokkaido and the Izu Islands, which lay outside its natural habitat (cf. Inoue 1989). Boar were probably transported to the Izu islands when young to provide food; while eventually left to run feral, they were presumably kept in pens at some stage (Hudson 1988, 50–52). Based on the distribution of Jōmon boar outside of its natural habitat and on finds of juvenile boar burials, Katō (1980) has argued that some sort of semi-domestication may have been practiced in the Jōmon.

Age profiles of boar excavated from Yayoi sites have suggested more intensive management. Since growth decreases dramatically after a certain age, it is uneconomical to keep domesticated animals after that stage, and maximum returns can be gained by slaughtering just before maturity. A large number of juveniles excavated from a site, therefore, may indicate the exploitation of domesticated animals. As shown in Table 5.3, "boar" from the Middle Yayoi Ikegami site in Osaka have a quite different age profile than do those of the Final Jōmon Saihiro site in Chiba, but the profile is similar to that of domesticated pigs from the Chinese Neolithic site of Hemudu. Confirmation of the presence of domesticated pigs in the Yayoi came in 1989 with Nishimoto's analysis of the well-preserved *Sus* skulls from Shimogōri-kuwanae in Ōita. On the basis of eight morphological criteria, Nishimoto (1989a) concludes that the remains from this site were pig rather than wild boar. Pigs are now known from at least seven other Yayoi sites: Nabatake

TABLE 5.3

PERCENTAGES OF AGED *SUS* REMAINS FROM IKEGAMI (MIDDLE YAYOI), SAIHIRO (FINAL JŌMON), AND HEMUDU (EARLY CHINESE NEOLITHIC)

	IKEGAMI	SAIHIRO	HEMUDU
0–1 year	23.3%	8.2%	few
1–2 years	53.3%	30.3%	54%
0–1 years	20.0%	52.7%	34%
over 3 years	3.3%	9.8%	10%

Compiled from data in Harunari (1990, 86–87).

and Yoshinogari (Saga), Karako (Nara), Ikegami and Kamei (Osaka), Asahi (Aichi), and Ikego (Kanagawa); they are probably also present at Magarita (Fukuoka), Tsuboi (Nara), Yotsuike (Osaka), and Nishikawazu (Shimane) (Nishimoto 1991, 1993). There is no reason to assume that such sites were unique, and domesticated pigs were probably widely distributed in the Yayoi. Although chickens have also been identified at one Yayoi site, at least (Nishimoto 1993), pigs appear to have been the main domestic animal exploited by the Yayoi people.

Stages to Agriculture

The development toward agriculture in the Japanese Islands can be divided into two main stages. Stage 1 saw limited exploitation of a number of plants, some native to the Islands, some introduced. None of the Stage 1 cultigens appear to have served as major food sources, a pattern by no means unusual in the history of plant domestication (see Farrington and Urry 1985; Hayden 1990). Rice was possibly cultivated in upland fields in several regions of western Japan from the end of the Late Jōmon, but it was not until approximately 400 BC that full-scale wet-rice farming began in the Islands in Stage 2. It is of course possible that the late-Jōmon rice cultivation should be regarded as a third stage. In view of the aim of this section to determine to what extent the Jōmon people developed agriculture independently, this is a crucial problem. While future finds may overturn any provisional conclusions made here, however, I do not believe that the Jōmon people were moving along an inexorable path toward agriculture. I see the late Jōmon cultivation of rice as a part of Stage 1 rather than as a separate stage of "incipient agriculture."

Following Spriggs (1996), I have argued on theoretical grounds that it is important to distinguish between small-scale *cultivation*—which is widely practiced by hunter-gatherers—and full-scale farming or *agriculture* (Hudson *in press* a). Jōmon cultivation appears typical of the sort of economic activity practiced by many foraging groups, whereas the agriculture that appeared in the Islands in the Yayoi clearly marks a revolutionary break with preceding subsistence patterns. Finds of possible cultigens from Jōmon deposits are extremely rare compared with later periods. Furthermore, it is crucial to note that there is no evidence that Jōmon society was undergoing fundamental changes as a result of "incipient agriculture." In fact, many late Jōmon sites with evidence of rice are characterized by what might be termed a "conservative" material culture. I have suggested that this conservatism may be explained by the Jōmon people's ideological acceptance of cultivation but rejection of agriculture (Hudson *in press* a).

A full understanding of the beginnings of rice cultivation in the Japanese Islands awaits further research. While in theory the full-scale farming that characterizes Stage 2 could have resulted from in situ intensification, the evidence for immigration discussed in the previous two chapters makes the introduction of a wet-rice agricultural complex with Peninsular migrants a much more likely scenario. Thus, the presence of some limited rice cultivation in the late Jōmon should not be seen as evidence against the model of Japanese ethnogenesis proposed here, since that cultivation appears to have been preempted by the immigration of Peninsular farmers with an intensive agricultural complex.

THE ARCHAEOLOGY OF THE INITIAL YAYOI

The earliest stage of Yayoi culture—the Initial phase—saw the sudden appearance of a wet rice-farming complex based on bunded paddy fields. On present evidence, the antecedents of this wet-rice complex cannot be found in the Jōmon. The discussion below will demonstrate that many specific material culture parallels exist between Kyushu and the Korean Peninsula, and a strong Peninsular influence in the formation of Yayoi culture is clear. The Initial Yayoi overlaps with the *tottaimon* (notched appliqué band)-pottery phase of the late Final Jōmon. *Tottaimon* ceramics were found throughout western Japan, but usually only sites with evidence for wet rice cultivation are termed "Initial Yayoi" (Table 5.4). No secure date exists for the beginning of the Initial Yayoi and thus for the start of wet rice farming in the Islands. A few transitional radiocarbon dates have been published, but many are much

TABLE 5.4

FINAL JŌMON–EARLY YAYOI POTTERY TYPES

	KYUSHU	KINAI	TOHOKU
FINAL JŌMON	Hirota/Ōishi	Shigasato II	Ōbora B
	Koga	Shigasato IIIa	Ōbora B-C
	Kurokawa	Shigasato IIIb	Ōbora C1
INITIAL YAYOI	**Yamanotera**	Shigasato IV	Ōbora C2
	Yu'usu I		
EARLY YAYOI	Yu'usu II/	**Funabashi/**	+
	Itazuke I	**Kuchisakai II**	
	Itazuke IIa	Yayoi I (Old)	Ōbora A
	Itazuke IIb	Yayoi I (Middle)	Ōbora A'
	Itazuke IIc	Yayoi I (New)	**Sunazawa**

Bold type denotes first wet rice farming in each region.

TABLE 5.5

FINAL JŌMON–EARLY YAYOI RADIOCARBON DATES FROM NORTHERN KYUSHU

SITE	POTTERY TYPE	UNCAL. DATE	MATERIAL	REF.
Sakaizaki	Kurokawa	3620±100	charcoal	GAK-722a
Sakaizaki	Kurokawa	3560±100	shell	GAK-722b
Sakaizaki	Kurokawa	3630±90	charcoal	GAK-723a
Sakaizaki	Kurokawa	3520±100	shell	GAK-723b
Osayuki	Osayuki	2870±70	soil	N-4298
Nabatake 12	Yamanotera	4030±65	?	N-4598
Nabatake 10–11	Yamanotera	2680±80	?	N-4230
Nabatake 10	late Final	3030±40	wood	KSU-520
Nabatake L8	Yu'usu	3230±100	?	N-4600
Nabatake L8	end of Final	2630±30	wood	KSU-513
Nabatake 8	Yu'usu	2620±60	?	N-4229
Itazuke	Yu'usu	2400±90	charcoal	GAK-2358
Ukikunden	Yu'usu	2370±50	shell	Kuri-0053
Ukikunden	Yu'usu	2240±50	charcoal	Kuri-0054
Nabatake U8	Yu'usu/ Itazuke I	29600±90	?	N-4599
Itazuke	Itazuke	2560±100	shell	GAK-2360

too early (Table 5.5). Most Japanese scholars give 400 BC as an approximation for the start of the Initial phase, a figure reached by working back from Middle Yayoi artifacts cross-dated with the continent. More precise dating of this important transition awaits better radiocarbon data.

Pottery

Yayoi ceramics were once believed to be decoratively and technologically quite different from Jōmon pottery, but recent work has shown that this is not the case. The major difference between the two pottery types is vessel shape. The vast majority of Jōmon pottery falls into a type known as *fukabachi* (deep bowl); other vessels such as the *asabachi* (shallow bowl) and spouted "teapots" are much less common. In contrast, Yayoi pottery was marked by four major shapes, a wide-mouthed *kame* (pot), a *tsubo* (narrow-necked jar), a *hachi* (bowl), and a *takatsuki* (pedestaled dish) (Barnes 1990b; Sahara 1975, 118–121; Hudson 1990a, 78–82) (Fig. 5.4). The *kame* is thought to have been the vessel primarily used for cooking and the *tsubo* for storing rice, but there are a few examples of soot-blackened *tsubo* that were probably used for cooking.

Yayoi pottery derived from Final Jōmon wares under the influence of the Korean Plain Pottery tradition. During the second millennium BC, Plain Pottery gradually replaced the preceding decorated Chŭlmun wares on the Peninsula. Using radiocarbon dates, Nelson (1993, 113–116) argues that Plain Pottery and dolmens appeared around 2000 BC, but most other scholars posit a later transition, at 1300 BC (Rhee and Choi 1992, 59) or 1000 BC (Ro 1992). Barnes (1993a, 160–161) notes that although Plain Pottery may appear as early as 1500 BC, bronze is not common until about 700 BC, and she proposes the term "Proto-Bronze Age" (1500–700 BC) for the period in which Plain Pottery was used before the Bronze Age proper (700 BC–AD 1). Plain Pottery is a coarse-tempered, thick-walled ware typified by wide-mouthed pots and narrow-necked jars. Decoration is not entirely absent but is mostly limited to incisions or punctates under the rim (Nelson 1993, 116–123). Various schemes exist for the subdivision of Plain Pottery, but many archaeologists posit three stages for the southern Peninsula: (1) an Early or Hunamni phase during which pots have punctates under the rim; (2) a Middle or Songgungni phase during which pots have no punctates but have slightly everted rims; and (3) a Late or Susongni phase during which pots have doubled-over or rolled rims (Gotō 1991; Harunari 1990, 101–103; Kataoka 1990; Yi

1991). The Initial Yayoi appears to have been contemporary with the late Early and the Middle phases.

There are three main aspects of the change from Jōmon to Yayoi pottery: vessel shape, decoration, and fabrication technique. As regards vessel shape, it is the appearance of the *tsubo* that is particularly significant: "It is, at present, not possible to find the source of the *tottaimon* jar-shaped pottery in Jōmon ceramics; from the red-burnishing technique and from similarities in shape, it seems more appropriate to look to the red-burnished wares of Korean Plain Pottery" (Yamazaki 1989, 349). Large jars, often red slipped and burnished, were particularly common in *tottaimon* sites in north Kyushu, sometimes comprising over 30 percent of all vessels. Such jars were much less common outside this area, though they are known to have existed as far as the Kinai. As the incidence of jars increased, the incidence of that typical Jōmon vessel the shallow bowl *(asabachi)* steadily decreased and, already rare at Initial Yayoi sites such as Notame, it had disappeared from western Japan by the Early Yayoi (Fig. 5.4).

In contrast to the jar and the shallow bowl, the cooking pot *(fukabachi* or *kame)* shows considerable continuity between Jōmon and Yayoi. Four main types of cooking pot have been defined at Initial Yayoi sites in the Karatsu and Fukuoka plains (Fig. 5.5). The first is a bullet-shaped vessel with a plain rim. The second has a shape similar to that of the first but with a notched appliqué ridge around the rim. The third type is the most typical Final Jōmon shape, a carinated deep bowl with notched ridges around the rim and the shoulder. The fourth has a shape similar to that of the first type but, instead of having an appliqué band, it has been notched directly onto the rim of the vessel (Yamazaki 1980; Fujio 1987; Harunari 1990, 35–41). It has been suggested that the last of these four types formed the prototype of the distinctive cooking pot of the Early Yayoi (Yamazaki 1980; Nakajima 1982). The presence of notching around the rim has led some archaeologists to argue that the origins of this so-called proto-Itazuke pot can be found in the Final Jōmon. A consideration of fabrication techniques, however, leads to a quite different conclusion. Since the 1960s, it had been known that Yayoi pottery was made with wider coils or strips of clay than was Jōmon pottery; the way these coils were fitted together was also known to be different. Work on Initial Yayoi ceramics by Yane Yoshimasa has shown these differences very clearly. Deep bowls of the Final Jōmon in western Japan were made with a series of narrow strips of clay some 1.5 to 2 cm wide. The vessels were built from the base upward, and new coils were added onto the *inside* of the previous strip. This

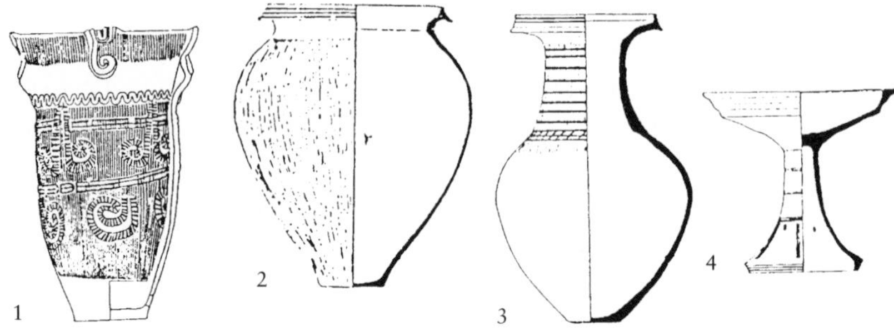

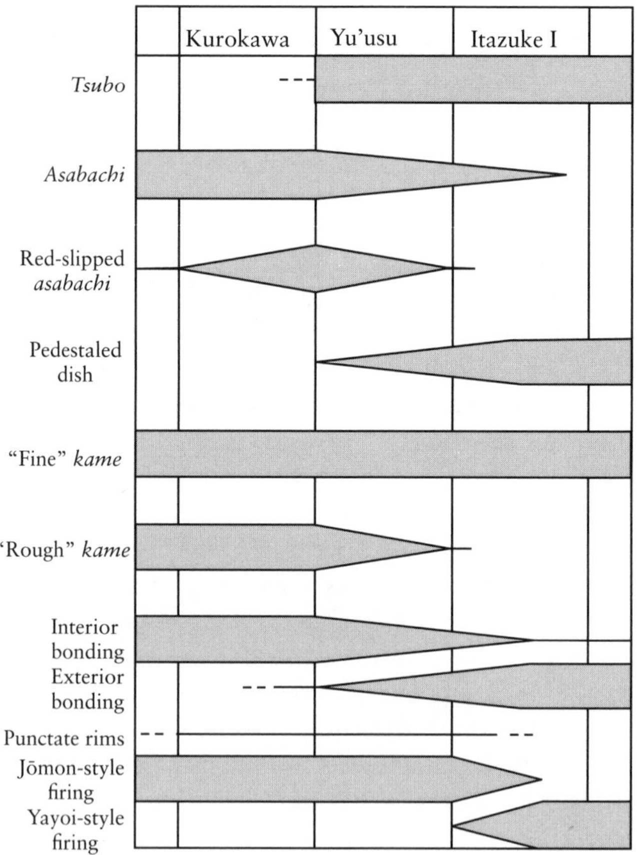

FIG. 5.4. Top: major Jōmon and Yayoi vessels shapes (1, Jōmon *fukabachi;* 2, Yayoi *kame;* Yayoi *tsubo;* 4, Yayoi *takatsuki*. Bottom: Vessel use in north Kyushu from the Jōmon to the Yayoi. Top: from Hudson (1990a). Bottom: modified from original by Tanaka Y. (1986).

technique is known as interior bonding and contrasts with Early Yayoi pottery, which was made of strips added onto the *outside* of the previous coil (exterior bonding). Wider strips of clay (4 to 5 cm) were also used in the Yayoi. According to Yane, the origin of this new fabrication technique is to be found in Korean Plain Pottery, which was also made by exterior bonding of 4- to 5-cm-wide coils. The switch to exterior bonding occurred gradually through the Initial Yayoi. At Nabatake, in the Yamanotera phase only 2 out of 85 vessels were made using this technique; by the Yu'usu phase this had increased to 33 out of 156. It was only in the Itazuke I phase of the Early Yayoi that exterior bonding became the norm (Yane 1984, 1987).

Similarities between Korean Plain Pottery and the proto-Itazuke pot are not limited to fabrication techniques. The presence of a finishing method known as *hakeme* involving smoothing with a wooden tool to create brush-like marks is also considered to have been derived from the Peninsula. The fact that *hakeme* seems to have been adopted at the same time as exterior bonding implies that they may have arrived together (Yokoyama 1979; Harunari 1990, 40). Despite these major influences from the Peninsula, however, the Itazuke I (Ongagawa) cooking pot is a clearly hybrid form. In particular, the everted, notched rim of this vessel is not found in Korean Plain Pottery but was derived from the Final Jōmon tradition.

Relatively few (several dozen?) actual Plain Pottery vessels appear to have been transported to Japan during the Final Jōmon and Initial Yayoi phases. In Japan, punctate-rim pottery has been found in an area stretching from Okinawa to Yamaguchi in the Kurokawa to Yu'usu phases, but most of this type of pottery are local vessels with the punctate decoration applied rather than Plain Pottery per se (Kataoka 1990, 78; Tanaka Y. 1986, 122). Peninsular-style red-burnished jars appear from the Yamanotera phase, but, again, most are thought to be of local manufacture (Tanaka Y. 1986, 122). Of course, the number of Plain Pottery vessels found in Japan cannot be used as a direct measure of immigration, since Peninsular immigrants may have made new vessels after their arrival instead of carrying fragile ceramics with them by boat. In this respect it is important to note that Yayoi ceramics made in the Peninsular *style* (sometimes with Jōmon influences) are much more common than are actual imported vessels.

Wooden and Stone Tools

The beginning of wet rice agriculture in the Islands is associated with a whole series of new tools: axes, adzes, and chisels for clearing forests and

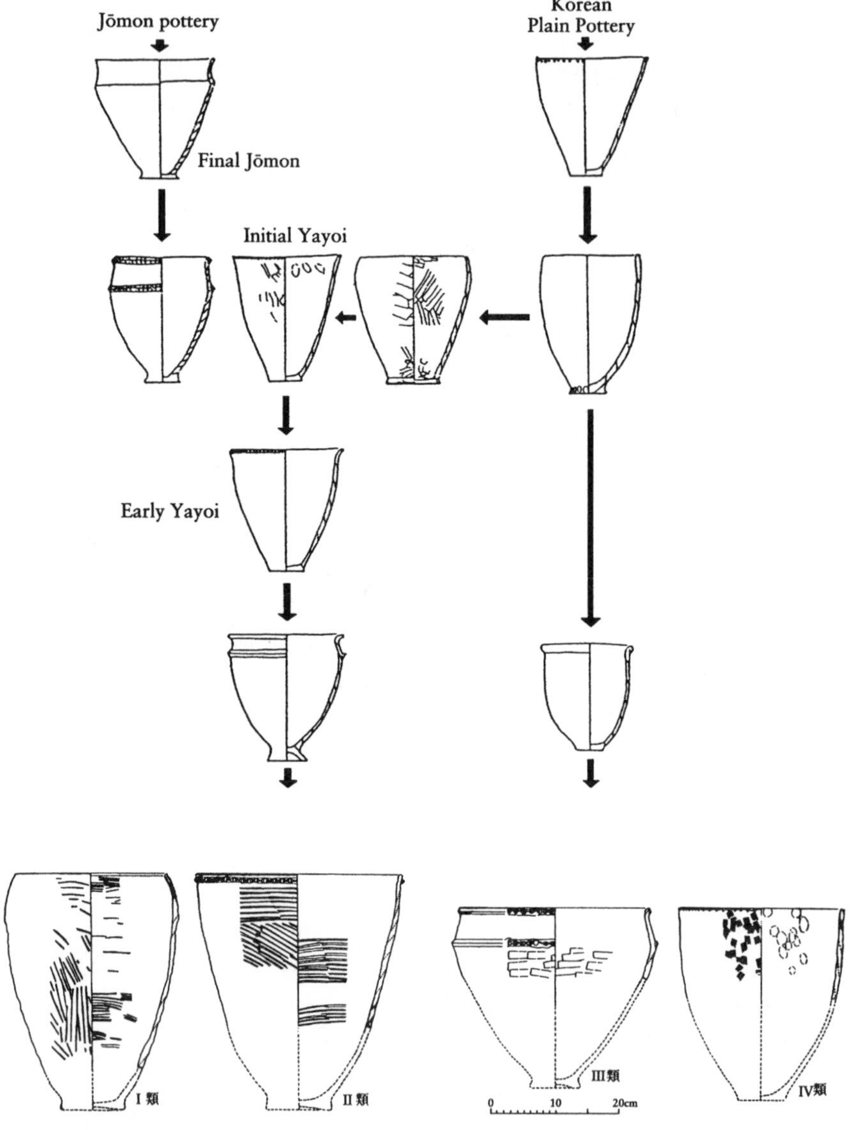

FIG. 5.5. Top: The development of the Yayoi cooking pot in north Kyushu. Bonding techniques shown in cross section. Bottom: Four cooking pot shapes found at Nabatake. I–III interior bonding, IV exterior bonding. Top: modified from Yane (1987). Bottom: from Harunari (1990, 36).

woodworking; hoes and spades for preparing paddy fields; reaping knives for harvesting; and mortars and pestles for processing grain. Almost all of these new tools first appeared in the Initial Yayoi, and many have known prototypes on the Asian mainland.

Prehistoric wooden agricultural tools have only recently been discovered in Korea, and their development there is still poorly known. Peninsular tools, however, most likely formed the prototypes for Yayoi examples. Hoes and rakes from Nabatake and Itazuke are the earliest wooden farming tools known in Japan (Fig. 5.6) (Yamaguchi 1991). Their presence in the Initial Yayoi implies that they were introduced as part of the wet-rice complex that was formed in that phase.

Although iron had largely replaced stone by the Late Yayoi, the early part of the period is marked by a distinctive lithic tool kit consisting of an *ishibōchō* (reaping knife), a bifacially beveled felling ax, a grooved columnar adze, a flat plano-convex sectioned adze, and a chisel-shaped adze. All of these distinctive types have been found at Bronze Age sites in Korea (Fig. 5.7). The adzes and the reaping knife were not known in the Jōmon and were clearly either brought from the Peninsula or else made following Peninsular prototypes. Most stone reaping knives have two circular holes for inserting a cord that was wrapped around the hand, but a few knives found at Initial Yayoi sites in northern Kyushu have a single narrow slit (Fig. 5.7). This type of knife disappeared by the end of the Initial phase, but similar knives are known in South Kyŏngsang province in Korea. Bifacial axes had existed in the Jōmon, but from the Initial Yayoi their typical triangular plan became more rectangular, and the cutting edge also became slightly wider. While these trends are regarded as showing continental influence, Japanese axes of this stage tend to be less rounded than their Peninsular counterparts, thus showing their hybrid ancestry (Harunari 1990, 107). Chon (1992, 168) argues that the lack of lithic parallels between south China on the one hand and south Korea/western Japan on the other suggests that the rice agriculture associated with these tools did not diffuse directly between these regions. Instead, Chon proposes (again on lithic parallels) that rice spread first to the Taedong and Jaeryong River valleys of northwest Korea and then into the southern Peninsula and Kyushu. Chon's (1990, 1992) studies of the distribution of stone tools have demonstrated that Yayoi lithics are very closely linked with the Korean Peninsula (Fig. 5.8).

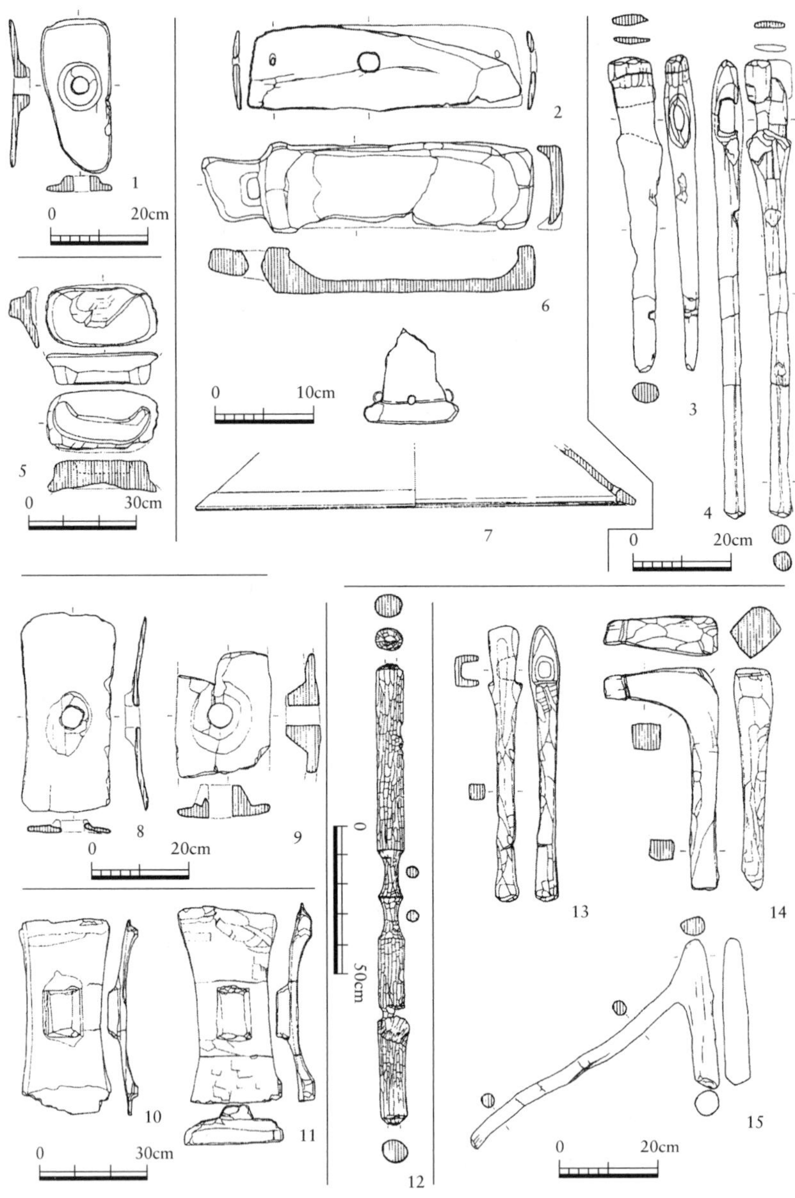

FIG. 5.6. Wooden farming tools from Nabatake, Initial-Early Yayoi. From Yamaguchi (1991).

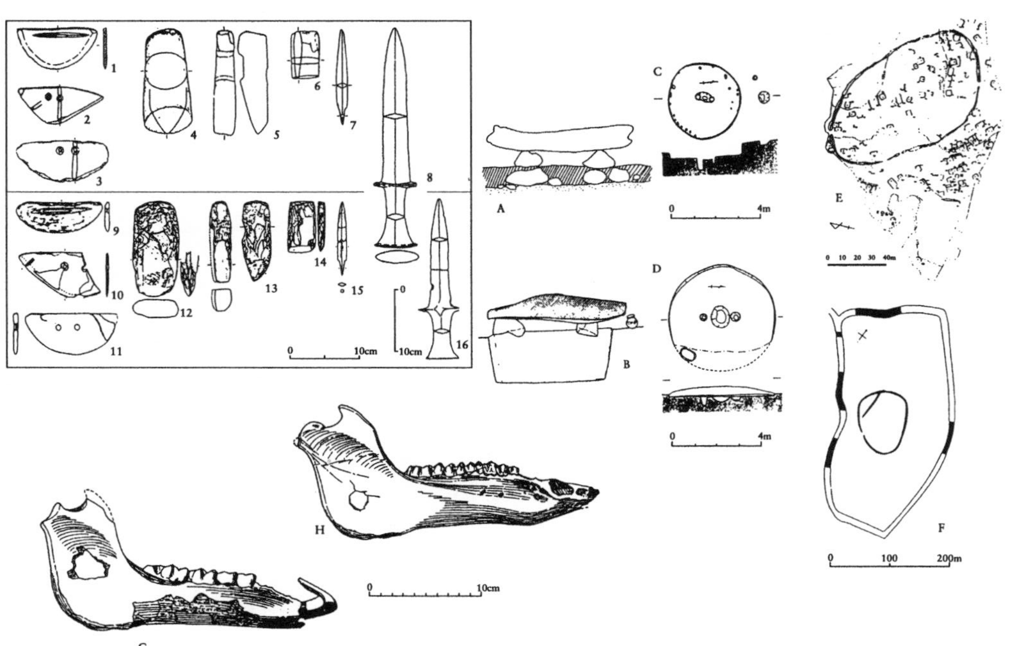

FIG. 5.7. Material culture parallels between Initial Yayoi Kyushu and the Korean Peninsula. **Lithics:** (1–8 from Korea, 9–16 from Japan): 1–3, 9–11 stone reaping knives; 4 and 12 bifacial axes; 5 and 13 cylindrical adzes; 6 and 14 chisel-shaped adzes; 7 and 15 polished arrowheads; 8 and 16 polished daggers. **Megalithic burials** from (A) the Peninsular and (B) Shinmachi. **Songgungni-type houses** from (C) Songgungni and (D) Shimohieda. **Ditched settlements** from (E) Komtalli and (F) Itazuke. **Pig ritual jawbones** from (G) Hogok and (H) Shimogōri-kuwanae.

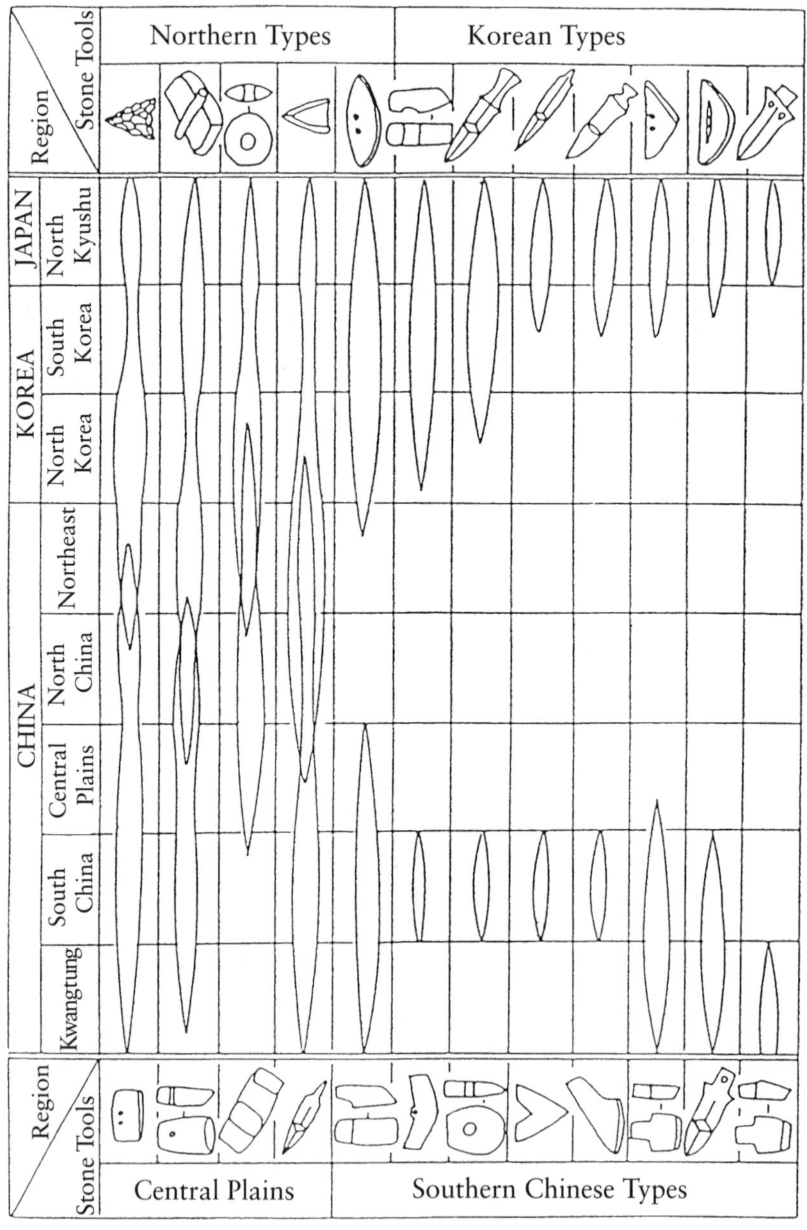

FIG. 5.8. Distribution pattern of stone tools in East Asia. From Chon (1992).

Metallurgy

At the Magarita site, a fragment of iron believed to be part of an ax was found in a pit building associated with Initial Yayoi pottery. An almost complete miniature iron ax found at Osayuki in Kitakyushu City may belong to the Kurokawa phase of the Final Jōmon. Other similar examples are known from the Early Yayoi (Harunari 1990, 14–17). In contrast, bronze was not introduced into the Islands on any large scale until the end of the Early Yayoi, although a few scattered finds are known from the first half of that phase. Bronze objects introduced in the late Early Yayoi include swords, spearheads, halberds, and geometric incised mirrors, most of which are known to have been brought from the Peninsula, though some local casting was already in operation by the end of the Early Yayoi. Many Japanese archaeologists believe bronze arrived not just as trade items but as part of an actual migratory process from the Peninsula. Finds of Korean Plain Pottery increase in Japan during the late Early Yayoi, and their distribution matches the extent of narrow-bladed weapons and geometric incised mirrors (Nishitani 1989). This suggests that Peninsular immigration was not limited to the Initial Yayoi but that it continued through the Early phase.

Settlements

Although both periods display considerable variation, two contrasting types of Jōmon and Yayoi settlement can be distinguished. Jōmon villages were typically marked by a concentric division of space with a central plaza, often with pit burials, encircled by dwellings that were in turn encircled by a garbage-discard zone. The Yayoi, in contrast, saw the development of a quite different settlement structure. Graves were now located outside the village in a separate cemetery. Though many settlements were undefended, large ditched villages were characteristic of the Yayoi. The origins of the Yayoi-type settlements are almost certainly to be found on the mainland.

A ditched site dated by radiocarbon to the sixth millennium BC was recently excavated at Xinglongwa in Liaoning province, northeast China (Nagashima 1994, 190), but at present this type of settlement is not known on the Korean Peninsula until much later. Currently, the only Peninsular ditched settlement that appears to predate the Yayoi is Komtalli, located about fifty km north of Pusan (Fig. 5.7). Komtalli has an oval-shaped moat about 120 m long; although only half of the buildings associated with the site are actually enclosed by the ditch, a defensive function is supported by its hilltop location.

Komtalli is thought to date to the fourth century BC (Nagashima 1994, 190). The earliest ditched settlements in Japan are found on the Fukuoka plain in north Kyushu. At Itazuke, a 1–4 m wide and 1–2.2 m deep ditch encircled an area of some 6,700 m^2. Yu'usu and Itazuke pottery were found together in the bottom of the ditch. In 1989, sections of an outer ditch were excavated at Itazuke; if this ditch continued around the whole site, it would encircle an area of 6.3 hectares. Three years later, a double ditch dating to the Yu'usu I stage was discovered at the Naka site about 1.5 km west of Itazuke (Yoshidome 1993). Ditched settlements were thus present from the very beginning of wet rice farming in Japan.

Final Jōmon house plans in north Kyushu were square or rectangular, but by the end of the Early Yayoi, circular plans had become the norm across western Japan (Nakama 1987, 597). Nakama looks to the Peninsula for the origin of Yayoi-period circular-pit houses, suggesting that they derive from the so-called Songgungni-type dwelling. This type of pit house is circular or nearly circular in plan and has two postholes adjoining a central oval pit. Similar dwellings are known at the Plain Pottery Songgungni site in southwest Korea (Nakama 1987, 597–598) (Fig. 5.7). Eleven pit buildings of this type have been excavated in an Initial Yayoi context at the Etsuji site in Fukuoka Prefecture (Shintaku 1992). Elsewhere in western Japan, thirty-nine Early and twenty-five Middle phase Songgungni-type houses are listed by Nakama (1987).

Domesticated Pigs

As discussed earlier in this chapter, Yayoi pigs seem to have been introduced from the continent rather than domesticated from existing wild boar. This interpretation is strengthened by the excavational context of *Sus* remains from many Yayoi sites. Mandibles are often found with a hole cut into the vertical ramus at the back of the jaw. A wooden pole onto which a number of mandibles were then hung was inserted into this hole. Pig jawbones still attached to such poles have been discovered at Nabatake and Karako (see Hudson and Barnes 1991, 232). This type of ritual practice is not known from the Jōmon, and it seems safe to assume that it was introduced in the Yayoi. Its presence at the Initial Yayoi site of Nabatake implies that this ritual arrived together with domesticated pigs as part of the agricultural package that was formed at that time. This has been interpreted as evidence for migration: "when rice agriculture was transmitted to Japan, it was not just a question of the transmission of rice technology and tools; we have to assume that a rice farming cultural system as a whole, with ritual included, was brought to Japan. This means the immigration of a large number of people who possessed that cultural system" (Nishimoto 1989b, 13).

The ritual use of pig jawbones is widely known from both archaeological and ethnographic contexts in China (Harunari 1993; Kim 1994), but so far only one example is known from the Korean Peninsula. This is the Plain Pottery Hogok site in the northeast corner of modern North Korea. The site produced two perforated *Sus* mandibles as well as a pile of pig skulls (Fig. 5.7). The context of the mandibles is unclear, but the skulls are from a building that can probably be dated to the late first millennium BC (Harunari 1993, 83–84). Nishimoto (1989b) and Harunari (1993) are probably correct in assuming that Yayoi pig rituals were introduced by continental immigrants, but it is not yet possible to securely assign the source of these rituals to the Korean Peninsula. The location of the Hogok site would seem to rule out any direct relationship with the Islands, although the same site has also produced oracle bones of the type known in Yayoi Japan (see Hudson 1992a, 152). If the Hogok mandibles date to the last stage of that site, then it is even theoretically possible that they postdate the Yayoi examples and were introduced from Japan.

Megalithic Burials

Megaliths or dolmens refer here to a type of burial chamber topped by a large capstone. The actual burial may be in an above-ground stone cist or else below the ground in an earthen pit or wooden or stone coffin. Though known in many parts of the world, in East Asia such graves are particularly numerous on the Korean Peninsula (Kim B-M 1982). In the Initial Yayoi this Peninsular burial custom spread to Kyushu. Though flourishing briefly, these dolmens were soon replaced by jar burials and did not enjoy the same popularity in Japan as they did in Korea.

Yayoi megaliths are found in a quite limited area of northwest Kyushu centering on the Karatsu and Itoshima plains and encompassing Saga and Nagasaki Prefectures. They are not known on the Fukuoka plain. Chronologically, they are mainly associated with the Yu'usu phase, although a few examples are known from as late as the Middle Yayoi in the Gotō Islands and in Kumamoto and Kagoshima Prefectures (Iwasaki 1987; Kōmoto 1982). Since the burial pit under many Japanese megaliths tends to be small, Mori (1969) argues that the Jōmon tradition of flexed burial continued to be common, showing that Jōmon people adopted the Peninsular megalithic custom themselves. Although small burial pits have also been found under Korean dolmens (Harunari 1990, 111), it is clear that in Japan these megaliths were not solely the graves of immigrants. The incidence of flexed burials and typical Jōmon artifacts such as clay figurines as grave goods increases as one moves away from the center of dolmen distribution in Saga. Skeletal remains with Jōmon characteristics have been discovered from Initial and Early Yayoi megaliths at the Shinmachi site in Fukuoka (Nakahashi and Nagai 1987).

Tooth Ablation

Ritual tooth ablation began in the Islands in the late Middle Jōmon and became widespread in the Late and Final phases (Han and Nakahashi 1996; Harunari 1986).[3] The custom continued through to the Middle Yayoi and even to the Kofun period in some areas, but there were noticeable changes in ablation patterns between the Jōmon and the Yayoi. Three major types of Yayoi-period ablation are known (Harunari 1987). In Harunari's terminology, these are known as 4I, C, and I^2. The 4I and C types both start from the removal of the upper canines but then divide into two lineages. Both are common Jōmon patterns, but, whereas in the Final Jōmon type 4I was very rare in eastern Japan, in the Yayoi it became quite common in the area from the Tokai to the southern Tohoku (Harunari 1986, 1987). Harunari (1987, 81) suggests that this may reflect eastward migration from the Tokai region in the Yayoi. In the area from north central Kyushu to Nagoya, the Jōmon C type is found with a completely new I^2 type wherein the upper lateral incisors, but *not* the canines, are removed. Since I^2 ablation is not found in the Jōmon, it is thought to have been an introduced type, an interpretation supported by the fact that many immigrant-type skulls have I^2 ablation. Exceptions to this (i.e., Jōmon-type skulls with I^2 ablation) are thought to represent intermarriage between the two populations (Harunari 1987, 83–86). The origin of I^2 type ablation is not known. Upper lateral incisor extraction was the most common type of tooth ablation in ancient China, and a mainland origin for the Yayoi custom is suggested by Han and Nakahashi (1996) and Harunari (1987, 85–86, 1990, 101), but, as these authors point out, there are no contemporary skeletal remains from Korea or China to test this theory.

To summarize the above discussion, the Final Jōmon phase saw increased interaction between the Korean Peninsula and Kyushu from the Kurokawa phase onward, culminating in the Initial Yayoi Yamanotera and Yu'usu phases with the establishment of wet rice farming and the arrival of a complex of items and influences from the Peninsula as evidenced at sites such as

Nabatake, Itazuke, and Etsuji: narrow-necked storage jars, exterior bonding in pottery fabrication, stone reaping knives and adzes, wooden agricultural tools, polished stone daggers and arrowheads, ditched settlements, the Songgungni-type dwelling, pig jawbone ritual, and megaliths. Initial Yayoi culture was concentrated in north Kyushu but was also found in other parts of western Japan. Initial Yayoi paddy fields have been identified at Tsushima-Edō in Okayama, wooden farming tools from the Sasai site, Fukuoka and Hayashi-Bōjiro on Shikoku, and stone reaping knives have been found at Kigawa, Fukuoka, and Kuchisakai, Hyōgo (for summaries of Initial Yayoi finds see Harunari [1990] and Hudson [1990a]). These sites do not mean, however, that wet rice cultivation was already being practiced throughout western Japan. Initial Yayoi sites are rare, isolated occurrences outside of north Kyushu. As all the components of the Initial Yayoi complex are not present at these non-Kyushu sites, Harunari (1990, 14) argues that they represent the adoption of rice cultivation by local Jōmon groups. An alternative explanation might be that these sites are small frontier colonies of Yayoi farmers. Whichever interpretation is correct, the following Early Yayoi phase saw clear population expansion from Kyushu and the establishment of full-scale agriculture across western Japan.

OUT OF KYUSHU: YAYOI EXPANSION

After a period of "incubation" (Barnes 1993b) in north Kyushu, Yayoi culture spread through much of western Japan and into parts of the eastern archipelago during the Early Yayoi (ca. 300–100 BC). The following Middle Yayoi (ca. 100 BC–AD 1) saw further expansion and massive population growth in many regions; chiefdom-level societies were present in at least western Japan by this stage. Yayoi culture never extended to Hokkaido and the Ryukyus, although both of these areas were influenced by contact with the Yayoi mainland.

The most distinctive archaeological phenomenon of the Early Yayoi is the expansion of Ongagawa-type ceramics from northeast Kyushu around the Inland Sea. Traditionally, the areal extent of Ongagawa ware was thought to be coterminous with the initial spread of rice cultivation; in contrast, the spread of rice farming into eastern Japan was seen as a much slower process that involved a great deal of assimilation with local Jōmon populations (e.g. Akazawa 1982). Over the past decade, this traditional picture has seen considerable modification as a result of the discovery of Initial Yayoi rice-farming sites dating to before the Ongagawa expansion and of paddy fields in northern

Honshu dating to the Early Yayoi. To a large extent, however, the importance of Ongagawa has remained, because of its association with the spread of a fully developed Yayoi culture.

The earliest Early Yayoi pottery (the Itazuke I type) developed in central north Kyushu in the Fukuoka and Karatsu plains. Neighboring northeast Kyushu, however, seems to have been the primary source of the Ongagawa ceramic culture that spread to the Inland Sea and Kinai regions. This northeastern Kyushu zone is usually seen as derivative from the Itazuke zone. In the Fukuoka and Karatsu plains, and also in central and south Kyushu, Itazuke pottery commonly coexists with Yu'usu ware at the same site, but in northeast Kyushu and western Yamaguchi Itazuke is not found associated with Yu'usu pottery, implying a different developmental process.

Hashiguchi Tatsuya has argued that population pressure in the area around Ogōri in northeast Kyushu led to an eastward expansion at the beginning of the Itazuke II phase (Harunari 1990, 73). Since Ongagawa pottery displays a remarkable uniformity across its distribution, it has been widely interpreted as evidence for the actual movement of people out of northeast Kyushu, an interpretation strengthened by the speed with which Ongagawa wares spread to the Kinai region (Bleed 1972, 10; Kanaseki and Sahara 1978, 20–21). Everywhere, however, Ongagawa pottery coexisted with *tottaimon* wares to some extent, either at the same site or in the same region. In Kyushu, south of the Fukuoka plain the *tottaimon* tradition continued despite influences from the north: at some sites over 90 percent of *kame* were of *tottaimon* tradition and less than 10 percent were of Itazuke type (Harunari 1990, 41). In Wakayama Prefecture the *tottaimon*-derived "Kii-type pot" continued until the mid-Middle Yayoi (Miyata and Ōno 1991, 225–226).

Some of the best data for connections between *tottaimon* and Ongagawa pottery come from the Kinai region. Four types of sites can be recognized, depending on their ratio of *tottaimon* (Nagahara) and Ongagawa wares (Harunari 1990, 68–69):

(1) **Nagahara only**: Kuchisakai, Itami; Nishiurabashi and Suzu-no-miya, Sakai.

(2) **Mainly Nagahara, small quantity of Ongagawa**: Nagahara, Osaka; Kitoragawa, Higashi Ōsaka; Sadō, Yao; Ōta, Wakayama

(3) **Ongagawa only**:
   (a) Yayoi I (Early): Yoshida and Katayama, Kobe;
   (b) Yayoi I (Middle) and later: Higashinara, Ibaraki; Kamei, Yao; Tamatsutanaka, Kobe; Katsube, Toyonaka; Ama, Takatsuki; Uriyudō, Higashi Ōsaka; Uriwari, Osaka

(4) **Mainly Ongagawa, small quantity of Nagahara:** Otoshiyama and Daikai, Kobe; Kami-no-shima and Tanō, Amagasaki; Onitsuka, Higashi Ōsaka; Yamaga and Kyūhōji, Yao; Yotsuike, Sakai; Karako, Nara

At sites where both types are known, it is not just a question of the adoption of foreign stylistic traits. At Nagahara and Kitoragawa, the temper of Nagahara and Ongagawa sherds was clearly different, implying the trade of ceramics produced in different areas. Sites with mainly Nagahara pottery were concentrated in different places from those with mainly Ongagawa ceramics. Nagahara sites were most numerous along the western foothills of the Ikoma mountains; Ongagawa sites, in contrast, were densest along the Yodo River and in the Nara Basin (Nakanishi 1984).

Settlement patterns in the Kinai suggest some residential separation between Jōmon and Yayoi groups at the beginning of the Early Yayoi, but interaction between these groups is shown by stylistic influences between Jōmon and Yayoi pottery. One example is a cooking-pot rim sherd found at Miwa, Nara Prefecture. This rim is not everted like typical Ongagawa examples, and it has a *tottaimon* band below the rim. Unlike Final Jōmon pottery, however, the gap between the lip and the appliqué band is unusually big (1.5 cm), the interior and exterior surfaces were finished by wiping with a soft material, and the sherd was fired harder than normal Final Jōmon vessels were (Okita 1993, 143). All this suggests that the sherd is a mixture of Jōmon and Yayoi traditions produced during the Old or Middle subphase of the Early Yayoi. Okita (1993, 143) goes on to conclude that "This proves that the main actors who developed the Yayoi culture . . . were the Jōmon people," but such an interpretation is applicable only to pottery and cannot necessarily be extended beyond the Miwa site.

The Ongagawa expansion did not involve only pottery; evidence for rice cultivation also increases dramatically during this stage. Paddy fields dating to the beginning of the Early Yayoi are known at Tsushima in Okayama and Tamura in Kōchi. The whole range of Yayoi wooden and stone tools found in Kyushu has also been discovered at these and other Early-phase sites throughout the Inland Sea region. There can be no doubt that during the Early Yayoi a fully developed and rapidly expanding agricultural society was first established in large parts of the western archipelago. Earlier conclusions that Yayoi expansion into eastern Honshu was slow and primarily along inland routes (e.g. Akazawa 1981, 245) are not supported by recent discoveries. Ongagawa pottery has been found at at least twenty-four sites in eastern Honshu (Sahara 1987c). Based on temper analysis, some of these are thought to have been imported from western Japan and some to have been made locally (Shimizu 1987). The distribution of this pottery, which includes the Tabara site on Niijima in the Izu Islands, suggests movement by sea up both the Pacific and the Japan Sea coasts. From decorative similarities, Sahara (1987c) suggests that Early Yayoi groups from the coastal areas of Shimane and Kyoto "leapfrogged" up the Japan Sea to Akita and Aomori, where Ongagawa pottery is especially common. Early Yayoi paddy fields at Sunazawa in Aomori may support this interpretation, although Harunari (1990, 65-66) notes that the Yayoi lithics and wooden implements known from western Japan are absent; in this respect sites such as Sunazawa, which have impressive paddy fields but few of the other features of Yayoi culture, resemble Initial Yayoi sites in the Inland Sea region (Harunari 1990, 65-66).

The expansion of Japanese farmers continued well after the end of the Yayoi in the north and south of the Islands. As noted, Hokkaido and the Ryukyus fell outside the geographical extent of Yayoi culture, since wet rice farming was not practiced in these regions until much later. In Hokkaido, a basically hunter-gatherer Epi-Jōmon culture seems to have continued until about AD 700 (Crawford and Takamiya 1990). By the following Satsumon period (ca. 700-1200), the cultivation of barley, wheat, and broomcorn and foxtail millet seems to have been common, at least in the Ishikari plain (Crawford and Yoshizaki 1987), but it is not clear if Satsumon Hokkaido can be termed fully agricultural. Japanese farmers did not colonize Hokkaido until the late nineteenth century, partly because trade in marine and other products was more profitable than agriculture in what was a climatically marginal zone (Hudson *in press* a).

In the 1950s, ethnographer Yanagita Kunio argued that rice cultivation had spread north up the Ryukyu Islands into Japan (Yanagita 1978). Though severely criticized by both archaeologists and linguists, this theory has been extremely influential, and Yanagita's Ryukyuan route still commonly appears on maps showing possible paths of diffusion of rice into Japan. All the available evidence, however, suggests that agriculture spread south from Kyushu into Okinawa rather than the other way around. The exact chronology of this process, though, is still unknown. From an account given by two Korean castaways who were in the Ryukyus from 1477-1479, we know that rice, foxtail, and broomcorn millet, *mugi* (barley or wheat) and taro were being cultivated there by the fifteenth century (see Matthews et al. 1992, 30). The few finds of rice that have been made in archaeological contexts in Okinawa date to the twelfth century AD at the earliest (Kishimoto 1991). A cultural transition did occur in the Ryukyus at about 100 BC with the shift from the Early to the Late

Shellmound period. As in mainland Japan, there was a move from the basic Jōmon deep pot to three main vessel forms: the *tsubo* jar, the *hachi* bowl, and the *kame* pot (Pearson 1996, 101–102). Over thirty Okinawan sites have produced a total of several hundred sherds of Yayoi pottery (Kishimoto 1991). A few bronze objects have also been found in the islands, but the main defining elements of Yayoi culture are absent: there is no evidence of rice agriculture, of large moated villages, or of social stratification. Most of the imported Yayoi pottery dates to the Middle Yayoi and can probably be linked with the trade in tropical shells to Kyushu (cf. Pearson 1990).

Late Shellmound period sites are often in sand dunes and have shell-midden deposits suggesting extensive use of lagoon resources (Pearson 1996, 102). It is theoretically possible, however, that rice or other plants may have been cultivated in backswamp areas behind the dunes, and Okinawan archaeologists such as Takamiya Hiroe (1991, 234) do not rule out the possibility that rice farming in the islands will be pushed back to the Yayoi. Takamiya Hiroto (1996a, 1996b, 149) has identified rice and wheat in eighth- to tenth-century deposits at the Nāzakibaru site near Naha airport. Excavations at the Uehara Nūribaru site in Ginowan City uncovered a series of four-meter-long ditches dating to the Final Jōmon of the mainland. These features could possibly have been used for some sort of plant cultivation, although soil analyses failed to confirm plant remains (Goya Yoshikatsu personal communication).

The Kanto Jōmon-Yayoi Transition

A large literature exists on the transition from Jōmon to Yayoi in each region of Japan. For several reasons, however, no attempt will be made here to discuss that literature in detail. First, the sheer quantity of data available means that several monographs would be required to cover each region effectively. Second, and more important, I believe that we are not in a position to fully test the model of agricultural colonization proposed in this book until we have resolved certain theoretical problems about the interpretation of ethnicity and population movements in the archaeological record. A preliminary attempt is made to discuss these questions in the following chapter, but, to put the problem as bluntly as possible, it is crucial not to lose sight of the forest for the trees: in other words, *changes in local ceramic sequences do not necessarily directly reflect the economic transition to farming or the spread of ethnic Japanese populations*. At the broadest level—and with the possible exception of Okinawa—the archaeological evidence supports a link between the expansion of agriculture and that of ethnic Japanese populations. This general conclusion is not invalidated by minor variations from this pattern that may have occurred in certain regions during the Jōmon-Yayoi transition.

For these reasons, therefore, detailed regional analyses will not be undertaken here, but what I do propose to do in the last section of this chapter is to briefly discuss some of the problems involved in understanding the archaeology of the Jōmon-Yayoi transition in the Kanto region. The Kanto includes the seven prefectures of Ibaragi, Tochigi, Gunma, Saitama, Chiba, Tokyo, and Kanagawa, which comprise an area of 39,785 km^2. Today, most of this area is highly urbanized, with a total population of over 37 million people. There are five main geographical zones: mountains, hills, terraces, lowland plains, and offshore islands. The region is dominated by a large plain, which at about 15,000 km^2 is the largest in Japan. Mountain ranges surround the plain with the highest peaks on the northern and western sides, limiting access to certain mountain passes.

The Jōmon-Yayoi transition in the Kanto is complicated by evidence of massive depopulation and subsistence stress in the region in the Final Jōmon. Site numbers dropped to a fraction of their Middle-phase highs. Of course, a decline in site numbers does not necessarily directly reflect population. Middle Jōmon sites may have served more specialist, nonresidential functions than did sites in the Final phase, thus increasing the site total. Alternatively, Final Jōmon groups may have been more mobile and thus built less-substantial houses, even though the basic population level was little changed. There is no evidence, however, that nonresidential sites were proportionately more common in the Kanto area in the Middle Jōmon than in later phases. If numbers of pit houses rather than just site numbers are compared, the Late/Final decline becomes even steeper (Fig. 5.9). The Final-phase dwellings that are known in the Kanto are substantial pit houses whose structure is little different from that of earlier stages, and the dwellings lend no support to the suggestion that the Kanto Final Jōmon people were more nomadic than their predecessors.

What might have caused such a catastrophic depopulation? Two main theories have been proposed. The first is that epidemic disease decimated Middle Jōmon populations, leading to lower levels in the following Late and Final phases (Kidder 1984; Koyama 1984, 195; Kobayashi 1989, 59). This theory has a number of problems that have not yet been thought through. Viral epidemic diseases need a large, dense human host in which to spread. Although the Chūbu and Kanto Middle Jōmon were marked by comparatively high population levels—2.40 and 2.98 persons per km^2, respectively, according to Koyama's (1984, 31) estimates—that density was probably not sufficient to create a major disease problem. Not confined to permanent urban centers, Jōmon groups were free to disperse, should the need arise. Since the Chūbu and Kanto were the most densely populated areas in the Middle Jōmon, we might expect any epidemics to be especially prevalent there. If the disease spread from the continent, however, we would also expect it to have affected the areas of western Japan closest to the mainland. Such was the case in the early historic period, when epidemics were clearly associated with routes of maritime transport (see Farris 1985, 58). In reality, though, population levels remained constant in western Japan but declined dramatically in the east, something which is not consistent with the spread of epidemic disease from Asia.

The second main theory that has been offered to explain the depopulation is that of climatic change. An obvious problem here is that although the population of central Honshu declined dramatically after the end of the Middle Jōmon, the more northerly Tohoku region—where temperatures would presumably have been even colder—did not undergo any such major transformation. As noted by Imamura (1996, 109), therefore, we have a contradiction: if we simply say it became too cold in the Chūbu region after the end of the Middle phase, we need to explain why a similar problem was apparently not encountered in the Tohoku. The answer to this contradiction must lie in the differing ecological adaptations of the regions. Two specific suggestions have been made relating to nuts and yams. As noted earlier in this chapter, the

TABLE 5.6

CHRONOLOGICAL PHASES USED IN THIS SECTION FOR THE KANTO JŌMON-YAYOI TRANSITION

PHASE	KINAI	TOKAI	CHUBU	KANTO	TOHOKU
I	I (Old)	Mamizuka	(Kōri I)	Sugita/Chiami	Ōbora A
II	I (Middle)	Kashiō	Kōri I	Arami 1	Ōbora A'
III	I (Late)	Suijinbira	Kōri II	Arami 2	Sunazawa
IV	II	Yanabe/ Mariko	Jijo	Ozakata Hse 15	Nimaibashi
V	III	Kaida-chō	Awabayashi	Suwada	Utetsu II
VI	IV	Takakura	Hyakuse	Miyanodai	Inakadate

In the standard Kanto terminology, phases I-III are assigned to the Final Jōmon and phases IV-VI to the Middle Yayoi. The late Final Jōmon of the Kanto, therefore, overlaps with the Early Yayoi of western Japan.

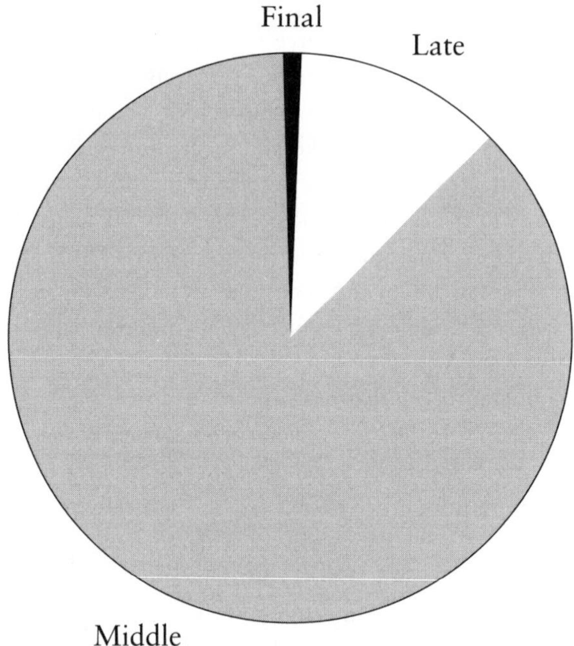

FIG. 5.9. Pit buildings from Middle-Final Jōmon sites in Tokyo, Kanagawa, and Saitama Prefectures. Collated from data in Suzuki (1985).

subsistence base of the Chūbu Middle Jōmon has long been a subject of debate, but there is little doubt that nuts were an important food source during this period. A project conducted by Koyama (1984, 97) has shown that deciduous nuts are very susceptible to climatic fluctuations. Deciduous nuts, therefore, could explain both the subsistence base of the Middle Jōmon florescence and its subsequent sudden decline. Imamura (1990, 1996, 106–109), however, has noted that storage facilities are scarce or absent in those regions where the Middle-phase florescence was strongest, namely the Chūbu and southwest Kanto, but that these regions have a comparatively large proportion of chipped stone axes. In the northeast Kanto and Tōhoku, these distributions are reversed. Imamura argues that a large quantity of nuts were not stored in the former regions in the Middle Jōmon. Instead, he takes the standard interpretation of the stone "axes" as digging tools and suggests that they were used for grubbing roots and tubers, proposing that a wild yam, *Dioscorea japonica,* was the basis of the Middle Jōmon economy in the

Chūbu and southwest Kanto. Imamura (1990, 77) notes that *Dioscorea* is unresistant to cold and was thus probably affected by the climatic cooling after the Middle Jōmon. Though all his evidence is circumstantial, Imamura does present a model that explains the archaeological data well. One weak point is the lack of detailed explanation of the post-Middle phase decline, but linking climatic fluctuations to specific plants is a step in the right direction.

The problems found in central Honshu after the Middle Jōmon were not experienced in the Tohoku region, where a more stable economy—thought to have been based on salmon (Sasaki 1991b, 239)—appears to have continued through to the Final phase. In the Kanto, the Late Jōmon saw a major shift of emphasis from the inland economy of the previous phase to coastal fishing and shellfish collecting around Tokyo Bay. Population levels were still quite high at 1.61 people per km^2 but became very low (0.24 per km^2) in the Final phase (Koyama 1984, 31). Zvelebil (1981, 12) defines population pressure as "a situation occurring when a society or a group of individuals perceive a lack of certain resources without which they feel unable to cope." Zvelebil goes on to argue that such pressure forces people to make one or more of the following choices: (1) adjusting by lowering standards of living or population; (2) finding suitable resource alternatives; (3) reorganizing resource procurement to increase production; (4) emigrating. The Final Jōmon Kanto people seem to have made at least the first three of these choices. Population levels were lowered, perhaps partly by emigration north. The search for resource alternatives is evidenced at a number of Final middens where layers of shell are suddenly replaced by bones of deer and wild boar. Such sites include Saihiro and Kainohana in Chiba and Shimotakabora D on Izu-Ōshima. Overexploitation of shellfish is a distinct possibility at these sites: although some climatic changes may have occurred, it is unlikely that the shells found earlier in the sequence at Saihiro completely disappeared from the area in the late Final phase, since the same species have been found from Yayoi and Kofun layers at a nearby site. Age composition analyses on deer teeth have also demonstrated a marked increase in hunting pressure at two Final Jōmon sites in the Kanto (Koike 1986, 1992; Koike and Ohtaishi 1985, 1987).

There is, therefore, evidence to suggest resource stress during the Kanto Final Jōmon, but that stress does not seem to have led to the intensification of plant cultivation in the region. The agricultural transition in the Kanto can be divided into two stages. The first dates to the Early and the first part of the Middle Yayoi of western Japan. A few sites from this stage have produced finds of rice, but all of these are in local Final Jōmon contexts, as at Arami near Narita Airport, where rice phytoliths were identified from a layer producing

Arami 2 pottery (Shitara 1991, 196). The Kanto was still sparsely populated, and sites from this stage are extremely rare. In contrast, the second stage, which begins in the late Middle Yayoi, sees a dramatic increase in site numbers and complexity. Ditched farming villages begin with the Suwada-phase Ikegami site in Saitama and become common in the following Miyanodai phase. As is clear from Table 5.7, population growth on a massive scale began in the Kanto region at this time. In Tokyo there are 50 percent more pit houses from the Miyanodai phase (which lasted perhaps sixty or seventy years) than from the whole 1,000-year span of the Final Jōmon. The Miyanodai is also marked by an explosive increase in large, clearly agricultural settlements, some of which are ditched (Shitara 1991, 200). Similarities between Miyanodai pottery and ceramic styles from along the Tokai coast have suggested large-scale immigration from the latter region into the Kanto during this stage (Shitara 1991, 201). As noted in chapter 3, immigrant-type Yayoi skeletons also make their appearance in the Kanto in the Miyanodai. Archaeologically, there is almost no overlap between sites of these two stages in the Kanto region, something that, again, may suggest immigration.

At a general level, therefore, the sequence from the Kanto region may be said to support the gradual expansion of Yayoi agricultural colonists through eastern Honshu and thus the model of Japanese ethnogenesis proposed here. While some admixture no doubt occurred, the genetic contribution of the Kanto Jōmon people may have been minor, since the region was sparsely populated in the Final Jōmon. Of course, at a detailed level there are still many unresolved problems. For example, the relative scarcity of land suitable for rice paddies means we have to be careful how we understand the agricultural history of the Kanto. The region's hills and terraces are both covered by volcanic ash deposits (the "Kanto loam"), which are "inherently infertile" and "notoriously deficient in water" (Trewartha 1965, 441). Many of the low marshy areas of the Kanto plain were also not developed for rice farming until quite late. The whole area of present downtown Tokyo was well known for its marshy reeds throughout medieval literature: the early eleventh-century *Sarashina Nikki* describes reeds around Takeshiba so high that the top of the bows of the mounted soldiers could not be seen (Morris 1975, 36).

While there are problems in overemphasizing the role of rice in the Kanto, however, it is equally important to avoid simplistic scenarios whereby people who did not farm continued their traditional Jōmon hunter-gatherer lifestyles. The spread of farming in the Islands would have engendered complex processes of economic specialization within an incipient market economy (cf. Kōmoto 1992a). Such processes are integral to any agricultural society and in

TABLE 5.7

PIT BUILDING NUMBERS IN FINAL JŌMON AND YAYOI TOKYO

	MOUNTAINS	HILLS	TERRACE	LOWLANDS	ISLANDS
Final Jōmon	0	2	18	0	1
Suwada	0	0	0	0	1
Miyanodai	0	11	19	0	1
Kugahara and Yayoi-chō	0	30	175	0	0
Maeno-chō	0	27	73	0	0
Late Yayoi	0	133	195	0	0
Final Late	0	0	55	0	0
Final Late/ Early Kofun	0	63	34	0	0
Yayoi (unspec.)	0	2	56	0	1
TOTAL					
Jōmon	0	2	18	0	1
Yayoi	0	266	607	0	3

Collated from Tokyo Board of Education (1988). The Yayoi figures represent minimums since (i) I was unable to locate a few (5–10 percent?) site reports to check building numbers; (ii) there are several large sites (such as Kugahara) where many unexcavated pit houses are known to exist; and (iii) scores of new Yayoi buildings will have been excavated since 1988, but I am unaware of any new Final Jōman dwellings.

no way undermine the model of Yayoi/Japanese colonization proposed in this book, though they certainly complicate the archaeological study of the Jōmon-Japanese transition. An example of this problem is provided by a series of Yayoi-period coastal cave sites on the Miura Peninsula in Tokyo Bay. Aikens and Akazawa (1992, 75) and others argue that these sites support "strong Jomon-Yayoi cultural continuity," showing "how a major dimension of ancient Jōmon tradition was incorporated into the new farming culture of the Yayoi age, and thus passed down ultimately to the present day." This interpretation is based primarily on the fact that the fishing gear from the caves is basically of Jōmon tradition. A number of theoretical models could, however, apply to the Miura sites: (1) a Jōmon population continued its traditional lifestyle with only minor influences from Yayoi groups; (2) a Jōmon population

TABLE 5.8

KANTO YAYOI PERIOD SITES WITH EVIDENCE OF RICE OR RICE CULTIVATION

SITE	EVIDENCE OF CULTIVATION	KANTO PHASE
1. Arami, CHIB	impression and soil phytoliths	III (2330±130 & 2350±120 BP)
2. Takarada Toba, CHIB	phytoliths (soil)	III
3. Iwana Tenjinmae, CHIB	impression	IV
4. Takeshi, CHIB	impression	IV
5. Namie-kita, GUN	paddy field	beginning of Late
6. Kozuka, GUN	carb. rice	VI
7. Oshide, GUN	impression	EY imported
8. Minami-otsuka, GUN	impression	EY
9. Izuruhara, TOCH	impression (x2)	V
10. Goshinden-Fujimae, TOCH	impression (x3)	VI
11. Nozawa-kita, TOCH	impression (x1)	V
12. Nozawa-kita, TOCH	impression (x1)	V
13. Utsunomiya Seiryō High School, TOCH	impression (x1)	VI
14. Nagayatsu, TOCH	impression (x1)	V
15. Ozakata, IBAR	impression (x2)	IV
16. Higashi-nakane, IBAR	carbonized rice (3 litres)	early LY
17. Ikegami-nishi, SAI	phytoliths (soil)	V
18. Ikegami, SAI	carbonized rice	V (2570±145 - 2160±75bp)
19. Kamifumen, SAI	impression	V
20. Tabara, TOK	impression	III C14

Collated from Maizō Bunkazai Kenkyūkai (1991). For phase chronology see Table 5.6. *Prefecture key:* CHIB = Chiba; GUN = Gunma; IBAR = Ibaragi; SAI = Saitama; TOCH = Tochigi; TOK = Tokyo.

entered into close (perhaps symbiotic) relations with a local Yayoi group, possibly providing fish in exchange for rice, but remaining basically autonomous; (3) any local Jōmon people were quickly assimilated by incoming farmers, and the Miura sites represent seasonal or other subsistence specializations by a basically Japanese population; (4) the Miura sites are the remains of a Japanese population who had only minor contacts with local Jōmon people. Choosing between these and other potential scenarios is by no means easy. The general interpretative problems involved form the subject of the next chapter, but many more specific questions also need to be approached. Are the Miura secondary burials really derived from the Jōmon tradition, as Aikens and Akazawa (1992, 78) suggest (cf. Ishikawa 1987; Shitara 1993; Hudson 1992a, 161–163)? Are the formal similarities between Jōmon and Yayoi fishhooks due to functional or cultural reasons (cf. Wada 1985)? How much significance should be given to the tooth ablation patterns in the area (cf. Harunari 1987)?

Local sequences such as the Miura Peninsula are an important part of obtaining a concrete picture of how the transition to the Yayoi was effected. In terms of the overall aims of this book, however, it must be stressed that it is the "big picture" that matters. In other words, any hypothetical population continuity from the Jōmon in one small area such as the Miura Peninsula cannot in itself be seen as either proving or disproving my model of Japanese agricultural colonization.

6

An Emerging Synthesis?

[T]he understanding of past societies on the basis of their material remains is surely one of the most complex philosophical problems which human beings have ever set themselves. In order to achieve it, we can and must take whatever help we can from wherever we can find it. Archaeology is hard work.

Julian Thomas and Christopher Tilley, "TAG and 'Post Modernism': A Reply to John Bintliff"

To what extent can the biological, linguistic, and archaeological data presented so far be used to support a model of initial Japanese ethnogenesis in the Yayoi period? The preceding chapter shows that a wide range of new cultural traits arrived in the Initial Yayoi phase: bunded paddy fields, new types of polished stone tools, wooden farming implements, iron tools, weaving technology, ceramic storage jars, exterior bonding of clay coils in pottery fabrication, ditched settlements, domesticated pigs and jawbone ritual, and megalithic tombs. In every case where the origin of these traits is known, they all clearly derive from the Korean Peninsula. Despite this evidence for discontinuity, however, many Japanese archaeologists have argued that the transition from Jōmon to Yayoi was in fact marked by strong cultural *continuity*. In particular, the hybrid nature of Yayoi ceramics has led to a widespread view of the transition as being a gradual, diffusionary process: "The formation of Yayoi culture did not involve the sudden change that has been envisioned until now. Rather, a situation where advanced culture from Korea gradually arrived from the Late and Final Jōmon periods, was accepted while fusing with indigenous elements, then gradually developed into Yayoi culture, is closer to what really happened" (Hashiguchi Tatsuya cited in Harunari 1990, 130). As shown in chapter 3, there is abundant anthropological data to support the arrival of a new population in the Islands in the Yayoi. This population has played the major role in the genetic makeup of the modern Japanese. Chapter 4 argues that the spread of a new language through the Islands in the Yayoi would fit well with this biological evidence for immigration and with the linguistic record itself. Is there not, therefore, a contradiction between the archaeology on the one hand and the biological and linguistic evidence on the other?

An archaeological theory of migration is central to this problem. How do we recognize migrations from the archaeological record? What happens when new colonists arrive in a given region? How do we distinguish between diffusion and migration in an archaeological context? While some traditional procedures for dealing with these questions exist, they remain poorly developed, and migrations have been largely ignored in the archaeological literature of the past three decades. For this reason, conclusions that the Jōmon-Yayoi transition was caused by diffusion rather than by immigration rest on rather shaky theoretical foundations. This chapter will attempt to show that the archaeological evidence is not necessarily inconsistent with the model of Japanese ethnogenesis proposed in this book.

POPULATION MOVEMENTS AND ARCHAEOLOGY

A "retreat from migrationism" (Adams et al. 1978) has been visible in recent archaeological theory in both Japan and the West. It is shown in Part I that since the 1930s Japanese archaeologists have favored endogenous explanations for the prehistory of their country. This has had a negative influence in terms of their reluctance to consider problems of prehistoric ethnicity and migrations. It has also encouraged an obsession with artifact typology and chronology at the expense of a consideration of what artifact variation may mean in social terms. In the West, the rise of neoevolutionism in postwar anthropology led to widespread criticisms of the diffusionist-migrationist paradigms of previous scholars. To take one typical example, Binford (1968) criticizes Sabloff and Willey's (1967) suggestion that the Classic Lowland Maya cultural collapse had been caused by an invasion of non-Classic Maya people. Following Hempel, Binford argues that an archaeological explanation must be not only general but also *predictive;* since cultural collapse is not always caused by invasion, it cannot be counted as a real explanation (Binford 1968,

268; cf. Sabloff 1992). Many other criticisms are equally polemical and extreme. Harris (1969, 378) writes, "As soon as we admit . . . that independent invention has occurred on a massive scale, diffusion is by definition not only superfluous, but the very incarnation of antiscience." Hill (1991, 48) cites one of the achievements of processual archaeology as the knowledge that "innovation, diffusion, and migration are insufficient, in themselves, to explain any aspect of cultural variability or change."

To some extent, these criticisms were useful in that they contributed to the rejection of the more extreme claims of long-distance migration and diffusion. Critics of migrationism have tended to caricature migrations as long-range movements of warlike people who sweep all before them in their journeys across continents or oceans; migrations are also typically seen as implying that "primitive" societies resist innovation and that change must come from the outside (Bellwood 1983b, 324). As Bellwood and others have stressed, however, the drainage of this very stagnant bathwater should not lead to the loss of the migrationist (or diffusionist) baby (Anthony 1990; Broodbank and Strasser 1991, 234; Renfrew 1987, 3). I also reject the idea that archaeological explanations have to be general or predictive and consequently that migration is "non-explanatory."

The postprocessual archaeologies of the 1980s and 1990s can be seen as historical/particularist reactions to the neoevolutionary generalizations of the New Archaeology. For this reason, we might expect to have witnessed an increased interest in the historical contexts of past population movements, but such interest has not emerged. One explanation for this absence is the postprocessual critique of ethnic identity in the archaeological record. Hodder (1990, 307) comments that "material culture often does not represent directly but only through poetry or myth. Thus migrations or indigenous development cannot be identified by archaeologists." Unlike processualists, who preferred endogenous evolution to migration, Hodder is suggesting that neither can be supported in the archaeological record, since such identifications necessitate a known link between ethnic groups and material culture, a link he does not believe possible. As a way out of this impasse, Collett (1987) has argued for a contextual approach to identifying migrations (see below), but most postprocessual archaeologists have ignored the topic of population movements altogether.

Identifying Archaeological Migrations

In spite of these trends, since the late 1980s there has been something of a return to migrationism within Western archaeology. As Gamble (1993, 37) puts it, "Migration and diffusion are back in town." Two broad approaches to the archaeological study of population movements can be discerned in the recent literature. The first emphasizes the use of migration theories derived from sociology, demography, ecology, and human geography. As Anthony (1990, 895) has said, "a methodology for examining prehistoric migration must be dependent upon an understanding of the general structure of migration as a patterned human behavior." The second approach focuses on the archaeological record and attempts to derive criteria by which archaeologists can recognize migrations (e.g. Rouse 1958, 1986; Trigger 1968, 39–46; MacWhite 1956). The main proponents of these approaches, Anthony and Rouse, respectively, see them as opposing rather than complementary. Anthony (1990, 908) writes, "It should be emphasized that the approach to migration advocated here is fundamentally different from the traditional culture-historical approach, in which normative "cultures" correspond to "peoples," and migrations were seen as the activities by which they played out their destinies on the world stage." Rouse (1986, 161–163) dismisses the relevance of social anthropological studies of migration to prehistory in equally unequivocal terms. I myself, however, fail to see how these two approaches can be anything but complementary. Archaeologists obviously cannot afford to ignore the sophisticated models of migration that colleagues in other disciplines have developed, but, on the other hand, Anthony (1990, 897) plays down the difficulties of actually testing such models in the archaeological record.

American prehistorian Irving Rouse has been particularly influential in developing archaeological approaches to migrations (Fig 6.1). Rouse's 1986 book *Migrations in Prehistory: Inferring Population Movements from Cultural Remains,* which includes a chapter on Japan, is the most detailed attempt made to date to deal with archaeological migrations at a methodological level. As a first step toward analysis, Rouse (1986, 14) stresses the strict classification of archaeological data on formal criteria. The problem here is agreeing upon exactly what his criteria refer to. Rouse's assumption that his archaeological units represent "complexes of norms, each indicative of a local people and its culture" (Rouse 1986, 14), is debatable, yet he simply states that "A people carries its culture with it when it migrates. We may therefore trace its movement by plotting the distribution of the norms that characterize its culture" (Rouse 1986, 4). Rouse's approach is very much a common sense one that is followed (at least as a preliminary step) by all archaeologists working on migrations. The problems with his approach, however, are well illustrated in his chapter on Japan (Rouse 1986, 67–105). The chapter is plagued by numerous factual inaccuracies; some are more serious than others, but here

I will focus on the methods employed by Rouse rather than on the data he uses. The first difficulty is that Rouse does not follow his own strict guidelines regarding the independent testing of linguistic, anthropological, and archaeological evidence. The biological record is barely mentioned at all, yet he concludes that "The linguistic, physical anthropological, and archeological tests *all* indicate that the traditional hypothesis of migration into Japan [in the Yayoi] is wrong" (1986, 101, emphasis added). Historical linguistics receives a more detailed treatment, but in his discussion of Miller's Early Jōmon theory Rouse gets lost in circular reasoning when he fails to distinguish between the linguistic side of the theory (a glottochronological estimate for Japanese/Korean separation prior to 2665 BC) and Miller's speculation that the arrival of the Japanese language in Kyushu may have been linked with Korean ceramic influences in the Early Jōmon.

> It is necessary to do five things in order to demonstrate adequately that a migration has taken place: 1) identify the migrating people as an intrusive unit in the region it has penetrated; 2) trace this unit back to its homeland; 3) determine that all occurrences of the unit are contemporaneous; 4) establish the existence of favorable conditions for migration; 5) demonstrate that some other hypothesis, such as independent invention or diffusion of traits, does not better fit the situation.
>
> (Rouse 1958, 64)
>
> [There are] a number of phenomena which, when occurring together, probably indicate an immigration of a new group of people: 1) a simultaneous occurrence of a number of attributes in different contexts of material culture, such as dwelling-types, burials, lithic assemblage, pottery, symbol and design, which are exogenous to the region and which can be related to another culture group (ethnically homogenous) or culture area (no ethnic homogeneity); 2) initial disappearance or reduction of the previously existing, indigenous traits; 3) shift in the location of settlements or in the entire settlement pattern; 4) where applicable, change in the genetic make-up of the population, detectable from the skeletal evidence; 5) the existence of a clear boundary within which such combination of new elements will be enclosed and beyond which only isolated elements would extend.
>
> (Zvelebil 1981, 15)

FIG. 6.1. Identifying migrations: Archaeological checklists.

Moving on to his archaeological tests, Rouse (1986, 91) proposes that ceramic similarities between south Korean and north Kyushu ceramics in the Initial Yayoi suggest local development rather than population movement of any sort. In eastern Japan, however, he argues for a much more clear-cut transition: "There was . . . almost complete replacement of the Kamegaokan diagnostics by the Yayoi diagnostics. This indicates migration rather than acculturation" (Rouse 1986, 93). These conclusions are the opposite of those espoused here. In contrast to Rouse, I see substantial migration into Kyushu but a considerable degree of acculturation in the Tohoku. Rouse (1986, 93) argues that Jōmon decoration on Tohoku Yayoi pottery is a "superficial" trait, yet he gives no explanation for that assumption. In the Kyushu case, a full consideration of the biological evidence indicates a level of immigration that Rouse is unable to pick up from the archaeology alone.

There are many examples of quite substantial migrations known from historical records that are barely visible in the archaeological record. Such cases do not mean that Rouse's type of approach can *never* work. In criticizing Ōno's (1990) theory that a migration of Tamil speakers reached Japan in the Yayoi, for example, one makes use of many of the principles espoused by Rouse: the danger of placing too much emphasis on superficial formal similarities, the importance of a tight chronology, the need to plot the route of a proposed population movement, and so forth (see Hudson 1992b). *The important point is that these methods do not always work and are not always sufficient to identify migrations.*

What, then, of the "alternative" approach advocated by Anthony? As noted, I believe that sociological and other models of migration can be usefully applied to prehistory, and a number of the models mentioned by Anthony have obvious relevance for the Yayoi. The need to study push and pull factors between the home and destination regions is one example. To understand Yayoi immigration, one needs to look closely at the archaeology of southern Korea as well as Kyushu and to attempt to relate the two. So far this has not been done: many studies have of course compared the archaeological records of Kyushu and Korea in some detail, but few have attempted to model actual social connections between the two regions. Several of the long-distance migratory patterns discussed by Anthony (1990, 902–904) are also present in the Yayoi. Leapfrogging of Yayoi farmers up the Japan Sea may explain the presence of Ongagawa pottery and very early paddy-field sites such as Sunazawa and Tareyanagi in northern Tohoku (Barnes 1993b, 183). Evidence for "migration streams" may exist in the fact that Yayoi culture tended to expand eastwards along certain well-defined routes rather than "filling up" all available space—although it must be said that these routes often mirror lines of information flow in the Final Jōmon (cf. Sakai 1990).

While there is no doubt, therefore, of the relevance of these models, I cannot accept—as Anthony (1990) appears to suggest—that they represent a viable alternative approach to a methodology based on the archaeological record. Let us take the example of Jizōden B, an Early Yayoi settlement in Akita City near the Japan Sea coast (Sugawara and Yasuda 1986). The site is one of the earliest Yayoi settlements in the Tohoku region and consists of three or four pit houses surrounded by an oval palisade. Outside the palisade were twenty-five graves with eight burial jars, some of which were of Ongagawa-type pottery. Jizōden B is interpreted as an agricultural village (Sutō 1988, 25). The palisade—a feature not known in Jōmon sites—recalls the ditched settlements of western Japan, and the Ongagawa vessels also suggest close contacts with the western Yayoi. Are we, then, justified in seeing Jizōden B as an example of the leapfrogging phenomena known from historic migrations? While such a hypothesis is a useful one for testing, we are reliant on the archaeological record to determine whether the site represents immigrant farmers or local Jōmon people who adopted rice cultivation and imported Yayoi pottery. Without some method of identifying migrations in the archaeological record, migratory models derived from other fields will remain untestable.

Although I do not rule out their value for future studies, therefore, the approach to population movements adopted in this chapter does not make use of models derived from social-science migration research on modern societies. Instead, I focus on the more fundamental problems of the relationship between anthropological, linguistic, and archaeological data and the interpretation of the archaeological record. In the next section I look briefly at three comparative cases of prehistoric migrations. My aim is to see how recent archaeologists have actually tackled the problem of migrations in general and the relationship between the archaeological, linguistic, and anthropological records in particular. All three examples considered here provide invaluable comparative perspectives on Yayoi immigration. From the three case studies a series of expectations are derived; these will be applied to the Yayoi in the following section.

Migrations in Action

Austronesians

The prehistoric expansion of the Austronesian-speaking peoples, particularly the Polynesians, has generated a large literature, and an exhaustive discussion cannot be attempted here. Rather, I intend to focus on the early stages of the Austronesian expansion and particularly on the debate between Bill Meacham and Peter Bellwood that took place at the 12th Indo-Pacific Prehistory Association Congress, which was subsequently published in *Asian Perspectives* (Meacham 1985, 1991; Bellwood 1985; see also Bayard 1994; Spriggs 1991; Kōmoto 1992b). As can be determined from the title of his paper, Meacham (1985) argues for the "improbability of Austronesian origins in South China." The main points of his argument can be summarized as follows:

(i) On a priori grounds, Meacham supports a local evolution model for south China (Meacham 1977) in opposition to diffusion/migration models, which he sees as discredited.

(ii) Meacham (1985, 92) is convinced that "linguistics has very little to contribute to the writing of prehistory, especially regarding population movements and cultural developments." Citing the (undeniable) time-space problems faced in linguistic reconstruction, Meacham argues that the archaeological record must take precedence in the study of prehistory.

(iii) More specifically, Meacham presents a detailed review of the archaeology of south China to argue that there is no archaeological evidence for a population expansion from south China to Taiwan that would correspond with the proposed first stage of the Austronesian expansion.

The first point made by Bellwood (1985) in his reply is that a polarized contrast between "migration" and "local evolution" is misleading: "[In the Austronesian case] I am discussing an expansion which took 4,000 years to reach completion; I am not talking about ferocious conquering migrants sweeping all before them. The Austronesian story was partially one of assimilation of other cultures, and, in Melanesia, partially one of being assimilated" (Bellwood 1983a, 80). Similar comments can be made about the hypothesis of Yayoi origins proposed in this book. Although at times the Yayoi farmers expanded quite rapidly (especially during the Early Yayoi), assimilation with/of Jōmon peoples was widespread, particularly in the eastern archipelago. The expansion of Japanese-speaking farmers into Hokkaido was only accomplished in the late nineteenth century. Thus, although the model proposed here may be described as favoring population expansion over local evolution, I see that expansion as a long and regionally variable process that took centuries (and over two millennia in the case of Hokkaido) to accomplish. In both the Japanese and the Austronesian cases, the length of the process does not, however, detract from population expansion as an overall explanatory framework.

Bellwood is also critical of Meacham's unequivocal dismissal of linguistics, pointing out that the origin and spread of the Austronesian language family is primarily a linguistic problem. In other words, it is important to keep separate, as far as possible, hypotheses derived from linguistics, archaeology, and other fields such as biological anthropology. These hypotheses can then be usefully tested against each another. In both the Austronesian and Yayoi cases it is possible to argue that the archaeological evidence does not support large-scale population expansion from proposed homelands in south China and southern Korea, respectively. In order to argue this, however, one also needs to privilege the archaeological record over the biological and linguistic evidence, a stance adopted by Kōmoto (1992b) as well as by Meacham. Such a decision seems, to say the least, premature, particularly as the relationships between material culture and ethnicity are still being hotly debated.

Despite recurring difficulties in interpreting the archaeological record, however, is it not reasonable to expect relatively clear material culture parallels where population expansions occurred? In answer to Meacham's third point about the absence of such parallels between south China and Taiwan, Bellwood argues that this expectation may be false. For example, later "Polynesian founder populations as seen in the archaeological record did not replicate with exactitude *any* homeland cultural configurations" (Bellwood 1985, 114, emphasis added). If exact material culture replication did not occur in the case of the Polynesians, then we cannot assume that the lack of such replication means the lack of a population movement. In this context, the many quite specific cultural parallels between southern Korea and Yayoi Japan may take on added significance, but the crucial point is that in many land-based migrations, few people actually move very far. If a population *grows* as it expands, then even if it moves only a short distance per generation, over several generations a population movement between two points can be said to have occurred. The material correlates of this type of population movement could be quite different from those of a rapid, long-distance migration.

Iroquois

The second example of prehistoric population movement considered here is that of the Iroquois Indians of eastern North America. The Iroquois were a group of tribes that shared a similar culture based on intensive maize horticulture, fishing, and hunting, and characterized by large fortified villages, longhouses, secondary burials, prisoner sacrifice, and a matrilineal kinship system (Trigger 1978a, 2; Wright 1972, 67).[1] The Iroquois also spoke a group of closely related languages that were distributed in a wedge-shaped area of the eastern Great Lakes between the Central and Eastern branches of the Algonquian language family. Until the 1950s, it was commonly believed that the Iroquois had moved north from the Mississippi basin as late as the sixteenth century AD (Parker 1916). Typological studies of Iroquois pottery by Ritchie and MacNeish (1949) and MacNeish (1952), however, appeared to confirm the in situ theory of Iroquois development proposed by Griffin (1944). The in situ hypothesis received theoretical support with the retreat from migrationism of the 1960s, and it became widely accepted (Fitting 1978; Fagan 1995, 453–460; Trigger 1976, 105, 1978b, 802; Tuck 1978).

As Chapdelaine (1992, 3) points out, "Le mérite de MacNeish a été de promouvoir l'idée que les groupes dans le Nord-Est pouvaient changer et qu'ils n'étaient pas statiques." There were, however, clear problems with the in situ hypothesis. First, it did not attempt to solve the question of the ultimate origins of the Iroquois (Snow 1992a, 5). Trigger (1976, 105), for example, citing the many gaps in our knowledge, writes that "it seems best to set aside the question of Iroquoian ethnic origins while surveying the developments that gave rise to the northern Iroquian cultural pattern." Second, it did not adequately take into account the linguistic situation, both in terms of the estimated date of separation of the branches of the Iroquois family and of the fact that Iroquois languages had divided an original Algonquian unity into two. Historical linguistics proved crucial in the establishment of an alternative to the in situ hypothesis in the late 1980s and early 1990s. Archaeologist Stuart Fiedel used the linguistic evidence to propose an integrated model of Algonquian and Iroquoian origins whereby Northern Iroquois expansion occurred in the second half of the first millennium AD, thus making "the *in situ* theory of Iroquoian development . . . untenable" (Fiedel 1990, 223; 1987, 1991). Glottochronological estimates for the breakup of Proto-Northern Iroquois at between 1,000 and 1,500 years ago (Lounsbury 1978, 336) seem to fit well with a proposed date for the Algonquian central-eastern divergence of around AD 570 (Fiedel 1991, 19). Snow (1990, 1991, 1992a, 1992b, 1995) has also proposed an intrusion hypothesis on archaeological grounds, positing an adaptive radiation from central Pennsylvania after AD 900.

It is not important here to attempt to decide which of these theories of Iroquoian origins is correct. What *is* important is the relevance of the Iroquois debate for the Yayoi. One of the most interesting things about this debate is the way interpretations have changed over the years with changing trends in archaeological theory. Another point worth noting is the way ceramic typology was used to support a theory of gradual cultural change and thus of in situ development. Ramsden (1992, 21) argues that assuming a direct link between pottery styles and Iroquois social evolution is like representing the development of modern America through the changing styles of TV sets. In both the Iroquois and the Yayoi cases there is a need for a greater consideration of the *meaning* of the ceramic record. Finally, recent consideration of the linguistic evidence has led to conclusions about Iroquoian origins that are quite different from those derived from ceramic evidence. In this respect, Fiedel (1991, 9) writes, "Language may be a more sensitive and reliable indicator, for purposes of historical reconstruction, than material culture, which can be rapidly and radically transformed due to new environmental pressures, borrowing from neighboring groups, and innovation."

Anglo-Saxons

The role of immigration in Anglo-Saxon England is perhaps the most controversial of the three examples considered here. Although it would be fair to say that the migration or "Germanic" hypothesis has traditionally dominated the literature, in the words of J. N. L. Myres (1989, 1), the era of the Anglo-Saxon settlements is a "void of confusion." Myres (1989, 1) begins Volume 2 of the new *Oxford History of England* with the following statement: "The period of some two centuries which lies between the collapse of Roman government in Britain and the arrival of St. Augustine in AD 597 has long been recognized as the most difficult and obscure in the history of this country." The obscurity of this period is due to the scarcity of good historical and archaeological evidence—a scarcity that contrasts with the quality of the evidence available from the Roman and later medieval periods. Particularly with respect to the question of Germanic immigration into Britain, the complex and often contradictory evidence from historical records, linguistics, and archaeology needs to be carefully interpreted to derive realistic models of the historical processes involved. This has ensured continued controversy, but the nature of this interpretive endeavor provides excellent comparative material for understanding Yayoi immigration.

The starting point for studies of the Anglo-Saxon migrations has always been the written sources, particularly the descriptions of the invasion by the British monk Gildas preserved in Bede's *Ecclesiastical History of the English Peoples* (AD 731). Gildas' account, which is thought to date to the early sixth century, relates mass migrations to Britain by tribes of Angles, Saxons, and

Jutes. Actual physical evidence of these peoples, however, has so far been poorly researched. According to Härke (1990, 40–41), immigrant Anglo-Saxon men were on average 4 cm taller than Romano-British men, and non-metric skeletal differences also exist between the two. Despite the lack of basic anthropological research, Reece (1989) stresses biological criteria above archaeological ones, writing that the only criteria that should really be used for calling an archaeological skeleton a Saxon rather than a Briton are the "chemical and material characteristics of the body"; in the absence of such information, a body buried in early-fifth-century Britain with Saxon-type brooches might as well be Chinese (Reece 1989, 234). Reece fails to distinguish the biological and social aspects of ethnicity: it is doubtful to what extent the type of biological data that typically comes from archaeological situations can be used to identify ethnicity where biological differences between groups are minor. Thus the absence of major skeletal differences may not necessarily rule out immigration in a given situation. Reece is surely correct, however, that in theory biological remains must be the most direct evidence for human population change.

The migrationist view of Anglo-Saxon settlement was given early support by linguistic research that showed only minimal British influences on the English language and on English place-names (Myres 1989, 29–45). British loan words attested in Anglo-Saxon number less than twenty (Jackson 1953). There is no doubt that language replacement took place in lowland Britain in the early medieval period, and many scholars have used this fact to support the migration hypothesis. For both language and place-names, the contrast between the continuity in post-Roman Gaul and the near complete replacement in England is remarkable. Only a few British place-names were adopted by the early English or else survived the invasions intact: the names "Kent," "London," "Devon," and "Thames" are all derived from Celtic sources, as are a number of other toponymic elements such as *cumb* (deep valley, e.g. Salcombe) and *torr* (high rock, peak, e.g. Torcross) (Baugh and Cable 1993, 73).

Recently, Higham (1992) has argued for basic *continuity* in population from Roman to early medieval times, proposing that the Britons adopted the English language and its place-names as part of an active process of anglicization: "English was not imposed on the indigenes but embraced by them as one element in a process of cultural integration which they believed offered advantages to themselves" (Higham 1992, 198). While British reactions to Anglo-Saxon culture were no doubt complex, the degree of language and place-name replacement experienced in early medieval England does not seem consistent with Higham's model of an elite takeover by a few continental barbarians.

Roman Britain and Anglo-Saxon England are, in many respects, two completely different systems: the continuities between them are complex and problematical, and for that reason they have often been treated as "mutually exclusive periods of history, each butt-ended against the other with a minimum of linkage or overlap" (Myres 1989, 24). To begin with, the two periods are dated quite differently. Coins provide relatively secure chronological indicators for many Roman sites, but they are scarce by the last quarter of the fourth century and nonexistent in the fifth (Reece 1989, 232–233; Millett 1990, 219). Early Anglo-Saxon deposits, in contrast, are usually dated by pottery or other artifacts that are themselves dated by reference to presumed continental prototypes. As Millett (1990, 221) notes, using this type of circular reasoning, it is "logically impossible to date an Anglo-Saxon burial urn in Britain to before the historically attested date for the migrations." The problem of chronology is an important one, since much of the debate over the degree of English immigration revolves around the degree of *continuity* visible in the archaeological record. Certainly the archaeological record of early medieval England contains enough evidence for migration to satisfy the criteria of Rouse and others. The incoming Germanic tribes are clearly intrusive; on historical, linguistic, and archaeological evidence they can be traced back to their homelands in Denmark, Schleswig-Holstein, and the Low Countries, and the route and general causes of the migrations are also known. When we look in detail at cemeteries, towns, or rural settlement, however, the relationship between Romano-Britons and Anglo-Saxons is often obscure. Limitations of space mean that only one example can be considered here, and I propose to briefly discuss towns.

The whole Roman system of urban settlement declined with the end of Roman occupation. In fact, the towns of Roman Britain had been in decline since the third century; by the fifth, many had been abandoned altogether. At best, settlement continued in the form of a few pit houses in the ruins of Roman towns, the inhabitants possibly making use of the rich soil accumulated within the city for agricultural purposes (Welch 1993, 104). All of this seems pretty clear evidence for upheaval and discontinuity in fifth-century England, yet archaeologists have by no means agreed on how to interpret this urban decay. Reece argues that lack of continuity in towns is not the same as discontinuity, which he defines as a "lengthy upheaval centring on a period of destruction, or a well-orchestrated replacement of one agricultural process by another" (Reece 1989, 232). He believes that the archaeological record does not contain evidence for discontinuity in his definition, and therefore it cannot be used to support two current immigration models, that is, that (i) the decline of Roman Britain led to abandonment and the immigration of Germanic tribes, or (ii) a Germanic invasion led to competition with the Britons who were eventually defeated and who retreated to the Celtic periphery. Reece himself sees basic population continuity and interprets the archaeological hiatus as a "period of indifference between the loss of interest in things Roman and the rise of interest in matters Saxon" (Reece 1989, 235).

What overall conclusions can be derived from the three case studies considered above? There are a number of points that help our understanding of the role of migration in Yayoi Japan. First, while migrations were obviously common in prehistory, the term "migration" covers a variety of complex processes that must be seen as merging with rather than replacing processes of "independent" evolution. Second, the sheer complexity of past population movements means we need to fully take into account all the relevant information from biological anthropology and linguistics as well as from archaeology. The study of human biology provides the most direct physical evidence for population movements. There is a need for both quality and quantity in such evidence, but in these respects Yayoi Japan is one of the best examples from anywhere in the prehistoric world. *It would be hard, in fact, without the preservation of soft tissue, to imagine an archaeological situation other than that of Yayoi Japan in which there was clearer evidence for biological change caused by immigration.* Despite this, there have been decades of controversy over the relationship between the Jōmon and Yayoi populations. While one might argue that our analytical methods only recently have become refined enough to allow us to be reasonably sure of the nature of the biological differences between the two groups, for many archaeologists, similarities in *material culture* between Jōmon and Yayoi are enough to cast doubt on the results derived from biological anthropology.

In the three case studies considered here, the linguistic evidence has played a major role in formulating hypotheses about past population movements. The social processes that lie behind language change are, in general, better understood than is the relationship between population movements and the archaeological record, and there is certainly no reason to privilege the archaeological over the linguistic record. If anything, the case studies imply that linguistic evidence may be a more direct indication of past population movements than the archaeological evidence is.

A number of archaeological phenomena are common to the three examples. Substantial changes in material culture between the beginning and end of migrations were found in the Austronesian and Anglo-Saxon cases. This process may be analogous to the "founder effect" known in biology, whereby migration to a new environment may result in the transfer of only selected genes from the parent population. Some archaeologists have proposed that the stress of migration may undermine processes of cultural transmission (e.g. Myres 1969, 21). Another approach would be to argue that migrations often result from adaptive radiations of populations that, for whatever reason, start to exploit a new ecological or cultural niche. In this case, differences between parent and colonizing populations would be natural, since those differences give the latter population its adaptive advantage and are thus part of the cause of the migration.

A more general conclusion based on the examples is that archaeological data is often not very useful in identifying population movements. In all three cases, the same archaeological evidence has been used to support ostensibly opposing interpretations of both migration and independent evolution. This does not mean that the "shopping list" criteria of Rouse and others are incorrect. Such criteria are important preliminary steps in any archaeological study of migrations; the problem is that they are not always sufficient. There are a number of reasons that it is often so difficult to identify population movements from the archaeological record. We have already noted that what we loosely term "migration" frequently involves complex processes of population movement, expansion, and interaction. While in theory such processes can be described separately (e.g. Gamble 1993, 45), in practice they most likely combine with each other and do not leave the clear-cut traces that archaeologists expect. Second, the technomic artifacts that archaeologists study—be they pottery, lithics, or TV sets—often do not encode the type of social or ethnic information that would enable us to be sure a change in population has taken place. For example, it has been argued that ceramic styles roughly correlate with historic Ontario Iroquois tribal divisions, but not with those of neighboring Algonquian Indians (Wright 1972, 92). Wright (1972, 92–94) proposes a plausible explanation for this in terms of differing patterns of social structure and marriage, but Engelbrecht's (1974, 1978) work has not shown clear links between Iroquoian pottery and tribal groupings, and without independent documentary evidence we can probably never be sure of the meaning of such differences from the archaeology alone: "While there are many cases in which there is a high correlation of cultural boundaries with linguistic, ethnic or religious entities, there are just as many non-coincidences" (Chapman and Dolukhanov 1993, 7).

The archaeological identification of population movements relies on a link between material culture and ethnic identity. Since the 1930s, this link has traditionally been made in terms of archaeological "cultures," which were thought to be the material representation of past ethnic groups. We now know, partly through ethnoarchaeological studies such as Hodder (1982), that material culture does not always directly reflect ethnicity. More theoretical criticisms of the culture concept have also existed for some time (e.g. MacWhite 1956; Phillips and Willey 1953; Renfrew and Bahn 1991, 407–409; Shennan 1989). Some archaeologists have argued that the concept of "culture" as used in archaeology is more confusing than explanatory, and that it should therefore be abandoned as a taxonomic unit (Shennan 1978). As noted by Chapman and Dolukhanov (1993, 8), however, the concept continues to be widely used—even though there is no agreement on how we should approach the social meanings of archaeological cultures. Unfortunately, the approach espoused by Rouse relies on a firm knowledge of the parameters of the relationship between archaeological units and actual people. If there was always a one-to-one relationship between an archaeological unit and a past social group, then recognizing the movement of that group would be relatively easy. The fact that such a relationship does not always exist is probably the major flaw of the traditional archaeological approach to migrations.

A contextual approach may be one solution to this problem. In other words, we need to ask in what situations and in what ways is social or ethnic identity linked with material culture. Collett (1987) looked at two series of migrations by the Ngoni and Kololo peoples in south and central Africa. His data show that (a) only some aspects of material culture may change after a migration, e.g. settlement patterns but not ceramics, and (b) that types of cultural change cannot be typologically linked with types of migration (Collett 1987, 114). The cases in which Collett shows ceramic continuity despite the arrival of a new group are particularly interesting from the perspective of this book. Collett (1987, 115) concludes: "If archaeologists want to infer a migration then they must undertake a detailed contextual analysis to establish the cultural significance of different aspects of material culture and then try to show that the new system of beliefs represented in the material culture is more easily derived from elsewhere." While not denying that contextual interpretations in purely prehistoric situations can be extremely difficult, where sufficient evidence exists this may be the best approach to linking the archaeological record with past social groups.

To conclude the discussion so far, consideration of the sparse theoretical literature on prehistoric migrations and a brief look at how archaeologists have approached some population movements has led to a number of preliminary conclusions:

(1) Human population movements were common in prehistory.

(2) Both the causes and the conduct of these movements can be enormously complex, and we must therefore expect their archaeological signatures to be equally complex.

(3) Human physical remains provide the most direct evidence for migrations, but we need to be sure that observed biological changes cannot be attributed solely to environmental causes.

(4) In many cases, linguistic evidence may provide more direct evidence for past population movements than does the archaeological record. To some extent, this conclusion relies on the assumption that processes of language change are likely to have been simpler in nonstate than in state societies (e.g. fewer or no pidgins/creoles), but on present evidence this assumption appears justified.

(5) Identifying migrations from the archaeological record is extremely difficult, largely because we are unsure of the relationship between units of archaeological classification (cultures, assemblages, etc.) and past social groups. Thus, plotting the changing distribution of archaeological units may or may not relate directly to population movements. The traditional checklist approach used by Rouse and others is not wrong, but in itself it cannot be regarded as sufficient proof for the existence of migrations.

(6) While the last point may seem unduly pessimistic, the way forward is clear: it is the realization that the traditional migration *versus* independent evolution divide is damaging, and the espousal of a multidisciplinary approach making full use of biological anthropology and historical linguistics as well as archaeology. Where possible, a contextual approach to material culture may help us understand its relationship with past social groups. As the fourth-century Roman critic Symmachus put it, *Uno itinere non potest perveniri ad tam grande secretum.*[2]

YAYOI IMMIGRATION AND COLONIZATION

Using the above provisional conclusions, this section attempts to evaluate the evidence for the immigration and expansion of a Peninsular population into the Japanese Islands in the Yayoi period. The place to begin is obviously with biological anthropology, and it must be emphasized again that we have a whole battery of different but complementary techniques that all say the same thing: the Yayoi saw the arrival of a new population that expanded at the expense of the indigenous Jōmon people to form the basis of the modern Japanese—notwithstanding some interbreeding between the two groups, the importance of which varied according to region. Despite all this evidence, however, it has proven difficult to relate the biological anthropology to the archaeological remains of the Yayoi. One problem is the nature of the skeletal sample we have. Almost all Yayoi skeletons have come from jar-burial and sand-dune sites in north Kyushu and western Yamaguchi, respectively, leading to both a geographical and chronological bias. The chronological bias is particularly serious, as all specimens used to support immigration theories date to the end of the Early Yayoi or later, and no skeletal remains with immigrant characteristics are known from the Initial Yayoi.

Notwithstanding this sample bias, the lack of any transitional skeletal samples that would correspond to transitional Initial Yayoi archaeological sites such as Nabatake is puzzling. The Doigahama cemetery contains at least one Jōmon-type individual (Matsushita 1994, 36–40), and the Doigahama population as a whole is reported to be slightly closer to the Jōmon than to Kanenokuma (Dodo et al. 1992). Despite this, the populations at these and other north Kyushu/Yamaguchi sites are clearly *qualitatively* different from contemporary Jōmon-type populations. While they may have been formed through interbreeding with native groups since the Initial Yayoi, that mixing process had already reached such an advanced stage that these Yayoi people were morphologically closer to modern Japanese than to their neighbors along the coast in northwest Kyushu. Archaeologically, there is no reason to see sites such as Doigahama and Kanenokuma as colonies, but based on the skeletal evidence alone, such a conclusion would be quite reasonable.

At present, only one site can shed any sort of light on the formation process of the immigrant Yayoi population. That site is Shinmachi in western Fukuoka Prefecture, only a few kilometers from Magarita. Skeletal remains of fourteen individuals were excavated there in 1986. Shinmachi's megalithic graves date to the Yu'usu phase of the Initial and the Itazuke I phase of the Early Yayoi, and the skeletal remains thus represent unique specimens. Of the fourteen, only one individual (No. 9) was well preserved; seven of the others were only fragmentary remains. Analysis of these remains showed that they are similar to Jōmon-type populations from northwest Kyushu and quite different from the immigrant population known at Kanenokuma. This conclusion was reached by studying the skulls of the better-preserved specimens, on the basis of stature (average of 157.1 cm for three males), and on the basis of the presence of Jōmon-style tooth ablation on five individuals. Contrary to our expectation, therefore, this Initial/Early Yayoi site, despite its Peninsula-inspired burials, would seem to contain the remains of neither an immigrant nor even a transitional population, but of a Jōmon one (Nakahashi and Nagai 1987), although Tanaka (1991, 493–496) argues that the eye sockets of skull No. 9 are of immigrant type and thus that some degree of population mixing had already occurred.

What is needed here is a way of modeling the interaction that occurred between the native and immigrant populations in the Yayoi. Despite a large theoretical literature on acculturation and culture contact (e.g. Lathrap 1956), little work of this sort has been done. Many Japanese archaeologists appear to assume that there is a direct relationship between the number of immigrants and the degree of material acculturation—with the high level of acculturation of Initial Yayoi ceramics seen as evidence for only a small number of immigrants (e.g. Yane 1993, 316). The implication is that clear-cut separation between Jōmon and Yayoi would have been the norm if immigration had occurred on a large scale. Even a superficial survey of what happens to material culture in colonial contexts, however, shows that this is not usually the case. The archaeology of early European colonialism in Asia, America, and Africa demonstrates that whatever the ultimate fate of the native peoples, very close interaction with the incoming Europeans was initially the norm. Excavations at European colonial sites regularly produce native artifacts: at Oudepost I, a Dutch site in South Africa occupied between 1669 and 1732, Schrire (1987, 442; 1991, 82) found stone tools, bone spear points, Khoikhoi pottery, and an eggshell bead; in the Caribbean, elements of Taino (Arawak) food and cooking techniques were adopted by early Spanish colonists (Pons 1992, 137); and English settlers in Newfoundland adopted several items of Inuit culture, including sealskin boats and dog traction (Firestone 1992). Material acculturation did not take place everywhere in the same way. In northeast America, despite the close links with the Indians that the complex nature of the fur trade encouraged (Schrire and Merwick 1991, 14), native artifacts were rare at French, Dutch, and English colonial sites (Deagan 1991, 105). A similar difference exists in lexical acculturation, whereby Native American languages influenced by Spanish speakers adopted many Spanish loan words, whereas languages influenced by English or French tended to use native words for new items and concepts (Brown 1994). Brown argues that this difference relates to the degree of bilingualism of the Indian groups. The degree of acculturation between European colonial and indigenous societies depended on a variety of factors including, of course, the type of settlement by the Europeans. Equally or perhaps more important were "the qualities of the indigenous society which profoundly influenced the kind of settler society which could be superimposed upon it, or which might entirely replace it" (Denoon 1983, 27). Agricultural societies such as the Maori displayed a much higher "survival rate" than did foraging societies such as the Australian Aborigines (Denoon 1983, 27).

Archaeologically, native-settler interaction can be reflected in a number of ways, but I propose to look at pottery in some detail here, since it is the supposed mixing of Jōmon and Peninsular ceramics that is widely seen as evidence *against* population movement into Kyushu during the Jōmon-Yayoi transition. One of the most interesting comparative cases for Yayoi pottery is provided by the syncretic Hispanic-Indian wares of the New World. The first European town in the Americas was La Isabela on Hispaniola, established on Columbus' second voyage and used from 1494 to 1496. At La Isabela, kilns were built to produce *mudejar* ware of the type then in common use in Spain. At Concepción de la Vega, which was founded two years after La Isabela, however, syncretic Hispanic-Indian pottery was already in evidence (Deagan 1988, 206–210, 1992). From then on, "the Spaniards adopted locally produced non-European wares as their primary kitchen pottery throughout the circum-Caribbean region and . . . this trend persisted throughout the colonial period" (Deagan 1988, 214–215). Further support for this conclusion comes from Deagan's work at the colonial St. Augustine site in Florida. In the excavated eighteenth-century levels, the utilitarian pottery was mainly aboriginal, accounting for as much as 66 percent of total ceramics (Deagan 1983, 84). Deagan explains this as a result of the high rate of intermarriage between Spaniards and Indians, particularly Spanish men and Indian women. In these *mestizaje* households, the highest proportion of Indian influence was reflected in activities such as food preparation and pottery production that were handled by the Indian women. One 1580 estimate suggests that over 25 percent of domestic households in St. Augustine had an Indian woman as a member (Deagan 1983, 103). Parish registers between 1735 and 1750 record that 11 percent of all marriages were between Indian or *mestizo* women and Spanish men, although Deagan (1983, 103) notes that the real figure was probably much higher, as many weddings would have taken place at mission villages for which records no longer exist.

Beginning with Kanaseki Takeo (1971), there have been various suggestions that Yayoi immigrants were mainly males who took local Jōmon women as wives. If Yayoi pottery was made by women, then this might explain the ceramic continuities between the Final Jōmon and the Yayoi. Kōmoto (1978) argued that, except for weaving, all Yayoi cultural traits introduced from the continent can be associated with mens' work, whereas the objects and activities held over from the Jōmon were mainly associated with women. An obvious problem here is that unless Final Jōmon women only married immigrant males, it is hard to imagine why the latter had such a large genetic influence. One theoretical explanation is the presence of widespread polygamy in Yayoi society, so that immigrant males had many native wives. The third-century *Wei zhi* does, in fact, mention that "Ordinarily, men of importance have four or five wives; the lesser ones, two or three" (Tsunoda and Goodrich 1951, 12), although this may reflect Chinese beliefs in a mythical land in the eastern ocean rather than actual Yayoi customs. Polygamy was also known in early historic Japan (Morris 1979, 232; Torao 1993, 429–430). Of course, none of this makes it certain that polygamy was practiced in the Initial Yayoi—some six centuries before the *Wei zhi*—yet the reproductive co-option of Jōmon women by immigrant males is a distinct possibility. On the evidence of tooth ablation and burial goods, Harunari (1984b, 1991) has suggested that there was a shift from matrilocal to bilateral postmarital residence in western Japan during the Final Jōmon to Yayoi periods. A possible explanation for this might have been the need to incorporate more labor into the society with the increased demands of rice farming (cf. Miles 1990).

Barnes (1993b) takes up Dennell's (1985) models of migration/assimilation and adoption/imitation, originally developed for the European Mesolithic-Neolithic transition (Table 6.1). Barnes argues that the Kyushu Initial Yayoi best fits the latter model, whereby hunter-gatherers adopt agriculture to increase their production. While this no doubt happened in some instances, however, I believe the migration/assimilation model to be the more likely scenario for the western Yayoi. According to Barnes (1993b, 184), the Kyushu transition satisfies several of the criteria of Dennell's adoption/imitation model: "indigenous intensification of food production prior to the adoption of agriculture; long-distance seafaring abilities to bring distant agricultural communities within reach; the emergence of a hybrid material culture; and the absence of a clear transition point between the Mesolithic and Neolithic (Final Jōmon and Initial Yayoi, in the case of Japan)." We see in chapter 5 that there is no evidence that western Jōmon groups were "more familiar with and oriented to plant foods" (Barnes 1993b, 184) than were their eastern neighbors. Furthermore, while Dennell's two models are in themselves useful ways of looking at the Mesolithic-Neolithic boundary, I see no reason for them to be exclusive of each other. Hunter-gatherer need to increase productivity could

TABLE 6.1

SCHEMATIC REPRESENTATION OF DENNELL'S (1985) ALTERNATIVE MODELS FOR THE SPREAD OF AGRICULTURE

MIGRATION = ASSIMILATION	ADOPTION = IMITATION
Geographic proximity of	*Geographic distance between*
Foreign agriculturalists (AG) with:	Foreign agricultural communities with:
donor material culture	several donor cultures
different ethnicity	year-round settlement
year-round settlement	small annual territories
small annual territories	high productivity
high productivity	
Resident hunter-gatherers (HG) with:	Resident horticulturalists:
knowledge of local resources	food production experimentation
status of supplier of mates	mobile
strategic mobility	eclectic borrowing
Interaction at AG settlement	*Reasons for interaction at AG settlement*
AG trade crops for goods	AG need for goods
AG receive mates	HG need to increase productivity
HG trade goods for staples	
HG receive novel objects	
Results	*Results*
AG co-opt reproductive HG	HG acquire technology and reproduce it through imitation
AG expand settlements at expense of HG	HG increase productivity through gradual transformation of subsistence system
HG lose mates	
HG abandon foraging	
Therefore:	*Therefore:*
Spread of AG culture	Emergence of new eclectic/hybrid AG culture among former HG
Disappearance of HG culture	First evidence for this appears in subsistence realm

From Barnes (1993b) with minor modifications.

just as well have led to their assimilation as to independent imitation. The unarguable eclecticism of Initial Yayoi pottery can, in my view, be better explained through Dennell's assimilation model, whereby agriculturalists receive mates, than through his imitation model. Finally, Barnes' (1993b, 185) argument that "paddy field, canal and tool remains [appear in] Final Jōmon . . . contexts that otherwise are Jōmon in nature and contain no non-agricultural aspects of Peninsular material culture" is incorrect, since dolmens, moated settlements, Songgungni-type buildings, and pig rituals all appear as a set in Initial Yayoi Kyushu.

In short, therefore, I believe Dennell's migration/assimilation model may be appropriate for the Jōmon-Yayoi transition in northern Kyushu. This model does not overlook the Jōmon people as historical actors. It hypothesizes that in some cases they made their own choice to assimilate with the incoming migrants, which partly explains the reproductive success of the Japanese at the expense of the indigenous Jōmon people. Another likely factor is the massive population growth experienced by most societies in the change from hunter-gathering to farming. Clear evidence of Yayoi population increase is known in many areas. Maritime activity also seems to have been important in the Yayoi (Hudson 1990b) and this no doubt further contributed to the spread of immigrant genes. The degree of mobility may have been greater and the incidence of regional intermarriage higher in the Yayoi than they were at any other time in Japanese history until the twentieth century.

As well as reproductive co-option, there are several possible reasons explaining why the Final Jōmon and immigrant people should have lived together in the same settlements. If certain Final Jōmon populations were already engaged in rice cultivation, then they may have sought out close relations with the incoming farmers. Forager-farmer interactions in prehistory are currently a topic of debate in archaeology. While such interactions are known to exist ethnographically (see references in Gregg 1988, 2), they are not easy to identify from the archaeological record, a difficulty that Gregg never really resolves in her own study of Neolithic Europe. If the hybrid nature of Initial Yayoi ceramics can be explained by the cohabitation of migrants and indigenes in north Kyushu, then this may imply that those ceramics were not an important locus for signifying ethnic identity. *Tottaimon* pottery was marked by a high level of uniformity across western Japan. Similar uniformity continued through the Early Yayoi but was thereafter quickly replaced by a proliferation of local styles. The uniformity of the Early Yayoi Ongagawa style can be attributed to its spread out of Kyushu with a population of agricultural colonists; the *tottaimon* uniformity is more problematical. Japanese archaeologists typically explain it as the result of intense interregional communication at that time (e.g. Morioka 1990, 208). Hodder (1979, 1982) has criticized the view that stylistic similarity is directly proportional to increased interaction between ethnic groups. Instead, pottery decoration (or the lack of it) may be linked with its role in identity signaling: "What is important to the maintenance of [ethnic] boundaries is not the totality of cultural traits contained by them but those traits that the groups utilize as symbols of their identity separate from other groups. These symbols may be behavioral or material in form" (McGuire 1982, 160).

I propose the hypothesis here, therefore, that pottery in western Japan in the Initial Yayoi was not an important medium for signifying ethnic identity. The sparse Initial Yayoi ceramic decoration contrasts strongly with the intricate carved and erased cordmarked decorations of the Final Jōmon Kamegaoka pottery of the eastern archipelago. Mizuno (1990, 97–104) has argued that the dominant symbolic framework of the Yayoi was one of ditches, moats, and boundaries. Archaeologically, these are represented by the ditches surrounding paddy fields, by village moats, and by moated burial precincts. We might develop Mizuno's scheme further by pointing out that rectilinear boundaries and "compounds" are also found on some categories of Yayoi material culture. Suwada pottery of the Kanto Middle Yayoi and the design panels of *dōtaku* bronze bells are two examples. Such designs are noticeable in their absence, however, on pottery from the western Initial and Early Yayoi. Of course, the difficulty with this contextual explanation is that the trend toward low-key ceramic decoration began in western Japan in the Late Jōmon (Kobayashi 1992, 90). One is thus forced to argue that the western Jōmon people and the Peninsular Plain Pottery people had a similar aversion to "displaying" their identity on pottery. This complicates the issue but does not necessarily disprove my hypothesis, and it is possible that Peninsular Plain Pottery had already influenced western late Jōmon ceramics in their decorative simplification.

Notwithstanding the complexity of Initial Yayoi ceramics, it is clear that there is a general fit between the expansion of agriculture and the expansion of the Japanese core population as defined in this book. As noted already, however, one area in which no such agreement appears to exist is the Ryukyu Islands. Do the Ryukyus therefore disprove my hypothesis of Japanese ethnogenesis? I believe not, for several reasons. The linguistic evidence shows that Ryukyuan and Japanese split from a common ancestor in the early centuries AD or thereabouts. Discounting a move in the opposite direction as extremely unlikely, the Ryukyu language must have spread from mainland Japan, replacing the preexisting Okinawan language(s). We do not know by what social process this language replacement took place. Theoretically, an elite dominance or lingua franca model associated with the medieval Ryukyuan state is possible, but the linguistic evidence points to a much earlier spread of the language. On present evidence, the subsistence/demography model applied here to explain the spread of the Japanese language through the mainland cannot yet be dismissed with respect to the Ryukyus.

It is noted in chapter 3 that anthropologists do not agree on the amount of Japanese immigration into Okinawa in ancient times; it is therefore too early to rule out a substantial level of population movement into the islands. There appears to be little archaeological evidence for such immigration, but this chapter has shown that the archaeology of migration needs careful interpretation. It is also difficult to make a link with agricultural colonization, but, since it is not known when and how farming began in the Ryukyus, such a link cannot be ruled out. At present, therefore, a subsistence/demography model for the spread of Ryukyuan is at least as likely as is any other scenario.

CONCLUSIONS

The identification of ethnosocial units and their movements from the archaeological record is one of the most difficult problems facing the historical sciences. While making no pretense of offering a solution, this chapter has argued a need for "lateral thinking." In emphasizing a multidisciplinary approach, it was suggested that far from privileging archaeological data, the biological and linguistic records are, in many cases, of more direct relevance to understanding prehistoric migrations. The traditional archaeological approach to identifying migrations, though it sometimes works in practice, cannot be used as a sufficiently rigorous test of migrations. In Japan, for example, sites with a majority of Korean Plain Pottery are known in parts of north Kyushu during the late Early Yayoi and are believed to be immigrant colonies (Kataoka 1990, 97–102). The fact that such clear separation of material culture appears absent during the Initial Yayoi, however, does not mean that immigration did not also occur during that phase.

In their research on the Jōmon-Yayoi transition, Japanese archaeologists have been guilty of privileging not just the archaeological record as a whole but the ceramic evidence in particular. As discussed in detail in chapter 5, most other aspects of Initial Yayoi material culture show quite marked discontinuities between Jōmon and Yayoi. In contrast, Initial Yayoi ceramics are clearly hybrid in form, but we cannot assume that ceramic traits can be mapped directly onto past social units. This chapter has proposed several reasons why incoming Peninsular migrants could have used pottery made by local Jōmon people. Of course, after one generation, Yayoi pottery would have been made by *Japanese* potters for whom, whatever their ethnic identity, a hybrid ceramic style was the norm.

In short, therefore, I believe that biological anthropology, historical linguistics, and archaeology all support my model of initial Japanese ethnogenesis in the Yayoi period. The ceramic evidence implies that in north Kyushu there was close contact between the Japanese and Jōmon populations and that *in the first generation of settlement* much Yayoi pottery was made by Jōmon people, but this evidence cannot be used as a direct indication of the relative number of immigrants *versus* indigenes.

PART III

Post-Yayoi Interaction and Ethnogenesis

7

Ethnicity and the Ancient State

A Core/Periphery Approach

State formation triggers uneven development—i.e., it both creates and perpetuates circumstances in which societies can develop at different rates. This means that, at any instant and depending on one's perspective, some societies appear "backward" or "peripheral" while others possess "advanced" or "metropolitan" features. Uneven development provides a rich medium for both ethnocide and ethnogenesis.

Thomas C. Patterson, *Tribes, Chiefdoms and Kingdoms in the Inca Empire*

Part II of this book argues that the first stage of Japanese ethnogenesis occurred in the Yayoi period, when farmers from the Korean Peninsula and their descendants began to spread their genes, language, and agricultural lifestyle through the Islands. Part III moves on to analyze the processes of ethnic change and construction that occurred on the basis of the Japanese core population established during the Yayoi. Most existing approaches to this problem have assumed ethnic groups to be natural, sui generis communities. Particularly in the case of peripheral groups such as the Emishi and Hayato, it has been proposed that they represent either relict cultures, essentially unchanged from the Jōmon, or else peoples of exotic origin—the Hayato, for example, being commonly seen as of Indonesian stock. The *isolation* of these groups from the Japanese core is thought to explain their retention of different ethnicities (e.g. Otomasu 1970, 90). In contrast, it will be argued here that these groups were formed through the complex processes of *interaction* that occurred between core and periphery. The approach used here has its basis in recent discussions of premodern world-systems and in anthropological and historical studies of the influence of the state in ethnogenesis. This chapter looks at the influence of the state on ethnic differentiation during the Yayoi, Kofun, and Nara periods; the following chapter analyzes the ethnogenesis of the Ainu in medieval Hokkaido.

WORLD-SYSTEMS AND ETHNOGENESIS

Wallerstein (1987, 309) proposes that world-systems analysis is not a theory but a *protest*. In other words, it is foremost a reaction to the traditional historical and anthropological view of distinctive "societies" and "cultures" that "spin off each other like so many hard and round billiard balls" (Wolf 1982, 6). In a world-systems approach, the scale of analysis is not supposedly self-contained units such as the Late Dorset Eskimo, the Umayyad caliphate, or the Yamato state, but the larger system in which these units are located. Such systems are defined not by their internal cultural homogeneity but through their webs of interconnections (Chase-Dunn and Hall 1991a, 10). World-systems can thus be defined as "intersocietal networks in which the interactions (e.g. trade, warfare, intermarriage) are important for the reproduction of the internal structures of the composite units and importantly affect changes that occur in these local structures" (Chase-Dunn and Hall 1993, 855).

Wallerstein's comment that world-systems analysis is not a theory emphasizes the still-immature nature of that approach. This is particularly true for premodern world-systems that have been given little attention in Wallerstein's own work. A growing literature now exists on premodern world-systems, but many problems and disagreements remain. Most scholars working on the premodern era use the concept of regional world-systems to analyze their particular area of interest (e.g. Algaze 1993; Blanton and Feinman 1984; Dincauze and Hasenstab 1989; Edens 1988; McGuire 1989). While this basic approach is also adopted here, a parallel debate exists over the global scope of the world-system. Three main positions can be identified within this latter debate. The first is Wallerstein's (1974) proposal that there has only been one world-system that began in Europe in the sixteenth century; this world-system coincides with the capitalist mode of production, and previous systems—which Wallerstein terms "mini-systems" and "world-empires"—were therefore of a qualitatively different nature. The second position, typified by Abu-Lughod (1989, 1990), is that there have been several successive world-systems, such as the one that developed in Eurasia in the thirteenth century. The third argues for a *single* Eurasian world-system that has evolved over the past five millennia (Frank 1990, 1993; Gills and Frank 1991; Frank and Gills 1993). Frank and Gills propose that the supposed differentiating characteristics of the post-1500 system—the accumulation of capital, core/periphery hierarchies, A/B cycles of economic expansion and contraction, and imperialism—were also present in antiquity (see also Ekholm and Friedman 1982). To some extent, this controversy can be sidestepped by using the concept of a nested hierarchy of world-systems. Whatever the theoretical value of a single Eurasian system, in practical terms, prior to 1500, events in East Asia usually had a more direct influence on the Japanese Islands than did events further afield. At the same time, however, the debate over the global extent of the world-system is important for two reasons. First, it forces us to face the analytical problem of structural differences between modern and premodern systems, something which will be discussed in more detail below. Second, it offers an explanation for why both Western and Japanese scholars have so far been slow to apply world-systems theory to Japan.

The traditional view of recent Japanese history, held by both Marxist and non-Marxist scholars, has been that Japan's modernization was the direct result of her forced incorporation into the modern world-system in the nineteenth century. It is the view that "The magical power that drew the histories of isolated peoples together and welded them into one world for the first time was modern capitalism" (Hattori 1980, 18). Of course, recent years have seen a growing trend toward searching for "proto-capitalist" roots in the Tokugawa era. Sanderson (1991) even argues that the economic growth experienced by Tokugawa Japan supports the conclusion that too much emphasis has been given to world-system interactions in accounting for the development of capitalism as a whole:

> [O]ne might say that Japanese society underwent its own transition from feudalism to capitalism. . . . the extraordinary thing about this transition was that it was a *completely endogenous process*. Indeed, it had to be, because Japan sealed itself off from the rest of the world between 1638 and its "opening" in the middle of the nineteenth century. *During this time Japan was not part of any world-system, or even of any much looser world-network of societies* (Sanderson 1991, 184–185, emphasis added).

In a more recent paper, Sanderson (1994) recognizes the presence of some Tokugawa contacts with the outside but still explains the transition to capitalism there through endogenous preconditions. A similar argument is made by Kawakatsu (1991) who contrasts the Tokugawa *sakoku* (closed country) system with the modern world-system based in Europe, proposing a type of convergent evolution between the two. Because of its emphasis on the independent evolution of a single "civilization," Kawakatsu's book represents the very antithesis of world-systems theory. Though a reaction to the Eurocentric nature of traditional theories of modernization, it has simply adopted a new Japanocentric perspective (cf. Morris-Suzuki 1993a).

In my opinion, Sanderson and Kawakatsu's writings demonstrate the futility of trying to argue that the magical power of capitalism and European contact were behind the formation of a qualitatively different world-system. The Tokugawa economy cannot be seen in isolation. In fact, one can make a good case that Japan became part of a *single* world-system after the mid-sixteenth century (Hudson 1994b, 140). Precious metals were central to this global trade (cf. Yamamura and Kamiki 1983; Flynn and Giráldez 1995). By the early seventeenth century, Japan was producing as much as 150,000 to 187,500 kg of silver in certain years (Atwell 1982, 71), accounting for a third of world silver output at that time (Katō 1987, 47). Atwell (1982) has even argued that fluctuations in Japanese bullion flows may have contributed to the fall of the Chinese Ming dynasty in 1644. Within this context, the decision by the Tokugawa shogunate to close the country in the 1630s can be seen as an attempt to limit the economic power of peripheral chieftains who had been engaged in profitable trade with regions such as Southeast Asia. The same basic process of capital imperialism continued, however, within the Islands. Hechter (1975, 349) proposes that external colony, internal colony, and peripheral region should be seen as part of a continuum and that, while the degree of integration differs, basically similar processes are at work in all three. Economic penetration of Hokkaido and even of Sakhalin by Japanese merchants played a role in Tokugawa agricultural growth in its provision of herring fertilizer (see Howell 1995; Morris-Suzuki 1995). The conquest of the Ryukyu Islands by the Satsuma domain in 1609 greatly enhanced the wealth of the latter as it tapped the overseas trade of the Okinawans who were allowed a facade of independence; the power thus obtained was instrumental in Satsuma's leading role in the Meiji revolution (Calman 1992, 44–45).

Overemphasis on the magical power of European capitalism would therefore seem to go some way in explaining the lack of interest in world-systems theory shown by historians of Japan. Those scholars who have reacted to the Eurocentrism inherent in the traditional approach to modernization have tended to focus on developments within Japan, mirroring the Japanocentric emphasis on endogenous change maintained by Japanese archaeologists. Debate on East Asian international relations in the premodern period has been dominated by the traditional Chinese concepts of investiture *(cefeng;* J. *sakuhō)* and the civilization-barbarian dichotomy *(hua-yi;* J. *ka-i)* (e.g. Nishijima 1983, 1994; Arano 1988). One area of Japanese scholarship that does have links to the approach used here is work on ancient imperialism. Ishimoda (1972) has applied Lenin's theory of imperialism to antiquity, an analysis developed further by Ishigami (1987). Ishigami (1987, 65) writes that the Japanese state exaggerated physical and cultural differences between the ethnic Japanese and groups such as the Emishi and Hayato for its own political ends. In my view, however, Ishigami does not take this analysis as far as he might, emphasizing political and ideological factors at the expense of economic ones.

The lack of interest in world-systems theory among Western historians of Japan is also probably best explained by an emphasis on endogenous change. Although there are exceptions, including work by Moulder (1977), Toby (1984), Batten (1997), and Murai (1997), as a generalization, this remains valid. The tone was set here by John Whitney Hall, the leading Western historian of Japan in the postwar era. As Mass (1992, 2) notes, for Hall "Japan is important because of what it achieved without excessive outside influence." Hall's influence is also visible in his approach to regionality, whereby the region is significant because it "contains all the institutional ingredients of the larger national community" (Hall 1966, vii). For Hall, "local history is a reflection of national history; regional differences reflect distance from the center as much as anything else and do not in any case add up to 'different' histories" (Mass 1992, 8). While again there are several exceptions (e.g. Philip Brown 1993; Trott 1995; Wigen 1995), Western historiography has tended to focus on the institutions of the center at the expense of the political economy of the periphery, and our understanding of Japanese history has suffered as a result (Hudson 1995).

As noted, world-systems theory takes as its basis of analysis not small, bounded societies—or even larger ones such as the ancient Japanese "empire" discussed by Ishimoda (1972) and Ishigami (1987)—but the wider system in which they are all embedded. How then are we to study particular ethnic units within a world-system? One of the few theoretical contributions to this problem is Hechter's (1975) work on internal colonialism in the British Isles.

Hechter argues that the uneven spread of industrialization across a state creates an unequal distribution of power and resources, which is reproduced by the development of distinctive ethnic identities; these identities are institutionalized by the core to maintain its centrality and are strengthened in the periphery by assertiveness against the political and economic inroads of the core. While Hechter focuses on industrialization—and has thus been criticized for the limited applicability of his model (e.g. Smith 1981, 33)—the basis of his model can be transferred to preindustrial societies if we concentrate on the inequalities brought about by the Agricultural Revolution rather than by the Industrial Revolution.

Hechter contrasts his internal colonial scheme with what he describes as the traditional diffusionist model of ethnic formation whereby interaction leads to commonality, a contrast that mirrors the one between the modernization theory and the dependency approach on which Hechter's model is based. In the diffusionist model, "The type of social structure found in the developing core regions will, after some time, diffuse into the periphery. Since the cultural forms of the periphery were evolved in isolation . . . contact with modernizing core regions will transform these cultural forms by updating them, as it were" (Hechter 1975, 7). This type of diffusionist model has been commonly employed in Japan, with peripheral ethnic groups such as the Ainu and Okinawans seen as relict leftovers from the Jōmon. While these populations may retain some elements of a Jōmon inheritance, it will be argued here that their social formation is better explained as the result of political and economic interactions with the mainland Japanese.

It can be said that Hechter's internal colonial model succumbs to some of the pitfalls associated with dependency theories, including a rather passive view of peripheral ethnicity derived from an overemphasis on the role of external factors (cf. Boutilier 1989, 27; Shannon 1989, 144–145). Anthony Smith (1981, 33) argues that Hechter's model "possesses little relevance for most non-western areas [where] there was little capitalism or industry. . . ." To the extent that (as far as I am aware) no one has actually applied the model to preindustrial societies, Smith's criticisms remain untested, but I believe that, as Schneider (1977, 20) has commented about Wallerstein's work, Hechter's model can be said to suffer from a too-limited application of its own theory. With certain modifications, the model can be usefully applied to ancient societies. As already noted, the most important modification we need to make is that of focusing on agriculturalization—the differential spread of farming—rather than on industrialization. While there is little doubt that the uneven spread of agriculture could lead to significant imbalances in wealth and complexity, however, we need first to consider to what extent industrial economies were structurally different from their agrarian predecessors. This is, of course, a basic problem in the study of premodern world-systems, relating to the substantivist/formalist debate in economic anthropology. If, as Wallerstein suggests, the modern world-system is fundamentally different from what went before, then world-systems prior to 1500 must have had different internal structures. If, on the other hand, we accept Frank and Gills' argument that changes within the Eurasian world-system(s) have only been quantitative, then the basic systemic structures would be the same in antiquity as in the modern world.

What, then, are the major structural differences that need to be considered when applying Hechter's theory to the premodern Japanese Islands? One problem is the extent to which premodern systems are dominated by political and ideological factors as opposed to the supposedly pure free-market economic basis of the modern world-system. Samir Amin argues that the shift from a tributary to a capitalist mode of production around 1500 was manifested "in a fundamental reversal: the dominance of the economic replaces that of the political and ideological" (Amin 1993, 250). Many scholars working on the premodern era, however, would disagree with this statement. For example, though they are dismissed by Wallerstein (1974, 20–21) as being of little systemic significance, the importance of prestige goods in antiquity has been emphasized by several writers (Schneider 1977; Ekholm 1977; Frankenstein and Rowlands 1978). Conversely, items considered luxury goods, such as sugar, spices, and tobacco, also played a significant role in the modern world-system until as late as the nineteenth century (Brewer 1980, 4–6). Despite Amin's simplistic trajectory, the difficulties in separating economic from political and ideological factors within any world-system are clear, and there is certainly a need to consider political and ideological as well as economic dependence between core and periphery in antiquity (Champion 1989b, 12; Woolf 1990, 49; Schortman and Urban 1994). Pollard (1994, 79) writes that, "Political authorities have two fundamental goals for the survival of their centralized power: (1) the economic exploitation of populations and resources, and (2) the protection of the integrity of the state frontiers." Both of these can lead to ethnic changes (Pollard 1994, 79), and the ways in which the realization of these two goals affected ethnogenesis in ancient Japan is the subject of this chapter. Closely linked to political dependency is the question of ideology. Schortman and Urban (1994, 402) argue that the economic, political, and ideological dimensions of dependency need not necessarily coincide, but in many cases *state* ideology (often the only type for which documents remain) will be inseparable from politics. In Japan, the ideological concept of inside purity/outside impurity was a crucial aspect of the ancient and medieval state (Murai 1985; Yoshie 1995). Since this dichotomy has obvious relevance for the problem of identity, the ideological dimension of core/periphery relations must be considered.

Kohl (1987a, 1987b) has argued that primitive technology and transportation placed severe limits on the relationship between economic development and dependency in ancient states: "the development of underdevelopment in [antiquity] was sharply constrained or itself underdeveloped. Critical technologies, such as metal working, could diffuse relatively easily and new means of transportation and sources of power, such as horses, could be raised in peripheral zones and radically restructure this ancient world system" (Kohl 1987a, 23). To some extent, Kohl's conclusions are borne out by the Japanese evidence. For example, Uno (1991) has proposed that technological transfers to the provinces in the Nara period triggered regional economic growth, undermining the Ritsuryō system. The role of locally produced gold and horses in the economic power of the early medieval Tohoku region will be discussed later in this chapter. Although the most agriculturally advanced Kinai region remained the overall center of the Japanese world-system until industrialization in the nineteenth century, technology transfers seem to have been partly responsible for shifting core/periphery hierarchies in the premodern Islands, and they thus deserve our attention here.

A final modification that must be made to Hechter's model is the adoption of a world-systems perspective. Wallerstein's world-systems theory was in part a reaction to the rather narrow geographic focus of the dependency approach upon which Hechter's model is based. Japanese scholars such as Ishigami (1987) have also tended to assume that political empires were commensurate with an economic system. Thus, instead of only looking at relations between core and periphery, this chapter aims to situate those relations in the wider regional framework of East Asia. I shall attempt to show how the dominance of the Kinai core was partly due to links with China and the Korean Peninsula and how, at the same time, its control of peripheries within the archipelago was to some extent limited by those peripheries' relations with other continental states.

CORE AND PERIPHERY IN THE JAPANESE ISLANDS

The first step in our analysis is to determine the existence of core and peripheral regions in ancient Japan. Comparative ethnography suggests that various types of regional identities are possessed by hunter-gatherer groups at the most primitive (i.e., low-density and mobile) level (cf. Peterson 1976). Such tribalism is likely to have been particularly developed in the affluent and sedentary Jōmon culture, although its precise nature awaits further study (cf. Kobayashi 1992). It seems clear, however, that ethnic behavior became more prominent with the development of chiefdom- and state-level political organization (Fried 1975, 1983; Gailey and Patterson 1987; Brumfiel 1994; Pollard 1994). For this reason the terms "core" and "periphery" are probably not appropriate in Japan before the protohistoric era: although some areas of the Jōmon archipelago had higher populations than others, "uneven" development, that is, the economic and political exploitation of certain regions by others, began with the Yayoi. While the most affluent Jōmon cultures had been located in the eastern archipelago, in the Yayoi the emphasis shifted west, with core regions developing around the Inland Sea. This westward shift reflects, in addition to ecological factors, participation in East Asian systems of trade and tribute centered on the Chinese court.

Premodern East Asia was a world with China at its center. Although the power to enforce it varied from period to period, the Chinese practice of investiture was a crucial aspect of the East Asian world-system after about 200 BC (see Yü 1967; Rossabi 1983). In this system, surrounding barbarian states received official titles and gifts in return for the offer of tribute and political allegiance to the emperor. Barbarian groups were attracted by the prestige items that could be obtained in this way. For the Chinese, the main attraction was political, since investiture was a way of obtaining allegiance for a nominal outlay. Insular participation in the Chinese investiture system is recorded from AD 57. Prior to this, indirect Chinese influence reached the Islands through Korea, especially after the establishment of four Han commanderies on the Peninsula in 108 BC (Barnes 1990d, 124–126; Gardiner 1969, 18–28; Pai 1989a, 1989b; Pearson 1976–1978). The commanderies had an important influence on Yayoi Japan in terms of the increased importation of continental material culture.

Within the Chinese investiture system, the distribution of prestige goods was politically motivated but resulted in a type of elite trade between the countries participating in the system. In Yayoi Japan, Chinese-derived prestige goods, such as bronze mirrors, textiles, and seals, were central to the reproduction of social inequalities (e.g. Barnes 1986b; Stark 1989). The procurement of these items is described in some detail in the *Wei zhi*:

> In the sixth month of the second year of Jingchu [AD 238][1], the Queen of Wa sent the grandee Nashonmi and others to visit

> [Taifang], where they requested permission to proceed to the Emperor's court with tribute. . . . In answer to the Queen of Wa, an edict of the Emperor . . . said as follows: "Herein we address Pimiko, Queen of Wa, whom we now officially call a friend of Wei. [Your embassy has] arrived here with your tribute, consisting of four male slaves and six female slaves, together with two pieces of cloth with designs, each twenty feet in length. You live very far away across the sea; yet you have sent an embassy with tribute. Your loyalty and filial piety we appreciate exceedingly. We confer upon you, therefore, the title "Queen of Wa Friendly to Wei," together with the decoration of the gold seal with purple ribbon. . . . We have granted them audience in appreciation of their visit, before sending them home with gifts. The gifts are these: five pieces of crimson brocade with dragon designs; ten pieces of crimson tapestry with dappled pattern; fifty lengths of bluish-red fabric; and fifty lengths of dark blue fabric. These are in return for what you sent as tribute. As a special gift, we bestow upon you three pieces of blue brocade with interwoven characters, five pieces of tapestry with delicate floral designs, fifty lengths of white silk, eight taels of gold, two swords five feet long, one hundred bronze mirrors, and fifty catties each of jade and of red beads . . . you may exhibit them to your countrymen in order to demonstrate that our country thinks so much of you as to bestow such exquisite gifts upon you (Tsunoda and Goodrich 1951, 14–15, reromanized in Pinyin).

All the important elements of the investiture system are described in this passage: the unequal "exchange" of goods; the official granting of status to polities such as Wa; the role of displaying the goods received as evidence of the power of both sides. While silk and other fabrics are only rarely preserved in archaeological contexts in Japan, Chinese bronze mirrors are commonly excavated from Yayoi and Kofun sites. Six triangular-rimmed beast-deity mirrors bearing inscriptions and Wei dynasty reign dates corresponding to AD 239 and 240 have been found in Japan. Debate continues, however, as to whether the mirrors given to Pimiko were actually of this type, of which around 340 examples are known from *kofun*.

As well as purely material exchanges between China and her neighbors, the associated ideological concept of *hua-yi* (the civilized core surrounded by barbarians) was also important. The Chinese model of territorial space can be

FIG. 7.1. Major sites mentioned in Part III. 1, Tobinitai; 2, Moyoro; 3, Shibechari chasi; 4, Nibutani and Iruekashi; 5, Suehiro and Tapkop; 6, Benten; 7, Usu 10; 8, Setanai chasi; 9, Matsumae; 10, Tosaminato; 11, Shirihachi tate; 12, Hiraizumi; 13, Taga; 14, Kamakura; 15, Tsuruga; 16, Kyoto; 17, Tsubai Ōtsukayama; 18, Nara; 19, Tsukuriyama; 20, Tatetsuki; 21, Kusado Sengen; 22, Kōjindani; 23, Hakata; 24, Dazaifu; 25, Yoshinogari; 26, Hirota.

described as a series of regular tetragons with the capital at the center and the most savage barbarians at the edge. By at least the eighth century, the Japanese had also adopted this spatial model with respect to their own peripheral peoples within the Islands (cf. Senda 1980, 113–115).

Within the Islands, a network of regional chieftains began to appear from the Yayoi period. Those who had access to productive agricultural land or contacts with the advanced civilizations of the continent became powerful and extended their domains. There is not space here for a detailed discussion of the formation of the protohistoric Japanese core around the Inland Sea. Although it became more integrated over time, this core should be seen as a series of competing polities: "The center need not be a single political unit which would, in fact, require an extraordinary degree of direct control over the accumulation process. More often it tends to consist of a number of competing/exchanging political units, one of which may exercise hegemony within the center" (Ekholm and Friedman 1982, 93). Two lines of evidence suggest that by the third century AD the Inland Sea region was home to just such a series of cores, with one polity—Yamato—in an ostensibly dominant position. The first is the *Wei zhi* account of the kingdom of Yamatai and the second the archaeological record of the expansion of standardized keyhole-shaped tomb mounds around the Inland Sea at the start of the Kofun period.

The *Wei zhi* describes a number of *guo/kuni* (countries) in the Islands in the third century AD, most of which are said to be under the control of the kingdom of Yamatai, which was then ruled by a Queen Pimiko.[2] Yamatai is the longest and most-debated historiographic problem in Japanese history (cf. Young 1958; Saeki 1971, 1972; Kakubayashi 1980, 162–176; Edwards 1996). The location of Yamatai cannot be determined from the Chinese accounts, which place it out in the Pacific Ocean. Scores of different locations have been proposed, but north Kyushu and the Kinai have been the main contenders. The Kinai theory derives from the similarity of the word "Yamatai" (Middle Chinese **i̯a-ma-d'ậi* or **i̯a-ma-t'ậi*) with "Yamato" (OJ *Yamatö*), the name of the Nara Basin, and from the fact that the most powerful polity of the Kofun period was in fact found in the Kinai. The Kyushu theory derives support from that island's role as an important Yayoi center and from the identification based on place-name evidence of several of the "countries" controlled by Yamatai with places in north Kyushu.[3]

Apart from the *Wei zhi* account, we have no reason to believe that north Kyushu or the Kinai were themselves under the control of a single polity, and the dominance of all of western Japan by Yamatai is highly unlikely. In recent years, however, Japanese scholars have argued for an alliance or confederacy centered on the Kinai and symbolized archaeologically by the spread of standardized keyhole mounds (e.g. Shiraishi 1991; Yamao 1990). While the absolute chronology of the first keyhole tombs is still being hotly debated, there is a growing trend toward placing them in the second half of the third century, a date that would fit well with the *Wei zhi* account of Yamatai. Both the major attraction and the major problem with the concept of a Yamato "alliance" is its vagueness. Exactly what type of organization are we dealing with? How much real power did Yamato possess? In theory, the alliance could have been a rather loose affair without a dominant leader, perhaps somewhat similar to the Huron and Iroquois confederacies of northeastern America. The fact that the standardized *kofun* system first originated in the Kinai, where the largest such tombs are located, however, suggests that Yamato was in fact the leader of the alliance, a *primus inter pares*.

Apart from Yamato, the major protohistoric political centers around the Inland Sea were north Kyushu, Kibi (Okayama and east Hiroshima), and Izumo (Shimane) (Fig. 7.1). In the Yayoi period, north Kyushu was home to a number of small chiefdoms known from the Chinese histories and from archaeological distributions of burials and settlements (Stark 1989; Takashima 1993). Yamao (1990, 122) speaks of a "Tsukushi *seiken*," a vague term meaning a "north Kyushu polity," as early as the third century. In reality, it is not clear to what extent north Kyushu ever became a unified polity, although from 527–528, Iwai, the *kuni no miyatsuko* (provincial governor) of Tsukushi, managed to gain short-lived control of a wide area of the northern island in a revolt against Yamato (cf. Delmer Brown 1993, 149–151; Aston 1972 [1896], II:15–17).

The importance of both Kyushu and the Izumo region in the Yamato chronicles has long been recognized, and one third of the *Kojiki* and *Nihon Shoki* legends are said to have come from Izumo (Piggott 1989, 62; for details see Aoki 1971).[4] Large keyhole-shaped tombs over 100 m long are unknown in Izumo, and until recently the archaeological record of the region had seemed somewhat at odds with its mythological importance. The past decade, however, has seen a dramatic increase in our understanding of ancient Izumo and of its local Yayoi culture in particular (Piggott 1989; Mori 1991; Ueda 1986, 1993). Considering both the archaeological and historical data, it now seems likely that Izumo was not fully incorporated into the Yamato state until the sixth or seventh century. Even after that time, Izumo's continuing status is shown by the role of the Izumo myths in the Yamato chronicles and by the importance of Izumo Taisha, which is still one of the main Shinto shrines.

The Kibi region presents a considerable contrast with Izumo, since the former has many large *kofun*, including Tsukuriyama. At 360 m long, it is the fourth-largest keyhole tomb in Japan, yet it gets comparatively little mention in the *Kojiki* and the *Nihon Shoki* (Makabe 1993, 83). Like Izumo, however, Kibi is also known for its Late Yayoi mound burials, which include the famous Tatetsuki mound (Kondō 1986). The hybrid nature of the early Yamato *kofun* system is shown by its adoption of tomb-mound facing stones and the ritual jars and stands that evolved into *haniwa* figures from Kibi (Kondō 1986; Kondō and Harunari 1967). Kibi seems to have been incorporated into the Yamato kingdom at a relatively early stage, but it still retained a regional identity and was the location of several uprisings in the fifth century.

The reasons Yamato became the dominant polity in protohistoric Japan are still poorly understood. Military superiority in the so-called Wa Unrest is one possibility (Shiraishi 1991).[5] Both the cause and the effect of Yamato's success was its apparent ability to control access to continental trade and exchange. In the Yayoi period, for example, Chinese mirrors are mostly known from sites in Kyushu, but in the Kofun era they become much more common in the Kinai. A similar switch seems to occur with finds of iron, and this metal, originally obtained from southern Korea, was essential to Yamato's power (Shiraishi 1991, 50–53). An earlier interpretation of this evidence, based on the *Nihon Shoki* account of the "emperor" Jimmu, was that a Kyushu kingdom moved east to the Kinai at the start of the Kofun era and established a new government there (Watsuji 1920; cf. Egami 1964; Ledyard 1975; Kakubayashi 1987). The approach adopted here suggests a shift in hegemony between Kyushu and the Kinai is a better explanation than is military conquest, but if anything a Kinai subjugation of Kyushu is more likely than the other way around. Shin (1993a, 1993b) argues that the arrival of a new ruling elite in the Peninsular kingdom of Kaya in the late third century was linked to the establishment of the Yamato alliance. At around this time, bronze spearheads and imitation Chinese mirrors from north Kyushu are replaced by typically Kinai goods such as bronze cogwheel ornaments and stone arrowheads in Kaya sites (Shin 1993a, 1993b, 143–151). While Shin (1993b, 150) quite rightly stresses the importance of iron to Yamato, it is not clear how Yamato managed to obtain its dominant position vis à vis access to the Peninsular source of that raw material, although divisions and conflict between the various north Kyushu polities may have left them open to outside intervention.

Within the Japanese Islands, various core-periphery systems served to bolster Yamato's power. Many of these systems had complex and varied histories, which are well illustrated by the example of shell bracelets. Although shell bracelets are also known in the Jōmon (Hashiguchi 1994, 126–132), in the Yayoi period tropical shells from the Ryukyu Islands were used to make bracelets for chiefs in north Kyushu. The shells include *imogai (Conidae), gohōra (Tricornis),* and *suijigai (Harpago);* of these, *imogai* and *gohōra* are only found south of Amami Ōshima and the latter only at depths of fifteen meters or more on the open sea side of coral reefs (Pearson 1990, 915). Bracelets made from these shells are most common in north Kyushu where their role as prestige goods is clear from burial contexts at sites such as Tateiwa and Yoshinogari. The bracelets appear to have been processed in the Ryukyu Islands, and several probable production sites have been identified (Pearson 1990, 919). Although it is not clear what was obtained in exchange for the bracelets, the trade seems to have been associated with some degree of increased social complexity in the Ryukyus, at least on Tanegashima, which is marked by rich burials at the Hirota site (cf. Ikehata 1990a).

The shell trade between Okinawa and Kyushu reached its peak in the Middle Yayoi, but after that time shell bracelets began to be replaced by bronze and then jasper imitations (Fig. 7.2). Prestige goods, of course, derive their significance from the ability of local leaders to monopolize their supply (Chase-Dunn 1992, 316). If it was possible to copy the goods concerned or even to replace them with other objects, then their status—and thus the status of the chiefs who used them—was undermined. Local production of prestige goods enables a much more direct manipulation of the prestige economy. As Barnes (1986b, 90) puts it, "Since importation is essentially *substitutive* while local craft production and specialisation are *additive,* the structural elaboration of a polity would be advanced more by the latter than by the former." The local production of originally imported prestige goods is a distinctive feature of protohistoric Japan. Another example of a switch from importation to local production, besides the replacement of shell bracelets by bronze and jasper imitations, is provided by bronze mirrors. Well over 3,000 mirrors have been discovered at protohistoric sites in Japan (Tanaka Migaku 1991, 154). Mirrors seem to have played a particularly important role in the Islands, much more so than on the Korean Peninsula where mirrors are comparatively rare. So-called geometric incised mirrors from the Peninsula were the first to arrive in the Islands in the late Early Yayoi, followed by Han Chinese examples from the second half of the Middle Yayoi. From the beginning, the importance of these mirrors as prestige goods is made clear by their presence in high-status burial contexts. Local casting of bronze mirrors began in Kyushu in the Late Yayoi. As noted already, mirrors are rare in the Kinai in the Yayoi but become very common in the Kofun era. It seems probable that the Kinai core obtained a measure of control over the production of bronze mirrors from the third century, although exactly how much control remains an extremely controversial problem. The most controversy has revolved around triangular-rimmed beast-deity mirrors. These mirrors are found in Early Kofun tomb mounds from Kagoshima in the south to Fukushima in the north but are especially common in the Kinai. Many are sets cast from the same mould (Fig. 7.3). According to Kobayashi's (1961) analysis, 81 percent of the same-mould sets are represented in the Kinai region, 14.6 percent at one particular tomb—Tsubai Ōtsukayama in Kyoto Prefecture. If actual numbers rather than sets of mirrors are considered, the Kinki region has 49.7 percent (n=93) and Tsubai Ōtsukayama 11.2% (n=21) (calculated from Table 1 in Edwards' [1995] translation of Kobayashi [1961]).

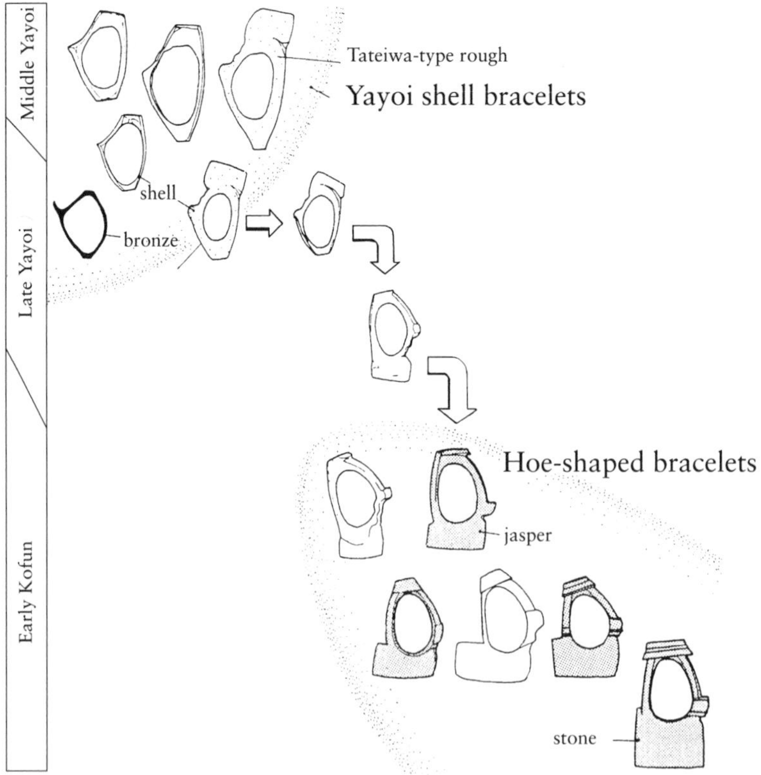

FIG. 7.2. The switch from Yayoi-period shell bracelets to jasper and stone imitations in the Kofun. Modified from Kinoshita (1994).

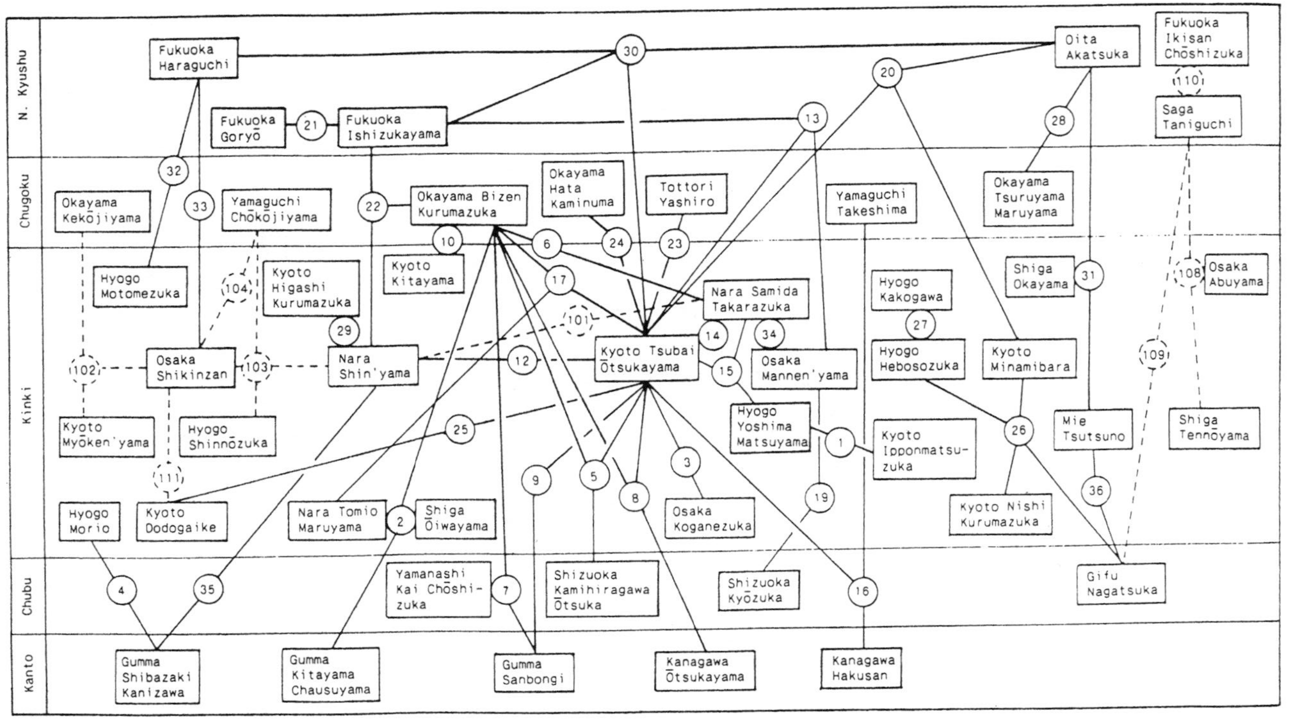

FIG. 7.3. Tombs linked directly or indirectly with Tsubai Ōtsukayama *kofun* through shared sets of duplicate mirrors. From Edwards (1995).

A number of interpretations of this evidence are possible. Kobayashi (1961) argues that the mirrors were distributed to regional chieftains in exchange for allegiance to Yamato. Central to the evaluation of this hypothesis is the question of where the triangular-rimmed mirrors were made. Until recently, it was assumed that they were Chinese imports and could be linked with the mirrors given Pimiko by the Wei emperor in 239. This type of mirror is not known on the mainland, however, and Wang (1981) proposed that they may have been made by south Chinese craftsmen from the state of Wu living in Japan. While debate continues over the place of production, the importance of the Kinai in the *distribution* of the mirrors seems clear.

The distribution of triangular-rimmed beast-deity mirrors was intimately related to the expansion of keyhole-shaped tombs. Standardized keyhole tombs spread from the Kinai at the beginning of the Kofun period (Tsude 1992; Hojo 1989; Hudson 1992a, 170–171). Although Barnes (1986b) has proposed that the spread of these tombs may simply represent a shared elite material culture, most Japanese archaeologists argue that similarities between the tombs suggest that the technology and the permission to build them was granted by Yamato in exchange for allegiance. Of course, the fact that the differences between the *kofun* of the core and periphery was only one of degree implies that Yamato would go to great lengths to obtain regional allegiance. If the tombs themselves were a type of prestige good, they were not limited to the central elites. The *kofun* tomb system typifies core/periphery relationships in the early part of the Kofun period in that it was based on a "discontinuous or chiefly hierarchy where most territories were locally controlled and relations between levels were of an allegiance nature, the higher level having access only to the representatives of the local areas but not to the individuals under the latter's jurisdiction" (Barnes 1987, 86). As the Kofun era wore on, however, the Yamato state was increasingly successful in establishing a continuous hierarchy with direct access to local producers. The establishment of the *be* system from the late fifth century was one of the most important means by which this was accomplished. The *be* were occupational groups that produced goods and foodstuffs for the court (Barnes 1987; Hirano 1983; Vargo 1979). In several cases *be* comprised immigrant specialists from the Peninsula, their distinct ethnicities and lack of local ties probably facilitating Yamato control.

Although the *be* and similar systems worked to increase the political and economic power of the Kinai core, as discussed by Barnes (1987) the Late Kofun period also saw a noticeable increase in regional economic production that served to strengthen the power of the peripheries. One example is provided by government pastures used to produce horses for transport and military uses. The Kanto was an important center for these official pastures, and Peninsular immigrants also appear to have played a significant role in the development of horse-breeding there (cf. Matsui 1991; Ōtsuka 1992). The long-term result of this intervention in the Kanto economy, however, was not a permanent periphery but rather the development of a new core—or perhaps a hegemonic shift within the core region—in the early medieval era. Horses were central to the power of this new Kanto core. As Farris (1992, 60) puts it, "It was no accident that twelfth-century warriors *(bushi),* such as the Shida, Chichibu, Mochizuki, Sara, and Kodama, had their origins in pastures established under the Taiho [Ritsuryō] system."

The Nara period (710–784) saw the realization of a bureaucratic state based on Chinese models. Under this Ritsuryō state, intricate tax and revenue systems successfully exploited surpluses from the provinces (see Naoki 1993; Torao 1993). Available evidence, which now includes a growing number of inscribed *mokkan* (wooden tablets) used as baggage labels for tax shipments, suggests that the influence of the Ritsuryō state was a pervasive one, and not just in the Kinai region. From *mokkan* excavated in the Nara capital, for example, we know that in just one year (735) Izu province supplied at least 250 kg of bonito as tax (Hudson 1994d). A traditional interpretation of the Ritsuryō economy has been that internal growth led to the transfer of power back from the court into the provinces. In contrast, Farris (1985) has argued that economic backwardness was more characteristic of the Ritsuryō system. The issues are complex, and Farris (1985, 144–145) himself notes that the two approaches may be complementary. Archaeological evidence suggests that in some cases technology shifts to the provinces did in fact trigger economic growth in protohistoric peripheries (Uno 1991), and more research is needed to elucidate core/periphery relations in Ritsuryō Japan.

ETHNIC GROUPS AND THE ANCIENT STATE

While only the briefest of summaries has been attempted here, a variety of core/periphery systems—political and ideological as well as economic—were thus present in ancient Japan. As it grew in power, the Yamato state began to define a system of ethnic relations whereby ethnic differences in the Inland Sea core region were played down to emphasize state unification, while ethnic differences with the non-Yamato periphery were stressed to provide further justification for Yamato expansion. The latter process in turn appears to have led to heightened ethnic solidarity in those regions that actively opposed incorporation by Yamato.

The most important aspect of Insular ethnicity as related in the Nara texts was between groups that actively opposed the growing power of Yamato and those who did not. The Chinese ideology of a central kingdom surrounded by barbarians in the four cardinal directions was adopted by the Japanese. While the etymology of the names of the various ethnic minorities that appear in the Nara texts is complex, terms such as 蝦夷 and 蝦狄 used to refer to the Emishi of eastern Honshu and Hokkaido reflect the Chinese concept of Eastern and Northern barbarians (東夷・北狄) (Lewin 1967, 306–307). Itō (1991, 69–70) argues that the inhabitants of the Ryukyu Islands may have been seen as *Nanban* (Southern barbarians). Another possibility is that the first character of the names of the main ethnic groups (Kumaso 熊襲、Hayato 隼人、and Emishi/Ebisu 蝦夷) were a symbolic representation of state control of the three realms of the earth (熊 *kuma* [bear]), the air (隼 *hayabusa* [peregrine falcon]) and the water (蝦 *ebi* [shrimp]) (Ōbayashi 1975, 22–24).[6]

Two of the main ethnic minorities mentioned in the Nara texts are the Kumaso (OJ *Kumaso*) and the Hayato (OJ *Paya-pitö*) of southern Kyushu, and many scholars see a basic continuity between the Kumaso and the Hayato, the former term being applied to the people who opposed the Yamato state and the latter used after their submission (Ōbayashi 1975, 28; Kamimura 1984, 14; Nakamura 1993a, 20–21). The exact relationship between the two groups is unknown, but as Nakamura (1993a, 21) notes, there is no unequivocal evidence that they were separate tribes. The *Kojiki* and the *Nihon Shoki* personify Yamato's defeat of the Kumaso as a fight between the princess Yamato-takeru-no-mikoto and the elder and younger Kumaso-takeru (Philippi 1968, 234–235; Aston 1972[1896], I: 200–201). Although both chronicles have earlier, possibly anachronistic references, Nakamura (1993b, 8) argues that the term "Hayato" was first used during the reign of the emperor Temmu (672–686). Some Hayato were taken to the Kinai and served as imperial guards, probably also from the time of Temmu.

We see in chapter 3 that the skeletal evidence suggests that Jōmon-type populations continued as late as the Kofun era in the more remote, mountainous parts of southern Kyushu. Whatever their biological identity, however, the little we know about the Kumaso and Hayato suggests that culturally these peoples cannot simply be seen as "leftovers" from the Jōmon or as the result of regional isolation. Neither can their social formations be fully explained by ecological factors. While much of southern Kyushu is mountainous, and Kagoshima is plagued by infertile volcanic soils, similar problems were experienced elsewhere in the Islands. The Kumaso are known from the *Kojiki* and the *Nihon Shoki* exclusively as a people who opposed the Yamato state. This is suggested archaeologically by the late spread of keyhole-shaped tombs into southern Kyushu and by their relative scarcity in Kagoshima and southern Kumamoto (Ikehata 1990b, 1992a).[7] Though the etymology of the term "Kumaso" is much debated, a common theory sees it as a combination of two place-names: Kuma county in Higo province and So county in Ōsumi province. If correct, this would make it likely that "Kumaso" was a name—and thus an identity—imposed from outside, rather than the ethnonym of a single ethnic group. There is thus a case for seeing Kumaso ethnicity as essentially a *reaction* to Yamato expansion, and the same conclusion can be made regarding the Hayato.

The forced removal of groups of Hayato to the Kinai was clearly an attempt to weaken their political power in southern Kyushu (Inoue 1978, 170). The Hayato's position as palace guards is an excellent example of what Enloe (1980, 23) calls the "Gurkha Syndrome." Many states have created special military units from ethnic groups, one of the most famous examples being the Nepalese Gurkhas of the British Army:

> By making military vocations an integral part of a group's sense of its own ethnicity, the central state élite hopes not only to make the military recruiter's task easier, but to wed ethnicity to state allegiance. The consequence for the group targeted to be a "martial race" is often an increased sense of ethnic cohesion bought at the price of growing vulnerability to state manipulation (Enloe 1980, 25).

Typically, such martial groups are found at the margins of a state, often in remote or mountainous areas; they have often originally waged war against the state. Militarily, they are seen as special units and socially as somewhat exotic, bounded tribes; usually they are stationed away from their homeland (Enloe 1980, 26–30). These points are all applicable to the Hayato. The *Nihon Shoki,* for example, relates that they "do not leave the enclosure of the Imperial Palace" (Aston 1972, I: 100), although later they were resident in at least eight provinces of the Kinai (Mori 1975, 165) and were even used in Kyushu on at least one occasion, as a reconnaissance team during the 740 revolt of Fujiwara no Hirotsugu (Farris 1992, 61). The martial behavior of the Hayato may have stemmed from long resistance to Yamato in their Kyushu homeland, a resistance that continued until their last revolt in 720–721. Although the sources do not permit a firm conclusion, it is also possible that Yamato attempted to exoticize the Kinai Hayato. We know that the Hayato had an important ritual function, performing doglike barks and howls at certain major palace ceremonies and funeral lamentations around the tomb of King Yūryaku (cf. Aston 1972, I: 101 and 375).[8] Based in part on the proposed presence of women in the howling *imaki* (newcomer) Hayato, Nakamura (1993a, 273–285) argues that the Kinai Hayato rituals may have had deep roots in southern Kyushu. At the same time, however, we cannot ignore the ritual significance of border lands and people within the Ritsuryō system. Various ritual activities, including divination, were conducted to counter the perceived impurity of areas beyond the Ritsuryō state (see Hashiguchi 1994, 143–144). Within this system, it seems unlikely that the major ritual role of the Kinai Hayato—a frontier people living in the ritually purest region around the capital—was not in part the result of state direction.

Although his exact role in the establishment of the Hayato palace guards is unknown, Temmu's ability in military matters has been widely commented upon. In particular, Temmu seems to have been responsible for the development of a category of *sakimori* (border guards) who were sent from their homeland in the eastern provinces (Kanto) to serve in north Kyushu (Farris 1992, 46 and 54–55). The *sakimori* can also be seen as "ethnic soldiers" of the type described by Enloe, and it would not have been strange for Temmu to have used the same principle for the Hayato guards.

I am not suggesting here that Kumaso and Hayato ethnicity was totally due to the influence of the Yamato state. Of course, since our only sources are the Yamato chronicles, we have no information on how these groups viewed their own ethnicity—or even if they did in fact see themselves as distinct ethnic categories. If the Kuna of the *Wei zhi* can be identified with the Kumaso or with a location in southern Kyushu, then that would imply a certain degree of ethnic cohesion as early as the third century AD. However, in my view, such an identification is unlikely precisely because there appears to be little or no evidence for such a degree of regional social complexity at that stage. The Kumaso and the Hayato cannot be seen as relict Jōmon cultures, but neither did the expansion of the Japanese core lead simply to the reproduction of central culture in southern Kyushu. Instead, new tribal or ethnic formations resulted from peripheral resistance to the attempted domination of the core. Yamato's role in the *demise* of these groups is, if anything, clearer than its role played in their formation. Whether the Kumaso were renamed as the Hayato or were simply defeated and assimilated, their fate was intimately tied to Yamato policies. Similarly, the Hayato were no longer differentiated as a separate ethnos after about 800, when they were allowed to become *ryōmin* (commoners) and to enter the *handen-sei* (Ritsuryō land-allotment system) rather than paying tribute as barbarians (Nagayama 1992; Nakamura 1993b, 16–24).

Several Japanese scholars, beginning with Torii (1918) and Nishimura (1922), have argued that the Hayato and (more rarely) the Kumaso were populations of Southeast Asian origin (cf. Ōbayashi 1975, 29–34). This theory may be seen as being in direct conflict with my own approach: if they really were distinct ethnic groups who had migrated from Southeast Asia, then that would seriously undermine my theory of Yamato intervention as a primary cause of ethnogenesis. The actual evidence for Southeast Asian links, however, is not very convincing. Proposed linguistic cognates include linking "Hayato" with *hayi*, (south, south wind) in Ryukyuan, Proto-Austronesian **paRi* or Proto-Oceanic **fai* (stingray; Southern Cross) (Sakiyama 1996, 350) and Proto-Malayo-Polynesian **pat'iγ* (seashore) (Miller 1967, 170). Various shared myth motifs with Southeast Asia and Oceania have been proposed, especially the lost fishhook story in the *Kojiki/Nihon Shoki* story of Hayato origins (Slawik 1955, 217–218; Schaumann 1980; Kakubayashi 1996). Other proposed cultural influences include the custom of lighting a fire near women in childbirth (cf. Kojima 1990, 146–147).

From these points of similarity, Kakubayashi (1996, 37) argues that the "Austronesian-language speaking Kumaso (or Hayato), who were racially different from the mainstream Yamato tribe" must have migrated directly to Japan from Southeast Asia. If the Kumaso and Hayato really were Austronesian-speaking populations, then we would have to think seriously about such a scenario. At present, however, we have no way of proving the linguistic identity of these peoples. The same problem holds for the biological status of the Kumaso/Hayato, since it is by no means clear to what extent they were "racially different" from the Yamato Japanese. Although some cultural influence from Southeast Asia may well have reached southern Kyushu in the Kofun period, there is no reason to see the Kumaso or the Hayato as a distinct ethnic group that had migrated from the former region. I have argued that it is difficult to see any evidence of population movements from Austronesian-speaking areas into the Japanese Islands in late prehistory (Hudson 1999). This does not, of course, constitute proof that such a migration never took place, but those who argue for a Southeast Asian link need to develop more explicit historical models than have been used so far.

The Emishi

Apart from the Kumaso and Hayato, the other main ethnic group distinguished by the Yamato state was the Emishi of northeast Honshu. Two competing theories have traditionally been used to explain the Emishi: (1) Emishi as Ainu, and (2) Emishi as non-Ainu or as Japanese (Kikuchi 1984, 349–398; Kudō 1989a, 143–145). Underpinning the debate over these theories has been a tendency to see the Emishi as a bounded, discrete ethnos. Thus, for example, the fact that horse riding was present among the Emishi but not among the Ainu is sometimes seen as evidence against the Emishi=Ainu theory. The approach taken here is a more dynamic one; it argues that, notwithstanding basic genetic and linguistic continuities between Jōmon, Emishi, and Ainu populations, the ethnicity of each of these groups needs to be seen in its own terms.

Like "Hayato" and "Kumaso," the etymology of the term "Emishi" (OJ *Emisi*) is enormously complex and cannot be discussed here in detail (see Kitakamae 1991; Kikuchi 1989). Whatever its origins, as used in the sources, "Emishi" was clearly a label applied by the Yamato court to the "barbarians" of the northeast rather than the ethnonym of a distinct ethnic group. The Emishi were not remnant hunter-gatherers continuing their millennia-long lifestyle unaffected by the agricultural Japanese society to the south. While the Epi-Jōmon people of Hokkaido did retain a foraging subsistence base, iron tools from Honshu were used together with stone artifacts. Despite regional and chronological variations, however, the Tohoku Emishi appear to have been basically agricultural. Wet rice cultivation was present in Aomori from the Early Yayoi but seems to have disappeared in the northern Tohoku from about the fourth century AD, and it reappears only in the seventh century (Kudō 1991, 39–40). The reason for the southward retreat of rice cultivation during the Kofun era is unknown, but a climatic explanation is possible. Rice farming may have been marginal so far north during the Yayoi, and perhaps only with the early medieval phase of climatic warming did agriculture finally become fully established in the north (Iwate 1985, 196). Some Japanese scholars now argue that despite minor differences, the subsistence basis of the Tohoku from the late Kofun was more or less the same as that of the rest of Japan (Iwate 1985, 196). Others, however, point to the documented importance of hunting and nonrice cultivation in the region in historic times: as Kudō (1990, 7) puts it, "Without doubt the ancient Emishi of the Tohoku practised rice cultivation. But it does not therefore follow that they depended only on rice cultivation or that they abandoned (traditional) Jōmon hunting, gathering and fishing activities." The available documentary evidence backs up this view of Emishi subsistence diversity (Imaizumi 1992, 165–167).

"Emishi" was primarily a political category whose meaning changed over time: by around the twelfth century, when the inhabitants of the Tohoku had been brought under the influence of Japanese culture, the same word—

now pronounced "Ezo" instead of "Emishi"—was used to refer to Hokkaido, the Kurils, and Sakhalin (cf. Kaiho 1987, 10–36). Yamato recognized several different types of Emishi. On a tribute mission to the Tang court in 659, Yamato envoys were asked by the Chinese emperor, "'How many tribes of Yemishi are there?' The Envoys answered respectfully, saying:—'There are three kinds. The most distant are called Tsugaru, the next Ara-Yemishi, and the nearest Nigi-Yemishi'" (Aston 1972, II: 261–262). Aston (1972, II: 261–262), referring to their degree of assimilation, notes that *ara* and *nigi* mean rough and soft, respectively. A few pages after this passage, the *Nihon Shoki* also mentions the Emishi of "Watari-shima," thought to mean the Oshima Peninsula area of Hokkaido (Aston 1972, II: 264). A further distinction is made between *san'i* (mountain Emishi) and *den'i* (field Emishi)—in other words between those who farmed and those who did not (Niino 1991, 78–90). The important point, however, is that none of these can really be described as *ethnic* categories. While the chronicles do contain evidence—some of it clearly exaggerated—for cultural differences between the Emishi and the Kinai Japanese, such differences were of less relevance to the Yamato court than was the degree of political allegiance of the Emishi. The Taga Fort stele (AD 762) mentions only two borders to the north of modern Sendai, that of the Emishi country and that of the Mohe of eastern Manchuria. This again implies that "Emishi" was a political label superimposed by Yamato with the intention of masking actual regional diversity.[9]

Militarily, the Emishi were more than a match for the Yamato armies (Farris 1992, 82–119; Friday 1994; Lewin 1967). Campaigns against the Emishi continued from the late seventh until the early ninth centuries, and a series of forts and palisades were constructed across the Tohoku region (Kudō 1989a). The Emishi were particularly known as skillful horse riders. Sources mention gifts of horses from the Emishi to the Yamato court from the eighth century onward. Debate continues over whether some of these horses may have arrived via a northern route from the Asian mainland or were rustled from the Yamato armies, but either way, the military skills of the Emishi represented a major departure from preceding cultural adaptations in the Tohoku. The private trading of horses by the Emishi was banned four times between the early eighth and the mid-ninth centuries (Imaizumi 1992, 166), implying that the trade was quite common at that time.

As with the Hayato, it is not my purpose here to suggest that Emishi ethnicity be totally attributed to the influence of the Yamato state. Biologically and probably linguistically, the Ainu were derived from Jōmon ancestors, and there can be little doubt that such proto-Ainu groups were included in the category of Emishi. However, the presence of any ethnic "reality" behind the Emishi is in a sense irrelevant, since the concept of Emishi was itself an artificial construct, imposed from outside. Thus, for example, when the Emishi were accepted into the Ritsuryō system, they were referred to as *fushū* or *ishū*, i.e., former captives or prisoners of war, implying either that ethnic differences between the Emishi and Japanese were not very great or else that such differences were not considered important in this context.

In terms of Hechter's model, it may appear as if the Tohoku region became a political periphery before it was an economic one. In reality, however, it was the relatively underdeveloped agricultural base of the Tohoku that prevented its developing a degree of social complexity equivalent to the Kinai and that was thus ultimately responsible for its political peripheralization. Actual economic exploitation of the Tohoku by the core region came later and only gradually with the incorporation of the Emishi into the Ritsuryō state. That economic exploitation was short-lived. With the decline of the Ritsuryō system in the Heian era, power shifted back to regional chieftains, such as the Northern Fujiwara who ruled northeast Honshu as an effectively independent kingdom in the twelfth century. The economic power of the Northern Fujiwara was due to horses, gold mined in the Tohoku, and trade with other regions of Japan and the Asian mainland.

The Song financial revolution led to a massive influx of Chinese coins into Japan (Elvin 1973, 149), stimulating an increase in nonofficial trade in the Islands (Yamamura 1990, 358–360). The extent of this trade has been demonstrated by excavations at Hiraizumi, the Northern Fujiwara capital, which has more Chinese porcelain than any other contemporary Japanese site except Kyoto and Hakata (Miura 1993, 79; see also Saitō 1993, 334–336; Hudson 1997). Hiraizumi became the political and economic metropolis of northern Japan and was one of the most advanced cultural centers outside Kyoto. Thus, in the twelfth century the Tohoku region transformed itself into a semiperiphery; although Northern Fujiwara power was destroyed at the establishment of the Kamakura shogunate, this economic role continued through the medieval era.

Ethnic Groups within the State

Based on the above examples, we can conclude that in ancient Japan more attention was given to determining which peoples were *not* Japanese than to deciding the defining elements of Japanese ethnicity. Murai (1985) has discussed this process with respect to the ritual pure/impure division of the medieval state. Howell (1994, 72–74) notes a similar phenomenon in the Tokugawa era, and such boundary behavior is an integral part of ethnic identity (Barth 1969). However, I believe Wilmsen (1995, 309) goes too far in arguing that ethnicity is always imposed from the outside and that consequently "dominant groups are never ethnicities [i.e., ethnoi]," because as well as shaping ethnicities at its frontiers, the state has also to work to create an acceptable level of ethnic uniformity within its borders. The most important ethnic group found within the borders of the Yamato state and mentioned in the early chronicles is the Tsuchigumo (OJ *Tutigumo*). Most references to these people locate them in Kyushu, but they were also found in the Kanto and the Kinai. As with the Hayato and Emishi, there have been centuries of debate over the identity of the Tsuchigumo (cf. Mizuno 1984, 309–314). The name itself—literally "earth spiders"—is thought to mean people who lived in pit dwellings *(murö)* but may have been used as a more general derogatory term. Tails and other physical peculiarities were often attributed to the Tsuchigumo (Aston 1972, I: 130; Philippi 1968, 174). Mizuno (1984) argues that the Kyushu Tsuchigumo were a fishing people of Southeast Asian origin, but there is no unequivocal evidence that they were ever a specific ethnic group, and a Southeast Asian origin is as unlikely as it is for the Kumaso and the Hayato. I prefer to see the Tsuchigumo as an example of the Yamato language of political allegiance, whereby people who opposed the state were assigned the status of barbarian.

Ōbayashi (1991, 17) argues that "the groups of people who in the Nara period were regarded by the inhabitants of the central parts of Japan as alien peoples possessed non-wet rice growing cultural traditions and still retained the legacy of Jōmon traditions in regard to their physical characteristics." While it would be premature to downplay these factors, I prefer to take a more dynamic approach to protohistoric ethnicity, placing greater emphasis on the ways in which the Yamato state "created" ethnic identities out of such material. The suggestion that political factors were more important to the construction of protohistoric identity than were physiognomy or language is supported by the apparent ease with which new Peninsular immigrants were assimilated into Japanese society. A large number of immigrants from China and from the Peninsular states of Koguryŏ, Paekche, Kaya, and Silla arrived in the Islands in the Kofun period. Although low-status economic migrants were probably also common, many were "official" migrants, craft specialists, and high-status refugees from the Peninsular wars, who were quickly assimilated into the social structure of the Yamato state. According to the *Shinsen Shōji Roku* (AD 814–815), of the 1,182 aristocratic clans in the Kinai, almost one-third were of immigrant origin (Hirano 1993, 99; Wada 1994, 234). The Yamato chronicles call these immigrants *kikajin* and other similar terms meaning "people who have undergone a (grateful) change of allegiance" (Carter 1983). The ethnocentricity inherent in such terms is itself important evidence for the active assimilatory processes conducted by the state. Although most *kikajin* lived in the Kinai, many were settled in the provinces, often with tax-free lands (Carter 1983). The following entry for the fifth year of King Tenchi (AD 666) is a typical example of the resettlement of these immigrants (although the large number of persons here is rather unusual): "Over 2000 [Paekche] people, men and women, were settled in the East country [Kanto]. Without distinction of black and white ["i.e. of priests and laymen" (Aston)], they were all maintained at government expense for three years beginning [in 663]" (Aston 1972, II: 285). Sansom (1973, 222) writes that,

> Aliens were freely allowed, if not encouraged, to become Japanese subjects, and aliens who in their own country had been slaves became free upon settling in Japan. This liberal treatment of foreigners seems very creditable to the Japanese of those days. It tends to show that racial feeling was not strong, and there is a good deal of other evidence to support the view that Korean and Chinese settlers of all classes were as a rule welcomed, and indeed invited, no doubt because most of them could contribute something to Japan in learning, or in arts and crafts.

In recent years, much archaeological evidence relating to these immigrants has come to light. In contrast to the Initial Yayoi in north Kyushu, the archaeological record suggests that these immigrants sometimes formed more or less distinct settlements separate from the ordinary Japanese (e.g. Hanada 1993; Kirihara 1989; Ōtsuka 1992). Watsuji Tetsurō argued that the assimilation of immigrants into ancient Japan was easy because of basic similarities between Insular and Peninsular populations (Hirano 1993, 8). Of course we know almost nothing about what today would be called race relations at the local, everyday level, but it seems to me that an equally good case can be made for assimilation by government decrees *despite* a fair degree of ethnic difference that can only have been reinforced by residential separation. Ancient Japan was probably marked by considerable ethnic heterogeneity. As Wada (1994, 234) notes, for example, the *Man'yōshū* phrase *kotosaheku*, meaning "the echo of words difficult to understand" and used as a pillow word for Kara (Kaya or Tang China) and Paekche, implies that the languages of those places were commonly used in the Islands in the eighth century.

Lewin (1962, 134–144) describes two important seventh-century measures in the assimilation of the immigrants. The first was the abolition of the *be* in 646 and the second the reformation of aristocratic ranks and surnames in 685. Ironically, in doing away with the *be* (cf. Aston 1972, II: 206), the Yamato court was attempting to limit local power and prestige—the very reason for the initial establishment of the *be* system. Although *kikajin* were barred from the highest levels, one important result of the reformation of the *kabane* rank system (cf. Aston 1972, II: 364–365; Miller 1974) was "the integration into the lower echelons of Japanese society of substantial numbers of immigrant communities who . . . hitherto had achieved only an ambivalent status in Yamato society" (Wheatley and See 1978, 215). Later surname regulations in the mid-eighth century also made it easier for immigrants to hide their origins and thus to gain access to higher official positions than would otherwise have been available to them (Kiley 1969). According to Lewin (1962, 144), the immigrants had become fully Japanized by the ninth century.

A further example of the importance placed on assimilation by the Yamato state is provided by Emishi resettlement policies. From the northern frontier, Emishi groups were settled right across the country in as many as forty-four out of sixty-four provinces excluding Mutsu and Dewa (Imaizumi 1992: 196). In contrast to, say, Indian resettlement in the American West, the Yamato seem to have made a real effort to make this policy work, although several uprisings on the part of these resettled Emishi are recorded. In one instance, a group of Emishi settled in mountainous Kai province was again transferred to Suruga to enable them to continue their presumably traditional occupation as fish and salt producers (Imaizumi 1992, 166).

CONCLUSIONS

Until recently, ethnicity as an aspect of state formation has received little attention from archaeologists. A small but growing literature now exists that attempts to investigate ethnogenesis in ancient states. Many of these works use the concept of uneven development or core/periphery exploitation and, while the application of such schemes to premodern societies offers many theoretical problems, the potential of this type of model for understanding ancient ethnicity is clear. This chapter has attempted to analyze the processes by which the Kinai region became the dominant core in the Japanese Islands and to determine the role of that core in the development of peripheral ethnicities in the ancient era. As the most explicit model linking ethnicity with core/periphery relations, Hechter's (1975) internal colonial scheme was used as the starting point for the analysis, although in adapting this model for ancient Japan, several major modifications were made. At the most basic level, premodern core and peripheral regions were determined by the differential spread of agriculture in the Yayoi and Kofun periods. Though its actual ability to do so was often constrained, the core attempted to institutionalize differences between core and periphery, at least as long as peripheral groups opposed the state. The expansion of state society also appears to have led to heightened ethnic awareness among groups such as the Emishi and the Kumaso, who conducted successful military opposition. Not all aspects of ancient ethnicity in the Islands can be explained through core/periphery relations, yet this chapter has demonstrated the central role of the Kinai core in that ethnic development, and it illuminates a promising area of future research. More work is, of course, needed, particularly on the documentary sources, to further support the model proposed here.

The late Heian warlord Fujiwara no Kiyohira (1056–1128), founder of the Northern Fujiwara clan, serves as an effective personification of the themes of this chapter and indeed of this book as a whole. The rise and fall of the Northern Fujiwara shows the value of a world-systems perspective with, for example, the effects of the East Asian medieval economic revolution forming an essential factor in the development of their power. The structural instability of premodern core/periphery systems is also well illustrated by the Northern Fujiwara, as is the role of outside contacts in reformulating core/periphery hierarchies. With respect to ethnicity, a subject-oriented approach would see the Northern Fujiwara as Emishi. Kiyohira spoke of himself as "distant chief of the eastern barbarians" and "highest chief of the (barbarian) captives [*fushū*]." In what was an extremely rare practice in Japan, the bodies of the four generations of Fujiwara leaders were intentionally mummified in the Chūsonji temple in Hiraizumi (Asahi Shimbun 1950; Sakurai and Ogata 1980; Hudson 1996). Anthropological investigations of these mummies suggest that the Northern Fujiwara family derived originally from Kyoto (Hanihara 1993), enabling us to pose the question of why Kiyohira should have identified himself with the eastern barbarians. I have argued in this chapter that the basic structure of Emishi ethnicity was largely a result of interaction with the Yamato and Ritsuryō states. Once created, however, this ethnicity was not static and could be reconstructed and interpreted by both sides. Perhaps such an interpretation was what Kiyohira was attempting when he identified himself with the Emishi, using their history of military opposition to empower his own opposition. As noted by Yiengpruksawan (1993, 51), Kiyohira's mausoleum, the Konjikidō of the Chūsonji temple, is a complex mix of Emishi and Japanese elements, a pastiche and a pun "fraught with inversion and twists of meaning." The Konjikidō is more than a Japanese temple acculturated to the barbarian northeast and more than a barbarian mausoleum acculturated to Japanese Buddhism. It is a locus of ethnic and cultural constructions that shows the complexity and fluidity we must strive to understand if we are to write the history of Japanese ethnogenesis.

8

The Unbroken Forest? Ainu Ethnogenesis and the East Asian World-System

Savage life, in its general features, is much the same all over the world. In studying the Ainu, we see mirrored the habits of our primitive fathers in the woods and swamps of northern Europe in the days when Caesar met a man who had been travelling for two months in the unbroken forest.

William Elliot Griffis, *The Japanese Nation in Evolution: Steps in the Progress of a Great People*

A view of the Ainu as a primitive, hunter-gathering people essentially unchanged since the Jōmon has long dominated the Western literature. Bicchieri's (1972, 448) comment that "Despite historical contact with the Japanese, the culture of the mainland had little impact upon the lives of the Ainu until Japanese colonization . . . in the late nineteenth century" is typical of many. Rouse writes that the medieval Japanese "developed both commercial and political relationships with the two outlying peoples [of Hokkaido and the Ryukyus], *but did not influence them strongly enough to affect their separate identities*" (Rouse 1986, 72, emphasis added). Even Hechter (1975, 48) ironically suggests that his model of ethnogenesis through interaction is not applicable to "such culturally enveloped groups as the Ainu of Japan. . . ." In complete contrast to such assertions, this chapter argues that the formation of an Ainu etic ethnos was due to contacts with surrounding peoples. Elsewhere in this book it has been argued that the Ainu are biologically and probably linguistically derived from Jōmon ancestors; what I am suggesting here is that the social and cultural aspects of Ainu ethnogenesis were in large part the result of interaction with the Japanese to the south and with various other peoples to the north.

On the face of it, the very idea that the Ainu were a "culturally enveloped" group is a surprising one, since European writers had noted evidence to the contrary since the sixteenth century. Though he never visited Hokkaido himself, Englishman John Saris, who was in Japan in 1613, obtained his information from "a Iapanner who had bene there twice." According to this source, the Ainu obtained rice, cotton, iron, and lead from the Japanese, who received payment in "silver and sand gould," although Saris notes that "In March they bring downe Salmon, and dried fish of sundrie sortes, and other wares, for which the Iaponners barter: which the Iaponners rather desire then silver" (Ōtsuka 1941, 245–246). Many other, more detailed descriptions of Ainu trade and interaction exist, written by both Europeans and Japanese. The trend, contrary to such accounts, to see the Ainu as culturally isolated appears to result from attempts to situate the Ainu in evolutionary schemes whereby they were held to typify a more primitive stage of humanity. Nineteenth and early twentieth century interpretations of the Ainu, both in Japan and the West, relied on the notion of "primitive society" and assumed the Ainu were representative of such society and were therefore doomed to extinction in the face of the natural destiny of the Japanese to colonize Hokkaido and use its natural riches (see Ölschleger 1993, 141–143). With a language and culture of obscure origins, and widely seen as a "tiny island of alleged Caucasian people within a great Mongoloid sea" (Harrison 1954, 278), the *isolation* of the Ainu was central to the so-called "Ainu problem" (Harrison 1954, 278; Tamburello 1969, 95; Buffetaut 1976). Constructed as timeless paragons of earlier humanity, the Ainu were, to quote Wilmsen (1989, 10) on the Kalahari San, "permitted antiquity while denied history."

The persistence in the West of such views is no doubt attributable to the lack of recent in-depth studies of Ainu origins. Japanese scholarship has been much more aware of the historical context of the Ainu, but medieval Hokkaido has become an important focus of research only in the last ten to fifteen years. In particular, it is only during this period that Ainu archaeology has become a viable subject. Since Ainu origins are to be found in an essentially prehistoric era, a real understanding of Ainu ethnogenesis was not possible without the evidence of the archaeological record. Despite these recent advances, however, Japanese theoretical approaches to interregional relations and ethnogenesis in the medieval north remain poorly developed. Using a world-systems approach, this chapter will argue that the Ainu did not develop in isolation and that the "primitive" aspects of early modern Ainu culture did not result simply from the failure of advanced, metropolitan features to diffuse north. The historical (under)development of Ainu society must be seen as a direct result of interactions within the East Asian world-system.

AINU CULTURE: ARCHAEOLOGY AND IDENTITY

We must begin by defining exactly what we mean by "the Ainu." Documentary evidence is little help in this respect. The word "Aino" (later "Ainu") apparently first appeared in writing in a 1591 Latin manuscript entitled *De Yezorum insula.* This document gives the native name of Hokkaido as "Ainomoxori," i.e., *Ainu mosir,* the "land of the Ainu" (Kreiner 1993, 15–16). "Aino/Ainu" did not come into common usage in European and Japanese sources until the early nineteenth century: of the works listed in Adami's (1991) European-language bibliography, for example, the word first appears in a title in a German encyclopedia article of 1819. Neither European nor Japanese sources can be said to have conceived of the Ainu as a distinct ethnic group before about the late eighteenth century.

If the Ainu are the biological descendants of the Jōmon people, then they must have lived in Hokkaido for a very long time, possibly since the Pleistocene, and ancestral forms of the Ainu language may also have been spoken there for an equivalent amount of time. The cultural pattern of Ainu society as known ethnographically, however, only seems to date to about the twelfth century AD. Archaeologically, therefore, the terms "Ainu period" and "Ainu culture" refer to the cultural stage following the Satsumon era and lasting until the Japanese colonization of Hokkaido (ca. 1200–1870). Prior to this, Hokkaido was home to rather different cultural adaptations: the Epi-Jōmon (ca. 100 BC–AD 700), Satsumon (ca. 700–1200), Okhotsk (ca. 500–1000) and Tobinitai (ca. 1000–1200). In terms of the theoretical concepts discussed in the introduction to this book, these cultures may all be assigned to the level of etic ethnos, but our understanding of these units varies considerably. Best known is the Ainu culture after about 1800, since ethnographic records enable us to flesh out the archaeology. Furthermore, because the defining elements of the Ainu archaeological culture can be related to historically known social processes, that culture does appear to represent an actual social entity. This does not, of course, necessarily mean that the members of that Ainu culture saw themselves as forming a single emic ethnos.

The Ainu Cultural Complex

Watanabe (1972b) argues that the kernel of Ainu culture can be found in what he calls the "bear ceremony cultural complex" (cf. Utagawa 1992a, 256–260). Utagawa (1992a, 260) notes that the fully developed bear ceremony *(iyomante)* only appears to date from the late eighteenth century and suggests that this marks the transition between a "Proto Ainu culture" beginning at the end of the Satsumon period and a "New Ainu culture" (Utagawa 1988, 320, 1992a, 260).[1] Utagawa (1980, 162–168, 1992a, 260–263) elaborates on Watanabe's research to propose his own "Ainu cultural complex" (Fig. 8.1). Utagawa's scheme is not intended to be exhaustive:

> If my . . . proposal for an Ainu cultural complex is accepted, the question arises as to whether all of its constituent elements are necessary before an "Ainu culture" can be recognized. . . . Let it suffice to note that Ainu culture is too complex a subject to permit any all-encompassing definitions or norms. Many aspects of Ainu culture not considered in my primarily archaeological approach are of great relative importance in Ainu culture, particularly those pertaining to the provinces of folklore and ethnography: nonmaterial elements of ritual and daily life such as songs *(yukar, upopo)* and dances (*rimse*); technological aspects such as toolmaking and construction methods; and elements relating to various rites of passage (Utagawa 1992a, 263–264).

An ever-evolving culture can never be *totally* described and defined. Although Utagawa's cultural complex is the closest we have come to a definition of Ainu culture in its archaeological sense, all elements of the scheme underwent changes over the course of the Ainu period. Taking those changes into account, this section briefly discusses the archaeology of several of the most important elements of the Ainu cultural complex: houses, pottery, *chasi* (forts), and the bear ceremony. Space prevents discussion of other major elements of the complex such as burial forms (cf. Hirakawa 1984) or the salmon gaff (cf. Deriha 1989).

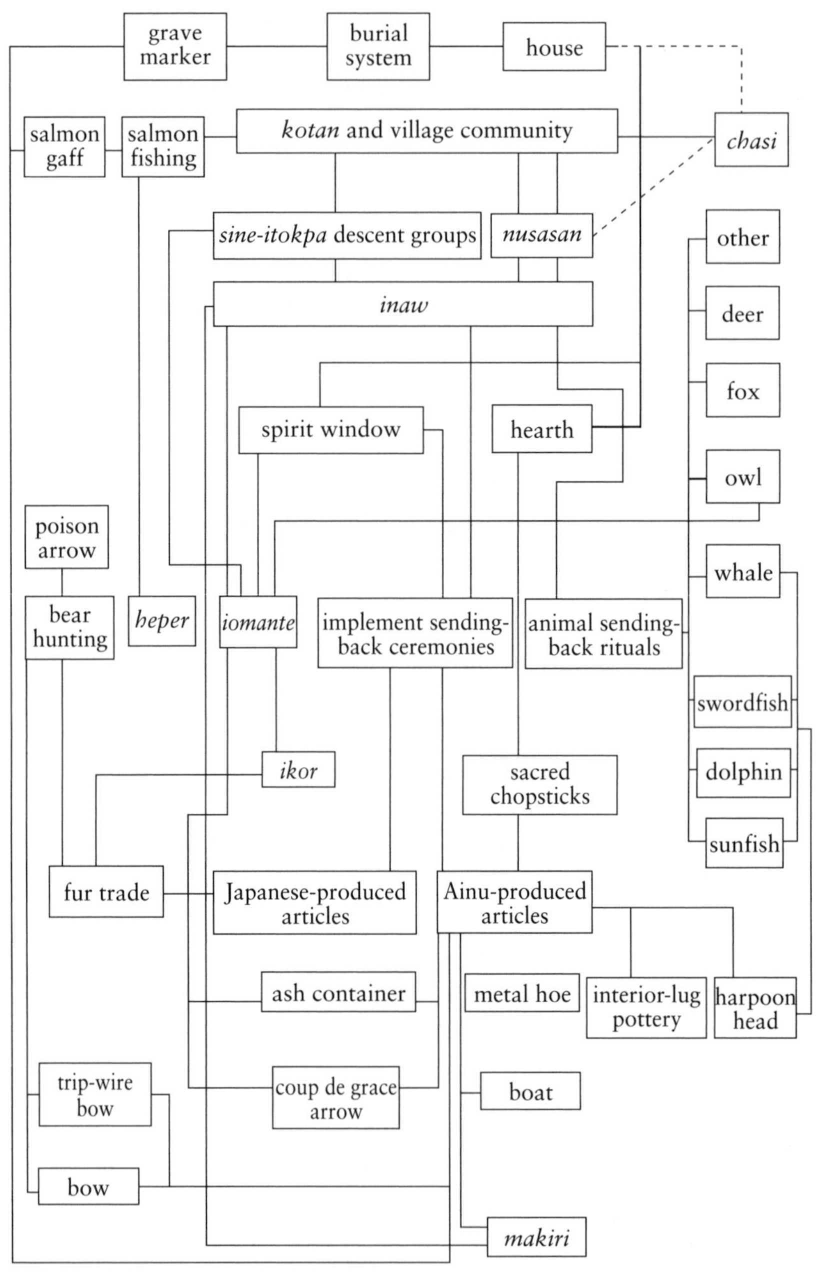

FIG. 8.1. Utagawa's Ainu cultural complex. From Utagawa (1992a).

Archaeologically, the formation of Ainu culture must be seen as a continuation of earlier processes of interaction with mainland Japan and with the regions to the north. The term "Epi-Jōmon" is used by archaeologists for the culture found in Hokkaido during the Yayoi and Kofun periods in Honshu. The absence of farming in Epi-Jōmon Hokkaido is the most important difference between that region and mainland Japan. Iron tools, however, appear to have been used in the Epi-Jōmon to some extent, although actual finds are still quite rare (Utagawa 1988, 184–185). Hokkaido was by no means isolated from the rest of Japan, and tropical shell bracelets from the Ryukyus have been found at the Epi-Jōmon Usu 10 site (Ōshima 1989). By the eighth century, Epi-Jōmon pottery gave way to Satsumon ceramics, which developed under the influence of Japanese Haji wares; *kamado* (built-in ovens) also diffused from the south, and some iron forging took place (Kikuchi 1984, 88–191; Yokoyama 1990; Yoshizaki 1986, 313–318). Most significantly, the cultivation of barley and millet is known from several Satsumon sites (Crawford and Yoshizaki 1987; Crawford and Takamiya 1990).

Ancient Hokkaido was not influenced only from the south. During the Satsumon period, the Okhotsk Sea coast of northeast Hokkaido was home to the Okhotsk culture, which appears to have originated in Sakhalin and to have spread south to Hokkaido and the Kuril Islands (Fujimoto 1986, 1990; Ohyi 1975). Skeletal remains support the conclusion that the Okhotsk culture people were an intrusive, non-Jōmon population (Ishida 1988, 1994; Kozintsev 1992). Broadly speaking, Ainu culture can be seen as a mixture of Satsumon and Okhotsk elements, although of the two, the Satsumon contribution was more significant.

Segawa (1989, 1994) argues that the basic cultural pattern of Ainu society was established in the Satsumon; he suggests that the term "Epi-Satsumon" could be applied to what is here called the Ainu period (Segawa 1994, 269). Segawa is no doubt correct that many aspects of Ainu culture were formed in the Satsumon period: intensive salmon fishing for exchange may have been one such element. This chapter, however, argues that there were *qualitative* differences between the Satsumon and the Ainu periods. During the Ainu period itself there were further quantitative changes with, for example, Japanese trade goods becoming much more visible in Ainu sites after the sixteenth century (Table 8.1). The transition between the Satsumon and the Formative Ainu periods can be defined by a move from pit buildings to surface dwellings and by the disappearance of locally produced ceramics (Ishizuki 1979; Takasugi 1982). The move to surface dwellings began in

TABLE 8.1

JAPANESE TRADE GOODS FROM MAJOR AINU-PERIOD SITES IN HOKKAIDO

SITE	SWORDS and KNIVES	PORCELAIN and CHINA	IRON POTS	COINS	LACQUERED VESSELS	OTHER METAL	PIPES	DATE
Setanai Chasi	53	2682	33	22	92	144	44	15–20C
Osatsuto 1	1	0	1	0	0	1	1	Early Ainu
Notoro misaki	6	0	0	0	3	3	0	ca. 1600
Iruekashi	31	5	63	0	?	121	19	16–17C
Umegawa 3	6	0	1	0	5	6	0	16–17C
Yuoi Chasi	10	1	5	5	1	14	1	Pre Ta-b
Poromoi Chasi	13	1	2	1	1	25	1	Pre Ta-b
Nibutani	57	+	18	9	16	85	1	Pre Ta-b
Morikawa B	0	0	0	0	0	0	1	pre-1640
Bibi 8	2	11	7	1	13	16	1	Pre Ta-b
Bibi 8	0	1	0	1	5	10	1	Between Ta-a & Ta-b
Bibi 7	1	0	0	0	0	0	1	Between Ta-a & Ta-b
Osatsu 2	2	0	0	0	0	3	0	Pre Ta-a
Usakumai	6	0	0	2	0	2	0	Pre Ta-a
North Kamuyekashi Chasi	1	0	0	0	0	1	0	Early 17C
Tapkop	4	0	4	5	0	6	1	17–19C
Suehiro	51	11+	10	9	25	57	1	17–18C?
Nakajima matsu 7	2	0	0	0	0	2	1	Late 17C?
Satsukari	2	0	0	0	0	1	0	Early Tokugawa
Charanke Chasi	1	0	0	0	0	3	2	Tokugawa
Tennaisan	2	4	1	0	0	4	1	Tokugawa
Toya 2 Chasi	21	1	5	0	0	60	4	Tokugawa
Horikabu	6	0	2	4	0	21	1	Tokugawa
Yukanboshi E3-B	5	0	0	0	0	0	0	Tokugawa
Opau Shinai 1	3	0	0	0	7	21	1	Tokugawa

SITE	SWORDS and KNIVES	PORCELAIN and CHINA	IRON POTS	COINS	LACQUERED VESSELS	OTHER METAL	PIPES	DATE
Oshoro Shrine	1	13+	1	0	0	8	4	18–19C
Yasawa	8	0	6	6	+	40	3	Ainu
Yusu Oya-kotsu	10	0	5	3	+	36	0	Ainu
Uebetsugawa	2	0	0	0	0	0	0	Ainu
Usakumai group	12	0	0	1	5	28	2	Ainu
Ponma	0	0	2	5	0	11	0	Ainu
Furetoi	9	4	0	1	0	11	2	Early 19C
Benten	5+	2000+	90+	71	+	12500+	10+	19C
Uchizono	0	13	6	0	0	3+	0	Meiji
Hamabekkai	3	0	0	0	0	2	0	Meiji

Sites known to be mainly occupied by Japanese colonists were omitted. "Swords and knives" includes all blades, though some may have been recast by the Ainu using imported iron. All objects include fragments, and the figures thus represent maximum numbers of individual items. Ta-a and Ta-b are volcanic ash deposits dating from 1739 and 1667, respectively.

the late Satsumon on the Oshima Peninsula but took longer to spread into eastern Hokkaido (Yokoyama 1990, 50–51). The new surface dwellings were very similar to *chise* (traditional Ainu houses). One of the most important aspects of those houses was the replacement of built-in ovens by a central open hearth. Satsumon ovens were usually built against the eastern wall of the dwelling instead of the western side, which was the norm on Honshu. This difference can probably be linked with later Ainu ritual beliefs about fire (Utagawa 1988, 313), but such behavior seems to have become more pronounced in the Formative Ainu period. The fire god *ape-kamuy* was one of the most important in the Ainu pantheon (Utagawa 1992a, 260–261; Ohnuki-Tierney 1974a, 89). A whole series of ritual activities were associated with the hearth, and while determining cause and effect is difficult, the introduction of Japanese-made iron pots at the end of the Satsumon period and the subsequent disappearance of locally produced ceramics appear closely linked to this fire complex. The iron pots were designed to be suspended over open fires, replacing the large ceramic pots that were placed in ovens (Fig. 8.2). Although iron pots from the Satsumon era have not yet been excavated in Hokkaido, their spread into north Tohoku in the twelfth to the thirteenth centuries, and the presence of late Satsumon pottery vessels with interior lugs that seem to be copies of iron pots, suggest they also spread into Hokkaido at this time (Utagawa 1988, 321). Two sites in Aomori Prefecture have produced iron pots in association with Satsumon pottery; one of these sites also produced interior-lug pottery (Utagawa 1992b, 139). By 1984, more than 150 iron pots (or fragments thereof) had come from over 100 pre-Meiji sites in Hokkaido (Koshida 1984). The wide availability of these vessels is further supported by the disappearance of interior-lug pottery in Hokkaido in the Formative Ainu phase. In the Kuril Islands and southern Kamchatka and on Sakhalin, however, interior-lug pottery continued to be made as late as the eighteenth and early nineteenth centuries, respectively (Fukuda and Hendei 1974; see also Chard 1956, 288–289).

During the Formative Ainu phase, therefore, the long tradition of pottery making in Hokkaido came to an end as a result of Japanese imports of iron, porcelain, and lacquered vessels. Local craft specialization was undercut by the import of these finished goods. As well as their obvious utilitarian function, lacquered vessels also served—together with swords and other imported articles—as *ikor* (treasures). As prestige goods or symbols of wealth, *ikor* became essential ritual paraphernalia for the bear ceremony (Watanabe 1972b, 52; Utagawa 1992a, 258; Hudson *in press* b). The Ainu obtained *ikor* through trade in furs, feathers, and marine products with the Japanese. Growing dependence on this trade appears to have stimulated an increasingly ritualized bear ceremony complex based around the *ikor*. Bear ceremonialism of various sorts is widely distributed in Northeast Asia (Hallowell 1926). In Japan, sending-back rituals, whereby the spirits of animals, plants, and implements were gratefully returned to the heavens, appear to date to the Jōmon period (Utagawa 1989, 4–5). However, the specific roots of the Classic-phase *iyomante* are still debated. Some influence from the bone mounds of the Okhotsk culture seems hard to deny (cf. Watanabe 1974), though Satō (1993) has recently argued for a greater Satsumon component than has hitherto been accepted. Increasing Ainu acquisition of *ikor* would have led to various social tensions. Ohnuki-Tierney (1976, 321) argues that while the bear ceremony, and the *ikor* used therein, of the Sakhalin Ainu "functioned to reduce both the accumulation of property and the difference between the wealthy and the poor, the bear ceremony among the Hokkaido Ainu encouraged the accumulation of treasures for the occasion." In Hokkaido in recent

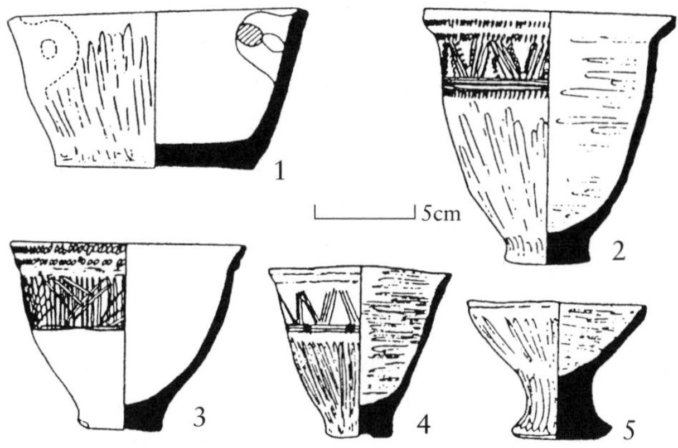

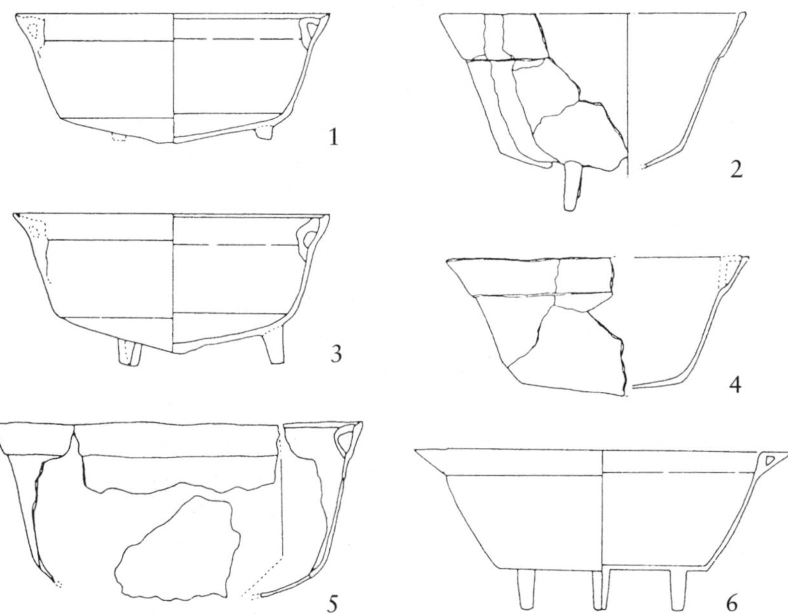

FIG. 8.2. *Top:* Interior-lug (1) and Satsumon pottery (2–5). *Bottom:* Interior-lug iron pots from Ainu sites in Hokkaido (approx. one-fifth actual size). Top: from Utagawa (1992a). Bottom: from Koshida (1984).

times, the *ikor* were in practice retained as the property of wealthy Ainu households (Uchida Yūichi, personal communication), though they were ideologically incorporated into the continual ceremonial return to the gods. The role of *ikor* in Ainu society clearly merits further study, but there is little doubt that they were crucial in the elaboration of that most distinctive Ainu ritual, the Classic-phase *iyomante* (Fig. 8.3).

Another important element of the Ainu cultural complex that has diverse roots is the *chasi* (hilltop fortifications that were also used for ceremonial and other purposes) (Utagawa 1992c). Over 520 *chasi* have been identified in Hokkaido, and they are also known from southern Sakhalin and the Kurils. In Hokkaido, *chasi* are thought to date from the sixteenth to the eighteenth centuries (Utagawa 1992b, 156–157). Several theories exist as to their origin, but no consensus has been reached. *Chasi*-like structures, such as the Russian *gorodische,* are relatively common on the Northeast Asian mainland (Egami 1949; Tamburello 1969, 106). *Chasi* are also known on the Kamchatka Peninsula, although Suzuki (1965) regards these as an independent development. A late Okhotsk period *chasi* has recently been excavated at Belokamennaya in southern Sakhalin (Hirakawa 1994). Of course, since *chasi* are basically only ditched, defensive features, they may simply have been reinvented by the Ainu and may not be directly derived from any other region.

While many aspects of Ainu *chasi* remain enigmatic, it is widely accepted that their primary function was defensive in the face of growing Japanese encroachment in Hokkaido. Vries describes *chasi* he saw in eastern Hokkaido in 1643 in the following terms:

> These forts were made as follows: on the mountain on which they were placed was a small road steep to climb, and round on the four sides palisades were placed of the height . . . of 1½ man's length; within this stood two or three houses. There were large fir doors in the palisades with strong clamps; when they were closed, two stout bars were passed through the clamps and thus fastened to them. At two corners of these . . . palisades, a high scaffolding is made of fir planks, for a lookout (Cited in Bickmore 1868b, 368).

In 1669, soon after Vries' voyage, the Shakushain war broke out between the Ainu and the Japanese (cf. Alber 1977, 41–112). The Shibechari *chasi* in Shizunai is mentioned in several contemporary Japanese sources relating to this conflict. Part of what is thought to be this actual *chasi* has been excavated and dated to the same time period as that in which the Shakushain war took place, linking the two unequivocally (see Utagawa 1992b, 157–159). As discussed later in this chapter, warfare probably played a significant role in the development of Ainu identity vis à vis the Japanese, and for this reason *chasi* were a significant component of the Ainu cultural complex.

FIG. 8.3. Hokkaido Ainu bear ceremony *(iyomante)* in the late Tokugawa period. Painting by Hirasawa Byōzan. Courtesy of Hakodate Municipal Library.

The Ainu and the East Asian World-System

In the previous chapter it was argued that the introduction of agriculture into the Japanese Islands and the social complexity thus engendered led to the formation of a political and economic core in the Kinai region. This core became powerful enough to institutionalize ethnic identities in peripheral regions of the Islands in a process broadly comparable to Hechter's (1975) model of ethnogenesis. The premodern dominance of the Kinai was tempered by structural factors that permitted certain peripheral regions to achieve considerable power, one such region being the northern Tohoku under the twelfth-century Northern Fujiwara. The relative power of both core and periphery was further affected by relations within the larger East Asian world-system. All these factors are important to an understanding of Ainu ethnogenesis. The Kinai core remained the ultimate center of the Japanese system, but the northern Tohoku under various chieftains continued to play a crucial role. Interaction within the wider East Asian world-system was equally significant; in fact, Hokkaido may be seen as a periphery of both Japan *and* the states of north China/Manchuria, although it was far more dependent on the former than on the latter. The first part of this chapter has shown that the formation of Ainu culture in Hokkaido was intimately connected with the spread of Japanese goods into that island. The background to the growth in Honshu-Hokkaido trade will be discussed in this section.

The expansion of commerce in medieval Japan resulted from numerous complex causes (Yamamura 1990). A massive influx of coins from Song China led to widespread monetization of the Japanese economy, particularly in cities. This further stimulated markets and specialist workshops, which were already enjoying increased popularity thanks to a rise in agricultural production. Urban development on a scale not previously seen in the Islands resulted from the general upswing in economic conditions as well as the decline of official towns and ports such as Dazaifu following political decentralization. The medieval era saw the rise of the Japan Sea as a major shipping and trading zone, a role it continued to play in the Tokugawa era (see Flershem 1964, 1966). In modern Japan, the Pacific coast has taken economic precedence over the Japan Sea, but in ancient and medieval times the opposite was true. The Japan Sea coast was generally safer for ships and closer to the continent, and it conveniently linked the Kyoto capital region with both the Inland Sea and the north.

The important role played in the Hokkaido trade by the dominant clans of northern Tohoku has long been recognized (e.g. Harrison 1954, 280), but recent archaeological research has enabled us to discuss the economies of these clans with more confidence. I shall argue here that uneven development between Hokkaido and the northern Tohoku had the most direct influence on Ainu ethnogenesis. In other words, while within the Japanese Islands the Tohoku was a political and ideological periphery of the Kinai, the economic power obtained by certain medieval clans in the northern Tohoku means that the region took on a semiperipheral status with respect to Hokkaido. Schortman and Urban (1994) distinguish what Whalen terms "attached" and "autonomous" peripheries:

> Attached peripheries follow the classic model, being closely bound to the core by a web of ideological, economic, and political ties. These areas suffer various forms of political and economic domination by the core polity, resulting in decentralization and underdevelopment of their own economic and political systems. In contrast, autonomous peripheries interact with cores in looser, less comprehensive ways without suffering either economic and political exploitation or diminished development (Whalen 1994, 421).

In economic terms, in the early medieval era northern Tohoku can be seen as an autonomous periphery of the Kinai and Hokkaido and as an attached periphery of north Tohoku. This relationship altered somewhat in the Tokugawa period when the shogunate, now based in Edo, gained more power over the northern clans.

The most powerful clans in northern Tohoku in the early medieval era were the Northern Fujiwara and the Andō. Elsewhere I have argued that the rise of the Northern Fujiwara was the primary catalyst behind the Satsumon-Ainu transition (Hudson in press c). The Northern Fujiwara were the first to develop significant economic wealth based on extensive trade both with the north (Hokkaido and beyond) and the south (Japan) (Saitō 1992, 32). This trade followed the breakdown of the tribute-based Ritsuryō system and the development of more regular economic relations. The possibility that the Northern Fujiwara may have obtained horses, which were crucial to their economic power, directly from northeast Asia is mentioned in chapter 7. Tax collection from the northern Tohoku estates of Kyoto-based noble Fujiwara no Yorinaga was controlled by the second-generation Northern Fujiwara chieftain Motohira (1105?–1157). Tax from these estates included eagle feathers and seal furs that must have been obtained from Hokkaido or regions to the north, testifying to Northern Fujiwara involvement in trade with Ezo

(Ōishi 1993, 127–129). Japanese iron pots may have moved north into Ezo in return for such goods. Interior-lug iron pots were used in eastern Honshu, especially in the north Tohoku, whereas tripod and flanged pots were used in western Japan (Isogawa 1992). Kikuchi (1984, 208–209, 1992) has argued that it was interior-lug iron pots from twelfth-century northern Tohoku that moved north to Satsumon Hokkaido. One such vessel has been excavated from Hiraizumi, and it seems likely that the spread of iron pots may be linked with the Northern Fujiwara's attempts to increase trade with the north.

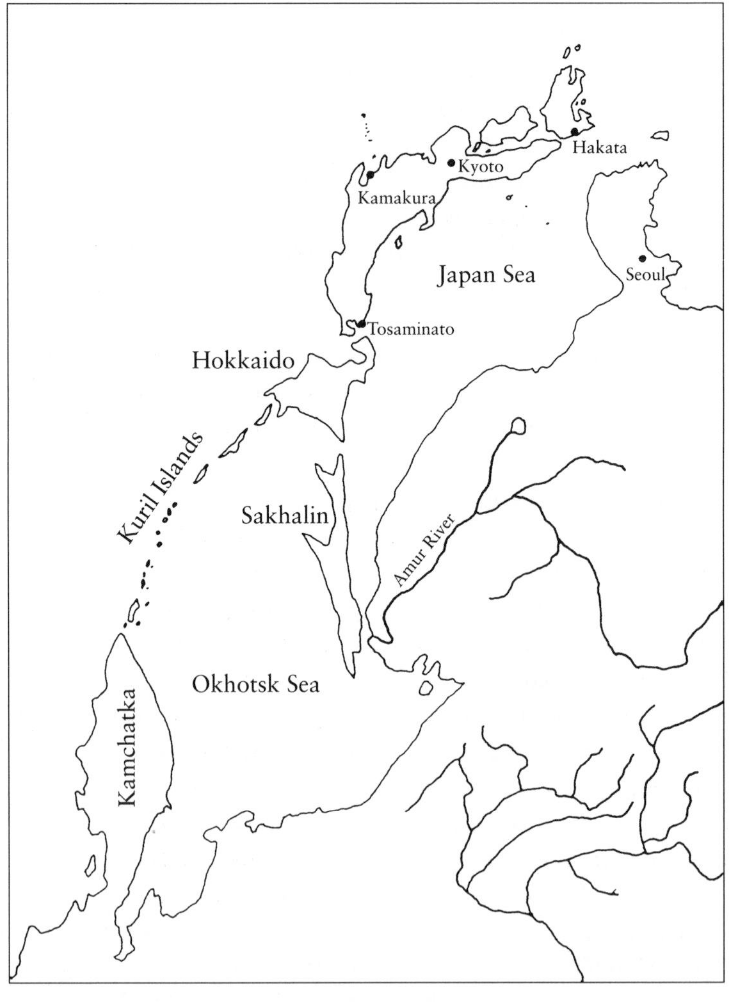

FIG. 8.4. Ezo seen from Northeast Asia.

The trading pattern with the north begun by the Northern Fujiwara was continued from the thirteenth century by the Andō. As a result of the scarcity of relevant historical records, the Andō remain rather elusive, but they are known to have been a powerful, semi-independent clan centered in Aomori (Ōishi 1990; Kaiho 1987, 128–145; Alber 1977, 13–19). The Andō appear to have been divided into several branches, including one based in southern Hokkaido after 1442, but during the thirteenth to fifteenth centuries they can be considered to have been an autonomous periphery region based on the port of Tosaminato in northwest Aomori. As a central link in the Japan Sea coastal trade, Tosaminato connected Hokkaido, Sakhalin, and the north with the markets of the Kinai and the Inland Sea. The Andō's political connections with the Kinai testify to their reliance on the Japan Sea economy (Kaiho 1989, 198), and there is also no doubt that their trading activities extended to Hokkaido. In 1423, for example, tribute sent by the Andō to Ashikaga Yoshikazu included 5,000 bird feathers, 30 sea otter furs, and 500 bundles of *konbu* sea tangle (*Laminariaceae*)—all items thought to have originated in Hokkaido or regions to the north (Kaiho 1987, 138). A probable direct link between Tosaminato and the Ainu is provided by a seventeenth-century lacquered plate from the Shibechari *chasi* in Shizunai, which bears the inscription 十三—almost certainly the first two characters of Tosaminato 十三湊 (Utagawa 1992b, 159). Documentary evidence relating to Tosaminato is sparse, but archaeological excavations have shown that the florescence of Tosaminato occurred from the thirteenth to fourteenth centuries under the Andō clan (Senda 1994). Clues to the wealth of the Andō include the fact that more imported than domestic porcelain was excavated at the late fourteenth to late fifteenth century Shirihachi-date site in Aomori; the only other site in eastern Japan in which the same phenomenon has occurred is Kamakura itself (Ōishi 1990, 329). The pivotal role of Tosaminato and the Japan Sea trade in socioeconomic developments within Hokkaido is confirmed by the distribution of archaeological finds of medieval trade ceramics. As can be seen from Fig. 8.5, there is a clear difference between the distribution of these ceramics along the Pacific and the Japan Sea coasts of northern Japan. While all regions reach a peak between the fifteenth and sixteenth centuries, the number of sites among the Pacific prefectures of Ibaragi, Chiba, and Miyagi increase considerably in the thirteenth century, whereas along the Japan Sea coast the increase is more gradual until the fifteenth century. In terms of both chronology and of comparative quantity of ceramics, Hokkaido conforms with the Japan Sea rather than with the Pacific pattern.

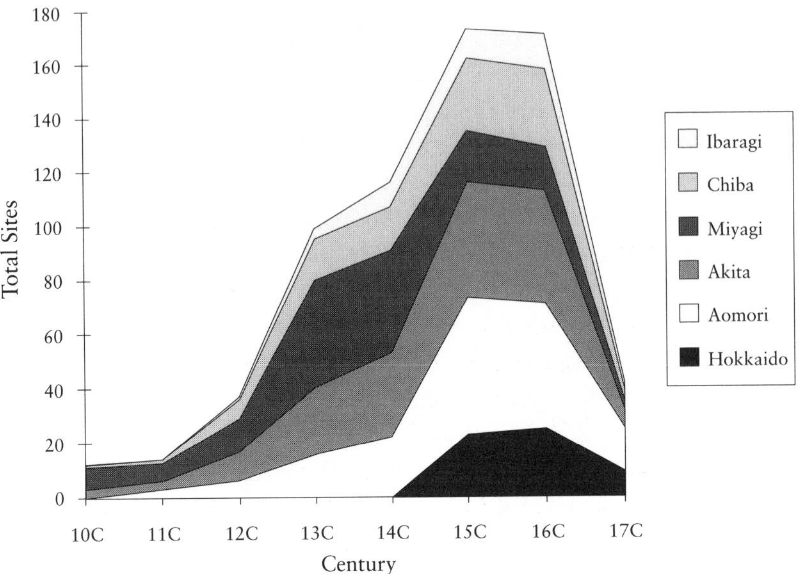

FIG. 8.5. Area graph of sites with excavated trade ceramics from selected prefectures on the Pacific and Japan Sea sides of Honshu, tenth–seventeeenth centuries. The vertical axis gives the *total* number of sites; the width of each band denotes the number of sites from that prefecture. Thus, for example, in the fifteenth century there are a total of 173 sites of which Hokkaido has 23, Aomori 50, Akita 43, Miyagi 19, Chiba 27, and Ibaragi 11. The relative quantity of ceramics from each site is not included as a variable. The category "trade ceramics" comprises Chinese, Korean, and nonlocal Japanese wares. Graph compiled from data in *Nihon Shutsudo no Bōeki Tōji, Higashi Nihon 1,* National Museum of Japanese History, Sakura 1994. (Sites in Sakhalin and the Kurils listed in the Hokkaido chapter of this catalogue were not used for the graph).

This may be an appropriate point at which to summarize the discussion so far. The archaeological changes that mark the end of the second half of the first milleneum AD appear to be socially significant, since the new culture that was formed as a result is closer to Ainu culture as known ethnohistorically than to the preceding Satsumon culture. Archaeologically, the Satsumon-Ainu transition was primarily the result of influences from Japan. The best understood of these influences is the replacement of locally made pottery by iron, lacquered, and porcelain vessels obtained through trade with the Japanese. Historical documentation on trade between Hokkaido and Honshu at this stage is sparse, but the emergence of powerful peripheral kingdoms such as the Northern Fujiwara and the Andō was almost certainly linked to their exploitation of the north. As well as furs, the Japanese were keen to obtain eagle feathers for arrows, and *konbu,* salmon, and other marine products. Trade down the Japan Sea to the Kinai markets further stimulated economic exploitation of the north. Finds of salmon and cod bones in late medieval deposits at Kusado Sengen (Hiroshima Prefecture) on the Inland Sea show that goods obtained in the Japan Sea trade were transported through the Kinai to other areas of western Japan (Matsui 1994).

We have seen that culturally the Satsumon-Ainu transition appears to have been a major turning point, but we can only speculate as to how that transition affected perceptions of Ainu ethnic identity on the parts of both the Japanese and of the Ainu themselves. While the approach used here may seem to place too much emphasis on outside economic factors, it must not be forgotten that ethnicity is also a subjective phenomenon that can be manipulated for individual advantage. The Andō are a case in point. I have suggested that the Andō clan was largely responsible for the spread of Japanese (material) culture into Hokkaido in the thirteenth and fourteenth centuries, yet its ethnic status is ambiguous. The Andō were possibly descended from the Abe clan and of Emishi extraction (Ōishi 1990, 320–326), but, as discussed in chapter 7, the meaning of the term "Emishi" is unclear, particularly in contexts such as this. Howell (1994, 78) follows Kaiho (1987, 124–145) in seeing the Andō titles of *Ezo no kanrei* (governor of Ezo) and *Hinomoto no shōgun* (Shogun of Hinomoto) as self-appointed rather than official: "[The Andō] assumed titles that placed them within the central institutional hierarchy or outside it as political or economic conditions warranted" (Howell 1994, 78). The term "Hinomoto" is particularly problematical. Based on a 1436 decree to Andō Yasusue from the emperor Go-Hanazono, which refers to him as "Northern Tosaminato Hinomoto (no) shōgun Abe [*sic*] Yasusue" (see Kaiho 1987, 138–139), the fact that this term was linked to the Andō is clear. "Hinomoto" was also used, however, as a general term for northern Tohoku and eastern Hokkaido. The *Suwa Daimyōjin E-kotoba* (Suwa Shrine Scroll) of 1356 mentions three types of Ezo: Karako, Watari-tō, and Hinomoto. Of these, Kaiho believes that Hinomoto refers to eastern Hokkaido; the southern Oshima Peninsula, partly ruled by the Andō, was also home to the Watari-tō ("crossing party")—Japanese who migrated to Hokkaido (Kaiho 1987, 154–172). "Hinomoto" therefore seems to have been a somewhat vague term for various regions of northern Japan. Though it may have originated in the Japanese court, like the term "Emishi," it was used by groups such as the Andō who wished to stress their Otherness to Japan (though ironically, of course, *Hinomoto* 日（之）本 was usually written with the same characters as was *Nihon*, sometimes with a possessive conjunction in the middle).

From the fifteenth century, Japanese settlement of the Oshima Peninsula became more intensive with the establishment of forts known as *tate* (Alber 1977, 19–21; Edmonds 1985, 46–49). The case of the Andō suggests that a strict Japanese/Ainu ethnic dichotomy is too simplistic here, yet it is likely that the Watari-tō included a large proportion of immigrants from western Japan (Kaiho 1987, 172). The growing influence of the Japanese also led to military conflicts that almost certainly increased ethnic differentiation on both sides. Conflict began in 1457 with the Koshamain War and continued intermittently until the Kunashir-Menash revolt of 1789 (Alber 1977; Kaiho 1989; Hanazaki 1996). Just as military campaigns against Ritsuryō armies had probably stimulated ethnic self-awareness among the Emishi and the Hayato, revolts by the medieval Ainu appear to have further distilled their ethnic identity: "according to Emori Susumu [1982, 157–159], military conflict with the Japanese encouraged the Ainu to close cultural and linguistic ranks, which resulted in greater uniformity within a culture that was, after all, an amalgam of Satsumon and Okhotsk elements spread thinly over a broad geographical area. In other words, the threat posed by the intrusion of the Japanese made the Ainu more coherent as an ethnic group than they would have been otherwise" (Howell 1994, 77; see also Utagawa 1992b, 149; Kikuchi 1994, 60). The importance of *chasi* in Ainu society between the sixteenth and eighteenth centuries can also be related to increased military conflicts with the Japanese. As discussed in more detail in the following section, the Ainu appear to have come into conflict with the Okhotsk people as well as with the Japanese. Chiri Mashiho suggests that Ainu *yukar* (oral epics) of battles between the *yuankur* (people of the land) and the *repunkur* (people of the sea) may be a symbolic representation of such a conflict (see Philippi 1979, 40–44).

The formation of ethnic identities is clearly linked to ideological factors. As noted in the previous chapter, Schortman and Urban (1994) have argued that ideology should form a part of core/periphery analysis. There is evidence that in medieval Japan the Ainu were perceived in terms of the state ideology of inside purity/outside impurity. In several medieval texts and illustrations, including the *Shōtoku Taishi E-den*, an explicit link is made between the people of Ezo and various demons and outcastes, both of whom were conceived of as inhabiting the polluted realm beyond the border zone of Sotogahama in Aomori (Kikuchi 1994, 46–48). Naturally, such caricatures were really about defining Japanese ethnic identity vis à vis the "polluted" non-Japanese. Nevertheless this is a factor that cannot be ignored, and future work on the archaeological aspects of ideology may be able to add to the textual information relating to this problem.

Relations with the North

So far, this section has discussed Ainu ethnogenesis purely in terms of relations with Japan to the south. While undeniably important, however, this is only half the story: relations with the north also played a crucial role. A basic archaeological problem here is the date of the end of the Okhotsk culture. Recent research suggesting that it may have come to an end in Hokkaido by the tenth or late ninth century (Ushiro 1993a; Sugita 1992, 480) would seem to rule out earlier theories that thirteenth-century Mongol attacks on Sakhalin were responsible for the demise of the Okhotsk (Utagawa 1988, 301–306). In the north of Hokkaido, some Okhotsk groups may have been pushed to southern Sakhalin by Satsumon expansion (Ohyi 1975, 146), but elsewhere the Okhotsk culture appears to have been assimilated by the Satsumon. The eastern part of Hokkaido saw the development of a hybrid culture known as the Tobinitai that lasted until the twelfth or thirteenth century (Utagawa 1988, 306–309; Fujimoto 1984). A subsistence change from an emphasis on marine mammal hunting and offshore fishing to riverine salmon fishing appears to have been associated with the Tobinitai culture. Sugita (1992, 491) links this with a decline in the marine-mammal fur trade following the fall of Tang and Parhae and with the growing influence of Satsumon culture but does not elaborate on the causal processes involved.

In archaeological terms, therefore, we can posit the assimilation of Hokkaido Okhotsk culture by the Satsumon and the resulting formation of a new Ainu culture. The relationship between the actual populations, however, remains more controversial. Earlier in this chapter, it was noted that the Okhotsk people are thought to have been an intrusive, non-Jōmon population from the north. Various theories exist as to their identity, including Befu and Chard's (1964) suggestion that they were of Eskimo-Aleut origin. Many archaeologists link the Okhotsk people with the Nivkh (Gilyak) of north Sakhalin (e.g. Kikuchi 1992, 392; Vasilyevskiy 1978). While some cranial analyses support this identification (Kozintsev 1992, 109), others conclude a closer relationship with the Nanai and Ulchi people of the Amur and Sakhalin

(Ishida 1994, 266). More anthropological work needs to be conducted, but skeletal differences between Okhotsk and Ainu populations in both Hokkaido and Sakhalin would seem to disprove Fujimoto's (1965; 1990, 86) proposal that there was a close relationship between the two.

The origins of Ainu culture in Sakhalin and the Kurils remain much more poorly understood than do those of Ainu culture in Hokkaido. In both of the former regions, Okhotsk pottery is followed by interior-lug ceramics, which are thought to mark the beginning of the local Ainu culture (Yoshizaki 1963, 142; Chard 1956). It has long been assumed that Ainu populations from Hokkaido expanded into Sakhalin and the Kurils, replacing or pushing out the Okhotsk people. While such a migration has yet to be proven, based on available evidence, it is the most parsimonious hypothesis. To begin with, the alternative explanation that the Okhotsk culture/people of southern Sakhalin and the Kurils transformed themselves into the Ainu culture/people of those regions seems unlikely. The expansion within Hokkaido of late Satsumon culture at the expense of the Okhotsk was probably the beginning of the process of Ainu colonization. Historical data may also support Ainu expansion into Sakhalin. The unsuccessful invasions of Kyushu launched by the Mongol Yuan dynasty in 1274 and 1281 are well known, but what is less widely realized is that the Mongols also made several attacks on Sakhalin, beginning in 1264 and continuing until 1308. The *Yuan shi* relates that from their bases at the mouth of the Amur, Mongol forces attacked the Guwei people who were located across water, presumably on Sakhalin. The Guwei of the *Yuan shi* can be linked with the Gui and Guwu of the Ming and the Kuye of the Qing. This word is most probably related to *kuγi*, the name given to the Sakhlain Ainu by their Nivkh and Nanai neighbors (Wada 1938, 81). Related names seem to have been in wide use in the region. The Kuril Ainu, for example, called themselves *koushi* (Torii 1919, 33–34), a word that may have been Russianized to form "Kuril." The etymology of this group of terms is debated, but it is reasonably certain that they do refer to the Ainu (see Hora 1956, 81–97; Kikuchi 1989).

The identification of the Guwei with the Sakhalin Ainu is possibly supported by descriptions of them in the Chinese sources. The late Ming *Liaodong zhi* relates: "The Ku-wu [Guwu] live to the east of the Nu-êrh-kan Sea. The people are hairy. They wear bear-skins on their heads and coloured clothes on their bodies. They use wooden bows; . . . as the arrow-head is smeared with poison, every animal hit dies" (Wada 1938, 81). Ainu body hair may have been a distinctive trait compared to their relatively hairless Tungusic neighbors. Use of poisoned arrows was another Ainu trait. It is mentioned in the late-twelfth-century Japanese *Shūchūsho,* although this custom was also practiced by several Manchurian tribes (see Kikuchi 1984, 248–251). A Guwei chief called Yu Shannu mentioned in a *Jingshi Dadian* entry for 1308 may have had a typical Ainu male name ending in *-aynu.*[2]

Mongol attacks on the Guwei resulted from the latter's raids on the neighboring Jilimi people, who had already submitted to the Mongols. The Jilimi can be linked with the Gillemi of the Nanai and Orochi, i.e., the later Gilyaks now known as Nivkh (Wada 1938, 65; Hora 1956, 82–84). During the past few centuries, the Nivkh have lived in northern Sakhalin as well as in the lower Amur, but it is not clear how long they have occupied Sakhalin. Japanese scholars such as Wada (1938, 82–83) and Hora (1956, 93–95) argue that the Jilimi were already present on Sakhalin as well as on the mainland in Yuan times. The sources are ambiguous, but perhaps more problematical is the fact that "Jilimi" appears to have been used in the Yuan and Ming to refer to a variety of tribal groups, including "wild" Jurchen (Wada 1938, 78). The mention of four separate Jilimi tribes in the *Kaiyuan Xinzhi* and the *Liaodong zhi* at first seems to contradict the ethnographic picture of a uniform Nivkh culture (cf. Black 1973, 3), but it must be remembered that substantial changes may have occurred in Nivkh society since the thirteenth century.

Summarizing the evidence of the Chinese texts, the following points stand in order of reliability: (1) the Guwei fought against the Jilimi between 1264 and 1308; (2) the Guwei can be linked with the Sakhalin Ainu; (3) the Jilimi were also located on the island of Sakhalin; and (4) the Jilimi can be linked with the later Nivkh. If the Jilimi were indeed found on Sakhalin at this stage, then the Yuan and Ming sources would support our archaeological scenario of Ainu expansion and conflict with the Okhotsk people in late-thirteenth-century Sakhalin.[3] In other words, in order to link the Jilimi with the people of the Okhotsk *culture* it is not neccessary to connect the Jilimi with modern tribes such as the Nivkh.

Why did the Mongols invest so much effort in subduing Sakhalin, and what fueled the northward expansion of the Ainu at this time? As discussed by de Rachewiltz (1973), the Mongols believed that the right to rule the whole world had been conferred on them by Eternal Heaven; peoples not yet actually under their control were, therefore, rebels, and war against them was morally right. Economically, the conquest of new peoples provided further wealth for the tribute-based Mongol state. The role of trade in the equation is less clear but is likely to have been important. The Khitan Liao dynasty (947–1125) was the first state to control all of Manchuria (Ledyard 1983, 323). From its inception, the Liao depended on trade: horses, fox and marten furs, brocade, lumber, and slaves from Manchuria were traded for silk, tea, ginger, weapons, and other Chinese goods (Shiba 1983, 97–100). The same pattern continued under the Jurchen Jin dynasty (1115–1234). The Jurchens acquired massive amounts of silver from the Northern Song, which they defeated in the 1120s. This silver helped stimulate the Jin economy, and paper money became widely used through Manchuria (Shiba 1983, 102). Trade is thought to have been less significant to the Mongols themselves, but the Mongol conquests created a vast zone of interaction unlike anything that had been seen previously. Abu-Lughod (1989) has proposed the existence of a Eurasian world-system between 1250 and 1350. While the Mongol attacks on Sakhalin may have been motivated more by political or ideological factors than by economic ones, it may be significant that direct Chinese influence was first extended to Sakhalin precisely at the time of this thirteenth-century world-system.

At the moment, a link between Ainu ethnogenesis and a new intensity in trading relations with Manchuria must remain a hypothesis for further testing. Of course, Ezo had never been isolated from the mainland (see e.g. Kikuchi 1986; Fujimoto 1990), but neither the archaeological nor the historical records presently support a noticeable increase in trade between Sakhalin and Manchuria during the era of Mongol influence on Sakhalin (1264–1320). However, archaeological research in Sakhalin remains poorly developed, and little work has been done on the historical sources relating to this remote outpost of the Yuan world. Rossabi (1982, 7) criticizes earlier views that the Mongol conquests had a totally negative effect on the economy of Manchuria: "Though the Mongols devastated Jurchen territory in their initial conquests, they generally sought, during more than a century of rule, to encourage the economic revival of Manchuria" (Rossabi 1982, 54). Archaeological study of trade with Sakhalin is complicated by the fact that most of the products involved are likely to have been perishable materials such as furs, feathers, and textiles.

The Amur and Sungari rivers were the major transportation routes across north Manchuria in ancient times and were the focus of political power in the region (Wada 1938, 44). Sakhalin's position at the mouth of the Amur thus predetermined its importance in Manchurian affairs. The basic geography of the region means that as long as trade, in furs and others items, occurred between Manchuria and China, Sakhalin is likely to have played a role in that trade. We know that the Manchurian fur trade was important even during periods when the Chinese did not actually occupy the Amur, for instance during the late Ming (Kawachi 1992, 592–656). It is not until the eighteenth century, however, that historical records enable us to discuss the so-called Santan trade between Ezo and the peoples of the Amur in some detail (Harrison 1954; Stephan 1971, 21–29). Brocades came from Yangzi cities such as Nanjing and Hangzhou via Manchuria, furs and eagle feathers flowed both ways from Sakhalin, and iron pots and tools traveled north from Japan. This Santan trade may have reached its peak during the eighteenth century (Ohnuki-Tierney 1974a, 8), but its roots are much older. A mention of "Ezo brocade" in a Japanese document of 1143 suggests that the basic pattern of the trade may date back to at least the twelfth century (see Kaiho 1990, 270).[4]

On present evidence, therefore, it is somewhat harder to link early medieval Ainu ethnogenesis with core/periphery relations with Sakhalin and Manchuria than it is to link it with the much stronger process of uneven development between Hokkaido and Japan. Even during Yuan times, however, it is clear that the proper scale for the study of the Ainu is one that includes Manchuria and the Maritime Provinces. During the Ming and Qing, the volume of the Santan trade increased, and the Ainu, especially in Sakhalin, were more and more exploited by both their northern and their southern neighbors. Eventually, in the early nineteenth century, the Japanese paid off Ainu debts owing in the trade (Takakura 1960, 66–67), instituting a new stage in Ainu ethnicity whereby the Santan trade became linked with direct Japanese control and thus with the Japanization of the Ainu.

Climate Change

The world-systems approach proposed here naturally does not rule out other, complementary perspectives on Ainu ethnogenesis. One such perspective—climate change—is too important to be totally ignored and will be discussed here very briefly. Japanese environmental scientists propose the existence of a warm stage, two to three degrees C higher than the present, lasting from about the eighth to the thirteenth or fourteenth centuries, followed by a cold stage that lasted until about 1900 (Sakaguchi 1982, 1983; Yamamoto 1976; Yoshino 1982). Though exact dates vary by region, these stages appear to have worldwide correlations, the first corresponding to the so-called Neo-Atlantic and the second to the so-called Little Ice Age (cf. Bryson and Padoch 1981, 12–13). In Hokkaido, the two stages correspond very closely with the Satsumon and the Ainu period, respectively.

In order to derive environmental explanations for the past, historians need to do two things: (1) reconstruct the palaeoclimate of the region in question in as much detail as possible, since the labels "cold" and "warm" can encompass considerable variation in precipitation and other factors; and (2) propose specific models for how climate change may have influenced human behavior, bearing in mind that the same climatic event can lead to quite different cultural reactions. Recent work by Akamatsu and Ushiro (1992) on the species composition of Okhotsk shell middens is a good example of research in the first category, but Ushiro's (1993a, 55) proposal of Okhotsk exploitation of Hokkaido's east coast—which was free of sea ice—during the warm stage needs to be matched with an explanation of why the Okhotsk people should have migrated *north* with the return of the ice. With respect to the Ainu, it has been argued that the deteriorating climate made agriculture more difficult in the northern Tohoku and Hokkaido, forcing people north in search of trade goods (Kikuchi 1984, 222). I believe that such factors very probably played a role in Ainu ethnogenesis, but there are still several problems that need to be addressed. While wet rice cultivation may have been affected by climatic cooling, for instance, what was the effect on millet and other cold-adapted crops? To what extent did the Satsumon people ever become dependent on full-scale farming? Answers to these and other questions will help our understanding of Ainu origins, but by themselves they are unlikely to tell us the whole story, and they need to be fitted into a wider, cultural framework.

CONCLUSIONS

Like all ethnic groups, the Ainu have always been in the process of becoming. This chapter has argued that, at the same time, the end of the Satsumon period marks a decisive stage in that process. I have proposed that world-systems theory is a useful way of modeling the social processes that led to the formation of an Ainu etic ethnos in about the twelfth to the thirteenth century. According to this approach, the Ainu are not seen as a relict Stone Age culture, surviving in the remote north because of their lack of contact with the outside. Instead, the development of economic and political core and semiperipheral regions in the Kinai and the northern Tohoku and in Manchuria led to extensive contact with the Ainu and to the exploitation of Ezo through trade and eventual colonization. The extent of economic exploitation of Ezo altered with the rise and fall of core regions within the larger East Asian world-system, but, broadly speaking, Ezo became increasingly peripheralized over the course of the Ainu period.

A world-systems approach does not mean that all change has to come from the outside or be a mere reaction to outside change; it does not deny the role of the Ainu in creating their own identity. Economic and other interactions within the world-system were crucial to its reproduction and transformation, but both the Ainu and the Japanese attributed meanings and intentions to the cultures thereby formed. In terms of identity, for example, Ainu trade and expansion to the north seem to have been matched by a Japanese perception of Chinese influences spreading south. The three types of Ezo inhabitants named in the Suwa Shrine Scroll (1356) have been mentioned already. Of these, the term "Karako" 唐子 clearly derives from a word for China (Kara=Tang) and, by extension, with the more general meaning of "foreign." A similar name, of uncertain but at least Tokugawa antiquity, was given to Sakhalin by the Japanese: Karafuto, derived from Kara-*hito* or "Kara" (person). Originally written 唐太, the first character was changed to one meaning "birch" (樺) in the 1860s, since the earlier meaning of "China" was seen as inconsistent with Japanese territorial claims to the island (Kaiho 1987, 161). Kaiho (1987, 160–162) and others argue that the "Karako" of the Suwa Shrine Scroll were basically Ainu in western Hokkaido *influenced by* the Chinese and other peoples to the north. The picture is complicated by the Japanese belief, held as late as the seventeenth century, that Hokkaido was connected to Manchuria by land (see Kamiya 1994).

Clothing provides another example of the complexities of identity construction. The Ainu obtained secondhand ceremonial brocade robes from China via the north. Though prestige goods worn only by chiefs, brocade robes became so closely associated with the Ainu that in the early seventeenth century the founder of the Matsumae domain, Kakizaki Yoshihiro, wore one to a meeting with Tokugawa Ieyasu in order to represent himself as suzerain of the Ainu (Howell 1994, 79). Like the Andō and the Northern Fujiwara before him, Yoshihiro used the discourse of ethnicity to reinforce his power as a middleman between Japan and Ezo. Interestingly, there is documentary and pictorial evidence from the eighteenth century onward that Japanese peasants also wore *attush* (Ainu bast fiber cloth garments) in Aomori as well as Hokkaido (Ōtsuka 1993). The Nanbu and Matsumae domains both attempted to ban this custom; indeed the Matsumae went to great lengths to maintain ethnic separation between ordinary Japanese and Ainu, since its very existence depended on its control of the Ainu as an ethnic minority (Howell 1994, 85). Ōtsuka (1993) may be correct in attributing the spread of *attush* among the Japanese to "fashion"; we can only speculate on possible reasons that Japanese peasants adopted symbols of Ainu ethnicity, but that they should have done so only confirms that ethnic groups are not bounded, static phenomena.

This chapter has concentrated on the social and cultural aspects of Ainu etic ethnicity. The research summarized in chapter 3 appears to leave little doubt that there has been basic biological continuity in Hokkaido since the Jōmon, notwithstanding some possible minor genetic input from the Okhotsk people.[5] This biological continuity makes linguistic continuity highly probable because it is simply difficult to imagine when and by what process the Jōmon language of Hokkaido could have been replaced by another language prior to Japanese colonization. These biological and linguistic continuities were in turn no doubt mirrored by cultural ones. While the Satsumon-Ainu transition marks a major qualitative transformation, it is not my intention to argue that all elements of Ainu culture derive from that stage. The prototype of Ainu designs can probably be traced back to Epi- or Final Jōmon ceramics; the importance of the bear in Ainu culture may also have roots in the Epi-Jōmon as symbolized by the carved bears on the famous antler spoons from Usu 10 (Ōshima 1990).

The archaeological/ethnohistoric model of the Ainu etic ethnos used in this chapter is necessarily simplistic. My major concern has been with the first stage of Ainu ethnogenesis, and I have made no attempt to incorporate the question of the regional diversity of Ainu society across Ezo or of Ainu emic identities (cf. Kōno 1931, 1932; Kaiho 1974). The emphasis of this chapter, and indeed of the book as a whole, should not be thought to imply that self-identities are epiphenomena, somehow less important than the genes, languages, and material culture. My argument is simply that all these factors are crucial to an understanding of ethnicity. To give an example, in the northern Kuril Islands, the Ainu were heavily influenced by the Russians starting from the eighteenth century such that after their relocation to Shikotan in the south of the chain by Japanese authorities in 1884, these Ainu "clung tenaciously to their Russian heritage. They continued to speak a peculiar dialect of Russian. They treasured their Russian surnames, . . . wore Russian dress, and built steam baths close by their Japanese-style houses" (Stephan 1974, 108). It is the historian's task, not to deny the assumed identity of these people, but to point out that they had not always been "Russian," and (had they not been exterminated by Japanese colonial policies) they would not have remained Russian or even Ainu or Japanese forever. Contemporary Hokkaido Ainu views of their identity stress their status as an ecologically aware "indigenous people." Leading Ainu activist Kayano Shigeru's recent autobiography is called *Our Land Was a Forest,* a title that implies a virginal, snow-covered land untouched by the outside until Japanese colonization (cf. Kayano 1994). While not denying the suffering and oppression of the Ainu people in recent times, this chapter has shown that the Ainu forest was never totally pristine and unbroken.

9

Japanese Ethnicity

Some Final Thoughts

I would like to suggest an answer to the question, What is the essence of Japanese culture? or, to put almost the same question in another way, What is Japan?

I view Japanese culture as contained in the synthesis of the opposition between Jōmon and Yayoi cultures.

Umehara Takeshi, "Nihon to wa nan na no ka: Nihon kenkyū no kokusaika to Nihon bunka no honshitsu"

In this book, I have discussed ethnogenetic processes in the Japanese Islands from the Yayoi until the early medieval era. I argue that the analysis of ethnogenesis in premodern contexts cannot begin with current standard definitions of an ethnos as an emic self-identity or as an essentialist cultural unit. The proper place to begin is with the available biological and linguistic evidence that may be used to determine the existence of what have been termed "core populations." A core population may correspond to an ethnos or may simply be a group of people with shared genetic and linguistic components; historical or ethnographic records are needed to determine its wider significance. In chapter 8, it was shown that a reasonably detailed ethnographic and archaeological record makes it possible to trace back an Ainu etic ethnos to as early as the twelfth century. In this last chapter, I want to consider whether the Japanese core population can also be termed an ethnos in either the etic or emic sense. Some preliminary speculations will be attempted with respect to two questions: has the population here termed "Japanese" seen itself as a separate ethnic unit since its formation in the Yayoi? If not, then can we retrospectively propose any criteria that give it a social and cultural continuity?

Let us begin with the second question of to what extent the Japanese core population can be said to have formed an etic ethnos. It must be stressed that I am not suggesting that we search for any sort of immutable essence that is Japaneseness. Like the Ainu cultural complex discussed in chapter 8, a model of Japanese etic ethnicity would necessarily be simplistic, yet it would nevertheless contain a series of distinctive cultural elements that could mark off the Japanese in time and place. How should one approach this question? Should we immerse ourselves in a sea of details such as those in Braudel's unfinished "total history" of *The Identity of France* (1988–1990)? Should we adopt a relativist approach such as that taken in Ruth Benedict's pathbreaking *The Chrysanthemum and the Sword* (1954), a book that Geertz (1988, 117) has argued is a deconstruction of the West as well as of Japan? Or is a more poetic, even mystical perspective more appropriate, resembling, like Carlos Fuentes' reflections on Spanish identities, a flamenco cry that is "not beneath words but above them, when words are not enough" (Fuentes 1992, 31)? Probably all of these approaches and others will be necessary. Perhaps the greatest theoretical challenge is that of how to overcome the existing discourses of what Moeran (1990) has termed "Japanism." Japanism is Said's Orientalism in Japanese garb; it is the ways in which Japan is dominated and controlled by Western constructions of the country as exotic and unique *and also* the ways in which Japan seeks to escape that control by reinventing its own exoticity as traditional and superior. In the West, Japan is popularly portrayed as a topsy-turvy land of opposites, feudal yet postmodern, peaceful yet violent, diligent yet frivolous. Japan is the "Outnation" (Rauch 1992), quite unlike anywhere else. In Japan itself, depictions of Japanese culture are more varied and more numerous, with Befu (1993, 109) estimating that over 1,000 works on the nature of Japanese culture (i.e., *Nihonjinron*) were published between 1945 and 1990. Whether Japanese culture is explained by Confucianism, by the psychology of dependence, or by the lack of meat in the diet of its people, however, a shared assumption is that the culture is not only "uniquely unique" but that it is superior to that of the West (Dale 1986).

A further problem is that of time. Debate continues even over the defining elements of postwar Japanese culture, yet this chapter seeks a cultural core that goes back to the formation of the Japanese people around

400 BC. Recently, archaeologists have shown renewed interest in the history of the long term (e.g. Chang 1992; Hodder 1987, 1990), but as used by the postprocessualists this approach falls into an idealism that seems disturbingly reminiscent of *Nihonjinron* discourse.[1] Of course, many things that we think of as typically Japanese are relatively recent in origin. Kabuki and Noh drama and the culture of tea and of flower arrangement all date from the medieval era and gained popularity through the Tokugawa. Many typical Japanese foods are even more recent, sukiyaki having only become common with the spread of beef and egg consumption in the Meiji era, and tempura and sushi dating to the Tokugawa (Sasaki 1991b, 14–16). Many of the most distinctive aspects of contemporary Japanese culture derive from the mixing of Western and indigenous elements and as such date back at most to just over a century. Furthermore, it is becoming increasingly clear that the Cold War was responsible for a series of extraordinary political and economic conditions that have underlain the spectacular success of "Japan, Inc." during the last fifty years. This is not to say that the Japanese people had no part in their success but rather that some of the distinctive social structures of the period have tended to be wrongly attributed to traditional Japanese culture, when in many cases their origins lie in specific political circumstances of the 1940s and 1950s (see e.g. Buruma 1994).[2] The incredible success of the postwar ideologies of Japaneseness can in turn be largely attributed to the role of the mass media (see Ivy 1988; Kogawa 1988; Oblas 1995).

Amino (1992a, 132–133) has argued that Japanese culture continues to be explained around four main themes: insularity, rice monoculture, a unified state based on the emperor, and a homogeneous ethnos. Of these, the last is the very variable we are trying to analyze. The state and emperor only developed a millennium after the formation of the Japanese and cannot be used as a defining element of that population. Similarly, though Japan's insularity has influenced Japanese culture and identity, it cannot be used as a defining criterion, since insularity is not culture specific. The problem of rice merits special attention here since the presence of agriculture is one of my defining elements of the Japanese population. There is no doubt that rice has been of great importance to the Japanese people ever since the Yayoi period; this importance was not just dietary but also political, cultural, and spiritual. The difficulty lies in deciding how much emphasis should be placed on rice and rice farmers as opposed to on other crops and other types of farmers and indeed on fishermen, hunters, and craftsmen. Watabe (1993, 150) argues that the Japanese have only been a "rice-eating people" since World War II; before that they should rather be described as a "people who prayed for rice" (*beishoku higan minzoku*). Insufficient documentary and archaeological evidence exists to enable us to determine how much rice was actually consumed (and by whom) through much of Japanese history, but for most people, the consumption of rice was probably the exception rather than the rule. Even today, rice is not as ubiquitous as it might seem: a recent survey of museum employees in Yamanashi Prefecture found that only 21.8 percent and 6.7 percent of those surveyed ate white rice for their midday and evening meals, respectively (Kobayashi 1994, 59).

Ohnuki-Tierney (1993) has argued that rice has served as a metaphor of the Japanese Self since the Yayoi period. While this is undoubtedly so in contemporary Japan, nothing in her analysis convinces me that it is not a relatively recent development. Obviously, rice was important in ancient times, playing a significant role in imperial rituals, for instance. Since agricultural surpluses provided the basis of state power, it is not surprising that rice and rice fields developed a ritual significance. To go beyond this, however, and argue that rice has always served as a metaphor for Japanese identity, is pure speculation that itself relies on the premise of a unified sense of Japaneseness in the first place. What is lacking from existing works on rice is an explanation of why the contemporary Japanese view of "rice as self" should have become so pervasive, and also of why this should have led to the marginalization of non-rice-farming peoples. Amino's (1994, 1) classic Marxist formulation that the ideology of rice is a "false consciousness" is unconvincing, since rice is linked directly to the ideology of the emperor, whereas in reality, as Ohnuki-Tierney (1993, 94) herself notes, some Japanese opponents of the imperial system, no longer aware of the traditional rice/emperor link, also oppose the importation of foreign rice. Ohnuki-Tierney's symbolic analysis of the role of rice in Japanese identity is theoretically more sophisticated than is Amino's approach, but in taking the "rice as self" metaphor back to the Yayoi, Ohnuki-Tierney is in effect perpetuating the rice-centered ideology, since her scheme has no historical basis at that early stage.

It seems to me, therefore, that it is difficult to identify any culturally specific traits that can be assigned to the Japanese population across the whole of its history. Thus, in terms of the analytical categories discussed in the introduction, the establishment of a core Japanese population in the Islands cannot be seen to correspond with a single etic ethnos, except in the broadest sense of a predominantly agricultural society on the periphery of the Chinese sphere of influence. Instead, there are several Japanese etic ethnoi corresponding with the Yayoi, Kofun, Ritsuryō, medieval, Tokugawa, and modern eras. Perhaps the only cultural unity of the Japanese as a whole is the precedence of what are perceived as the layers of a common, evolving history. The Japanese have always been in the process of becoming.

The other question posed at the beginning of this chapter is that of whether the Japanese core population has seen itself as a separate ethnos since its formation in the Yayoi. Again, this is an enormously complex and controversial problem, and I can do little more than scratch the surface here. With the possible exception of Okinawa, most Japanese alive today would regard themselves as part of an ethnic nation, but this perception of being Japanese is a norm that covers considerable individual variation. In other words, what it means to be Japanese is not agreed upon by all who consider themselves so. Furthermore, it cannot be assumed that an inclusive belief in a shared Japanese identity has a particularly long history.

A considerable literature exists on premodern nationalism, but this literature tends to be highly Eurocentric and suffers from a predominant emphasis on the formation of modern nations and nationalism. Even Anthony Smith—who argues that these latter phenomena have ancient ethnic roots—is primarily concerned with explaining why premodern ethnic states were not nations rather than with discussing those earlier states for their own sake (e.g. Smith 1991, 43-70). Most scholars conclude that the nation-state is a modern development, dating to the late eighteenth and nineteenth centuries. Of course, national development was a gradual process, and work by Weber (1976), for example, has shown that anything approaching full integration of the French nation was not accomplished until World War I. Nation-states rely on industrial, mass culture to spread nationalist sentiment to every regional and social component of a state. In contrast, preindustrial nations are constrained by regionalism and by the fact that ethnic solidarity is usually confined to the aristocracy. Given these crucial parameters of the premodern world, as it stands without further explanation, Fujitani's (1993, 82) statement that "It is obvious to sensible historians today . . . that during the Tokugawa period the common people had [no] strong sense of national identity" is almost a tautology.

In medieval Europe, the concept of Christendom was a powerful focus of loyalty that to some extent overrode local identities. In the words of St. Thomas Aquinas, "Though one distinguishes peoples according to diverse dioceses and states, it is obvious that as there is one Church there must also be one Christian people" (Hertz 1972, 76).[3] Although a universalistic Buddhist worldview became important in medieval Japan (Vande Walle 1994), there was no East Asian equivalent of Christendom. Europeans could claim equal status before God as members of the one Church, but the universal worldviews of East Asia—be they Indian or Chinese—saw Japan as a minor, barbarian kingdom. While there are many examples of Japanese writers of both the Buddhist and Confucian traditions accepting a second-class position within these schemes, a Japan-centered perspective was also common (see e.g. Tyler 1994). Just as Japanese intellectuals of the early twentieth century counteracted Western Orientalism by creating their own Orient *(Tōyō)* that excluded Japan (see Tanaka 1993), the ancient Japanese amended the Chinese civilization-barbarian dichotomy to place themselves as the civilized center of a small empire.

From the establishment of the Ritsuryō state in the late seventh century, there existed the concept of a country or nation *(kuni)* of *Nihon,* which extended over the three main islands except for the northern Tohoku. The borders of this nation changed over time, especially in the east, but the concept continued to be used throughout premodern Japanese history (Murai 1985, 40).[4] In the medieval era, a concept of ritual pollution was also applied to the areas beyond the borders of the state (Yoshie 1995). However, both of these concepts were clearly imposed by the central elites, and the problem lies in deciding to what extent the court or aristocratic concept of *Nihon* was actually shared by its inhabitants.

Smith (1991, 52–54) divides premodern ethnoi (what he terms "ethnic communities") into lateral and vertical types. In the former, ethnic solidarity is primarily limited to the elites, whereas the latter also includes the peasant class. Ancient Japan would seem to fall into the first of these categories. The eighth-century *Kojiki* and *Nihon Shoki* accounts of descent from the gods provide the basis for concepts of the innate superiority of the Japanese. For example, the *Jinnō Shōtoki* ("A Chronicle of the Direct Descent of Gods and Sovereigns"), a history of Japan written in 1339, began "Great Japan is the divine land. The heavenly progenitor founded it, and the Sun Goddess bequeathed it to her descendants to rule eternally. Only in our country is this true; there are no similar examples in other countries. That is why our country is called the divine land" (Varley 1980, 49). In view of the apparent continuity with the official ideology of the Japanese state from 1868 to 1945, it would be easy to place too much emphasis on such ideas, but there are several reasons why this would be a mistake. First, until the modern era only a tiny minority of Japanese people would have even been aware of such concepts. Second, we need to carefully consider the context in which these ideas were propounded. The *Jinnō Shōtoki* and its author, Kitabatake Chikafusa, provide an excellent example. As a key player in the Nanbokuchō dispute between the Northern and the Southern courts (1336–1392), Chikafusa stressed the continuity of imperial succession to bolster the claims of the Southern court at the expense of the *bakufu*-dominated Northern court (Varley 1980, 30–31; 1990, 456–457). Varley notes that Chikafusa's writings were more influential in later times than they were in the fourteenth century: "With his call for the restoration of [real power to the emperor], Chikafusa was already an anachronism in his own lifetime" (Varley 1990, 457). However similar Chikafusa's ideas may appear to those of the ideologues of the early Showa state, their contemporary significance cannot be assumed to have been the same.

The idea of Japan as a *shinkoku* (divine nation) took root slowly during the Nara and the Heian periods. The term first appears in the *Nihon Shoki* account of Jingo's attack on Korea (cf. Aston 1972, I: 230). Following this example, many early uses of the term took the sense of "the nation protected by the gods" (Okada 1987, 34). The threat of foreign attacks on the Islands led to an increased perception of a nation that differed from its neighbors. The Tang-Silla alliance of the late seventh century was the first such threat, and Ōbayashi (1984) is no doubt correct in seeing this period as a crucial one in the formation of Japanese identity. The concept of *shinkoku* "reached its greatest height of propagation in the midst of the national crisis surrounding the Mongol invasions" of the late thirteenth century (Okada 1987, 33), and there is evidence that the threat of the Mongol invasions led to an increased sense of shared identity by some Japanese (Brown 1955, 25–30). Even at this time, though, links with identity were complex, since in an age of often-open conflict between religious groups, the reading of *chingo kokka kyō* (nation-protecting sutras) was emphasized by Buddhist sects because they brought direct state support to the particular sect (Rodd 1980, 9). Potential financial reward by the Kamakura *bakufu* led to both Buddhist and Shinto establishments exaggerating the role of the gods in defeating the Mongols (Hori 1974, 186–187), thus promoting the rhetoric of *shinkoku*. Nichiren (1222–1282), founder of the Lotus sect of Japanese Buddhism, used the crisis of the Mongol invasions to promote his own sect, declaring that the opposing Shingon sect's "rituals cannot be expected to ensure the defeat of the powerful Mongol nation" (Rodd 1980, 18).

Much of the literature on ethnicity has argued, following Barth (1969), that ethnic "groups tend to define themselves not by reference to their own characteristics but by exclusion, that is, by comparison to 'strangers'" (Armstrong 1982, 5). Thus, episodes of war, invasion, and intense contact with foreign peoples tend to increase feelings of national sentiment (Hertz 1972;

Smith 1986, 37–41). A classic example would appear to be the Meiji Restoration, a movement fueled by the nationalistic sentiment of *sonnō jōi* (revere the emperor, expel the barbarian!). Prior to the modern nation-state, however, it cannot be assumed that there was an inclusive feeling of identity at the level of the nation. For example, Bolitho (1993) has argued that the 1868–1869 military opposition by the Tohoku region to the new Meiji government was motivated not by traditional support for the Tokugawa regime but by resentment of outside influence in domain affairs and by a general fear of outsiders—especially soldiers from the western provinces. "Even in the late Tokugawa period—and especially in the Tohoku—anybody from a different domain was a foreigner" (Bolitho 1993, 9). Of course, a group of Greeks or Maori moving into the region would have been regarded with even more suspicion than the Kyushuans would have been, but the importance of local identities in the premodern context remains.

Tokugawa Japan is particularly apposite to the study of premodern ethnicity, since it is widely seen as a classic example of "proto-nationalism" (e.g. Smith 1991, 105). After a century of civil war, the country was unified at the beginning of the seventeenth century by the Tokugawa *bakufu*. As with earlier periods, however, historians continue to debate the extent of power enjoyed by the Tokugawa state (e.g. Berry 1986; Philip Brown 1993; White 1988). The *bakufu* stood at the apex of 260 largely self-governing domains *(han)*. Fearful that these domains would join together in military revolt, the Tokugawa regime instituted various policies that had the effect of both fostering and undermining national identity. On the one hand, domain pluralism was an essential part of the "divide and rule" strategy; on the other, measures such as the *sankin kōtai* system (whereby domain lords had to spend alternate years in residence at Edo) encouraged the national exchange of culture (Vaporis 1997). There can be no doubt that a highly urbanized and educated society, as well as the increasing popularity of pilgrimages and recreational travel (Vaporis 1994), were important in the development of a shared sense of Japaneseness such that it may be appropriate to speak of Japan beginning in the Tokugawa era as a "vertical ethnic community," to use Anthony Smith's terminology. At the same time, though, it is clear that local differences persisted. As late as 1837, a French economist writing about the central Pyrenees noted that "Every valley is still a little world that differs from the neighboring world as Mercury does from Uranus. Every village is a clan, a sort of state with its own patriotism" (Weber 1976, 47). Itself a complex mosaic of mountains and valleys, premodern Japan was little different in this respect.

There are several axes of diversity that need to be considered within the Japanese Islands. The first is ecological. While writing this book, I was lucky enough to travel from the coral reefs and sandy beaches of Hateruma Island in the south to the icy, wind-battered Okhotsk Sea town of Abashiri in the north. Some 80 percent of the Japanese Islands is mountainous, and traditional upland lifestyles were markedly different from those of the rice farmers of the coastal plains or those of the fishermen and traders of the seas. The division between the broadleaf evergreen forests of the western archipelago and the deciduous forests of the east partly explains a major east-west split that is visible as early as the Palaeolithic. In the main islands in the historic era, this east-west division occurs in a variety of cultural elements that cannot all be attributed to ecological factors: dry-field cultivation, horse transportation, and pork consumption in the east versus wet rice, boats, and beef in the west (see Hayashiya 1973; Amino 1992b; Ōishi 1987; Ōbayashi 1990a).

In Amino's writings, east and west Japan appear as almost separate "states," each with its own links to the continent (e.g. Amino 1992a). This question of how the diversity of premodern sociopolitical units in the Islands related to ethnic identity is one that needs careful consideration. Johnson and Earle (1987, 249) argue that medieval and Tokugawa Japan was "populated with communities ranging from simple to complex chiefdoms, with many areas not integrated beyond the family level or the local group." Following the decline of the Ritsuryō system, regional polities developed that may perhaps best be termed chiefdoms, but the political authority of many of these polities was in part derived from political association with the emperor and the traditional power structures of the Kinai, and all were to some degree economically interrelated.

For our present purposes, two questions need to be asked with respect to regional political formations in premodern Japan. First, to what extent were these units regarded as separate countries (to use the vaguest possible term) as opposed to simply administrative subdivisions within a greater *Nihon?* Of course, the court and provincial perceptions of such units would no doubt have been quite different. Second, at the level of the peasantry, to what extent was there a perception of belonging to a unit greater than the local village or valley? Lack of sources makes it impossible to answer either of these questions with any confidence, but further research on the relevant documentary evidence would result in more sophisticated guesswork than will be possible here.

The main candidate for a regional ethnos in premodern Japan is the Ryukyu Islands, which were home to a politically autonomous state from the fifteenth to the early seventeenth century (see Pearson 1996b, 1997). The main ethnic minorities of the ancient Japanese state are discussed in chapter 7. Groups such as the Kumaso and the Emishi probably saw themselves as ethnically different to some extent, but the nature of that ethnic identity is not known. As noted, terms such as "Emishi" must be seen as complex, shifting loci of identity rather than as fixed ethnonyms. The term "Hinomoto" is an excellent example: not only do we not know whether it was an indigenous or an outsiders' name, we are not even sure exactly to what location it referred—indeed, it seems to have meant different places at different times. The history of the Korean Yi dynasty *(Yijo Shillok)* records the late-fifteenth-century visit of an envoy from the "King of Ezo-ga-Chishima." This king may possibly be associated with the Andō clan and thus with Hinomoto (Kaiho 1987, 194–198), but he is not mentioned in Japanese sources.

One of the most explicit threats to the ancient Japanese state came from the Kanto uprising of Taira no Masakado (d. 940). The causes of this revolt are poorly understood, but local resentment against economic exploitation by the court seems to have been a major factor (Rabinovitch 1986, 20–27). After his armies gained control of the Kanto, Masakado was crowned "New Emperor" by his supporters in 12/939, but he does not seem to have used his local power base to develop a sense of ethnic solidarity in the region. Interestingly, Masakado's influence in this respect may have been greater after his death, since, from the fourteenth century, he was revered by the local populace as the guardian deity of Edo (see Rabinovitch 1986, 3).

A rather different, more pan-regional ethnic group seems to have existed in the Wakō pirates of the medieval era. The character 倭 (*Wa* in the modern Japanese reading, which is used hereafter) appears in Chinese sources relating to Japan from the third century. Rather than a separate ethnos, Wa was probably a general label for those inhabitants of the Japanese Islands known to the Chinese (Hudson 1989). In ancient times, "Wa" was also used to refer to people of other regions, including Manchuria and the south Chinese coast (Inoue 1991). Later "Wa" became commonly prefixed to a word meaning "pirate"; these Wakō reached their peak of activity between the fourteenth and the sixteenth centuries, terrorizing both coastal and inland areas around the East China Sea. Though literally meaning "Japanese pirates," the Wakō also included large numbers of Koreans and Chinese (Tanaka 1987, 147–155). Like the ancient Wa, the medieval Wakō were a population that overrode national or ethnic boundaries (Murai 1993, 39). Despite this, it seems likely that the Wakō merchants and pirates from Iki, Tsushima, and other parts of western Japan would have possessed quite different views of their identity than those held by the Japanese of the Kinai or of the eastern provinces.

This book has argued that a Japanese "core population" was established in the Islands in the Yayoi period. Prior to the nation-state of the twentieth century, it may have been during this very first stage in which a sense of shared identity was strongest. As Bellwood (1993b, 57) puts it, "I suspect that any society which is actively undergoing colonization, especially into regions where prior populations, however small, exist, will tend to be identity conscious." Over time, this hypothetical early unity would have diverged into various regional societies; but then in the Kofun period the process of state formation seems to have led to some degree of ethnic solidarity. By definition, this solidarity would have been primarily limited to the aristocracy and would have contained considerable regional variation in its degree of integration. Furthermore, the proposed Japanese ethnos based on the Kinai was matched by separate ethnic formations, most notably in the case of the Ryukyuans who, although they may have derived from the same core Japanese population, had formed their own ethnos by the medieval era. At times, other Insular groups also developed identities opposing that of the central Japanese, but since these groups have left insufficient documentary records, they remain poorly understood.

Given the parameters of premodern ethnicity, and compared with the states of western Europe, the Japanese can probably be said to have possessed a relatively high degree of ethnic solidarity before the establishment of a modern nation-state in Meiji times. This is not a conclusion that I come to lightly, since it could easily be misused for nationalistic ends. Fujitani (1993, 81) shies away from study of the whole history of the Japanese imperial system, "for such a project, even if it were to be a critical one, would have the inadvertent consequence of contributing to the myth of the imperial institution's continuity." Fujitani appears to be saying that the myths of Japanese uniqueness are too strong, too ingrained to be assaulted by the historian's pen. Perhaps he is right; perhaps I am naive to believe that the apparent contradiction between the existence of a *comparatively* well-developed level of ethnic sentiment in premodern Japan and the almost certain fact that the Japanese people as a whole never saw themselves as a single ethnos before the arrival of the railway, mass education, conscription, and other trappings of Meiji nationalism, will be easily overcome.

It has been proposed in this book that the elements of ethnicity typically seen as more objective—that is, genes and language—are crucial to any real understanding of that phenomenon. This is not because these elements necessarily constrain a people's perception of their identity but because they provide a means by which to debate the relationship between perception and reality. The prehistoric past will probably never be known in full, but it does not therefore follow, as Kaner (1996) argues, that the search for prehistoric ethnicity is futile. Instead, the reality gains importance in the contemporary world as an alternative rather than a hegemonic truth. In other words, whether the modern Japanese have their roots in the Jōmon or in the Yayoi is perhaps less important than is our using currently available scientific research to lay bare those elements of Japaneseness that are clearly pure imagination. We may never know the exact proportion of Jōmon and Yayoi genes possessed by the modern Japanese, but the research presented in this book has shown that a greater Yayoi heritage seems likely and thus that current Japanese perceptions of the Jōmon people as the original Japanese need to be reevaluated. Once exposed, the ruins of identity may then be rebuilt in a different way.

Postscript

It was a late June morning, hot and clear after the end of the rainy season. I had arrived at Hitoyoshi on the early train from Kumamoto, the track hugging the fast-flowing waters of the Kuma River up into the mountains. A car from the Menda Board of Education was waiting at the station, and after brief introductions we set off on the twenty-minute ride to Menda Township. One member of the welcoming party was a woman who had spent time in Bournemouth and spoke the type of natural English that is still rare in Japan. Her presence was welcome, since I was having trouble with the dialect spoken by the other two men. Before long, we passed a painted sign announcing "Menda: town of pottery and the gilt mirror." The car turned off up a small lane and parked under a tree.

Menda is a town of 6,300 people in central Kumamoto Prefecture, Kyushu. I had gone there after reading a newspaper report that the town office was planning to use archaeology to improve the image of the Kumaso—the ancient, warlike inhabitants of the region who still retain a certain primitive air in the minds of many Japanese. The late Otomasu Shigetaka, professor of archaeology at Tokyo's Kokugakuin University and himself from Menda, had named a distinctive type of Late Yayoi pottery after the town. The Menda area is also thought to have been an important center of the Kumaso people during the Kofun era.

I was taken first to a series of fields sown with dry rice and taro. My guides showed me where Menda pottery had been discovered in the past and where they planned to dig later that summer. Since none of them were archaeologists by training, Professor Mori Kōichi from Kyoto would supervise the project. As we stood beneath the blaring cicadas, our thoughts moved down to the dry soil, and we imagined the past under our feet, awaiting discovery in a few weeks' time.

The sun was getting hotter and hotter as midday approached, and I was glad of the suggestion that we head into the center of the town "before you think Menda is all fields and farmhouses." The town office was a solid brown cube that must have housed over 100 employees. Several artifacts and large color photos of the attractive Menda-type pottery were displayed in the entrance area, where a group of men sat in a cloud of smoke waiting to conduct their business. Upstairs I was introduced to Mr. Ogata, the head of the Board of Education and an amiable, bearlike man who somehow fitted the popular image of the Kumaso. Mr. Ogata gave me his name card, which was embossed, like those of several other members of the Board of Education, with a color photograph of the gilt bronze mirror found in the Saizon burial mound in the town. According to the detailed explanation on the back of the card, the mirror has a diameter of 11.67 cm and was cast in southern China in the early fifth century AD. Another name card I received bore the words *Kumaso densetsu* (legend[s] of the Kumaso) next to the photo of the mirror.

Most Japanese people, Mr. Ogata explained, continue to have a bad impression of the Kumaso, viewing them as a warlike tribe of barbarians who opposed the Yamato state from their remote mountain home in southern Kyushu. The Kumaso are, he suggested, viewed rather like the American Indians, although I suspect that many Americans today may not share the negative image Mr. Ogata thought this implied. In short, the time had come to do something about this negative stereotyping, and it had been decided to use archaeology to achieve this goal. Through education and excavation, the town office hoped to make people more aware of the sophisticated culture of the ancient Kumaso. With their links to China demonstrated by the gilt mirror, it was the non-Yamato identity of the Kumaso that seemed of most interest to the modern inhabitants of Menda. In addition to planning the excavations, the Board of Education had hosted lectures on archaeology and ancient history given by famous scholars. Mr. Ogata had even visited China in search of his Kumaso ancestors.

Later that afternoon, I sat relaxing in a small public bath back in the hot-spring town of Hitoyoshi. It was an old, wooden bathhouse, possibly even prewar. A thin layer of moss on the bottom of the stone bath was strangely comfortable against my tired feet. As an anthropologist, I couldn't help feeling uneasy about what I had seen and heard in Menda. Little is known for certain about the Kumaso, and there is no guarantee that they were the ancestors of the present people of Menda. Was the town really the center of the distribution of Menda pottery? If it were, what did that mean in social or ethnic terms? Why were the Mendans identifying themselves with the Kumaso but not with the Hayato? Other problems came to mind, but they all seemed somehow unimportant and evaporated with the steam from the bath.

Across the street from the bathhouse was a large hotel with a beer garden on the rooftop. It was just after five, and the only other customers were a couple of still-subdued salarymen. I sat under a line of gay paper lanterns and looked out over the mountains toward Menda. Though Japan's beer industry was still dominated by the four big corporations, that summer had seen the growing popularity of "regional" beers. The one I was drinking had been "Brewed in Kyushu for Kyushuans." To me, it tasted little different from most other Japanese beers but, as I was learning during my short visit to Menda, sometimes the label is more important than the contents.

From my bag I fished out a booklet about Menda that I had been given that morning. On the cover, "Menda" was written in Roman letters, and below it were small characters that read, *Menda-chō Chōsei Yōran* (A Survey of the Resources of Menda). The booklet was divided into two parts: tables of statistics at the back and glossy color photos and text at the front. In their own very different ways, both sections were effective at giving Menda a sense of community. With lists of everything from population to average temperature, from the number of vaccinations administered to the number of pigs raised, the statistics lent the impression of an enormously detailed picture of the day-to-day existence of the town. Reading through the figures, one could imagine Menda as a community in which every year 1,077 tons of trash are collected, 1,218 people use the town's badminton courts, and 1,485 women hold driver's licenses.

In complete contrast to this were the rather sentimental photos and text that began the book. A young girl puts her ear to a paper cup: "Listen! The footsteps of the Twenty-first century." To meet that approaching century, we must endeavor to "revive distinctive cultural activities appropriate to Menda." Part of this process was outlined under a section entitled *Kumaso fukken* (the rehabilitation of the Kumaso). After reading once again about how important the Menda area was in ancient Japan, I was somewhat surprised to turn the page and find the "*Menda Illust Map*" sporting a cartoon family with blonde hair and decidedly European features. Other photos depicted a woman milking a cow and a barber blow-drying a man's hair. What was the link between these people and the ancient Kumaso?

One of the villages that neighbors Menda is Suye Mura, the site of the first Western anthropological study of a Japanese community.[1] John Embree's 1939 monograph on Suye describes a village that is now much changed, yet at the same time significant tracks of continuity remain navigable between the two times and places. In Western Japanology, Suye is one of the most important topoi of Japanese identity, and I found it interesting that no one had mentioned the proximity of the village during my visit. It was possible that many were unaware of Embree's work. I suspected that most Mendans would certainly have felt an uncomfortable distance from the lives of the people in the photographs in the Suye monograph—despite the fact that several of the men I had met that day would have been born in the 1930s. Given this distance from the Japan of several generations past, why were the Mendans identifying themselves with the even more remote Kumaso?

Like many rural towns in Japan, Menda faces the challenge of how to revitalize itself and lure its young people back from the cities without losing sight of the changes of the new global information age. In this context, the Kumaso are a suitably malleable symbol of the town's identity. Identity is built from both biology and culture. The cultural elements are often assigned the status of tradition but could be better described as silent culture—elements that have only loose connections to the present and that can therefore easily be claimed for the purpose of identity building. Archaeological ruins are the silent culture par excellence, sleeping beneath the soil with none of the social anxieties born of precedence, waiting for the rediscovery and reinterpretation of each new generation. The Kumaso left no photographs or voices; their footsteps are gone forever and are now only audible in that perfect symbol of modern consumerism, the paper cup. I remembered Bashō walking through the summer grass at Hiraizumi. Nobody knew what lay beneath the taro fields in Menda, but whatever was found in the excavations later that summer, I felt sure that the dreams of the Kumaso would live on.

Notes

CHAPTER 1: INTRODUCTION

1. I am not suggesting here that such assumptions are only found in Japan. Forsythe (1989), for example, discusses similar attitudes held by Germans. What is perhaps unusual about the Japanese case is the level of support for such ideas. As Oblas (1995, 1) puts it, "If the Japanese myth of racial origins was an automobile, one might hear the consumer refrain that it outperforms the western model in terms of long-term reliability, flexible handling ability and attractive features."

2. (Moore 1994a, 15–16) argues that the political climate of the Cold War prevented American scholars from making full use of the Soviet approach to ethnogenesis. While political factors no doubt played a role, however, Gjessing (1975, 331) notes that unlike in the USSR and Eastern Europe, the topic of ethnogenesis was not respected in west European archaeology. It is interesting that ethnicity hardly receives a mention in English-language texts such as Bloch's *Marxism and Anthropology* (1983) or Spriggs' *Marxist Perspectives in Archaeology* (1984) and only warrants a brief entry in McGuire's *A Marxist Archaeology* (1992a), despite this author's own work on ethnicity (McGuire 1982).

3. In this book "mainland Japan" refers to the islands of Kyushu, Shikoku, and Honshu.

CHAPTER 2: TALES TOLD IN A DREAM

1. As early as 1894, however, Yagi and Shimomura had posited a chronological relationship between two types of Jōmon pottery at the Atamadai site in Chiba (Teshigawara 1988, 42–43).

2. Teshigawara (1988, 53) notes that Nakayama's use of "Aeneolithic" was not as an evolutionary stage but as a term to describe the coexistence of a Stone Age Ainu tribe and an Aeneolithic Japanese/Yayoi tribe. The continued dominance of ethnic interpretations of prehistory at this time is clear from debates over *dōtaku* (bronze bells). The discovery of four bells in Hyōgo Prefecture in 1912, for example, led to suggestions that they were used by Qin Chinese (Kita Sadakichi), by Miao tribesmen (Numata Yorisuke), and by an Indonesian-type people (Torii Ryūzō) (see Teshigawara 1988, 50). A 1923 article on bronze bells by Torii provides an excellent example of archeological interpretation in that decade. Torii attempts to answer the question of who made the bells (which were at that time not specifically associated with the Yayoi). He begins by noting that since the bells had not been found in *kofun,* they must date to before the Kofun age (though he was correct here, it was of course possible that they were of Kofun date but were not buried in the tombs). Several early documentary accounts of bell discoveries (the earliest of which dates to 668) support the belief that these objects were indeed foreign to the Kofun people. Torii proceeds to a contextual analysis of the design elements of the bells and ethnographic comparisons with the bronze drums of Southeast Asia. This leads him to the conclusion that the bells were made by an "Indo-Chinese" people such as the Miao, the Karen, or the Shan. While noting similarities between designs found on both the bells and Yayoi pottery, Torii regards the bell users and the makers of Yayoi pottery as ethnically separate (Torii 1974b[1923], 71).

3. Akazawa's work on the Jōmon-Yayoi transition is well known in the West but has been more or less ignored in Japan and does not even receive mention in Harunari's (1990) book on the formation of the Yayoi or in the ten-volume *Yayoi Bunka no Kenkyū (Studies on Yayoi Culture)* series edited by Kanaseki and Sahara (1985–1989).

4. McGuire (1992b, 816) on the liberal view of Indians as Americans.

CHAPTER 3: BIOLOGICAL ANTHROPOLOGY AND THE DUAL-STRUCTURE HYPOTHESIS

1. These sites are not identified in Yamaguchi's paper.

2. *Gekkan Bunkazai Shutsudo Hakkutsu Jōhō,* March 1994, p. 3.

3. However, a recent conference paper reports a secular increase in tooth size between early (Initial-Early) and late (Middle-Final) Jōmon populations (Manabe et al. 1993).

CHAPTER 4: THE LINGUISTIC ARCHAEOLOGY OF THE JAPANESE ISLANDS

1. This is the total *including* Japanese, which thus accounts for almost half of the speakers of Altaic languages (Ruhlen 1987, 127).

2. Technically, Ryukyuan is a group of dialects found across the Okinawan islands, but as a whole this group is separate from the mainland Japanese dialects.

3. The use of those words does not necessarily mean that the *matagi* are an Ainu population who have recently switched to speaking Japanese. A genetic study by Matsumoto et al. (1977) found the *matagi* to be closer to the Japanese than to the Ainu.

CHAPTER 5: FROM JŌMON TO YAYOI: THE ARCHAEOLOGY OF THE FIRST JAPANESE

1. Buckwheat seeds have also been reported from the Final Jōmon Shinbukuji site in Saitama, but the context is unclear (Nasu 1981, 53).

2. Rice phytoliths have also been reported from the body of a sherd of Middle Jōmon pottery at the Himesasahara site in Mikamo Village, Okayama Prefecture, but, again, full details have yet to be published.

3. Tooth ablation in the Islands may possibly date as far back as Minatogawa Man, ca. 18000 BP (see Han and Nakahashi 1996, 48).

CHAPTER 6: AN EMERGING SYNTHESIS?

1. Strictly speaking, I deal only with the Northern Iroquois here. The Southern Iroquois or Cherokee lived in the Carolinas and Virginia. A recent summary of Northern Iroquois archaeology can be found in Bamann et al. (1992).

2. Translated by Myres (1989, 218) as "It is impossible to solve so great a puzzle by using one route only."

CHAPTER 7: ETHNICITY AND THE ANCIENT STATE: A CORE/PERIPHERY APPROACH

1. Thought to be a mistake for the third year of Jingchu, i.e., AD 239 (Ishihara 1985, 50).

2. Middle Chinese *pjię-mjię-χuo*. This name is usually rendered "Himiko" in modern Japanese, but the final voiceless uvular fricative χ ("suggests that the

final element of the unknown original term did not correspond to Old Japanese *-ko,* which is rendered elsewhere—in *Fiko,* for example—with Middle Chinese *-k-* as one would expect. The final element of this transcription, then, remains obscure." (Miller 1967, 22).

3. The phonological identification of "Yamatai" with "Yamato" is by no means certain. While the final *-ai* may represent an earlier form of OJ *-ö,* it is otherwise unattested. Miller (1967, 18) notes that "Many of the *man'yōgana* characters used for Japanese syllables in *-o* are to be associated with Chinese forms that we would reconstruct in Middle Chinese *-âi.* This helps to show that the Yeh-ma-t'ai [*pinyin* Yematai]=Yamato identification is actually on a sound basis." Miller does not mention, however, that there is argument over the original final character in this word, as the *Wei zhi* has Yemayi (MC **i̯a-ma -·i̯ĕt*).

4. For a recent analysis of Yamato use of myths from the Harima region, see Palmer (1996).

5. According to the *Hou Han shu,* the country of Wa was in a state of unrest during the reigns of Huan-di (147–168) and Ling-di (168–189), although the *Liang shu* narrows this down to the Guanghe era (178–185) of the latter reign. Both the Wei and Later Han histories state that Pimiko was made queen after this period of internal strife.

6. The complexity of the debate over these names is shown by the fact that Nakamura (1993b, 29–103) devotes over seventy pages to a discussion of the usages and meanings of the term "Hayato."

7. Ikehata himself prefers to interpret these *kofun* distributions as *religious* opposition to Kinai burial forms (Ikehata 1992b).

8. The Yūryaku reference may be anachronistic.

9. In Chinese sources the Mohe are identified with the Sushen who, according to the *Nihon Shoki,* raided the Japan Sea coast on several occasions. As discussed by Tao (1976, 3–6), however, this identification is problematical. Kaiho (1987, 55) argues that the Watarishima Ezo were included in the Mohe country.

CHAPTER 8: THE UNBROKEN FOREST?: AINU ETHNOGENESIS AND THE EAST ASIAN WORLD-SYSTEM

1. With apologies to Americanists, I use the terms "Formative" and "Classic" to refer to the Proto and New Ainu stages. It remains to be seen, however, whether this is really the most appropriate way to divide up the Ainu period. In practice, a mainland Japan medieval-Tokugawa division is

still useful in Hokkaido, not least because pre-seventeenth century Ainu sites are still few in number and poorly understood.

2. Kaiho (1987, 199) notes that the Japanese names of the later Ainu war chiefs Koshamain and Shakushain seem to fall into the same pattern. It must be noted, however, that rather similar names are recorded for two Jilimi chiefs in the same entry: Dou Shennu and Yi Jinu. The ending -nu (slave) was in fact not unusual in China at this time, reflecting Buddhist and even Islamic influences (Serruys 1958). The *Jingshi Dadian* reverses the two characters of Guwei and calls them "Weigu."

3. The problem of a Sakhalin location for the Jilimi is too complex to discuss here in detail. The evidence is circumstantial but suggestive. For example, the *Jingshi Dadian* relates that the Guwei attacked the mainland in Jilimi boats, implying that the latter were also on Sakhalin, although in theory the boats may have been obtained from Jilimi on the mainland.

4. The term "Santan," itself of uncertain derivation, is not found in the historical sources until the eighteenth century.

5. Over the past century there has, of course, been considerable intermarriage between the Japanese and the Ainu. From family registers, Omoto estimated a 40% admixture rate in the Shizunai area of Hidaka District in the 1960s (see Omoto 1997, 70).

CHAPTER 9: JAPANESE ETHNICITY: SOME FINAL THOUGHTS

1. Harding's (1993) chapter, "Bronze Age Chiefdoms and the End of Stone Age Europe," for example is subtitled "The Rise of the Individual," implying that European and by extension Asian mentalities date back to prehistory.

2. The irony here is that postwar Japan has also "built its identity around its novelty, its discontinuity with the immediate past" of the Pacific War (Trott 1993, 3; see also Aoki 1994, 2). Such attitudes may not be limited to Japan but seem in part a result of the information overload of the contemporary world: "Late Capitalism consumes the past with amazing rapidity, spews it out with such dizzying speed that it has the effect of obliterating the past, including [one might say *especially*] the past of even 20 years ago" (Lee 1992, 37). In a footnote, Lee (1992, 44) goes on to cite Lowenthal's (1985) "provocative discussion of how both selective and cultural amnesia and an obsession with the past characterize the contradictory contemporary views of history."

3. The opposite view was expressed by Dutch poet Jan van Boendale (1285–1365): *Kerstenheit es gedeelt in tween: / die Walsche tonge die es een, / d'andre die Dietsche al geheel* ("Christendom is divided in twain: / The Romance tongue it is one, / The other all the Germanic tongues.") (Cited in Huizinga 1972, 20).

4. Batten *(in press)* makes an important distinction between boundaries and frontiers. The former are well-defined political or legal borders characteristic of nation-states, whereas the latter are vague transitional zones in which one society merges into another. Batten argues that Japan's premodern borders must be understood primarily as frontiers.

POSTSCRIPT

1. The village name would now be romanized as "Sue," but I retain the earlier form here, since my main interest is in Suye as an idea rather than as a place.

Bibliography

ABBREVIATIONS

AA	*Arctic Anthropology*
AJPA	*American Journal of Physical Anthropology*
AP	*Asian Perspectives*
ARA	*Annual Review of Anthropology*
AS	*Anthropological Science*
BIPPA	*Bulletin of the Indo-Pacific Prehistory Association*
CA	*Current Anthropology*
JASN	*Journal of the Anthropological Society of Nippon*
JJHG	*Japanese Journal of Human Genetics*
JJS	*Journal of Japanese Studies*
MN	*Monumenta Nipponica*
TASJ	*Transactions of the Asiatic Society of Japan*

Macrons are used only for Japanese language references. The names of Japanese, Chinese, and Korean authors writing in English are standardized to the Western order of given name followed by family name. The abbreviation ES denotes a Japanese work that has an English summary.

Abu-Lughod, Janet L. 1989. *Before European Hegemony: The World System, AD 1250–1350*. New York: Oxford University Press.

———. 1990. Restructuring the premodern world-system. *Review* 13(2): 273–286.

Adami, Norbert R. 1991. *Bibliography of Materials on the Ainu in European Languages*. Sapporo: Sapporo-do Booksellers.

Adams, William Y., Dennis P. van Gerven, and Richard S. Levy. 1978. The retreat from migrationism. *ARA* 7: 483–532.

Aikens, C. Melvin. 1981. The last 10,000 years in Japan and eastern North America: Parallels in environment, economic adaptation, growth of societal complexity, and the adoption of agriculture. In *Affluent Foragers: Pacific Coasts East and West,* ed. Shuzo Koyama and David Hurst Thomas, pp. 261–273. Osaka: Senri Ethnological Studies 9.

Aikens, C. Melvin, and Akazawa Takeru. 1988. Jomon-Yayoi continuity: Language, culture, population. Paper presented at the *53rd Annual Meeting of the Society of American Archaeology*. Phoenix, Arizona, April 30.

———. 1992. Fishing and farming in early Japan: Jomon littoral tradition carried into Yayoi times at the Miura caves on Tokyo Bay. In *Pacific Northeast Asia in Prehistory: Hunter-Fisher-Gatherers, Farmers, and Sociopoloitical Elites,* ed. C. M. Aikens and Song Nai Rhee, pp. 75–82. Pullman: Washington State University Press.

Aikens, C. Melvin, and Higuchi Takayasu. 1982. *Prehistory of Japan*. New York: Academic Press.

Ajisaka Makoto. 1986. "Shin Kyōto gakuha" no Nihon bunkaron. *Bunka Hyōron,* May, pp. 97–114.

Akamatsu Morio and Ushiro Hiroshi. 1992. Hokkaidō oyobi minami Saharin no chūsei ondanki ni tsuite no ichi kōsatsu [A note on the Neo-Atlantic stage in the Middle Ages in Hokkaido and south Sakhalin]. In *1991 Nendo "Kita no Rekishi-Bunka Kōryū Kenkyū Jigyō" Chūkan Hōkoku,* pp. 91–108. Sapporo: Historical Museum of Hokkaido. (ES)

Akazawa Takeru. 1981. Maritime adaptation of prehistoric hunter-gatherers and their transition to agriculture in Japan. In *Affluent Foragers: Pacific Coasts East and West,* ed. Shuzo Koyama and David Hurst Thomas, pp. 213–258. Osaka: Senri Ethnological Studies 9.

———. 1982. Cultural change in prehistoric Japan: Receptivity to rice agriculture in the Japanese archipelago. In *Advances in World Archaeology,* Vol. 1, ed. Fred Wendorf and Angela Close, pp. 151–211. New York: Academic Press.

———. 1986a. Hunter-gatherer adaptations and the transition to food production in Japan. In *Hunters in Transition: Mesolithic Societies of Temperate Eurasia and Their Transition to Farming,* ed. Marek Zvelebil, pp. 151–165. Cambridge: Cambridge University Press.

———. 1986b. Regional variation in procurement systems of Jomon hunter-gatherers. In *Prehistoric Hunter-Gatherers in Japan: New Research Methods,* ed. Takeru Akazawa and C. Melvin Aikens, pp. 73–89. Tokyo: Tokyo University Press.

———. 1988. Variability in the types of fishing adaptation of the later Jomon hunter-gatherers, c. 2500 to 300 BC. In *The Archaeology of Prehistoric Coastlines,* ed. Geoff Bailey and John Parkington, pp. 78–92. Cambridge: Cambridge University Press.

———. 1990. Les premiers riziculteurs du Japon. *La Recherche* 218: 142–148.

Alber, Heinz Hugo. 1977. Die Aufstände der Ainu und deren geschichtlicher Hintergrund. *Beiträge zur Japanologie* 14.

Algaze, Guillermo. 1993. *The Uruk World System: The Dynamics of Expansion of Early Mesopotamian Civilization.* Chicago: University of Chicago Press.

Alonso, Ana Maria. 1988. The effects of truth: Representations of the past and imagining of community. *Journal of Historical Sociology* 1(1): 33–57.

Amin, Samir. 1993. The ancient world-system versus the modern capitalist world-system. In *The World System: Five Hundred Years or Five Thousand?*, ed. A. G. Frank and B. K. Gills, pp. 247–277. London: Routledge.

Amino Yoshihiko. 1984. *Nihon Chūsei no Hinōgyōmin to Tennō.* Tokyo: Iwanami.

———. 1992a. Deconstructing "Japan." *East Asian History* 3: 121–142.

———. 1992b. Tōgoku to Saikoku, Kahoku to Kanan. In *Ajia no Naka no Nihonshi IV: Chi'iki to Minzoku,* ed. Arano Yasunori, Ishii Masatoshi, and Murai Shōsuke, pp. 233–250. Tokyo: Tokyo University Press.

———. 1994. Emperor, rice, and commoners. *Japanese Studies* 14(2): 1–12.

———. 1995. Les japonais et la mer. *Annales* 50(2): 235–258.

———. 1996. Emperor, rice, and commoners. In *Multicultural Japan: Palaeolithic to Postmodern,* ed. D. Denoon, M. Hudson, G. McCormack, and T. Morris-Suzuki, pp. 235–244. Melbourne: Cambridge University Press.

Anazawa Wakō. 1990. Kiba minzoku wa yatte kita no ka. In *Sōten: Nihon no Rekishi 2,* ed. Shiraishi Taichirō and Yoshimura Takehiko, pp. 74–89. Tokyo: Shinjinbutsu Ōraisha.

Anderson, Benedict. 1991. *Imagined Communities: Reflections on the Origin and Spread of Nationalism.* 2d. ed. London: Verso.

Anthony, David W. 1990. Migration in archeology: The baby and the bathwater. *American Anthropologist* 92: 895–914.

Aoki Kenichi. 1994. Maximum likelihood fit of a gradual admixture model to clines of gene frequencies in the main islands of Japan. *AS* 102(3): 285–294.

Aoki Kenichi and Omoto Keiichi. 1980. An analysis of the ABO gene frequency cline in Japan: A migration model. *JASN* 88(2): 109–122.

Aoki Michiko Yamaguchi. 1971. *Izumo Fudoki.* Tokyo: Sophia University.

Aoki Tamotsu. 1988. *Bunka no Hiteisei.* Tokyo: Chūō Kōronsha.

———. 1994. Anthropology and Japan: Attempts at writing culture. *The Japan Foundation Newsletter* 22(3): 1–6.

Arai Hakuseki. 1906. *Arai Hakuseki Zenshū,* Vol. 3. Tokyo: Yoshikawa Kōbunkan.

Arano Yasunori. 1988. *Kinsei Nihon to Higashi Ajia.* Tokyo: Tokyo University Press.

Armstrong, John A. 1982. *Nations before Nationalism.* Chapel Hill: University of North Carolina Press.

Arutjunov, Sergej Aleksandrovich. 1962. *Drevnij vostochno-aziatskij i ajnskij komponenty v etnogeneze yapontsev.* Ph.D. dissertation, Moscow.

Asai Toru 1974. Classification of dialects: Cluster analysis of Ainu dialects. *Hoppō Bunka Kenkyū* 8: 45–136.

Asato Susumu. 1992. Ryūkyū ōkoku no keisei. In *Ajia no Naka no Nihonshi IV: Chi'iki to Minzoku,* ed. Arano Yasunori, Ishii Masatoshi and Murai Shōsuke, pp. 111–136. Tokyo: Tokyo University Press.

Aston, W. G. 1879. A comparative study of the Japanese and Korean languages. *Journal of the Royal Asiatic Society of Great Britain and Ireland* 11.

———. 1905. Archaeology. In *Things Japanese,* by Basil Hall Chamberlain, pp. 27–34. London: John Murray.

———, trans. 1972. Reprint. *Nihongi.* Tokyo: Tuttle. Original edition, Japan Society, 1896.

Atwell, William S. 1982. International bullion flows and the Chinese economy *circa* 1530–1650. *Past and Present* 95: 68–90.

Bamann, Susan, Robert Kuhn, James Molnar, and Dean Snow. 1992. Iroquoian archaeology. *ARA* 21: 435–460.

Bannai Makato, Katsushi Tokunaga, Tadashi Imanishi, Shinji Harihara, Kiyoshi Fujisawa, Takeo Juji, and Keiichi Omoto. 1996. HLA class II alleles in Ainu living in Hidaka District, Hokkaido, northern Japan. *AJPA* 101: 1–9.

Barnes, Gina L. 1982. Toro. In *Atlas of Archaeology,* ed. K. Branigan, pp. 198–201. London: Book Club Associates/MacDonald.

———. 1986a. Paddy field archaeology in Nara, Japan. *Journal of Field Archaeology* 13: 371–379.

———. 1986b. *Jiehao, tonghao:* Peer relations in East Asia. In *Peer Polity Interaction and Socio-Political Change,* ed. C. Renfrew and J. Cherry, pp. 79–92. Cambridge: Cambridge University Press.

———. 1987. The role of the *be* in state formation. In *Specialization, Exchange and Complex Societies,* ed. E. Brumfiel and T. Earle, pp. 86–101. Cambridge: Cambridge University Press.

———. 1988. *Protohistoric Yamato: Archaeology of the First Japanese State.* Ann Arbor: Museum of Anthropology and Center for Japanese Studies, University of Michigan.

———. 1990a. The "idea of prehistory" in Japan. *Antiquity* 64: 929–940.

———. 1990b. Paddy soils then and now. *World Archaeology* 22(1): 1–17.

———. 1990c. Ceramics of the Yayoi agriculturalists (300 BC–AD 300). In *The Rise of a Great Tradition: Japanese Archaeological Ceramics from the Jomon through Heian Periods (10,500 BC–AD 1185),* ed. Erica Weeder, pp. 28–39. New York: Agency for Cultural Affairs, Government of Japan and the Japan Society.

———. 1990d. Early Korean states: A review of historical interpretation. In *Hoabinhian, Jomon, Yayoi, Early Korean States: Bibliographic Reviews of Far Eastern Archaeology 1990,* ed. Gina L. Barnes, pp. 113–162. Oxford: Oxbow.

———. 1992. The archaeology of protohistoric Yamato. Paper presented at the international conference *Japanese Archaeology in Protohistoric and Early Historic Period: Yamato and its Relations to Surrounding Populations.* Bonn, September 23–25.

———. 1993a. *China, Korea and Japan: The Rise of Civilization in East Asia.* London: Thames and Hudson.

———. 1993b. Miwa occupation in wider perspective. In *The Miwa Project Report: Survey, Coring and Excavation at the Miwa Site, Nara, Japan,* ed. G. L. Barnes and M. Okita, pp. 181–192. Oxford: Tempvs Repartvm.

———. 1993c. Family and state: The negotiation of identity in early Japan. Paper presented at the international conference *Stirrup, Sail and Plough: Continental and Maritime Influences on Japanese Identity.* Canberra, September 20–23.

Barshay, Andrew E. 1988. *State and Intellectual in Imperial Japan: The Public Man in Crisis.* Berkeley and Los Angeles: University of California Press.

Barth, Fredrick. 1969. *Ethnic Groups and Boundaries.* London: Allen & Unwin.

———. 1984. Problems in conceptualizing cultural pluralism, with illustrations from Somar, Oman. In *The Prospects for Plural Societies,* ed. David Maybury-Lewis, pp. 77–87. Washington, DC: American Ethnological Society.

Batten, Bruce. 1997. Kyōkai to wa nanika. In *Kyōkai no Nihonshi,* ed. Murai Shōsuke, Satō Noburu, and Yoshida Nakayuki, pp. 162–176. Tokyo: Yamakawa.

———. *in press.* Frontiers and boundaries of premodern Japan. *Journal of Historical Geography.*

Baugh, Albert C., and Thomas Cable. 1993. *A History of the English Language.* 4th ed. Englewood Cliffs, NJ: Prentice Hall.

Bayard, Donn. 1994. Linguistics, archaeologists, and Austronesian origins: Comparative and sociolinguistic aspects of the Meacham-Bellwood debate. Paper presented at the *15th IPPA conference,* Chiang Mai, Thailand, January.

Beardsley, Richard K. 1955. Japan before history: A survey of the archaeological record. *Far Eastern Quarterly* 14(3): 317–346.

Befu Harumi. 1965. Yayoi culture: An attempt at interpretation. *University of Michigan Center for Japanese Studies, Occasional Papers* 9: 3–49.

———. 1983. Internationalization of Japan and *Nihon bunkaron.* In *The Challenge of Japan's Internationalization: Organization and Culture,* ed. H. Mannari and H. Befu, pp. 232–266. Nishinomiya and Tokyo: Kwansei Gakuin University and Kodansha.

———. 1993. Nationalism and *Nihonjinron.* In *Cultural Nationalism in East Asia: Representation and Identity,* ed. Harumi Befu, pp. 107–135. Research Papers and Policy Studies 39, Institute of East Asian Studies, University of California, Berkeley.

Befu Harumi and Chester S. Chard. 1964. A prehistoric maritime culture of the Okhotsk Sea. *American Antiquity* 30(1): 1–18.

Bellwood, Peter. 1983a. New perspectives on Indo-Malaysian prehistory. *BIPPA* 4: 71–83.

———. 1983b. On "diffusionists" and legitimate aims in Polynesia prehistory. *AP* 13(2): 323–325.

———. 1985. A hypothesis for Austronesian origins. *AP* 26(1): 107–117.

———. 1991. The Austronesian dispersal and the origin of languages. *Scientific American* 265(1): 88–93.

———. 1992. Southeast Asia before history. In *The Cambridge History of Southeast Asia,* Vol. 1, ed. Nicholas Tarling, pp. 55–136. Cambridge: Cambridge University Press.

———. 1993a. The Austronesian dispersal and the origin of language families. In *The Illustrated History of Humankind,* Vol. 2, ed. Göran Burenhult, pp. 138–139. New York: HarperCollins.

———. 1993b. An archaeologist's view of language macrofamily relationships. *BIPPA* 13: 46–60.

———. 1994. An archaeologist's view of language macrofamily relationships. *Oceanic Linguistics* 33(2): 391–406.

———. 1996. Early agriculture and the dispersal of the southern Mongoloids. In *Prehistoric Mongoloid Dispersals,* ed. Akazawa Takeru and Emöke Szathmáry, pp. 287–302. Oxford: Oxford University Press.

———. 1997. Prehistoric cultural explanations for widespread language families. In *Archaeology and Linguistics: Aboriginal Australia in Global Perspective,* ed. Patrick McConvell and Nicholas Evans, pp. 123–124. Melbourne: Oxford University Press.

Bellwood, Peter, and Gina Barnes. 1993. Stone age farmers in southern and eastern Asia. In *The Illustrated History of Humankind,* Vol. 2, ed. Göran Burenhult, pp. 122–143. New York: HarperCollins.

Benedict, Paul K. 1990. *Japanese/Austro-Tai.* Ann Arbor, MI: Karoma.

Benedict, Ruth. 1954. *The Chrysanthemum and the Sword: Patterns of Japanese Culture.* Tokyo: Tuttle.

Bentley, G. Carter. 1987. Ethnicity and practice. *Comparative Studies in Society and History* 29: 24–55.

Berry, Mary Elizabeth. 1986. Public peace and private attachment: The goals and conduct of power in early modern Japan. *JJS* 12(2): 237–271.

Bicchieri, M. G., ed. 1972. Introduction to *Hunters and Gatherers Today,* pp. 448–449. New York: Holt, Rinehart, and Winston.

Bickmore, Albert S. 1868a. The Ainos, or hairy men of Yesso. *American Journal of Science and Arts* 45 (135): 353–361.

———. 1868b. The Ainos, or hairy men, of Saghalien and the Kurile Islands. *American Journal of Science and Arts* 45 (135): 361–377.

Binford, Lewis R. 1968. Some comments on historical versus processual archaeology. *Southwestern Journal of Anthropology* 24: 267–275.

Black, Lydia. 1973. The Nivkh (Gilyak) of Sakhalin and the lower Amur. *AA* 10(1): 1–110.

Blacker, Carmen. 1988. Two Shinto myths: The golden age and the chosen people. In *Themes and Theories in Modern Japanese History,* ed. Sue Henry and Jean-Pierre Lehmann, pp. 64–77. London: Athlone.

Blanton, Richard, and Gary Feinman. 1984. The Mesoamerican world-system. *American Anthropologist* 86(3): 673–692.

Bleed, Peter. 1972. Yayoi cultures of Japan: An interpretive summary. *AA* 9(2): 1–23.

———. 1974. Patterns and continuity in protohistoric Japan. *AA* 11 (Suppl.): 177–181.

———. 1986. Almost archaeology: Early archaeological interest in Japan. In *Windows on the Japanese Past,* ed. R. Pearson, pp. 57–67. Ann Arbor: Center for Japanese Studies, University of Michigan.

Bloch, Maurice. 1983. *Marxism and Anthropology.* Oxford: Oxford University Press.

Boas, Franz. 1940. *Race, Language and Culture.* New York: Macmillan.

Bolitho, Harold. 1993. 1868—the war in the north. In *Kinsei Nihon no Seiji to Gaikō,* ed. Fujino Tamotsu Sensei Kanreki Kinenkai, pp. 1–10. Tokyo: Yūzankaku.

Boller, Anton. 1857. *Nachweis, daß das Japanische zum Ural-Altaischen stämme gehort.* Vienna.

Borlase, William Copeland. 1876. *Niphon and its Antiquities: An Essay on the Ethnology, Mythology, and Religions of the Japanese.* Plymouth, U.K.: W. Brendon.

Bornoff, Nicholas. 1991. *Pink Samurai: Love, Marriage and Sex in Contemporary Japan.* New York: Pocket Books.

Boutilier, James A. 1989. Metropole and margin: The dependency theory and the political economy of the Solomon Islands, 1880–1980. In *Centre and Periphery: Comparative Studies in Archaeology,* ed. T. C. Champion, pp. 22–39. London: Unwin Hyman.

Brace, C. Loring, M. L. Brace, and W. R. Leonard. 1989. Reflections on the face of Japan: A multivariate craniofacial and odontometric perspective. *AJPA* 78: 93–113.

Brace, C. Loring, and M. Nagai. 1982. Japanese tooth size: Past and present. *AJPA* 59: 399–411.

Brace, C. Loring, and David P. Tracer. 1992. Craniofacial continuity and change: A comparison of late Pleistocene and Recent Europe and Asia. In *The Evolution and Dispersal of Modern Humans in Asia,* ed. T. Akazawa, K. Aoki, and T. Kimura, pp. 439–471. Tokyo: Hokuensha.

Brace, C. Loring, David P. Tracer, and Kevin D. Hunt. 1991. Human craniofacial form and the evidence for the peopling of the Pacific. *BIPPA* 11: 247–269.

Braudel, Fernand. 1988–1990. *The Identity of France,* 2 vols. London: Collins.

Brewer, Anthony. 1980. *Marxist Theories of Imperialism: A Critical Survey.* London: Routledge and Kegan Paul.

Bromley, Yu. 1974a. Ethnos and endogamy. *Soviet Anthropology and Archeology* 13(1): 55–69.

———. 1974b. The term *ethnos* and its definition. In *Soviet Ethnology and Anthropology Today,* ed. Yu Bromley, pp. 55–72. The Hague: Mouton.

———. 1983. *Ethnic Processes.* Moscow: Social Sciences Today, USSR Academy of Sciences.

Broodbank, Cyprian, and Thomas F. Strasser. 1991. Migrant farmers and the Neolithic colonization of Crete. *Antiquity* 65: 233–245.

Brown, Cecil H. 1994. Lexical acculturation in Native American languages. *CA* 35(2): 95–117.

Brown, Delmer M. 1955. *Nationalism in Japan: An Introductory Historical Analysis.* Berkeley and Los Angeles: University of California Press.

———. 1993. The Yamato kingdom. In *The Cambridge History of Japan,* Vol. 1, *Ancient Japan,* ed. Delmer M. Brown, pp. 108–162. Cambridge: Cambridge University Press.

Brown, Philip C. 1993. *Central Authority and Local Autonomy in the Formation of Early Modern Japan: The Case of Kaga Domain.* Stanford, CA: Stanford University Press.

Brownlee, John S. 1988. The Jeweled Comb-Box: Motoori Norinaga's *Tamakushige. MN* 43(1): 35–61.

Brumfiel, Elizabeth M. 1994a. Factional competition and political development in the New World: An introduction. In *Factional Competition and Political Development in the New World,* ed. E. M. Brumfiel and John W. Fox, pp. 3–13. Cambridge: Cambridge University Press.

———. 1994b. Ethnic groups and political development in ancient Mexico. In *Factional Competition and Political Development in the New World,* ed. E. M. Brumfiel and John W. Fox, pp. 89–102. Cambridge: Cambridge University Press.

Bryan, J. Ingram. 1925. The origin of the Japanese race. *Transactions and Proceedings of the Japan Society, London* 22: 89–105.

Bryson, Reid A., and Christine Padoch. 1981. On the climates of history. In *Climate and History: Studies in Interdisciplinary History,* ed. R. I. Rotberg and T. K. Rabb, pp. 3–17. Princeton, NJ: Princeton University Press.

Buffetaut, Eric. 1976. L'origine des Aïnous: Un problème anthropologique obscur. *La Recherche* 73: 1085–1087.

Buruma, Ian. 1987. Umehara Takeshi-shi wa yahari Yamatoisuto. *Chūō Kōron* 10: 236–243.

———. 1994. Japan against itself. *New York Review of Books,* May 12, pp. 18–22.

Buxton, L. H. Dudly. 1925. *The Peoples of Asia.* London: Kegan Paul, Trench, Trubner.

Bynon, Theodora. 1983. *Historical Linguistics.* Cambridge: Cambridge University Press.

Calman, Donald. 1992. *The Nature and Origins of Japanese Imperialism: A Reinterpretation of the Great Crisis of 1873.* London: Routledge.

Caron, François, and Joost Schouten. 1935. *A True Description of the Mighty Kingdoms of Japan and Siam (1636).* Reprint of English edition of 1663. London: Argonaut Press.

Carter, William R. 1983. Kikajin. In *Kodansha Encyclopedia of Japan,* Vol. 4, p. 205. Tokyo: Kodansha.

Cavalli-Sforza, L. L., P. Menozzi, and A. Piazza. 1994. *The History and Geography of Human Genes.* Princeton, NJ: Princeton University Press.

Chamberlain, Basil Hall. 1887. The language, mythology and geographical nomenclature of Japan, viewed in the light of Aino studies. *Memoirs of the Literature College, Imperial University of Japan* 1.

———. 1895. Essay in aid of a grammar and dictionary of the Luchuan language. *TASJ* 23 (Supp.).

———. 1905. *Things Japanese, Being Notes on Various Subjects Connected with Japan.* 5th ed. London: John Murray.

Champion, Timothy C., ed. 1989a. *Centre and Periphery: Comparative Studies in Archaeology*. London: Unwin Hyman.

———. 1989b. Introduction. In *Centre and Periphery: Comparative Studies in Archaeology.*, ed. T. C. Champion, pp. 1–21. London: Unwin Hyman.

Chang, K. C. 1992. The circumpacific substratum of ancient Chinese civilization. In *Pacific Northeast Asia in Prehistory: Hunter-Fisher-Gatherers, Farmers, and Sociopolitical Elites,* ed. C. M. Aikens and Song Nai Rhee, pp. 217–221. Pullman: Washington State University Press.

Chapdelaine, Claude. 1992. "L'origine des Iroquoiens dans le nord-est." Remise en question de l'hypothèse *in situ. Recherches Amérindiennes au Québec* 22(4): 3–4.

Chapman, John, and Pavel Dolukhanov. 1993. Cultural transformations and interactions in Eastern Europe: Theory and terminology. In *Cultural Transformations and Interactions in Eastern Europe,* ed. John Chapman and Pavel Dolukhanov, pp. 1–36. Aldershot, England: Avebury.

Chard, Chester S. 1956. Chronology and culture succession in the northern Kuriles. *American Antiquity* 21(3): 287–292.

Chase-Dunn, Christopher. 1992. The comparative study of world-systems. *Review* 15(3): 313–333.

———. 1993. Comparing world-systems: Concepts and working hypotheses. *Social Forces* 71(4): 851–886.

Chase-Dunn, Christopher, and Thomas D. Hall. 1991a. Conceptualizing core/periphery hierarchies for comparative study. In *Core/Periphery Relations in Precapitalist Worlds,* ed. C. Chase-Dunn and T. D. Hall, pp. 5–44. Boulder, CO: Westview.

———, eds. 1991b. *Core/Periphery Relations in Precapitalist Worlds*. Boulder, CO: Westview.

Chew, J. J. 1976. The prehistory of the Japanese language in the light of evidence from the structures of Japanese and Korea. *AP* 19(1): 190–200.

———. 1989. The significance of geography in understanding the relationship of Japanese to other languages. *Bochumer Jahrbuch zur Ostasienforschung* 12, I: 13–49.

Chisholm, Brian, Koike Hiroko, and Nakai Nobuyuki. 1992. Carbon isotopic determination of paleodiet in Japan: Marine versus terrestial resources. In *Pacific Northeast Asia in Prehistory: Hunter-Fisher-Gatherers, Farmers, and Sociopoloitical Elites,* ed. C. M. Aikens and Song Nai Rhee, pp. 69–74. Pullman: Washington State University Press.

Choe Chong-Pil. 1990. Origins of agriculture in Korea. *Korea Journal* 30(11): 4–14.

Chon Young-Nai. 1990. Yayoi, inasaku bunka no genryū: Masei sekki o chūshin toshite. In *Kodai Chōsen to Nihon*, ed. Nishitani Tadashi, pp. 17–73. Tokyo: Meicho.

———. 1992. Introduction of rice agriculture into Korea and Japan: From the perspective of polished stone implements. In *Pacific Northeast Asia in Prehistory: Hunter-Fisher-Gatherers, Farmers, and Sociopoloitical Elites*, ed. C. M. Aikens and Song Nai Rhee, pp. 161–169. Pullman: Washington State University Press.

Clark, Donald W. 1992. "Only a skin boat load or two": The role of migration in Kodiak prehistory. *AA* 29(1): 2–17.

Cohen, Ronald. 1978. Ethnicity: Problems and focus in anthropology. *ARA* 7: 379–403.

Collett, David. 1987. A contribution to the study of migrations in the archaeological record: The Ngoni and Kololo migrations as a case study. In *Archaeology as Long-Term History*, ed. Ian Hodder, pp. 105–116. Cambridge: Cambridge University Press.

Cooper, Michael. 1965. *They Came to Japan: An Anthology of European Reports on Japan, 1543–1640*. London: Thames and Hudson.

———. 1973. *This Island of Japon: Jaõa Rodrigues' Account of 16th-Century Japan*. Tokyo: Kodansha.

Crawford, Gary W. 1983. *Paleoethnobotany of the Kameda Peninsula Jomon*. Anthropological Papers No. 73, Museum of Anthropology, University of Michigan.

———. 1992a. The transitions to agriculture in Japan. In *Transitions to Agriculture in Prehistory*, ed. A. B. Gebauer and T. D. Price, pp. 117–132. Madison, WI: Prehistory Press.

———. 1992b. Prehistoric plant domestication in East Asia. In *The Origins of Agriculture: An International Perspective*, ed. C. W. Cowan and P. J. Watson, pp. 7–38. Washington, DC: Smithsonian.

Crawford, Gary W., and Takamiya Hiroto. 1990. The origins and implications of late prehistoric plant husbandry in northern Japan. *Antiquity* 64: 889–911.

Crawford, Gary W., and Yoshizaki Masakazu 1987. Ainu ancestors and prehistoric Asian agriculture. *Journal of Archaeological Science* 14: 201–213.

Crone, Patricia. 1986. The tribe and the state. In *States in History*, ed. J. A. Hall, pp. 48–77. Oxford: Basil Blackwell.

———. 1993. Tribes and states in the Middle East. *Journal of the Royal Asiatic Society* 3(3): 353–376.

Crump, Thomas. 1991. *The Death of an Emperor: Japan at the Crossroads*. Oxford: Oxford University Press.

Dale, Peter N. 1986. *The Myth of Japanese Uniqueness*. London: Croom Helm.

D'Andrea, A. Catherine. 1992. *Paleoethnobotany of Later Jomon and Early Yayoi Cultures in Northeastern Japan: Northeastern Aomori and Southwestern Hokkaido*. Ph.D. dissertation, University of Toronto.

D'Andrea, A. Catherine, G. W. Crawford, M. Yoshizaki, and M. Kudo. 1995. Late Jomon cultigens in northeastern Japan. *Antiquity* 69: 146–152.

Daniel, Glyn. 1962. *The Idea of Prehistory*. London: C. A. Watts.

Deagan, Kathleen. 1983. *Spanish St. Augustine: The Archaeology of a Colonial Creole Community*. New York: Academic Press.

———. 1988. The archaeology of the Spanish contact period in the Caribbean. *Journal of World Prehistory* 2(2): 187–233.

———. 1991. Historical archaeology's contribution to our understanding of early America. In *Historical Archaeology in Global Perspective*, ed. Lisa Falk, pp. 97–112. Washington, DC: Smithsonian.

———. 1992. Europe's first foothold in the New World: La Isabela. *National Geographic* 181(1): 40–53.

Dennell, R. W. 1985. The hunter-gatherer/agricultural frontier in prehistoric temperate Europe. In *The Archaeology of Frontiers and Boundaries,* ed. S. W. Green and S. M. Perlman, pp. 113–139. London: Academic Press.

Denoon, Donald. 1983. *Settler Capitalism: The Dynamics of Dependent Development in the Southern Hemisphere*. Oxford: Clarendon.

de Rachewiltz, Igor. 1973. Some remarks on the ideological foundations of Chingis Khan's empire. *Papers on Far Eastern History* 7: 21–36.

Deriha Kōji. 1989. Ainu no dentōteki gyōgu (mareku) no seiritsu haikei ni kansuru ichi shiron. *Busshitsu Bunka* 51: 19–54.

Diamond, Jared. 1997. *Guns, Germs, and Steel: The Fates of Human Societies.* New York: W. W. Norton.

Dietler, Michael. 1994. "Our ancestors the Gauls": Archaeology, ethnic nationalism, and the manipulation of Celtic identity in modern Europe. *American Anthropologist* 96(3): 584–605.

Dincauze, Dena F., and Robert J. Hasenstab. 1989. Explaining the Iroquois: Tribalization on a prehistoric periphery. In *Centre and Periphery: Comparative Studies in Archaeology,* ed. T. C. Champion, pp. 67–87. London: Unwin Hyman.

Dodo Yukio. 1974. Non-metrical cranial traits in the Hokkaido Ainu and the northern Japanese of recent times. *JASN* 82(1): 31–51.

———. 1983. A human skull of the Epi-Jomon period from the Minami Usu Six site, Date, Hokkaido. *JASN* 91(2): 169–86.

———. 1986. Metrical and non-metrical analyses of Jomon crania from eastern Japan. In *Prehistoric Hunter-Gatherers in Japan: New Research Methods,* ed. Takeru Akazawa and C. Melvin Aikens, pp. 137–162. Tokyo: Tokyo University Press.

———. 1987. Supraorbital foramen and hypoglossal canal bridging: The two most suggestive nonmetric cranial traits in discriminating major racial groupings of man. *JASN* 95(1): 19–35.

Dodo Yukio and Ishida Hajime. 1987. Incidences of non-metric cranial variants in several population samples from East Asia and North America. *JASN* 95: 161–177.

———. 1990. Population history of Japan as viewed from cranial nonmetric variation. *JASN* 98(3): 269–287.

———. 1992. Consistency of nonmetric cranial trait expression during the last 2,000 years in the habitants of the central islands of Japan. *JASN* 100(4): 417–423.

Dodo Yukio, Naomi Doi, and Osamu Kondo. 1998. Ainu and Ryukyuan cranial nonmetric variation: evidence which disputes the Ainu-Ryukyu common origin theory. *AS* 106: 99–102.

Dodo Yukio, Ishida Hajime, and Saito Naruya. 1992. Population history of Japan: A cranial nonmetric approach. In *The Evolution and Dispersal of Modern Humans in Asia,* ed. T. Akazawa, K. Aoki, and T. Kimura, pp. 479–492. Tokyo: Hokuensha.

Dodo Yukio, Kida Masahiko, Ishida Hajime, and Matsumura Hirofumi. 1991. Hokkaidō Akkeshi-chō Shimodanosawa iseki shutsudo no Satsumon jidai jinkotsu [A human skeleton of the Satsumon period from the Shimodanosawa site, Akkeshi-chō, eastern Hokkaido]. *JASN* 99(4): 463–475. (ES)

Dönitz, W. 1887. Vorgeschichte Graeber in Japan. *Zeitschrift für Ethnologie* 19: 114–126.

Dower, John W. 1986. *War Without Mercy: Race and Power in the Pacific War.* New York: Pantheon.

Dragadze, T. 1980. The place of "ethnos" theory in Soviet anthropology. In *Soviet and Western Anthropology,* ed. Ernest Gellner, pp. 161–170. London: Duckworth.

Earl, David Magarey. 1964. *Emperor and Nation in Japan: Political Thinkers of the Tokugawa Period.* Seattle: University of Washington Press.

Edens, Christopher. 1988. Dynamics of trade in the ancient Mesopotamian "world system." *American Anthropologist* 94(1): 118–139.

Edmonds, Richard Louis. 1985. *Northern Frontiers of Qing China and Tokugawa Japan: A Comparative Study of Frontier Policy.* Chicago: University of Chicago, Dept. of Geography Research Paper 213.

Edwards, Walter. 1983. Event and process in the founding of Japan: The horserider theory in archaeological perspective. *JJS* 9(2): 265–296.

———. 1991. Buried discourse: The Toro archaeological site and Japanese national identity in the early postwar period. *JJS* 17(1): 1–23.

———. 1995. Kobayashi Yukio's "Treatise on Duplicate Mirrors": An annotated translation. *Tenri Daigaku Gakuhō* 178: 179–205.

———. 1996. In pursuit of Himiko: Postwar archaeology and the location of Yamatai. *MN* 51(1): 53–79.

———. 1997. Japan's new past. *Archaeology* March/April: 32–42.

Egami Namio. 1949. Ainu no chashi to Roshia no gorodische. *Minzokugaku Kenkyū* 13(3).

———. 1964. The formation of the people and the origin of the state in Japan. *Memoirs of the Research Department, Toyo Bunko* 23: 35–70.

Ekholm, Kajsa. 1977. External exchange and the transformation of central African social systems. In *The Evolution of Social Systems,* ed. J. Friedman and M. Rowlands, pp. 115–136. London: Duckworth.

Ekholm, Kajsa, and Jonathan Friedman. 1982. "Capital" imperialism and exploitation in ancient world-systems. *Review* 6(1): 87–109.

Elvin, Mark. 1973. *The Pattern of the Chinese Past: A Social and Economic Interpretation.* London: Eyre Methuen.

Embree, John F. 1939. *Suye Mura: A Japanese Village.* Chicago: University of Chicago Press.

Emori Susumu. 1982. *Hokkaidō Kinseishi no Kenkyū.* Sapporo: Hokkaido Shuppan Kikaku Sentā.

———. 1987. "Ezochi" no rekishi to Nihon shakai. In *Nihon no Shakaishi 1: Rettō Naigai no Kōtsū to Kokka,* ed. Amino Yoshihiko, pp. 313–351. Tokyo: Iwanami.

Engelbrecht, William. 1974. The Iroquois: Archaeological patterning on the tribal level. *World Archaeology* 6(1): 52–65.

———. 1978. Ceramic patterning between New York Iroquois sites. In *The Spatial Organization of Culture,* ed. Ian Hodder, pp. 141–152. London: Duckworth.

Enloe, Cynthia H. 1980. *Ethnic Soldiers: State Security in a Divided Society.* Harmondsworth: Penguin.

Esaka Teruya. 1977. Jōmon no saibai shokubutsu to riyō shokubutsu. *Dorumen* 13: 15–31.

Esaka Teruya, Kokawa Shōhei, and Fujiwara Hiroshi. 1978. Ine no denrai. In *Chika ni Rekishi o Horu: Nihon no Kōkogaku Hyakunen,* ed. Saitō Tadashi, pp. 151–184. Tokyo: Asahi Shinbunsha.

Fagan, Brian M. 1995. *Ancient North America: The Archaeology of a Continent.* 2d. ed. London: Thames and Hudson.

Farrington, Ian S., and James Urry. 1985. Food and the early history of cultivation. *Journal of Ethnobiology* 5(2): 143–157.

Farris, William Wayne. 1985. *Population, Disease, and Land in Early Japan, 645–900.* Cambridge, MA, and London: Council on East Asian Studies, Harvard University, and the Harvard-Yenching Institute.

———. 1992. *Heavenly Warriors: The Evolution of Japan's Military Elite, 500–1300.* Cambridge, MA, and London: Council on East Asian Studies, Harvard University, and the Harvard-Yenching Institute.

———. 1993. Diseases of the premodern period in Japan. In *The Cambridge World History of Human Disease,* ed. Kenneth F. Kiple, pp. 376–385. Cambridge: Cambridge University Press.

Fawcett, Clare. 1986. The politics of assimilation in Japanese archaeology. *Archaeological Review from Cambridge* 5(1): 43–57.

———. 1996. The practice of archaeology in Japan and Japanese identity. In *Multicultural Japan: Palaeolithic to Postmodern,* ed. D. Denoon, M. Hudson, G. McCormack, and T. Morris-Suzuki, pp. 60–77. Melbourne: Cambridge University Press.

Fiedel, Stuart J. 1987. Algonquian origins: A problem in archeological-linguistic correlation. *Archaeology of Eastern North America* 15: 1–11.

———. 1990. Middle Woodland Algonquian expansion: A refined model. *North American Archaeologist* 11(3): 209–230.

———. 1991. Correlating archaeology and linguistics: The Algonquian case. *Man in the Northeast* 41: 9–32.

Firestone, Melvin. 1992. Inuit derived culture traits in northern Newfoundland. *AA* 29(1): 112–128.

Fitting, James E. 1978. Regional cultural development, 300 BC to AD 1000. In *Handbook of North American Indians,* Vol. 15, *The Northeast,* ed. Bruce Trigger, pp. 44–57. Washington, DC: Smithsonian.

Flershem, Robert G. 1964. Some aspects of Japan Sea trade in the Tokugawa period. *Journal of Asian Studies* 23: 405–416.

———. 1966. Some aspects of Japan Sea shipping and trade in the Tokugawa period, 1603–1867. *Proceedings of the American Philosophical Society* 110(3): 182–226.

Flynn, Dennis O., and Arturo Giráldez. 1995. Born with a "silver spoon": The origin of world trade in 1571. *Journal of World History* 6(2): 201–221.

Forsythe, Diana. 1989. German identity and the problem of history. In *History and Ethnicity,* ed. E. Tonkin, M. McDonald, and M. Chapman, pp. 137–156. London: Routledge.

Foster, Robert J. 1991. Making national cultures in the global ecumene. *ARA* 20: 235–260.

Frank, Andre Gunder. 1990. A theoretical introduction to 5,000 years of world system history. *Review* 13(2): 155–250.

———. 1993. Bronze age world system cycles. *CA* 34(4): 383–429.

Frank, Andre Gunder, and Barry K. Gills, eds. 1993. *The World System: Five Hundred Years or Five Thousand?* London: Routledge.

Frankenstein, Susan, and M. J. Rowlands, 1978. The internal structure and regional context of Early Iron Age society in south-western Germany. *Institute of Archaeology Bulletin* 15: 73–112.

Friday, Karl F. 1994. The taming of the shrewd: the conquest of the Emishi and northern Japan. *Japan Foundation Newsletter* 21(6): 17–22.

Fried, Morton H. 1975. *The Notion of the Tribe.* Menlo Park, CA: Cummings.

———. 1983. Tribe to state or state to tribe in ancient China? In *The Origins of Chinese Civilization,* ed. David N. Keightley, pp. 467–493. Berkeley and Los Angeles: University of California Press.

Friedman, Jonathan. 1992. The past in the future: History and the politics of identity. *American Anthropologist* 94(4): 837–859.

———. 1994. On perilous ideas. *CA* 35(2): 173–174.

Fuentes, Carlos. 1992. *The Buried Mirror: Reflections on Spain and the New World.* London: André Deutsch.

Fujiguchi Kenji. 1986. Chōsen mumon doki to Yayoi doki. In *Yayoi Bunka no Kenkyū,* Vol. 3, ed. Kanaseki Hiroshi and Sahara Makoto, pp. 147–162. Tokyo: Yūzankaku.

Fujimori Eiichi. 1970. *Jōmon Nōkō.* Tokyo: Gakuseisha.

Fujimoto Tsuyoshi. 1965. Ohōtsuku bunka no sōsei ni tsuite. *Busshitsu Bunka* 6: 15–30.

———. 1984. Tobinitai bunka no iseki ritchi. In *Hokkaidō no Kenkyū 2: Kōkogaku II,* ed. Ishizuki Kisao, pp. 209–235. Ōsaka: Seibundō.

———. 1986. Ohōtsukukai o meguru kōryū. In *Nihon no Kodai 3: Umi o Koete no Kōryū,* ed. Ōbayashi Taryō, pp. 233–264. Tokyo: Chūō Kōronsha.

———. 1988. *Mō Futatsu no Nihon Bunka.* Tokyo: Tokyo University Press.

———. 1990. Ohōtsukukai engan no bunka. In *Umi to Rettō Bunka 1: Nihonkai to Hokkoku Bunka,* ed. Amino Yoshihiko, pp. 67–93. Tokyo: Shōgakukan.

Fujio Shin'ichirō. 1987. Inasaku juyōki no kamegata doki kenkyū. In *Higashi Ajia no Kōko to Rekishi,* Vol. 2, ed. Okazaki Takeshi Sensei Taikan Kinen Jigyōkai, pp. 293–323. Kyoto: Dōhōsha.

———. 1991. Suitō nōkō kaishiki no chi'ikisei. *Kōkogaku Kenkyū* 38(2): 30–54.

———. 1993. Seigyō kara mita Jōmon kara Yayoi [Jomon to Yayoi as seen through subsistence]. *Kokuritsu Rekishi Minzoku Hakubutsukan Kenkyū Hōkoku* 48: 1–66. (ES)

Fujita Hisashi. 1995. Geographical and chronological differences in dental caries in the Neolithic Jomon period of Japan. *AS* 103(1): 23–37.

Fujita Yoshiko, Tanimura Masako, and Tanaki Katsumi. 1978. The distribution of the ABO blood groups in Japan. *JJHG* 23: 63–109.

Fujitani Takashi. 1993. Inventing, forgetting, remembering: Toward a historical ethnography of the nation-state. In *Cultural Nationalism in East Asia: Representation and Identity,* ed. Harumi Befu, pp. 77–106. Research Papers and Policy Studies 39, Institute of East Asian Studies, University of California, Berkeley.

Fujiwara Hiroshi. 1976. Puranto opāru bunseki ni yoru kodai saibai shokubutsu ibutsu no tansaku [Investigation on the remains of crops in ancient times by plant opal analysis]. *Kōkogaku Zasshi* 62(2): 54–62. (ES p. 90)

———. 1982. Puranto opāru kara mita Jōmon kara Yayoi. *Rekishi Kōron* 74: 63–70.

———. 1987. Application of plant-opal analysis to archeological surveys of agricultural sites. In *Development and Isolation in the Pacific,* pp. 40–42. Osaka and Tokyo: IPPA, the Japanese Society for Oceanic Studies, and the National Museum of Ethnology.

———. 1988. Puranto opāru bunseki ni yoru nōkōseki no tsuikyū. In *Yayoi Bunka no Kenkyū,* Vol. 2, ed. Kanaseki Hiroshi and Sahara Makoto, pp. 117–123. Tokyo: Yūzankaku.

———. 1990. Puranto opāru ga shimesu Yayoi to "Jōmon." In *Saishin Nihon Bunka Kigenron,* pp. 92–95. Tokyo: Gakken.

———. 1993. Research into the history of rice cultivation using plant opal analysis. In *Current Research in Phytolith Analysis: Applications in Archaeology and Paleoecology,* ed. D. M. Pearsall and D. C. Piperro, pp. 147–158. Philadelphia: MASCA Research Papers in Science and Archaeology 10.

Fukuda Ryōsuke. 1965. *Nara Jidai Tōgoku Hōgen no Kenkyū.* Tokyo: Kazama Shobō.

Fukuda Tomoyuki and Hendei Kazurō. 1974. Kitachishima Paramushiru-tō hakken no doki ni tsuite. *Hokkaidō Kōkogaku* 10.

Furuta Masataka. 1968. Jōmon banki shotō no momigara atsukon doki. *Kōkogaku Jānaru* 24: 20–21.

———. 1972. Kureishibaru iseki: Jōmon banki nōkō seisan bunka no shisō. In *Hyakunin Iinkai Maizō Bunkazai Hōkoku* 7, pp. 1–72.

Gailey, Christine W., and Thomas C. Patterson. 1987. Power relations and state formation. In *Power Relations and State Formation,* ed. T. C. Patterson and C. W. Gailey, pp. 1–26. Washington, DC: American Anthropological Association.

Gamble, Clive. 1993. People on the move: Interpretations of regional variation in Palaeolithic Europe. In *Cultural Transformations and Interactions in Eastern Europe,* ed. John Chapman and Pavel Dolukhanov, pp. 37–55. Aldershot, England: Avebury.

Gardiner, K. H. J. 1969. *The Early History of Korea.* Canberra: Australian National University Press.

Geertz, Clifford. 1988. *Works and Lives: The Anthropologist as Author.* Stanford, CA: Stanford University Press.

Gellner, Ernest. 1983. *Nations and Nationalism.* Oxford: Basil Blackwell.

———. 1988. *Plough, Sword and Book: The Structure of Human History.* London: Collins-Harvill.

Giesen, Bernhard, ed. 1991. *Nationale und kulturelle Identität: Studien zur Entwicklung des kollektiven Bewußtseins in der Neuzeit.* Frankfurt: Suhrkamp.

Gills, Barry K., and Andre Gunder Frank. 1991. 5000 years of world system history: The cumulation of accumulation. In *Core/Periphery Relations in Precapitalist Worlds,* ed. C. Chase-Dunn and T. D. Hall, pp. 67–112. Boulder, CO: Westview.

Gjerdman, O. 1926. Word parallels between Ainu and other languages. *Le Monde Oriental* 20.

Gjessing, Gutorm. 1975. Socio-archaeology. *CA* 16(3): 323–341.

Gotō Hidehiko. 1991. Hokkaido no chashi. In *Hokkaido no Kenkyū 2: Kōkogaku II,* ed. Ishizuki Kisao, pp. 335–373. Ōsaka: Seibundō.

Gotō Tadashi. 1991. Nihon e no eikyō. In *Nikkan Kōshō: Yayoi Jidai Hen,* ed. Oda Fujio and Han Byong-sam, pp. 31–35. Tokyo: Rokkō.

Gregg, Susan Alling. 1988. *Foragers and Farmers: Population Interaction and Agricultural Expansion in Prehistoric Europe.* Chicago: University of Chicago Press.

Griffin, James B. 1944. The Iroquois in American prehistory. *Papers of the Michigan Academy of Science, Arts and Letters* 29: 357–374.

Griffis, William Elliot. 1886. *The Mikado's Empire,* 5th ed., 1st ed. 1876. New York: Harper.

———. 1907. *The Japanese Nation in Evolution: Steps in the Progress of a Great People.* London: George and Harrap.

Grootaers, Willem A. 1967. Dialectology. In *Current Trends in Linguistics,* Vol. 2, *Linguistics in East Asia and South East Asia,* ed. Thomas A. Seebeok, pp. 585–607. The Hague: Mouton.

———. 1983. Dialects. *Kodansha Encyclopedia of Japan*, Vol. 2, pp. 91-93. Tokyo: Kodansha.

Haga Tōru. 1993. Nichibunken. *Bunka Kaigi* November, p. 1.

Haguenauer, Charles. 1956. *Origine de la Civilisation Japonaise. Introduction à l'Étude de la Préhistoire du Japon. Part I.* Paris: Imprimerie Nationale.

Hall, John Whitney. 1966. *Government and Local Power in Japan, 500 to 1700: A Study Based on Bizen Province.* Princeton, NJ: Princeton University Press.

Hallowell, A. Irving. 1926. Bear ceremonialism in the northern hemisphere. *American Anthropologist* 28: 1-175.

Hammer, Michael F., and Satoshi Horai 1995. Y chromosonal DNA variation and the peopling of Japan. *American Journal of Human Genetics* 56: 951-962.

Han Kangxin and Takahiro Nakahashi. 1996. A comparative study of ritual tooth ablation in ancient China and Japan. *AS* 104(1): 43-64.

Hanada Katsuhiro. 1993. Toraijin no shūraku to bōiki. *Kōkogaku Kenkyū* 39(4): 69-96.

Hanazaki Kōhei. 1994. Tabi nikki—1993nen (2). *Misuzu* 401: 17-27.

———. 1996. Ainu Moshir and Yaponesia: Ainu and Okinawan identities in contemporary Japan. In *Multicultural Japan: Palaeolithic to Postmodern*, ed. D. Denoon, M. Hudson, G. McCormack, and T. Morris-Suzuki, pp. 117-131. Melbourne: Cambridge University Press.

Hanihara Kazuro. 1985. Origins and affinities of Japanese as viewed from cranial measurements. In *Out of Asia: Peopling the Americas and the Pacific*, ed. Robert Kirk and Emöke Szathmáry, pp. 105-112. Canberra: The Journal of Pacific History.

———. 1986. The origin of the Japanese in relation to other ethnic groups in East Asia. In *Windows on the Japanese Past*, ed. R. Pearson, pp. 75-83. Ann Arbor: Center for Japanese Studies, University of Michigan.

———. 1987. Estimation of the number of migrants to Japan: A simulative study. *JASN* 95(3): 391-403.

———. 1990. Emishi, Ezo and Ainu: An anthropological perspective. *Japan Review* 1: 35-48.

———. 1991. Dual structure model for the population history of the Japanese. *Japan Review* 2: 1-33.

———. 1992. Dual structure model for the formation of the Japanese population. In *Japanese as a Member of the Asian and Pacific Populations*, ed. Hanihara Kazuro, pp. 244-251. Kyoto: Nichibunken.

———. 1993. Miira kara mita Fujiwara yondai. In *Ōgon no Hiraizumi: Fujiwara Ichizoku no Jidai*, ed. Takahashi Katsuhiko, pp. 63-68. Tokyo: Nihon Hōsō Kyōkai.

Hanihara Tsunehiko. 1989a. Comparative studies of dental characteristics in the Aogashima islanders. *JASN* 97(1): 9-22.

———. 1989b. Comparative studies of geographically isolated populations in Japan based on dental measurements. 97(1): *JASN* 95-107.

———. 1990a. Affinities of the Philippine Negritos with Japanese and the Pacific populations based on dental measurements: The basic populations in East Asia I. *JASN* 98(1): 13–27.

———. 1990b. Dental anthropological evidence of affinities among the Oceania and the pan-Pacific populations: The basic populations in East Asia II. *JASN* 98(3): 233–46.

———. 1991a. The origin and microevolution of Ainu as viewed from dentition: The basic populations in East Asia VIII. *JASN* 99(3): 345–361.

———. 1991b. Dentition of Nansei islanders and peopling of the Japanese archipelago: The basic populations in East Asia IX. *JASN* 99(4): 399–409.

———. 1992. Dental and cranial evidence on the affinities of the East Asian and Pacific populations. In *Japanese as a Member of the Asian and Pacific Populations,* ed. Hanihara Kazuro, pp. 119–137. Kyoto: Nichibunken.

Harashima Reiji and Kanaizuka Yoshikazu, eds. 1994. *Kodai o Kangaeru: Tōgoku to Yamato Ōken*. Tokyo: Yoshikawa Kōbunkan.

Harding, Anthony. 1993. Bronze Age chiefdoms and the end of Stone Age Europe: The rise of the individual. In *The Illustrated History of Humankind,* Vol. 2, ed. Göran Burenhult, pp. 102–119. New York: HarperCollins.

Härke, Heinrick. 1990. "Warrior graves"? The background of the Anglo-Saxon weapon burial rite. *Past and Present* 126: 22–43.

Harootunian, H. D. 1988. *Things Seen and Unseen: Discourse and Ideology in Tokugawa Nativism*. Chicago: University of Chicago Press.

Harris, David. R. 1977. Alternative pathways toward agriculture. In *Origins of Agriculture,* ed. A. Reed, pp. 179–243. The Hague: Mouton.

Harris, Marvin. 1969. *The Rise of Anthropological Theory*. London: Routledge and Kegan Paul.

Harrison, G. A., and A. J. Boyce. 1972. Introduction: The framework of population studies. In *The Structure of Human Populations,* ed. G. A. Harrison and A. J. Boyce, pp. 1–16. Oxford: Clarendon.

Harrison, John A. 1954. The Saghalien trade: A contribution to Ainu studies. *Southwestern Journal of Anthropology* 10: 278–293.

———. 1955. Kita Yezo Zusetsu or A Description of the Island of northern Yezo, by Mamiya Rinso. *Proceedings of the American Philosophical Society* 99(2): 93–117.

Harunari Hideji. 1984a. Kiyono Kenji ron. In *Jōmon Bunka no Kenkyū,* Vol. 10, ed. Katō Shinpei, Kobayashi Tatsuo and Fujimoto Tsuyoshi, pp. 79–87. Tokyo: Yūzankaku.

———. 1984b. Yayoi jidai Kyūshū no kyojū kitei [Rules of residence in Kyushu district during the Yayoi period]. *Kokuritsu Rekishi Minzoku Hakubutsukan Kenkyū Hōkoku* 3: 1–40. (ES pp. 274–275)

———. 1986. Rules of residence in the Jomon period based on the analysis of tooth extraction. In *Windows on the Japanese Past*, ed. R. Pearson, pp. 293–310. Ann Arbor: Center for Japanese Studies, University of Michigan.

———. 1987. Basshi. In *Yayoi Bunka no Kenkyū,* Vol. 8, ed. Kanaseki Hiroshi and Sahara Makoto, pp. 79–90. Tokyo: Yūzankaku.

———. 1988. Kanaseki Takeo ron. In *Yayoi Bunka no Kenkyū,* Vol. 10, ed. Kanaseki Hiroshi and Sahara Makoto, pp. 94–105. Tokyo: Yūzankaku.

———. 1990. *Yayoi Jidai no Hajimari.* Tokyo: Tokyo University Press.

———. 1991. Shinzoku soshiki no henka. In *Yayoi Bunka: Nihon Bunka no Genryū o Saguru,* ed. Ōsaka Furitsu Yayoi Bunka Hakubutsukan, pp. 97–103. Tokyo: Heibonsha.

———. 1993. Buta no kagakkotsu kenka [The custom of exorcism in the Yayoi period]. *Kokuritsu Rekishi Minzoku Hakubutsukan Kenkyū Hōkoku* 50: 71–131. (ES)

Hasebe Kotondo. 1949. Nihon minzoku no seiritsu. In *Shin Nihonshi Kōza: Genshi Jidai.* Tokyo: Chūō Kōronsha.

———. 1975. Reprint. Nihonjin no ikitachi. *Rekishi Kyōiku* 2(3), in *Nihon Kōkogaku Senshū 15: Hasebe Kotondo Shū,* ed. Esaka Teruya, pp. 10–20. Tokyo: Tsukiji Shokan. Original edition, 1954.

Hashiguchi Naotake. 1987. Hatasaku no keitō: Yayoi jidai no Irima, Tama chiku no sekki o chūshin toshite. In *Saitama no Kōkogaku,* ed. Yanagita Keiji Sensei Kanreki Kinen Ronbunshū Kankō Iinkai, pp. 255–281. Tokyo: Shinjinbutsu Ōraisha.

———. 1994. The Izu islands: Their role in the historical development of ancient Japan. *AP* 33(1): 121–149.

Hattori Shirō. 1954. "Gengo nendaigaku" sunawachi "goi tōkeigaku" no hōhō ni tsuite: Nihon sogo no nendai [On the method of glottochronology and the time depth of proto-Japanese]. *Gengo Kenkyū* 26–27: 29–77. (ES)

———. 1959. *Nihongo no Keitō.* Tokyo: Iwanami.

———. 1961. The affinity of Japanese: Phonetic law and lexicostatistical "sounding." *Acta Asiatica* 2: 1–29.

———. 1964. *Ainugo Hōgen Jiten.* Tokyo: Iwanami.

———. 1976. Ryūkyū hōgen to Hondo hōgen. In *Okinawagaku no Reimei,* pp. 7–55. Tokyo: Okinawa Bunka Kōykai.

Hattori Shiso. 1980. Absolutism and historiographical interpretation. *The Japan Interpreter* 13(1): 15–35.

Hayashi Shihei. 1979. *Shinhen Hayashi Shihei Zenshū 2: Chiri.* Ed. Yamagishi Tokuhei and Sano Masami. Tokyo: Daiichi Shobō.

Hayashiya Tatsusaburo. 1973. East and west in Japanese culture. *The Japan Interpreter* 8(1): 38–54.

Hayden, Brian. 1990. Nimrods, piscators, pluckers, and planters: The emergence of food production. *Journal of Anthropological Archaeology* 9: 31–69.

Healey, Graham. 1983. Kokutai. In *Kodansha Encyclopedia of Japan,* Vol. 4, pp. 262–263. Tokyo: Kodansha.

Hechter, Michael. 1975. *Internal Colonialism: The Celtic Fringe in British National Development, 1536–1966.* Berkeley and Los Angeles: University of California Press.

Helliwell, Christine. 1991. Evolution and ethnicity: A note on rice cultivation practices in Borneo. *BIPPA* 10: 209–217.

Hertz, Frederick. 1972. The role of the medieval church. In *Nationalism in the Middle Ages,* ed. C. L. Tipton, pp. 75–78. New York: Holt, Rinehart, and Winston.

Higham, Nicholas. 1992. *Rome, Britain and the Anglo-Saxons.* London: Seaby.

Hill, James N. 1991. Archaeology and the accumulation of knowledge. In *Processual and Postprocessual Archaeologies: Multiple Ways of Knowing the Past,* ed. Robert W. Preucel, pp. 42–53. Center for Archaeological Investigations, Southern Illinois University at Carbondale, Occasional Paper No. 10.

Hill, Jonathan D. 1992. Contested pasts and the practice of anthropology. *American Anthropologist* 94(4): 809–815.

Hinuma Yorio. 1986. *Shin Uirusu Monogatari: Nihonjin no Kigen o Saguru.* Tokyo: Chūō Kōronsha.

———. 1993. ATL uirusu to Nihonjin no kigen. In *Nihonjin to Nihon Bunka no Keisei,* ed. Hanihara Kazurō, pp. 356–362. Tokyo: Asakura Shoten.

Hirakawa Yoshinaga. 1984. Kinsei Ainu funbo no kōkogakuteki kenkyū. In *Hokkaidō no Kenkyū 2: Kōkogaku II,* ed. Ishizuki Kisao, pp. 375–418. Ōsaka: Seibundō.

———. 1994. Hoppō chi'iki kara mita Ainu bunka no seiritsu. Paper presented at the conference *Ainu Bunka no Seiritsu o Kangaeru,* Hokkaido Museum of Northern Peoples, Abashiri, December 8.

Hirano Kunio. 1983. Be. In *Kodansha Encyclopedia of Japan,* Vol. 1, p. 147. Tokyo: Kodansha.

———. 1993. *Kikajin to Kodai Kokka.* Tokyo: Yoshikawa Kōbunkan.

Hobsbawm, E. J., and T. O. Ranger. 1983. *The Invention of Tradition.* Cambridge: Cambridge University Press.

Hodder, Ian. 1979. Social and economic stress and material culture patterning. *American Antiquity* 44: 446–454.

———. 1982. *Symbols in Action: Ethnoarchaeological Studies of Material Culture.* Cambridge: Cambridge University Press.

———. ed. 1987. *Archaeology as Long-Term History.* Cambridge: Cambridge University Press.

———. 1990. *The Domestication of Europe: Structure and Contingency in Neolithic Societies.* Oxford: Basil Blackwell.

Hoffman, Michael A. 1974. The rise of antiquarianism in Japan and western Europe. *AA* 11 (Suppl.): 182–188.

Hojo Yoshitaka. 1989. The study of keyhole shaped tombs and Japanese archaeology. *Archaeological Review from Cambridge* 8(1): 81–90.

Hokama Shūzen. 1977. Okinawa no gengo to sono rekishi. In *Iwanami Kōza Nihongo 11,* ed. Ōno Susumu and Shibata Takeshi, pp. 181–233. Tokyo: Iwanami.

———. 1981. *Nihongo no Sekai 9: Okinawa no Kotoba.* Tokyo: Chūō Kōronsha.

———. 1986. *Okinawa no Rekishi to Bunka.* Tokyo: Chūō Kōronsha.

Holland, Swinton C. 1874. On the Ainos. *Journal of the Anthropological Institute of Great Britain and Ireland* 3: 233–244.

Honda Toshiaki. 1935. *Kinsei Shakai Keizaigakusetsu Taikei: Honda Toshiaki Shū*. Tokyo: Seibundō.

Hora Tomio. 1956. *Karafutoshi Kenkyū: Karafuto to Santan*. Tokyo: Shingisha.

Horai Satoshi. 1990. Intraspecific nucleotide sequence differences in the major noncoding region of human mitochondrial DNA. *American Journal of Human Genetics* 46: 828–842.

———. 1992. Human mitochondrial DNA: A clue to the development and dispersion of Asian populations. In *Japanese as a Member of the Asian and Pacific Populations,* ed. Hanihara Kazuro, pp. 146–159. Kyoto: Nichibunken.

———. 1993. Idenshi kara mita Nihonjin no kigen. In *Nihonjin to Nihon Bunka no Keisei,* ed. Hanihara Kazurō, pp. 323–342. Tokyo: Asakura Shoten.

———. 1994. Idenshi kara mita Nihonjin. In *Senshi Mongoroido o Saguru,* ed. Akazawa Takeru, pp. 53–68. Tokyo: Nihon Gakujutsu Shinkōkai.

Horai Satoshi, Kenji Hayasaka, Kumiko Murayama, Noriyuki Wate, Hiroko Koike, and Nobuyuki Nakai. 1989. DNA amplification from ancient human skeletal remains and their sequence analysis. *Proceedings of the Japan Academy* 65 (B): 229–233.

Horai Satoshi, Kumiko Murayama, Kenji Hayasaka, Satoe Matsubayashi, Yuko Hattori, Goonnapa Fucharoen, Shinji Harihara, Kyung Sook Park, Keiichi Omoto, and I-Hung Pan. 1996. mtDNA polymorphism in East Asian populations, with special reference to the peopling of Japan. *American Journal of Human Genetics* 59: 579–590.

Hori Kyotsu. 1974. The economic and political effects of the Mongol wars. In *Medieval Japan: Essays in Institutional History,* ed. J. W. Hall and J. P. Mass, pp. 184–198. New Haven, CT: Yale University Press.

Horowitz, Donald L. 1975. Ethnic identity. In *Ethnicity: Theory and Experience,* ed. Nathan Glazer and Daniel P. Moynihan, pp. 111–140. Cambridge, MA: Harvard University Press.

Hoshikawa Kiyochika. 1983. Potatoes and Yams. In *Kodansha Encyclopedia of Japan,* Vol. 6, p. 231. Tokyo: Kodansha.

Hoshino Ryōsaku. 1980. *Kenkyūshi: Jimmu Tennō*. Tokyo: Yoshikawa Kōbunkan.

Howell, David L. 1992. Proto-industrial origins of Japanese capitalism. *Journal of Asian Studies* 51(2): 269–286.

———. 1994. Ainu ethnicity and the boundaries of the early modern Japanese state. *Past and Present* 142: 69–93.

———. 1995. *Capitalism from Within: Economy, Society, and the State in a Japanese Fishery*. Berkeley and Los Angeles: University of California Press.

Howells, W. W. 1986. Physical anthropology of the prehistoric Japanese. In *Windows on the Japanese Past,* ed. R. Pearson, pp. 85–99. Ann Arbor: Center for Japanese Studies, University of Michigan.

Hudson, Mark J. 1988. *Interaction and isolation in Japanese prehistory: The archeology of the Izu and Ogasawara Islands, Tokyo Metropolis*. M.Phil. dissertation, University of Cambridge.

———. 1989. Ethnicity in East Asia: Approaches to the Wa. *Archaeological Review from Cambridge* 8(1): 51–63.

———. 1990a. From Toro to Yoshinogari: Changing perspectives on Yayoi period archeology. In *Hoabinhian, Jomon, Yayoi, Early Korean States: Bibliographic Reviews of Far Eastern Archaeology 1990,* ed. Gina L. Barnes, pp. 63–111. Oxford: Oxbow.

———. 1990b. Sea people, rice people: The dual nature of Yayoi society. *Transactions of the International Conference of Orientalists in Japan* 35: 147–148.

———. 1991. The formation of Yayoi culture and the continent: Some recent archaeological approaches. *Transactions of the International Conference of Orientalists in Japan* 36: 197–199.

———. 1992a. Rice, bronze, and chieftains: An archaeology of Yayoi ritual. *Japanese Journal of Religious Studies* 19(2–3): 139–189.

———. 1992b. Tamil and Japanese: Ono's Yayoi Theory. *Asian and Pacific Quarterly of Social and Cultural Affairs* 24(1): 48–64.

———. 1992c. Yamato and Kai: Interpreting the Yayoi-Kofun transition. Paper presented at the international conference *Japanese Archaeology in Protohistoric and Early Historic Period: Yamato and its Relations to Surrounding Populations.* Bonn, September 23–25.

———. 1993. Wet-rice cultivation. In *The Illustrated History of Humankind,* Vol. 2, ed. Göran Burenhult, p. 143. New York: HarperCollins.

———. 1994a. The linguistic prehistory of Japan: Some archaeological speculations. *Anthropological Science* 102(3): 231–255.

———. 1994b. Constructing Japan: Diversity and unification, 400 BC–AD 600. In *The Illustrated History of Humankind,* Vol. 4, ed. Göran Burenhult, pp. 122–141. New York: Harper-Collins.

———. 1994c. The Nakamichi tomb cluster. In *The Illustrated History of Humankind,* Vol. 4, ed. Göran Burenhult, p. 127. New York: HarperCollins.

———. 1994d. The Ritsuryo state and bonito from Izu. In *The Illustrated History of Humankind,* Vol. 4, ed. Göran Burenhult, p. 131. New York: HarperCollins.

———. 1995. Power and the late Heian periphery: An archeological perspective. Paper presented at the *9th Biennial conference, Japanese Studies Association of Australia.* Brisbane, July 3–6.

———. 1996. The mummies of the Northern Fujiwara. In *Tombs, Graves and Mummies,* ed. P. G. Bahn, pp. 198–199. London: Weidenfeld and Nicolson.

———. 1997. Hiraizumi: Japan's gateway to the north. In *Lost Cities,* ed. P. G. Bahn, pp. 156–157. London: Weidenfeld and Nicolson.

———. 1999. Japanese and Austronesian: An archeological perspective on the proposed linguistic links. In *Interdisciplinary Perspectives on the Origins of the Japanese,* ed. K. Omoto, 267–279. Kyoto: Nichibunken.

———. in press a. The agricultural threshold in the Japanese islands. In *From the Jomon to Star Carr,* ed. L. Janik, S. Kaner, A. Matsui, and P. Rowley-Conwy. Oxford: Oxbow.

———. in press b. Ikor. In *Lost Treasures,* ed. P. G. Bahn. London: Weidenfeld and Nicolson.

———. in press c. Ainu ethnogenesis and the Northern Fujiwara. *Arctic Anthropology* 36, No. 1.

———. n.d. Ainu ethnogenesis and the Northern Fujiwara. Manuscript submitted.

Hudson, Mark J., and Gina L. Barnes. 1991. Yoshinogari: A Yayoi settlement in northern Kyushu. *MN* 46(2): 211-235.

Hudson, Mark J., and Yamagata Mariko. 1992. Introduction to Kobayashi Tatsuo's "Regional organization in the Jomon period." *AA* 29(1): 82-85.

Huizinga, Johan. 1972. Nationalism in the Middle Ages. In *Nationalism in the Middle Ages,* ed. C. L. Tipton, pp. 14-29. New York: Holt, Rinehart, and Winston.

Ikawa-Smith, Fumiko. 1982. Co-traditions in Japanese archaeology. *World Archaeology* 13(3): 296-309.

———. 1990. L'idéologie de l'homogénéité culturelle dans l'archéologie préhistorique japonaise. *Anthropologie et Sociétés* 14(3): 51-76.

Ikeda Jirō. 1974. Okinawa, Miyakojima gendai jinruikotsu no keisoku [Craniometry of Miyako Islanders, the Ryukyus]. *JASN* 82(2): 150-160. (ES)

Ikeda Jirō and Tagaya Akira 1980. Seitai keisokuchi kara mita Nihon rettō no chi'ikisei [Geographic variation of the anthropometric measurements in the Japanese Islands]. *JASN* 88(4): 397-409. (ES)

Ikehata Kōichi. 1990a. Kai no michi: Kai no bunka to Hirota iseki. In *Hayato Sekai no Shimajima,* ed. Ōbayashi Taryō, pp. 111-138. Tokyo: Shōgakukan.

———. 1990b. Takazuka kofun no nangen to sono chikuzō jiki. In *Kyūshū Jōdai Bunka Ronshū,* ed. Otomasu Shigetaka Sensei Koki Kinenkai, pp. 327-348. Kumamoto.

———. 1992a. The central power and the incorporation of south Kyushu: Archaeology of the Hayato. Paper presented at the international conference *Japanese Archaeology in Protohistoric and Early Historic Period: Yamato and its Relations to Surrounding Populations.* Bonn, September 23-25.

———. 1992b. Kōko shiryō kara mita Hayato no shūkyōkan [A religious view of the Hayato: An approach from archaeological relics]. *Kodai Bunka* 44(7): 23-33 (ES p. 55).

Im Hyo-Jai. 1992. Prehistoric rice agriculture in Korea. In *Pacific Northeast Asia in Prehistory: Hunter-Fisher-Gatherers, Farmers, and Sociopoloitical Elites,* ed. C. M. Aikens and Song Nai Rhee, pp. 157-160. Pullman: Washington State University Press.

Imaizumi Takao. 1992. Ritsuryō kokka to Emishi. In *Shinpan "Kodai no Nihon" 9: Tōhoku, Hokkaidō,* ed. Tsuboi Kiyotari and Hirano Kunio, pp. 163-198. Tokyo: Kadokawa.

Imamura Keiji. 1990. Gunshū chōzōketsu to dasei sekifu. In *Kōkogaku to Minzokushi,* ed. Watanabe Hitoshi Kyōju Koki Kinen Ronbunshū, pp. 61-94. Tokyo: Rokkō.

———. 1993. Shuryō saishū keizai no Nihonteki seikaku. In *Shinpan "Kodai no Nihon" 1: Kodaishi Sōron,* ed. Tsuboi Kiyotari and Hirano Kunio, pp. 95-116. Tokyo: Kadokawa.

———. 1996. *Prehistoric Japan: New Perspectives on Insular East Asia.* London: University College London Press.

Imanishi Kinji. 1976. *Shinka to wa Nani ka.* Tokyo: Kōdansha.

Inoue Fumio. 1992. Hōgen no tayōsei to Nihon bunka no nagare. *Nihongogaku* 11: 57-67.

Inoue Hideo. 1991. *Wa, Wajin, Wakoku: Higashi Ajia Kodaishi Saikento.* Kyoto: Jinbun Shoin.

Inoue Kiyoshi. 1963. *Nihon no Rekishi,* Vol. 1. Tokyo: Iwanami.

Inoue Masataka. 1989. Izu shotō shutsudo dōbutsu izontai no gaikan. *Musashi* 2: 17-33.

Inoue Tatsuo. 1978. *Kumaso to Hayato.* Tokyo: Kyōikusha.

Ishida Hajime. 1988. Morphological studies of Okhotsk crania from Ōmisaki, Hokkaido. *JASN* 96: 17-45.

———. 1990. Cranial morphology of several ethnic groups from the Amur basin and Sakhalin. *JASN* 98: 137-148.

———. 1994. Skeletal morphology of the Okhotsk people on Sakhalin island. *AS* 102(3): 257-269.

Ishida Hajime and Dodo Yukio. 1992. Differentiation of the northern Mongoloid: The evidence of cranial nonmetric traits. In *Japanese as a Member of the Asian and Pacific Populations,* ed. Hanihara Kazuro, pp. 79-93. Kyoto: Nichibunken.

Ishida Hajime, Hanihara Tsunehiko, Kondo Osamu, and Oshima Naoyuki. 1994. A human skeleton of the early phase of the Okhotsk culture unearthed at the Hamanaka-2 site, Rebun Island, Hokkaido. *AS* 102(4): 363-378.

Ishida Hajime and Kida Masahiko. 1991. An anthropological investigation of the Sakhalin Ainu with special reference to nonmetric cranial traits. *JASN* 99(1): 23-32.

Ishida Yoshifumi. 1993. Uirusu no bunpu to jinrui shoshūdan. In *Nihonjin to Nihon Bunka no Keisei,* ed. Hanihara Kazurō, pp. 363-375. Tokyo: Asakura Shoten.

Ishigami Eiichi. 1987. Kodai higashi Ajia chi'iki to Nihon. In *Nihon no Shakaishi 1: Rettō Naigai no Kōtsū to Kokka,* ed. Amino Yoshihiko, pp. 55-96. Tokyo: Iwanami.

Ishihara Michihiro, ed. 1985. *Shintei Gishi Wajinden, Hoka Sanhen.* Tokyo: Iwanami.

Ishikawa Hideshi. 1987. Saisōbo. In *Yayoi Bunka no Kenkyū,* Vol. 8, ed. Kanaseki Hiroshi and Sahara Makoto, pp. 148-153. Tokyo: Yūzankaku.

———. 1992. Kantō daichi no nōkō sonraku. In *Shinpan "Kodai no Nihon" 8: Kantō,* ed. Tsuboi Kiyotari and Hirano Kunio, pp. 73-94. Tokyo: Kadokawa.

Ishimoda Shō. 1972. Kodai no okeru "teikoku shugi" ni tsuite. *Rekishi Hyōron* 265: 43-55.

Ishimoto Goichi, and Kuwata Mieko. 1973. Red cell glutamic-pyruvic transaminase polymorphism in Japanese populations. *JJHG* 18(4): 373-377.

Ishizuki Kisao. 1979. Hokkaidō ni okeru doki bunka no shūen to futsū suru shomondai. *Chihōshi Kenkyū* 29(6): 1-13.

Isogawa Shinya. 1992. Kodai chūsei no itetsu imono [Cast-iron articles in the ancient and medieval ages]. *Kokuritsu Rekishi Minzoku Hakubutsukan Kenkyū Hōkoku* 46: 1-79. (ES)

Itō Jun. 1991. Emishi to Hayato wa doko ga chigau ka. In *Sōten Nihon no Rekishi* 3, ed. Yoshimura Takehiko and Yoshioka Masayuki, pp. 59-74. Tokyo: Shinjinbutsu Oraisha.

Ivy, Marilyn. 1988. Tradition and difference in the Japanese mass media. *Public Culture* 1(1): 21-29.

Iwai Tadakuma. 1986. Iwayuru "Nihongaku" o megutte. *Nihonshi Kenkyū* 285: 78-81.

Iwasaki Jirō. 1987. Shisekibo. In *Yayoi Bunka no Kenkyū, Vol. 8*, ed. Kanaseki Hiroshi and Sahara Makoto, pp. 91-97. Tokyo: Yūzankaku.

Iwata Keiji. 1991. The evolution of the *kami* cult. *Acta Asiatica* 61: 47-67.

Iwate Maibun [Iwate-Ken Maizō Bunkazai Sentā]. 1985. *Iwate no Iseki*. Tokyo: Morioka.

Izui H. 1952. Nihongo to Nantō shogo. *Minzokugaku Kenkyū* 17: 15-26.

Jackson, K. H. 1953. *Language and History in Early Britain*. Edinburgh: Edinburgh University Press.

Jansen, Marius B. 1985. Editor's Introduction to *The Culture of the Meiji Period,* by Irokawa Daikichi, pp. ix-xvi. Princeton, NJ: Princeton University Press.

Johnson, Allen W., and Timothy Earle. 1987. *The Evolution of Human Societies: From Foraging to Agrarian State*. Stanford, CA: Stanford University Press.

Johnson, Marshall. 1994. Making time: historic preservation and the space of nationality. *Positions: East Asia Cultures Critique* 2(2): 177-249.

Kadowaki Teiji. 1992. Nihonjin no keisei. In *Ajia no Naka no Nihonshi IV: Chi'iki to Minzoku,* ed. Arano Yasunori, Ishii Masatoshi and Murai Shōsuke, pp. 1-28. Tokyo: Tokyo University Press.

Kaempfer, Engelbert. 1906. *The History of Japan Together with a Description of the Kingdom of Siam, 1690-92*. Vol. 1. Translated by J. G. Scheuchzer. Glasgow: James MacLehose.

Kagawa Mitsuo. 1971. Jōmon banki nōkō no kigen ni kansuru kenkyū. *Beppu Daigaku Kōkogaku Kenkyū Hōkoku 2*.

———. 1972. *Nōkō no Kigen*. Tokyo: Kōdansha.

———. 1982. Jōmon banki nōkōron. *Kikan Kōkogaku* 1: 71-76.

———. 1984. Cultural origins and domesticated plants of the Jomon culture in western Japan. In *Proceedings of the 31st International Congress of Human Sciences in Asia and North Africa,* Vol. 2, ed. Yamamoto Tatsuro, pp. 925-926. Tokyo: Tōhō Gakkai.

Kaifu Yōsuke. 1992. Gunma-ken Iwatsubo dōkutsu iseki shutsudo no Yayoi jidai jinkotsu [Human skeletal remains of the Yayoi period from the Iwatsubo cave site in Gunma prefecture, Kanto district]. *JASN* 100(4): 449-483. (ES)

Kaiho Mineo. 1974. *Nihon Hoppōshi no Ronri.* Tokyo: Yūzankaku.

———. 1987. *Chūsei no Ezochi.* Tokyo: Yoshikawa Kōbunkan.

———. 1989. Ezo ga Chishima ō no Chōsen Kenshi. In *Yomigaeru Chūsei 4, Kita no Chūsei: Tsugaru, Hokkaidō,* ed. Kikuchi Tetsuo and Fukuda Toyohiro, pp. 219-220. Tokyo: Heibonsha.

———. 1990. Hoppō kōeki to Chūsei Ezo shakai. In *Umi to Rettō Bunka 1: Nihonkai Hokkoku Bunka,* ed. Amino Yoshihiko, pp. 255-286. Tokyo: Shōgakukan.

Kakubayashi Fumio. 1980. *A Study of the Historical Development of the Yayoi Period with Special Reference to Japanese-Korean Relations.* Ph.D. dissertation, University of Queensland.

———. 1987. Jimmu. Entry in *The Encyclopedia of Religion,* Vol.8, ed. Mircea Eliade, pp. 91-92. New York: Macmillan.

———. 1996. Japanese and Polynesian mythologies: A comparative study. In *Papers in East Asian Studies,* ed. K. Ono and W. Anasz, pp. 29-42. Palmerston North, New Zealand: Dept. of East Asian Studies, Massey University.

Kamei Meitoku. 1995. Nisō bōeki kankei no tenkai. In *Iwanami Kōza Nihon Tsūshi 6,* ed. Tamai Chikara, pp. 107-140. Tokyo: Iwanami.

Kamimura Toshio. 1984. *Hayato no Kōkogaku.* Tokyo: New Science Press.

Kamimura Yukio. 1965. Okinawa no hōgen. *Bungaku* 33: 722-726.

Kamiya Nobuyuki. 1994. Japanese control of Ezochi and the role of northern Koryo. *Acta Asiatica* 67: 49-68.

Kanaseki Hiroshi. 1986. The evidence for social change between the Early and Middle Yayoi. In *Windows on the Japanese Past,* ed. R. Pearson, pp. 57-67. Ann Arbor: Center for Japanese Studies, University of Michigan.

Kanaseki Hiroshi and Sahara Makoto. 1978. The Yayoi period. *AP* 19(1): 15-26.

Kanaseki Hiroshi and Sahara Makoto, eds. 1985-1989. *Yayoi Bunka no Kenkyū,* 10 vols. Tokyo: Yūzankaku.

Kanaseki Takeo, 1971. Nihon jinshu ron. In *Shinpan Kōkogaku Kōza.* Tokyo: Yūzankaku.

———. 1976. *Nihon Minzoku no Kigen.* Tokyo: Hōsei University Press.

Kaner, Simon. 1990. The western language Jomon: A review. In *Hoabinhian, Jomon, Yayoi, Early Korean States: Bibliographic Reviews of Far Eastern Archaeology 1990,* ed. Gina L. Barnes, pp. 31-62. Oxford: Oxbow.

———. 1993. The impact of internationalisation on Japanese prehistory. Paper presented at the conference *Stirrup, Sail and Plough: Continental and Maritime Influences on Japanese Identity.* Canberra, September 20-23.

———. 1996. Beyond ethnicity and emergence in Japanese archaeology. In *Multicultural Japan: Palaeolithic to Postmodern,* ed. D. Denoon, M. Hudson, G. McCormack, and T. Morris-Suzuki, pp. 46-59. Melbourne: Cambridge University Press.

Kasahara Yasuo. 1982. Japan. In *Biology and Ecology of Weeds,* ed. W. Holzner and M. Numata, pp. 285-297. The Hague: W. Junk.

Kataoka Kōji. 1990. Nihon shutsudo no Chōsenkei Mumon doki. In *Kodai Chōsen to Nihon,* ed. Nishitani Tadashi, pp. 75–116. Tokyo: Meicho.

Katayama Kazumichi. 1996. The Japanese as an Asian-Pacific population. In *Multicultural Japan: Palaeolithic to Postmodern,* ed. D. Denoon, M. Hudson, G. McCormack, and T. Morris-Suzuki, pp. 19–30. Melbourne: Cambridge University Press.

Katō Masayo. 1987. Kōzanshi gaisetsu. In *Kai-Kurokawa Kinzan: Dai'ichiji Chōsa Hōkoku,* ed. Imamura Keiji and Sano Hiroaki, pp. 47–48. Kurokawa Kinzan Iseki Kenkyūkai.

Katō Minoru and Ishida Hajime. 1991. Yamagata-ken Hinata I dōkutsu shutsudo no Yayoi jidai josei tōgai ni tsuite [A human cranium of the Yayoi period from the Hinata I cave site, Yamagata Prefecture]. *JASN* 99(2): 149–154. (ES)

Katō Shinpei. 1980. Jōmon jidai no dōbutsu shi'iku: Toku ni inoshishi no mondai ni tsuite. *Rekishi Kōron* 6(5): 45–50.

Kawachi Yoshihiro. 1992. *Mindai Jōshin-shi no Kenkyū.* Kyōto: Dōhōsha.

Kawakatsu Heita. 1991. *Nihon Bunmei to Kindai Seiyō: "Sakoku Saikō."* Tokyo: Nihon Hōsō Kyōkai Books, 627.

Kayano Shigeru. 1994. *Our Land Was a Forest: An Ainu Memoir.* Boulder, CO: Westview.

Kazar, Lajos. 1980. *Japanese-Uralic Language Comparison: Locating Japanese Origins with the help of Samoyed, Finnish, Hungarian, etc.: An Attempt.* Hamburg: Lajos Kazar-Tsurusaki.

———. 1989. Northern Inner Asia: Probable one-time home of the Japanese, Uralians and Altaians. *Bochumer Jahrbuch zur Ostasienforschung* 12: 149–184.

Keally, C. T., and Mutō Yasuhiro. 1982. Jōmon jidai no nendai. In *Jōmon Bunka no Kenkyū,* Vol. 1, ed. Katō Shinpei, Kobayashi Tatsuo, and Fujimoto Tsuyoshi, pp. 246–275. Tokyo: Yūzankaku.

Kedourie, Elie. 1960. *Nationalism.* London: Hutchinson.

Keene, Donald. 1955. *Anthology of Japanese Literature.* New York: Grove Press.

———. 1969. *The Japanese Discovery of Europe, 1720–1830.* Stanford, CA: Stanford University Press.

Kidder, J. Edward Jr. 1959. *Japan Before Buddhism.* London: Thames and Hudson.

———. 1984. Problems of Jomon population decline. In *Proceedings of the 31st International Congress of Human Sciences in Asia and North Africa,* Vol. 2, ed. Yamamoto Tatsuro, pp. 926–927. Tokyo: Toho Gakkai.

———. 1993. The earliest societies in Japan. In *The Cambridge History of Japan,* Vol. 1, *Ancient Japan,* ed. Delmer M. Brown, pp. 48–107. Cambridge: Cambridge University Press.

Kikuchi Isao. 1994. *Ainu Minzoku to Nihonjin: Higashi Ajia no naka no Ezochi.* Tokyo: Asahi Shinbunsha.

Kikuchi Tetsuo. 1984. *Hoppō Kōkogaku no Kenkyū.* Rokkō.

———. 1989. Emishi (Kai) setsu saikō. *Shikan* 120: 100–114.

———. 1992. Yanagi no gosho ato shutsudo no naiji nabe. In *Ōshū Fujiwara-shi to Yanagi no Gosho Ato,* ed. Hiraizumi Bunka Kenkyūkai. Tokyo: Yoshikawa Kōbunkan.

Kikuchi Toshihiko. 1986. Continental culture and Hokkaido. In *Windows on the Japanese Past,* ed. R. Pearson, pp. 149–162. Ann Arbor: Center for Japanese Studies, University of Michigan.

———. 1992. Hokkaidō o meguru hoppō shominzoku no kōryū.. In *Shinpan "Kodai no Nihon" 9: Tōhoku, Hokkaidō,* ed. Tsuboi Kiyotari and Hirano Kunio, pp. 371–398. Tokyo: Kadokawa.

Kiley, Cornelius J. 1969. A note on the surnames of immigrant officials in Nara Japan. *Harvard Journal of Asiatic Studies* 29: 177–189.

Kim Byung Mo, ed. 1982. *Megalithic Cultures in Asia.* Seoul: Hanyang University Press.

Kim Seung-Og. 1994. Burials, pigs, and political prestige in Neolithic China. *CA* 35(2): 119–141.

Kim Won-Yong. 1982. Discoveries of rice in prehistoric sites in Korea. *Journal of Asian Studies* 41(3): 513–518.

Kindaichi Kyōsuke. 1960. Kokugo to Ainugo to no kankei. In *Ainugo Kenkyū.* Tokyo: Sanseidō.

Kinoshita Naoko. 1996. *Nantō Kaibunka no Kenkyū.* Tokyo: Hōsei University Press.

Kirihara Takeshi. 1989. *Tsumi'ishizuka to Toraijin.* Tokyo: Tokyo University Press.

Kishimoto Yoshihiko. 1991. Nantō no inasaku ni tsuite. In *Kakuchi'iki ni Okeru Komezukuri no Kaishi,* Vol. 3, pp. 33–42. Fukuoka: Maizō Bunkazai Kenkyūkai Dai 30kai Kenkyū Shūkai Jikkō Iinkai.

Kita Sadakichi. 1936. "Abata" mo "ekubo," "ekubo" mo "abata": Nihon sekki jidai shūmatsuki mondai. *Minerva* 1(5).

———. 1972. Reprint. Nihon sekki jidai no shūmatsuki ni tsuite. In *Nihon Kōkogaku Senshū 8: Kita Sadakichi Shū,* ed. Saitō Tadashi, pp. 14–20. Tsukiji Shokan. Original edition, 1936. *Minerva* 1(3).

———. 1978. Yamato minzokushi gaisetsu. In *Nihon Minzoku Bunka Taikei 5: Kita Sadakichi,* ed. Ueda Masa'aki, pp. 211–316. Tokyo: Kōdansha.

Kitakamae Yasuo. 1991. *Kodai Emishi no Kenkyū.* Tokyo: Yūzankaku.

Kiyono Kenji. 1938. Kofun jidai Nihonjin no jinruigakuteki kenkyū. In *Jinruigaku, Senshigaku Kōza* 2, pp. 1–20. Tokyo: Yūzankaku.

———. 1949. *Kodai Jinkotsu no Kenkyū ni Motozuku Nihon Jinshuron.* Tokyo: Iwanami.

Klaproth, H. J., trans. 1832. *San Kokf Tsou Ran To Sets, ou Aperçu Général des Trois Royaumes.* Paris: Oriental Translation Fund of Great Britain and Ireland.

———. 1854. Aperçu de l'histoire mythologique des Japonais. In *Nippon O Daï Itsi Ran ou Annales des Empereurs du Japon.* Translated by Isaac Titsingh. pp. i–xxxvi. Paris: Oriental Translation Fund of Great Britain and Ireland.

Kobayashi Kōji. 1994. Kin, gendai. In *Tabemono no Kōkogaku,* special issue of *Yamanashi Kōko* 49: 57–70.

Kobayashi Tatsuo. 1989. Jōmon jidai no bunkaryoku. In *Jōmon Jidai to Gendai*, pp. 33-77. Tokyo: Tama-shi Bunka Kōshin Zaidan.

———. 1992. Regional organization in the Jomon period. *AA* 29(1): 85-95.

Kobayashi Yukio. 1961. Dōhankyōkō. In *Kofun Jidai no Kenkyū*, pp. 95-133. Tokyo: Aoki Shoten.

Koganei Yoshikiyo. 1896. Kurze Mittheilung über Untersuchungen an lebenden Aino. *Archiv für Anthropologie* 24: 1-39.

Kogawa Tetsuo. 1988. New trends in Japanese popular culture. In *The Japanese Trajectory: Modernization and Beyond*, ed. Gavan McCormack and Yoshio Sugimoto, pp. 54-66. Cambridge: Cambridge University Press.

Kohama Mototsugu. 1968. Nihonjin to Ainu. In *Nihon Minzoku to Nanpō Bunka*, ed. Kanaseki Takeo Hakase Koki Kinen Iinkai, pp. 19-39. Tokyo: Heibonsha.

Kohl, Philip L. 1987a. The ancient economy, transferable technologies and the Bronze Age world-system: A view from the northeastern frontier of the Ancient Near East. In *Centre and Periphery in the Ancient World*, ed. M. Rowlands, M. Larsen, and K. Kristiansen, pp. 13-24. Cambridge: Cambridge University Press.

———. 1987b. The use and abuse of world systems theory: The case of the pristine West Asian state. In *Advances in Archaeological Method and Theory*, Vol. 11, ed. Michael B. Schiffer, pp. 1-35. San Diego, CA: Academic Press.

Koike Hiroko. 1986. Prehistoric hunting pressure and paleobiomass: An environmental reconstruction and archaeozoological analysis of a Jomon shellmound area. In *Prehistoric Hunter-Gatherers in Japan: New Research Methods*, ed. Takeru Akazawa and C. Melvin Aikens, pp. 27-53. Tokyo: Tokyo University Press.

———. 1992. Exploitation dynamics during the Jomon period. In *Pacific Northeast Asia in Prehistory: Hunter-Fisher-Gatherers, Farmers, and Sociopoloitical Elites*, ed. C. M. Aikens and Song Nai Rhee, pp. 75-82. Pullman: Washington State University Press.

Koike Hiroko and Ohtaishi Noriyuki. 1985. Prehistoric hunting pressure estimated by the age composition of excavated sika deer *(Cervus nippon)* using the annual layer of tooth cement. *Journal of Archaeological Science* 12: 443-456.

———. 1987. Estimation of prehistoric hunting rates based on the age composition of sika deer (*Cervus nippon*). *Journal of Archaeological Science* 14: 251-269.

Koike Keiji and Suzuki Hisashi. 1955. Chiba-ken Awa-gun Sano dōkutsu shutsudo jinkotsu. *Nihon Jinruigaku, Minzokugaku Rengō Taikai Kiji* 9: 164-166.

Kojima Yoshiyuki. 1990. Kaijō no michi to Hayato bunka. In *Hayato Sekai no Shimajima*, ed. Ōbayashi Taryō, pp. 139-194. Tokyo: Shōgakukan.

Kōmoto Masayuki. 1978. Yayoi bunka no keitō. *Rekishi Kōron* 4(3): 48-56.

———. 1982. Megalithic monuments in ancient Japan. In *Megalithic Cultures in Asia*, ed. Kim Byung-mo, pp. 4-40. Seoul: Hanyang University Press.

———. 1992a. Umi to yama to sato no keisei. *Kōkogaku Jānaru* 344: 2-9.

———. 1992b. Tōnan Ajia kōkogaku kenkyū. In *Shinpojumu: Higashi Ajia no Bunmei no Seisui to Kankyō Hendō,* ed. Kanaseki Hiroshi, pp. 53-65. Tenri: Tenri University, Department of Archaeology.

Kondo, S., and K. Kobayashi. 1975. Microevolution and modernization of Japanese. In *Anthropological and Genetic Studies on the Japanese,* ed. S. Watanabe, S. Kondo and E. Matsunaga, pp. 5-14. Tokyo: University of Tokyo Press.

Kondō Takaichi. 1988. *Sankakubuchi Shinjukyō*. Tokyo: Tokyo University Press.

Kondō Yoshiro. 1962. Yayoi bunka ron. In *Iwanami Kōza Nihon Rekishi I: Genshi oyobi Kodai 1,* pp. 137-188. Tokyo: Iwanami.

———. 1986. The keyhole tumulus and its relationship to earlier forms of burial. In *Windows on the Japanese Past: Studies in Archaeology and Prehistory,* ed. Richard Pearson, pp. 335-348. Ann Arbor: University of Michigan Center for Japanese Studies.

Kondō Yoshiro and Harunari Hideji. 1967. Haniwa no kigen. *Kōkogaku Kenkyū* 13(3): 13-35.

Kōno Hiroaki. 1931. Bohyō no keishiki yori mitaru Ainu no shokeitō. *Ezo Ōrai* 4.

———. 1932. Ainu no ichi keitō sarunkuru ni tsuite. *JASN* 7(4).

Kōno Isamu, Egami Namio, Gotō Shuichi, Yamanouchi Sugao, and Yahata Ichirō. Reprint 1971. Zadankai: Nihon sekki jidai bunka no genryū to kagen o kataru. *Nihon Kōkogaku Senshū 20: Kōno Isamu Shū,* ed. Esaka Teruya, pp. 84-94. Tokyo: Tsukiji Shokan. Original edition, 1936. *Minerva* 1: 34-46.

Koshida Kenichirō. 1984. Hokkaidō no tetsunabe ni tsuite. *Busshitsu Bunka* 42: 14-38.

———. 1988. Hokkaidō ni okeru chū-kinsei kōkogaku no genjō to kadai. *Busshitsu Bunka* 50: 51-64.

Kossina, Gustav. 1902. Die indogermanische Frage archäologisch beantwortet. *Zeitschrift für Ethnologie* 34: 161-222.

Kotani Yoshinobu. 1981. Evidence of plant cultivation in Jomon Japan: Some implications. In *Affluent Foragers: Pacific Coasts East and West,* ed. Shuzo Koyama and David Hurst Thomas, pp. 201-212. Osaka: Senri Ethnological Studies 9.

———.1994. "Maundo kensetsusha ronsō" to "Korobokkuru ronsō" to. In *Senshigaku, Kōkogaku Ronkyū. Kumamoto Daigaku Bungakubu Kōkogaku Kenkyūshitsu Sōsetsu 20 Shūnen Kinen Ronbunshū,* pp. 399-405. Kumamoto: Ryūta Kōkokai.

Kouchi Makiko. 1983. Geographic variation in modern Japanese somatometric data and its interpretation. *Bulletin of the University Museum, University of Tokyo* 22.

———.1986. Geographic variations in modern Japanese somatometric data: A secular change hypothesis. In *Prehistoric Hunter-Gatherers in Japan: New Research Methods,* ed. Takeru Akazawa and C. Melvin Aikens, pp. 93-106. Tokyo: Tokyo University Press.

Koyama Shuzo. 1976. *Subsistence and Population of the Jomon Period*. Ph.D. dissertation, University of California, Davis. Published 1979 by University Microfilms International.

———.1984. *Jōmon Jidai: Konpyūta Kōkogaku ni Yoru Fukugen*. Tokyo: Chūō Kōronsha.

Kozintsev, Alexander G. 1990. Ainu, Japanese, their ancestors and neighbors: Cranioscopic data. *JASN* 98(3): 247–267.

———.1992. Prehistoric and recent populations of Japan: Multivariate analysis of cranioscopic data. *AA* 29(1): 104–111.

Kracht, Klaus. 1986. *Studien zur Geschichte des Denkens im Japan des 17. bis 19. Jahrhunderts: Chu-Hsi-Konfuzianische Geist-Diskurse*. Wiesbaden: Otto Harrossowitz.

Kreiner, Josef. 1980. Mō hitori no Shiiboruto. *Shisō* 672: 68–83.

———.1993. European images of the Ainu and Ainu studies in Europe. In *European Studies on Ainu Language and Culture,* ed. Josef Kreiner, pp.13–60. Munich: Iudicium Verlag.

Kudō Masaki. 1979. *Kenkyūshi: Nihon Jinshu Ron*. Tokyo: Yoshikawa Kōbunkan.

———.1984. Kita Sadakichi ron. In *Jōmon Bunka no Kenkyū,* Vol. 10, ed. Katō Shinpei, Kobayashi Tatsuo, and Fujimoto Tsuyoshi, pp. 71–78. Tokyo: Yūzankaku.

———.1989a. *Jōsaku to Emishi*. Tokyo: New Science Press.

———.1989b. Nihonjin kigenron no hen'yō to genkyō. *Kikan Yamataikoku* 38: 50–70.

———.1990. Kodai Emishi no shomondai. *Yoneshiro Kōko* 5: 1–16.

———.1991. Kōkogaku kara mita kodai Emishi no bunka. In *Michinoku Kodai: Emishi no Sekai,* pp. 1–64. Tokyo: Yamakawa.

Kumata Ryōsuke. 1994. Kodai kokka to Emishi, Hayato. In *Iwanami Kōza Nihon Tsūshi 4,* pp. 187–224. Tokyo: Iwanami.

Kuraku Yoshiyuki. 1991a. *Suiden no Kōkogaku*. Tokyo: Tokyo University Press.

———.1991b. Inasaku nōkō no hajimari. *Kikan Kōkogaku* 37: 14–16.

Kyoto University Department of Archaeology, eds. 1989. *Tsubai Ōtsukayama Kofun to Sankakubuchi Shinjukyō*. Kyoto: Kyoto University.

Lathrap, Donald W. 1956. An archaeological classification of culture contact situations. In *Seminars in Archaeology 1955*, ed. Robert Wauchope, pp. 1–30. Salt Lake City, UT: Society for American Archaeology.

Leach, Edmund R. 1954. *Political Systems of Highland Burma: A Study of Kachin Social Structure*. Cambridge, MA: Harvard University Press.

Ledyard, Gari. 1975. Galloping along with the Horseriders: Looking for the founders of Japan. *JJS* 1(2): 217–254.

———. 1983. Yin and yang in the China-Manchuria-Korea triangle. In *China Among Equals: The Middle Kingdom and its Neighbors, 10th–14th Centuries,* ed. Morris Rossabi, pp. 313–353. Berkeley and Los Angeles: University of California Press.

Lee Ki-Moon. 1964. Mongolian loan-words in Middle Korean. *Ural-Altaische Jahrbücher* 30: 104–120.

Lee, Richard B. 1992. Art, science, or politics? The crisis in hunter-gatherer studies. *American Anthropologist* 94: 31–54.

Lee, Richard B., and Irven Devore, eds. 1968. *Man the Hunter*. Chicago: Aldine.

Lees, Robert B. 1956. Shiro Hattori on glottochronology and proto-Japanese. *American Anthropologist* 58: 176–177.

Levin, M. G. 1961. The ethnic history of Japan. *AP* 5: 134–137.

———. 1963. *Ethnic Origins of the Peoples of Northeastern Asia*. Toronto: University of Toronto Press.

Lewin, Bruno. 1962. *Aya und Hata: Bevölkerungsgruppen Altjapans kontinentaler Herkunft*. Wiesbaden: Otto Harrassowitz.

———. 1967. Die japanischen Beziehungen zu den Emishi um das Jahr 800. *Oriens* 18–19: 304–326.

———. 1973. Japanese and the language of Koguryo. *Papers of the C.I.C. Far Eastern Language Institute* 4: 19–33.

———. 1976. Japanese and Korean: The problems and history of a linguistic comparison. *JJS* 2(2): 389–412.

———. 1980. Sprachkontakte zwischen Paekche und Yamato in frühgeschichtlicher Zeit. *Asiatische Studien* 34(2): 167–188.

Li Po-Ju. 1984. *Sino-Japanese Political Relations before the Fifth Century AD*. M.A. thesis, University of Arizona. Published by University Microfilms International, 1990.

Libby, Dorothy. 1962. Ethnohistory in the USSR. *AA* 1(1): 68–75.

Lockwood, William G., ed. 1984. Introduction to *Beyond Ethnic Boundaries: New Approaches in the Anthropology of Ethnicity*, pp. 1–10. *Michigan Discussions in Anthropology* 7.

Lounsbury, F. G. 1978. Iroquoian languages. In *Handbook of North American Indians*, Vol. 15, *The Northeast*, ed. Bruce Trigger, pp. 334–43. Washington, DC: Smithsonian.

Lowenthal, David. 1985. *The Past is a Foreign Country*. Cambridge: Cambridge University Press.

MacNeish, R. S. 1952. *Iroquois Pottery Types: A Technique for the Study of Iroquois Prehistory*. National Museum of Canada Bulletin 124, Anthropological Series No. 31.

MacWhite, Eoin. 1956. On the interpretation of archeological evidence in historical and sociological terms. *American Anthropologist* 58: 3–25.

Maher, John C. 1991. "North Kyushu creole": A hypothesis concerning the multilingual formation of Japanese. *International Christian University Public Lecture Bulletin* 6: 15–48.

———. 1996. "North Kyushu creole": A language-contact model for the origins of Japanese. In *Multicultural Japan: Palaeolithic to Postmodern*, ed. D. Denoon, M. Hudson, G. McCormack, and T. Morris-Suzuki, pp. 31–45. Melbourne: Cambridge University Press.

Maizō Bunkazai Kenyukai, eds. 1991. *Kakuchi'iki ni okeru Komezukuri no Kaishi*. Fukuoka: Dai 30 Kai Maizō Bunkazai Kenkyū Shūkai.

Makabe Yoshiko. 1993. Izumo to Kyūshū, Yamato, Kibi. In *Kodai o Kangaeru: Izumo,* ed. Ueda Masa'aki, pp. 82–109. Tokyo: Yoshikawa Kōbunkan.

Makita Sōjirō. 1896. Yayoi-shiki doki (kaizuka doki ni nite usude no mono) hakken ni tsuite. *Tōkyō Jinruigakkai Zasshi* 122.

Mallory, J. P. 1898. *In Search of the Indo-Europeans.* London: Thames and Hudson.

———. 1992. Migrations and language change. In *Peregrinatio Gothica III. Universitetets Oldsaksamlings Skrifter Ny rekke Nr. 14,* pp. 145–153.

Mamiya Rinzō. 1972. Kita Ezo Zusetsu. Reprint. In *Hokumon Sōsho,* ed. Ōtomo Kisaku, pp. 277–380. Tokyo: Kokusho Kankōkai.

Manabe Yoshitaka, Y. Kitagawa, J. Oyamada, A. Rokutanda, and K. Kato. 1993. Secular change of tooth size from the Initial-Early Jomon period to the Middle-Late-Final Jomon period based on tooth cervix measurements. *AS* 101(2): 225.

Mass, Jeffrey P. 1990. The Kamakura bakufu. In *The Cambridge History of Japan,* Vol. 3, ed. Kozo Yamamura, pp. 46–88. Cambridge: Cambridge University Press.

———. 1992. *Antiquity and Anachronism in Japanese History.* Stanford, CA: Stanford University Press.

Matsui Akira. 1991. Kachiku to maki: Uma no seisan. In *Kofun Jidai no Kenkyū,* Vol. 4, ed. Ishino Hironobu et al., pp.105–119. Tokyo: Yūzankaku.

———. 1992. Wetland sites in Japan. In *The Wetland Revolution in Prehistory,* ed. Byrony Coles, pp. 5–14. Exeter: The Prehistoric Society and WARP.

———. 1994. Kusado Sengen: A medieval town on the Inland Sea. In *The Illustrated History of Humankind,* Vol. 4, ed. Göran Burenhult, p. 134. New York: HarperCollins.

Matsumae Hironaga. 1979. *Matsumae-shi.* Reprinted in *Hoppō Mikōkai Kobunsho Shūsei,* Vol. 1, ed. Terasawa Kazu et al., pp. 85–240. Tokyo: Sōbunsha.

Matsumoto, H. 1920. Notes on the Stone Age people of Japan. *American Anthropologist* 23: 50–76.

Matsumoto Hideo. 1984. On the origin of the Japanese race: Studies of genetic markers of the immunoglobulins. *Proceedings of the Japan Academy* 60: 211–16.

———. 1988. Characteristics of Mongoloid and neighboring populations based on the genetic markers of human immunoglobulins. *Human Genetics* 80: 207–218.

Matsumoto Hideo, Tasuku Toyomasu, Kaoru Sagisaka, Kenkichi Takahashi, and Arthur G. Steinberg. 1977. Studies of red blood cell and serum polymorphisms among the matagi. *JJHG* 22: 271–280.

Matsumoto Hideo, Tokiko Miyazaki, Nakao Ishida, and Kazumichi Katayama. 1982. Mongoloid populations from the viewpoints of Gm patterns. *JJHG* 27: 271–282.

Matsumoto Nobuhiro. 1928. *Le Japonais et les Langues Astroasiatiques: Étude de Vocabulaire Comparé.* Paris: Librairie Orientaliste Paul Geuthner.

Matsumoto Shigeru. 1970. *Motoori Norinaga*. Cambridge, MA: Harvard University Press.

Matsumura Hirofumi. 1990. Geographical variation of dental characteristics in the Japanese of the protohistoric Kofun period. *JASN* 98(4): 439-449.

Matsumara Hirofumi, Nobuo Shigehara, and Eisaku Kanazawa. 1992. Dental characteristics of Japanese population. Paper presented at the *First World Conference on Prehistoric Mongoloid Dispersals*. Tokyo, November 16-21.

———. 1996. Dental characteristics of the Japanese population. In *Prehistoric Mongoloid Dispersals*, ed. T. Akazawa and E. Szathmáry, pp.125-136. Oxford: Oxford University Press.

Matsushita Takayuki. 1994. *Nihonjin to Yayoijin*. Tokyo: Shōdensha.

Matsushita Takayuki and Naitō Yoshiatsu. 1989. Chi'ikisei. In *Yayoi Bunka no Kenkyū*, Vol. 1, ed. Kanaseki Hiroshi and Sahara Makoto, pp.65-75. Tokyo: Yūzankaku.

Matsu'ura Takeshirō. 1982. *Teishi Tōzai Ezo Sansen Chiri Shuchō Nisshi*, Vol. 1. Sapporo: Hokkaidō Shuppan Kikaku Sentā.

Matthews, Peter. 1991. A tropical wildtype taro: *Colocasia esculenta* var. *aquatilis*. *BIPPA* 11: 69-81.

Matthews, Peter, Emiko Takei, and Taihachi Kawahara. 1992. *Colocasia esculenta* var. *aquatilis* on Okinawa Island, southern Japan: The distribution and possible origins of a wild diploid taro. *Man and Culture in Oceania* 8: 19-34.

McConvell, Patrick, and Nicholas Evans, eds. 1997. *Archaeology and Linguistics: Aboriginal Australia in Global Perspective*. Melbourne: Oxford University Press.

McCormack, Gavan. 1995. Growth, construction, and the environment: Japan's construction state. *Japanese Studies* 15(1): 26-35.

———. 1996. Kokusaika: Impediments in Japan's deep structure. In *Multicultural Japan: Palaeolithic to Postmodern*, ed. D. Denoon, M. Hudson, G. McCormack, and T. Morris-Suzuki, 265-286. Melbourne: Cambridge University Press.

McGuire, Randall H. 1982. The study of ethnicity in historical archaeology. *Journal of Anthropological Archaeology* 1: 159-178.

———. 1989. The greater Southwest as a periphery of Mesoamerica. In *Centre and Periphery: Comparative Studies in Archaeology*, ed. T. C. Champion, pp. 40-66. London: Unwin Hyman.

———. 1992a. *A Marxist Archaeology*. San Diego: Academic Press.

———. 1992b. Archeology of the first Americans. *American Anthropologist* 94(4): 816-836.

McKay, J. 1982. An exploratory synthesis of primordial and mobilizationist approaches to ethnic phenomenon. *Ethnic and Racial Studies* 5: 395-420.

Meacham, William. 1977. Continuity and local evolution in the Neolithic of south China: A non-nuclear approach. *CA* 18(3): 419-440.

———. 1985. On the improbability of Austronesian origins in south China. *AP* 26(1): 89-106.

———. 1991. Further considerations of the hypothesized Austronesian Neolithic migration from south China to Taiwan and Luzon. *BIPPA* 11: 398–407.

Menges, Karl H. 1968. *The Turkic Languages and Peoples: An Introduction to Turkic Studies*. Wiesbaden, Germany: Otto Harrassowitz.

———. 1975. *Altajische Studien, II: Japanisch und Altajisch*. Wiesbaden, Germany: Franz Steiner.

———. 1977. Dravidian and Altaic. *Anthropos* 72: 129–179.

Miles, Douglas. 1990. Capitalism and the structure of Yao descent units in China and Thailand: A comparison of Youling (1938) and Pulangka (1968). In *Ethnic Groups Across National Boundaries in Mainland Southeast Asia*, ed. Gehan Wijeyewardene, pp. 134–148. Singapore: Institute of Southeast Asian Studies.

Miller, Richard J. 1974. *Ancient Japanese Nobility: The* Kabane *Ranking System*. Berkeley and Los Angeles: University of California Press.

Miller, Roy Andrew. 1967. *The Japanese Language*. Chicago: University of Chicago Press.

———. 1976. The relevance of historical linguistics for Japanese studies. *JJS* 2(2): 335–388.

———. 1980. *Origins of the Japanese Language*. Seattle: University of Washington Press.

———. 1982. *Japan's Modern Myth: The Language and Beyond*. New York and Tokyo: Weatherhill.

———. 1986. Linguistic evidence and Japanese prehistory. In *Windows on the Japanese Past*, ed. R. Pearson, pp.101–120. Ann Arbor: Center for Japanese Studies, University of Michigan.

———. 1989. Where did Japanese come from? *Asian and Pacific Quarterly of Cultural and Social Affairs* 21(3): 1–25.

———. 1990. Archaeological light on Japanese linguistic origins. *Asian and Pacific Quarterly of Cultural and Social Affairs* 22(1): 1–26.

———. 1992. New light on Old Korean. *Asian and Pacific Quarterly of Cultural and Social Affairs* 24: 1–25.

Millett, Martin. 1990. *The Romanization of Britain: An Essay in Archaeological Interpretation*. Cambridge: Cambridge University Press.

Milne, John. 1880. Notes on stone implements from Otaru and Hakodate, with a few general remarks on the prehistoric remains of Japan. *TASJ* 8: 61–91.

———. 1881. The stone age in Japan. *Journal of the Royal Anthropological Institute of Great Britain and Ireland* 10: 389–423.

———. 1882. Notes on the Koro-pok-guru or pit-dwellers of Yezo and the Kurile Islands. *TASJ* 10: 187–198.

Minagawa Masao and Akazawa Takeru. 1992. Dietary patterns of Japanese Jomon hunter-gatherers: Stable nitrogen and carbon isotope analyses of human bones. In *Pacific Northeast Asia in Prehistory: Hunter-Fisher-Gatherers, Farmers, and Sociopolitical Elites*, ed. C. M. Aikens and Song Nai Rhee, pp. 59–68. Pullman: Washington State University Press.

Minamiki M., Nōjo S., Kogawa S., Kosugi S., and Suzuki M. 1986. Shokubutsu itai no kokankyō. In *Ikiriki Iseki,* ed. Tarami-chō Kyōiku Iinkai, pp. 44–53. Tarami: Tarami-chō Kyōiku Iinkai.

Mine Kazuharu, Ogata Takahiko, Takenaka Masami, and Kim Jin-Jeong. 1994. Human skeletal remains from Yean-ri site, Kimhae, Korea. *AS* 102(2): 182.

Miura Kenichi. 1993. Yanagi no Gosho ato o hakkutsu suru. In *Zusetsu Ōshū Fujiwara shi to Hiraizumi,* ed. Takahashi Tomio, Miura Kenichi, and Irumada Nobuo, pp. 61–92. Tokyo: Kawade Shobō.

Miyake Shuetsu. 1940. Nihonjin no seitai keisokugaku. In *Jinruigaku Senshi Kōza,* Vol. 19, ed. Nihon Jinruigakkai. Tokyo: Yūzankaku.

Miyake Yonekichi. 1974. Reprint. *Nihon Shigaku Teiyō 1.* Fukyū Shakan. In *Nihon Kōkogaku Senshū 1: Miyake Yonekichi Shū,* ed. Kishiro Shūichi, pp. 159–243. Tokyo: Tsukiji Shokan. Original edition, 1886.

Miyata Keiji and Ōno Sachio. 1991. Yayoi bunka to sono jidai. In *Wakayama-shi Shi,* ed. Wakayama-shi Shi Hensan Iinkai, pp. 213–268. Tokyo: Wakayama City.

Miyazaki Michio. 1988. *Arai Hakuseki no Shigaku to Chirigaku.* Tokyo: Yoshikawa Kōbunkan.

Miyazawa Akihisa and Yanagiura Shun'ichi. 1993. Kōjindani iseki no igi. In *Kodai o Kangaeru: Izumo,* ed. Ueda Masa'aki, pp. 48–81. Tokyo: Yoshikawa Kōbunkan.

Miyoshi Norio and Usui Yōsuke. 1976. Jōtō iseki (Okayama-ken) no kafun bunseki. In *Shōwa 51 Nendo Tokutei Kenkyū "Inasaku no Kigen to Denpa" Nenji Hōkoku,* pp. 30–35.

Mizoguchi Yuji. 1986. Contributions of prehistoric Far East populations to the population of modern Japan: A Q-mode path analysis based on cranial measurements. In *Prehistoric Hunter-Gatherers in Japan: New Research Methods,* ed. Takeru Akazawa and C. Melvin Aikens, pp. 107–136. Tokyo: Tokyo University Press.

———. 1988. Affinities of the protohistoric Kofun people of Japan with pre- and proto-historic Asian populations. *JASN* 96(1): 71–109.

Mizuno Masayoshi. 1990. *Bunmei no Dojō: Shimaguni no Genzō.* Tokyo: Kadokawa.

Mizuno Yu. 1973. *Nihon Minzoku no Genryū,* new ed. Tokyo: Yūzankaku.

———. 1984. Tsuchigumo to sono jittai. *Gendai Shisō* 22(8): 306–317.

Moeran, Brian. 1990. Rapt discourses: Anthropology, Japanism and Japan. Introduction to *Unwrapping Japan: Society and Culture in Anthropological Perspective,* ed. Eyal Ben-Ari, Brian Moeran, and James Valentine, pp. 1–17. Manchester: Manchester University Press.

Mongait, A. L. 1968. Archeological cultures and ethnic units (A contribution to research technique in historical archeology). *Soviet Anthropology and Archeology* 7(1): 3–25.

Moore, John H. 1994a. Ethnogenetic theory. *Research and Exploration* 10(1): 11–23.

———. 1994b. Putting anthropology back together again: The ethnogenetic critique of cladistic theory. *American Anthropologist* 96(4): 925–948.

Moratto, Michael J. 1984. *California Archaeology*. Orlando, FL: Academic Press.

Mori Katsumi. 1961. International relations between the 10th and the 16th century and the development of the Japanese international consciousness. *Acta Asiatica* 2: 69–93.

Mori Kōichi. 1975. Kinki chihō no Hayato: Toku ni kōkogaku shiten kara. In *Nihon Kodai Bunka no Tankyū: Hayato,* ed. Ōbayashi Taryō, pp. 163–188. Tokyo: Shakai Shisōsha.

———. 1989. *Umi o Watatta Hitobito*. Tokyo: Chūō Kōronsha.

———, ed. 1991. *Umi to Rettō Bunka 2: Nihonkai to Izumo Sekai*. Tokyo: Shōgakukan.

Mori Teijirō. 1969. Nihon ni okeru shoki shisekibo. In *Kim Chae-wan Paksa Haesin Kinyom Nonop*. Seoul: Ulya Munhwasa.

———. 1988. Torii Ryūzō ron. In *Yayoi Bunka no Kenkyū,* Vol. 10, ed. Kanaseki Hiroshi and Sahara Makoto, pp.47–52. Tokyo: Yūzankaku.

Morimoto Rokuji. 1933a. Nihon ni okeru nōgyō kigen. *Dorumen* 2(9).

———. 1933b. Yayoi-shiki bunka to genshi nōgyō. In *Nihon Genshi Nōgyō*. Special edition of *Kōkogaku.*

———. 1933c. Higashi Nihon Jōmon jidai ni okeru Yayoi-shiki narabi ni Iwabe-shiki kei bunka no yōso tekishutsu. *Kōkogaku* 4(1).

Morioka Hideto. 1990. Inasaku wa dono yō ni hirogatte itta ka. In *Sōten Nihon no Rekishi 1,* ed. Suzuki Kimio, pp. 203–219. Tokyo: Shinjinbutsu Ōraisha.

Moriwaki Kazuo. 1989. Idenshi kara mita hatsuka nezumi Nihon torai no michizuji. *Kikan Yamataikoku* 38: 159–167.

Moriwaki Kazuo and Yonekawa H. 1993. Idenshi kara mita Ajiasan hatsuka nezumi ashu no bunshi to bunpu. In *Nihonjin to Nihon Bunka no Keisei,* ed. Hanihara Kazurō, pp. 422–431. Tokyo: Asakura Shoten.

Morris, Ivan. 1975. *As I Crossed a Bridge of Dreams*. Harmondsworth, U.K.: Penguin.

———. 1979. *The World of the Shining Prince: Court Life in Ancient Japan*. Harmondsworth, U.K.: Penguin.

Morris-Suzuki, Tessa. 1993a. Rewriting history: Civilization theory in contemporary Japan. *Positions: East Asia Cultures Critique* 1(2): 526–549.

———. 1993b. The discovery of culture in Japan. Unpublished paper.

———. 1994. Creating the frontier: Border, identity and history in Japan's far north. *East Asian History* 7: 1–24.

———. 1995. Sustainability and ecological colonialism in Edo period Japan. *Japanese Studies* 15(1): 36–48.

Morse, E. S. 1879a. *Shell Mounds of Ōmori*. Memoirs of the Science Department, University of Tokio, Japan, Vol. 1, Part 1.

———. 1879b. Traces of an early race in Japan. *The Popular Science Monthly* 14: 257–266.

Moto'ori Norinaga. 1972. *Moto'ori Norinaga Zenshū* Vol. 8, ed. Ōkubo Tadashi. Tokyo: Chikuma Shobō.

Moulder, Frances. V. 1977. *Japan, China, and the Modern World Economy: Toward a Reinterpretation of East Asian Development, ca. 1600 to ca. 1918.* Cambridge: Cambridge University Press.

Mouri Toshio. 1986. *Tōgaikotsu no hikeisoku keishitsu kara mita Nihon rettō shoshūdan no chiriteki oyobi jidaiteki hen'i.* Ph.D. dissertation, University of Kyoto.

———. 1988. Incidences of cranial nonmetric characters in five Jomon populations from west Japan. *JASN* 96(3): 319–337.

Munro, Neil Gordon. 1911. *Prehistoric Japan.* Edinburgh: William Bryce.

Murai Shōsuke. 1985.Chūsei Nihon rettō no chi'iki kūkan to kokka. *Shisō* 732: 36–58.

———. 1993. *Chūsei Wajinden.* Tokyo: Iwanami.

———. 1997. *Umi kara mita Sengoku Nihon.* Chikuma Shinsho.

Murakoshi Kiyoshi. 1983. *Kamegaoka-shiki Doki.* Tokyo: New Science Press.

Murayama Shichiro. 1976. The Malayo-Polynesian component in the Japanese language. *JJS* 2(2): 413–431.

———. 1992. *Ainugo no Kigen.* Tokyo: Sanichi Shobō.

———. 1993. *Ainugo no Kenkyū.* Tokyo: Sanichi Shobō.

Murray, David. 1919. *Japan.* 6th ed. London: T. Fisher Unwin.

Myres, John L. 1930. *Who Were the Greeks?* Berkeley and Los Angeles: University of California Press.

Myres, J. N. L. 1969. *Anglo-Saxon Pottery and the Settlement of England.* Oxford: Clarendon.

———. 1989. *The English Settlements.* Oxford: Oxford University Press.

Nagashima Kimichika. 1994. Chōsen hantō. In *Saishin Kaigai Kōkogaku Jijō.* Gekkan Bunkazai Hakkutsu Shutsudo Jōhō Special Issue, (January) pp. 183–92.

Nagayama Shuichi. 1992. Hasseiki Hayato shihai no tokushitsu ni tsuite [An inquiry into the control of the Hayato by the central government in the eighth century]. *Kodai Bunka* 44(7): 13–22. (ES pp. 54–55)

Naitō Yoshiatsu. 1971. Seihoku Kyūshū shutsudo no Yayoi jidai jinkotsu [On the human skeletons of Yoyoi *(sic)* period excavated at the sites in north-western Kyushu]. *JASN* 79(3): 236–248.

———. 1989. Yayoi jinkotsu to Nihonjin no genryū. In *Saishin Yamataikoku Ron,* pp. 146–149. Tokyo: Gakken.

———. 1992. The skeleton of the Yayoi people. In *Japanese as a Member of the Asian and Pacific Populations,* ed. Hanihara Kazuro, pp. 94–95. Kyoto: Nichibunken.

Nakahashi Takahiro. 1990a. Toraijin no mondai: Keishitsu jinruigaku no tachiba kara. In *Kodai Chōsen to Nihon,* ed. Nishitani Tadashi, pp. 117–174. Tokyo: Meicho.

———. 1990b. Doigahama Yayoijin no fushuteki basshi [Ritual tooth ablation in Doigahama Yayoi people]. *JASN* 98(4): 483–507. (ES)

———. 1993. DNA kara Jōmonjin no rūtsu wa doko made wakaru ka. In *Shinshiten Nihon no Rekishi 1,* ed. Suzuki Kimio and Ishikawa Hideshi, pp. 283-288. Tokyo: Shinjinbutsu Ōraisha.

Nakahashi Takahiro and Nagai Masafumi. 1987. Fukuoka-ken Shima-chō Shinmachi iseki shutsudo no Jōmon, Yayoi ikōki no jinkotsu. In *Shinmachi Iseki,* ed. Hashiguchi Tatsuya. Fukuoka: Shima-chō Kyōiku Iinkai.

———. 1989. Keishitsu. In *Yayoi Bunka no Kenkyū*, Vol. 1, ed. Kanaseki Hiroshi and Sahara Makoto, pp. 23-51. Tokyo: Yūzankaku.

Nakai, Kate Wildman. 1980. The naturalization of Confucianism in Tokugawa Japan: The problem of Sinocentrism. *Harvard Journal of Asiatic Studies* 40(1): 157-199.

———. 1988. *Shogunal Politics: Arai Hakuseki and the Premises of Tokugawa Rule.* Cambridge, MA: Council on East Asian Studies, Harvard University.

Nakajima Hachiro, Okura Koji, Inafuku Seiko, Ogura Yoshio, Koyama Takashi, Hori Fumio, and Takahara Shigeo. 1967. The distribution of several serological and biochemical traits in East Asia. II. The distribution of ABO, MNSs, Q, Lewis, Rh, Kell, Duffy and Kidd blood groups in Ryukyu. *JJHG* 12: 29-37.

Nakajima Naoyuki. 1982. Shoki inasakuki no tottaimon doki. In *Mori Teijirō Hakase Koki Kinen: Kobunka Ronshū,* ed. Mori Teijirō Hakase Koki Kinen Ronbunshū Kankōkai.

Nakajima Naoyuki and Tajima Ryuta, eds. 1982. *Nabatake Iseki.* Karatsu, Saga: Saga-ken Kyōiku Iinkai.

Nakama Kenji. 1987. Songgungni-gata jūkyo: Wagakuni inasaku nōkō juyōki ni okeru tateana jūkyo no kenkyū. In *Higashi Ajia no Kōko to Rekishi,* Vol. 2, ed. Okazaki Takeshi Sensei Taikan Kinen Jigyōkai, pp. 593-634. Kyōto: Dōhōsha.

Nakamoto Masachie. 1981. *Nihongo no Genkei: Nihon Rettō no Gengogaku.* Tokyo: Kinkeisha.

———. 1990. *Nihon Rettō Gengoshi no Kenkyū.* Tokyo: Taishūkan.

Nakamura Akizō. 1993a. *Shintei Hayato no Kenkyū.* Tokyo: Maruyama Gakugei Tosho.

———. 1993b. *Hayato to Ritsuryō Kokka.* Tokyo: Meicho.

Nakamura Gorō. 1988. *Yayoi Bunka no Shokō.* Tokyo: Miraisha.

———. 1990. Yayoi doki kara Hajiki e. *Fukushima Kōko* 31: 55-58.

Nakamura Jun. 1981. Kafun kara wakaru inasaku no kutō. *Kagaku Asahi* 41(6): 44-47.

———. 1982. Kafun kara mita Jōmon kara Yayoi. *Rekishi Kōron* 74: 71-77.

Nakanishi Yasuto. 1984. Zenki Yayoi mura no futatsu no taipu. In *Jōmon kara Yayoi e.* Nara: Tezukayama Kōkogaku Kenkyūjō.

Nakao Sasuke. 1966. *Saibai Shokubutsu to Nōkō no Kigen.* Tokyo: Iwanami.

Nakayama Heijirō. 1917. Kita Kyūshū hokubu ni okeru senshi genshi ryōjidai chūkanki no ibutsu ni tsuite. *Kōkogaku Zasshi* 7(10) and (11), and 8(1 and 3).

Nakayama Seiji and Toyama Shuichi. 1991. Ine to inasaku no hakyū. *Kikan Kōkogaku* 37: 23-28.

Naoki Kōjirō. 1993. The Nara state. In *The Cambridge History of Japan,* Vol. 1, ed. Delmer Brown, pp. 221-267. Cambridge: Cambridge University Press.

Nash, Manning. 1989. *The Cauldron of Ethnicity in the Modern World.* Chicago: University of Chicago Press.

National Museum of Korea, ed. 1976. *Jo-do Shellmound.* Report of the Research of Antiquities of the National Museum of Korea, Vol. IX. Seoul. (In Korean and English).

Nei Masatoshi. 1995. The origins of human populations: Genetic, linguistic, and archeological data. In *The Origin and Past of Modern Humans as Viewed from DNA,* ed. Sydney Brenner and Kazuro Hanihara, pp. 71-91. Singapore: World Scientific Publishing.

Nei Masatoshi and Imaizumi Yoko. 1966a. Genetic structure of human populations: I. Local differentiation of blood group frequencies in Japan. *Heredity* 21: 9-35.

———. 1966b. Genetic structure of human populations: II. Differentiation of blood group gene frequencies among isolated populations. *Heredity* 21: 183-190.

Nelson, Sarah M. 1992. The question of agricultural impact on sociopolitical developments in prehistoric Korea. In *Pacific Northeast Asia in Prehistory: Hunter-Fisher-Gatherers, Farmers, and Sociopolitical Elites,* ed. C. M. Aikens and Song Nai Rhee, pp. 179-183. Pullman: Washington State University Press.

———. 1993. *The Archaeology of Korea.* Cambridge: Cambridge University Press.

Nichols, Johanna. 1992. *Linguistic Diversity in Space and Time.* Chicago: University of Chicago Press.

Nihon Kōkogaku Kyōkai, eds. 1978. Reprint, *Toro.* Tokyo: Tokyo-do. (ES) Original edition, 1954.

Niino Naoyoshi. 1991. Emishi no kuni no jitsuzō. In *Michinoku Kodai: Emishi no Sekai,* pp. 65-112. Tokyo: Yamakawa.

Niiro Izumi. 1991. Roku, nana seiki no henmei to chi'iki shakai no dōkō. *Kōkogaku Kenkyū* 38(2): 55-67.

Nishida Masaki. 1975. Shokubutsu tane no dōtei. In *Kyōto-fu Maizuru-shi Kuwagaishimo Iseki Hakkutsu Chōsa Hōkokusho,* ed. Watanabe Makoto, pp. 244-249. Kyoto: Heian Hakubutsukan.

———. 1983. The emergence of food production in Neolithic Japan. *Journal of Anthropological Archaeology* 2: 305-322.

Nishijima Sadao. 1983. *Chūgoku Kodai Kokka to Higashi Ajia Sekai.* Tokyo: Tokyo University Press.

———. 1994. *Yamataikoku to Wakoku: Kodai Nihon to Higashi Ajia.* Tokyo: Yoshikawa Kōbunkan.

Nishikawa Nagao. 1992. *Kokkyō no Kōekata.* Tokyo: Chikuma Shobō.

———. 1993. Interpretations of Japanese culture. Paper presented at the conference *Stirrup, Sail and Plough: Continental and Maritime Influences on Japanese Identity.* Canberra, September 20-23.

———. 1996. Interpretations of Japanese culture. In *Multicultural Japan: Palaeolithic to Postmodern,* ed. D. Denoon, M. J. Hudson, G. McCormack, and T. Morris-Suzuki, pp. 245-264. Melbourne: Cambridge University Press.

Nishimoto Toyohiro. 1989a. Shimogōri Kuwanae iseki shutsudo no dōbutsu itai. In *Shimogōri Kuwanae Iseki,* ed. Takahashi Nobutake, pp. 48-82. Ōita: Ōita-ken Kyōiku Iinkai.

———. 1989b. Buta to Nihonjin. *Rekihaku* 34: 12-13.

———. 1991. Yayoi jidai no buta ni tsuite [Pigs in the Yayoi period]. *Kokuritsu Rekishi Minzoku Hakubutsukan Kenkyū Hōkoku* 36: 175-189. (ES)

———. 1993. Yayoi jidai no buta no keishitsu ni tsuite [The physical character of the pig in the Yayoi period]. *Kokuritsu Rekishi Minzoku Hakubutsukan Kenkyū Hōkoku* 50: 49-63. (ES)

Nishimura Shinji. 1922. Yamato jidai. In *Kokumin no Nihonshi 1.* Tokyo: Waseda University Press.

Nishioka Hideo and W. Egbert Schenck. 1937. An outline of theories concerning the prehistoric people of Japan. *American Anthropologist* 39: 23-33.

Nishitani Tadashi. 1989. Yayoi jidai no seidōki. *Kikan Kōkogaku* 27: 14-17.

Nosco, Peter. 1990. *Remembering Paradise: Nativism and Nostalgia in Eighteenth Century Japan.* Cambridge, MA: Council on East Asian Studies, Harvard University.

Noto Takeshi. 1987. Jōmon nōkōron. In *Ronsō: Gakusetsu Nihon no Kōkogaku 3:* 1-29.

Oba T., Mizoguchi S., and Yamaguchi Bin. 1978. Human skeletal remains from the Etomo site, Muroran, Hokkaido. *Bulletin of the National Science Museum* D, 4: 1-23. (In Japanese with ES)

Ōbayashi Taryō. 1975. Minzokugaku kara mita Hayato. In *Nihon Kodai Bunka no Tankyū: Hayato,* ed. Ōbayashi Taryō, pp. 11-62. Tokyo: Shakai Shisōsha.

———. 1984. Minzoku keisei no jiki: Nihon minzoku o chūshin ni shite [The crucial time in the formation of the Japanese people]. *Minzokugaku Kenkyū* 48(4): 401-405 (ES)

———. 1990a. *Higashi to Nishi, Umi to Yama: Nihon no Bunka Ryūiki.* Tokyo: Shōgakukan.

———. 1990b. Nihon minzoku bunka no keisei to Nihongo no kigen. In *Nihongo no Keisei: The Formation of the Japanese Language,* ed. Sakiyama Osamu, pp. 23-43. Tokyo: Sanseidō.

———. 1991. The ethnological study of Japan's ethnic culture: A historical survey. *Acta Asiatica* 61: 1-23.

———. 1995. Postwar Japan from an anthropological perspective. *Japan Review of International Affairs* 9(2): 147-159.

Oblas, Peter B. 1995. *Perspectives on Race and Culture in Japanese Society: The Mass Media and Ethnicity.* Lewiston, NY: The Edwin Mellen Press.

Oda Fujio. 1988. Nakayama Heijirō ron. In *Yayoi Bunka no Kenkyū,* Vol. 10, ed. Kanaseki Hiroshi and Sahara Makoto, pp. 53-63. Tokyo: Yūzankaku.

Ohnuki-Tierney, Emiko. 1974a. *The Ainu of the Northwest Coast of Southern Sakhalin*. New York: Holt, Rinehart and Winston.

———. 1974b. Another look at the Ainu—a preliminary report. *AA* 11(Suppl.): 189-195.

———. 1976. Regional variations in Ainu culture. *American Ethnologist* 3(2): 297-329.

———. 1993. *Rice as Self: Japanese Identities through Time*. Princeton, NJ: Princeton University Press.

Ohyi Haruo. 1975. The Okhotsk culture, a maritime culture of the southern Okhotsk Sea region. In *Prehistoric Maritime Adaptations of the Circumpolar Zone,* ed. William Fitzhugh, pp.123-158. The Hague: Mouton.

Ōishi Naomasa. 1987. Tōgoku, Tōhoku no jiritsu to "Nihonkoku." In *Nihon no Shakaishi 1: Rettō Naigai no Kōtsū to Kokka,* ed. Amino Yoshihiko, pp. 227-256. Tokyo: Iwanami.

———. 1990. Kita no umi no bushidan: Andō-shi. In *Umi to Rettō Bunka 1: Nihonkai to Hokkoku Bunka,* ed. Amino Yoshihiko, pp. 318-342. Tokyo: Shōgakukan.

———. 1993. Chi'ikisei to kōtsu. In *Iwanami Koza Nihon Tsushi* 7, ed. Ishii Susumu, pp. 105-140. Tokyo: Iwanami.

Oka Masao. 1994. Reprint. Nihon minzoku bunka no keisei. *Ijin sono Ta,* ed. Ōbayashi Taryō, pp. 5-41. Tokyo: Iwanami. Original version, 1956. In *Zusetsu Nihon Bunkashi Taikei 1.*

Okada Shoji. 1987. The development of state ritual in ancient Japan. *Acta Asiatica* 51: 22-41.

Okamoto Takayuki. 1991. Sugihara Sōsuke to Yamanouchi Sugao no sōkoku. *Kanagawa Kōko* 27: 57-69.

Okamura Michio. 1992. The achievements of research into the Japanese Palaeolithic. *Acta Asiatica* 63: 21-39.

Okazaki Takeshi. 1993. Japan and the continent. In *The Cambridge History of Japan*, Vol. 1, *Ancient Japan,* ed. Delmer M. Brown, pp. 268-316. Cambridge: Cambridge University Press.

Okita Masa'aki. 1993. Jomon elements in Yayoi pottery at the Miwa site. In *The Miwa Project: Survey, Coring and Excavation at the Miwa Site, Nara, Japan,* ed. Gina L. Barnes and Masa'aki Okita, pp. 143-148. Oxford: BAR International Series 582.

Ölschleger, Hans Dieter. 1993. John Batchelor's contribution to Ainu ethnography. In *European Studies on Ainu Language and Culture,* ed. Josef Kreiner, pp. 137-150. Munich: Iudicium Verlag.

Omoto Keiichi. 1972. Polymorphisms and genetic affinities of the Ainu in Hokkaido. *Human Biology in Oceania* 1: 279-288.

———. 1978. Blood protein polymorphisms and the problem of genetic affinities of the Ainu. In *Evolutionary Models and Studies in Human Diversity,* ed. R. J. Meier, C. M. Otten, and F. Abdel-Hameed, pp. 333-341. The Hague: Mouton.

———. 1986. The distribution of red cell enzyme and serum protein types in a sample from Iwate, northern Japan, with description of geographical cline of Gc sub-types. *JASN* 94: 51–63.

———. 1992. Some aspects of the genetic composition of the Japanese. In *Japanese as a Member of the Asian and Pacific Populations,* ed. Hanihara Kazuro, pp.138–145. Kyoto: Nichibunken.

———. 1995. Genetic diversity and the origins of the "Mongoloids." In *The Origin and Past of Modern Humans as Viewed from DNA,* ed. Sydney Brenner and Kazuro Hanihara, pp. 92–109. Singapore: World Scientific Publishing.

———. 1997. Ethnicity survived: The Ainu of Hokkaido. *Human Evolution* 12: 69–72.

Omoto Keiichi and Naruya Saitou. 1997. Genetic origins of the Japanese: A partial support for the dual structure hypothesis. *AJPA* 102: 437–446.

Ōno Susumu. 1970. *The Origin of the Japanese Language.* Tokyo: Kokusai Bunka Shinkokai.

———. 1980. *Nihongo no Seiritsu. Nihongo no Sekai 1.* Tokyo: Chūō Kōronsha.

———. 1987. *Nihongo Izen.* Tokyo: Iwanami.

———. 1989. The genealogy of the Japanese language: Tamil and Japanese. *Gengo Kenkyū* 95: 32–63.

———. 1990. Yayoi bunka to minami Indo. In *Yayoi Bunka to Nihongo,* pp. 10–49. Tokyo: Kadokawa.

———. 1994. *Nihongo no Kigen,* new ed. Tokyo: Iwanami.

Ōshima Naoyuki. 1989. Hokkaido shutsudo no kaiwa ni tsuite. *Kōkogaku Jānaru* 311: 19–24.

———. 1990. Kita no bunka. In *Ningen no Bijitsu 2: Ine to Kenryoku,* ed. Sahara Makoto and Inokuma Kanekatsu, pp. 80–87. Tokyo: Gakushu Kenkyūsha.

Ossenberg, Nancy S. 1986. Isolate Conservatism and hybridization in the population history of Japan: The evidence of nonmetric cranial traits. In *Prehistoric Hunter-Gatherers in Japan: New Research Methods,* ed. Takeru Akazawa and C. Melvin Aikens, pp. 199–215. Tokyo: Tokyo University Press.

———. 1992a. Native people of the American Northwest: population history from the perspective of skull morphology. In *The Evolution and Dispersal of Modern Humans in Asia,* ed. T. Akazawa, K. Aoki, and T. Kimura, pp. 493–530. Tokyo: Hokuensha.

———. 1992b. Microevolutionary parallels in the population history of Japan and aboriginal North America: The evidence of cranial nonmetric traits. In *Japanese as a Member of the Asian and Pacific Populations,* ed. Hanihara Kazuro, pp. 64–77. Kyoto: Nichibunken.

Ōta Hiroki. 1994. *Saga-ken Chiyoda-chō Takuta Nishibun kaizuka iseki (Yayoi jidai) shutsudo no bunshi jinruigakuteki kaiseki.* M.Sc. thesis, University of Tokyo.

Ōta Hiroki and Mark Hudson. 1998. Senshi kōkogaku to DNA: Ōyō to hōhō [Prehistoric archaeology and the DNA revolution: applications and methods]. *Kōkogaku Kenkyū* 45(2):124–134.

Ōta Hiroki, Naruya Saitou, Takayuki Matsushita, and Shintaroh Ueda. 1995. A genetic study of 2,000-year-old human remains from Japan using mitochondrial DNA sequences. *AJPA* 98: 133–145.

Otomasu Shigetaku. 1970. Kumaso, Hayato no kuni. In *Kodai no Nihon 3: Kyūshū*, ed. Kagamiyama Takeshi and Tamura Enchō, pp. 90–111. Tokyo: Kadokawa.

Ōtsuka Hatsushige. 1992. Tōgoku no tsumi'ishizuka kofun to sono hisōsha [Stone-piled tumuli in Togoku and the persons buried therein]. *Kokuritsu Rekishi Minzoku Hakubutsukan Kenkyū Hōkoku* 44: 3–19. (ES)

Ōtsuka Kazuyoshi. 1993. Ainu fūzoku no Wajin shakai ni okeru juyō, mohō ni tsuite. In *Nihonjin to Nihon Bunka no Keisei*, ed. Hanihara Kazurō, pp.109–124. Tokyo: Asakura Shoten.

Otsuka Takanobu. 1941. *The First Voyage of the English to Japan, by John Saris.* Tokyo: The Toyo Bunko.

Ōyama Kashiwa. 1927. *Kanagawa-ken shita Shin'iso-mura Aza-Katsusaka Ibutsu Hōganchi Chōsa Hōkoku.* Tokyo: Komiyayama.

Oyamada Joichi. 1992. Tooth crown size of Yayoi people in the northwest and north of Kyushu. *JASN* 100(1): 83–100. (ES)

Oyamada Joichi, Manabe Yoshitaka, Kitagawa Yoshikazu, Rokutanda Atsushi, and Nagashima Seiji. 1995. Tooth size of the protohistoric Kofun people in southern Kyushu, Japan. *AS* 103(2): 178.

Ozawa Ichirō. 1993. *Nihon Kaizō Keikaku.* Tokyo: Kōdansha.

Pai Hyng Il. 1989a. Lelang and the "Interaction Sphere": An alternative approach to Korean state formation. *Archaeological Review from Cambridge* 8(1): 64–75.

———. 1989b. *Lelang and the Interaction Sphere in Korean Prehistory.* Ph.D. dissertation, Harvard University. Published by UMI 1993.

Palmer, Edwina. 1996. From coastal vessel to ship of state: The transformation of Harima leaders into Yamato monarchs. *New Zealand Journal of East Asian Studies* 4(1): 5–37.

Palmer, Jay W. 1994. The prehistoric migrations of the Cherokee. *North American Archaeologist* 15(1): 31–52.

Parker, Arthur C. 1916. The origin of the Iroquois as suggested by their archeology. *American Anthropologist* 18: 479–507.

Patrie, James. 1982. *The Genetic Relationship of the Ainu Language.* Honolulu: University of Hawai'i Press.

Patterson, Thomas C. 1987. Tribes, chiefdoms, and kingdoms in the Inca empire. In *Power Relations and State Formation*, ed. Thomas C. Patterson and Christine W. Gailey, pp. 117–127. Washington, DC: American Anthropological Association.

Pauly, Ulrich. 1980. Japan und die "Kultur aus dem Süden": Vermutete Beziehungen Japans zu Südostasien und nicht-Chiesischen Völkern Süd-und Ostchinas. *Bonner Zeitschrift für Japanologie* 2: 55–127.

Pearson, Richard J. 1976–1978. Lolang and the rise of Korean states and chiefdoms. *Journal of the Hong Kong Archaeological Society* 7: 77–90.

———. 1990. Chiefly exchange between Kyushu and Okinawa, Japan, in the Yayoi period. *Antiquity* 64: 912–922.

———. 1992. *Ancient Japan*. New York and Washington, DC: George Braziller and the Smithsonian.

———. 1996a. The place of Okinawa in Japanese historical identity. In *Multicultural Japan: Palaeolithic to Postmodern*, ed. D. Denoon, M. Hudson, G. McCormack, and T. Morris-Suzuki, pp. 95–116. Melbourne: Cambridge University Press.

———. 1996b. The Chuzan kingdom of Okinawa as a city-state. In *The Archaeology of City-States: Cross Cultural Aproaches*, ed. T. Charlton and D. Nichols, pp. 119–134. Washington, DC: Smithsonian.

Pearson, Richard J., and Kazue Pearson. 1978. Some problems in the study of Jomon subsistence. *Antiquity* 52: 21–27.

Peterson, Nicholas, ed. 1976. *Tribes and Boundaries in Australia*. Canberra: Australian Institute of Aboriginal Studies.

Petrova-Averkiera, Yu. 1980. Historicism in Soviet ethnographic science. In *Soviet and Western Anthropology*, ed. Ernest Gellner, pp. 19–27. London: Duckworth.

Philippi, Donald L. 1968. *Kojiki*. Tokyo: University of Tokyo Press.

———. 1979. *Songs of Gods, Songs of Humans: The Epic Tradition of the Ainu*. Princeton and Tokyo: Princeton University Press and Tokyo University Press.

Phillips, P., and G. R. Willey. 1953. Method and theory in American archeology: An operational basis for culture-historical integration. *American Anthropologist* 55: 615–633.

Pietrusewsky, Michael, Li Yongyi, Shao Xianqing, and Nguyen Quang Quyen. 1992. Modern and near modern populations of Asia and the Pacific: A multivariate craniometric interpretation. In *The Evolution and Dispersal of Modern Humans in Asia*, ed. T. Akazawa, K. Aoki, and T. Kimura, pp. 531–558. Tokyo: Hokuensha.

Piggott, Joan R. 1989. Sacral kingship and confederacy in early Izumo. *MN* 44(1): 45–74.

Plutschow, Herbert. 1981. Introduction. In *Four Japanese Travel Diaries of the Middle Ages*, by H. Plutschow and Hideichi Fukuda, pp. 1–24. Ithaca, NY: Cornell University East Asia Papers 25.

Polivanov, E. D. 1924. Toward work on musical accentuation in Japanese (in connection with the Malayan languages). Reprinted in *Selected Works*, compiled by A. A. Leonte'v. The Hague: Mouton, 1974.

Pollard, Helen Perlstein. 1994. Ethnicity and political control in a complex society: The Tarascan state of prehispanic Mexico. In *Factional Competition and Political Development in the New World*, ed. E. M. Brumfiel and John W. Fox, pp. 79–88. Cambridge: Cambridge University Press.

Pons, Frank Moya. 1992. The politics of forced Indian labour in La Española 1493–1520. *Antiquity* 66: 130–139.

Poppe, Nicholas. 1960. *Vergleichende Grammatik der altaischen Sprachen. Teil I, Vergleichende Lautlehre*. Wiesbaden: Otto Harrossowitz.

———. 1965. *Introduction to Altaic Linguistics*. Wiesbaden: Otto Harrossowitz.

Rabbitt, James A. 1940. Rice in the cultural life of the Japanese. *TASJ* 19: 187-258.

Rabinovitch, Judith N. 1986. *Shōmonki: The Story of Masakado's Rebellion*. Tokyo: Monumenta Nipponica, Sophia University.

Ramsden, Peter G. 1992. Regards sur l'hypothèse de l'origine *in situ* des Iroquoiens. *Recherches Amérindiennes au Québec* 22(4): 19-23.

Ramstedt, G. J. 1949. *Studies in Korean Etymology*. Helsinki: Suomalais-Ugrilainen Seura.

Rauch, Jonathan. 1992. *The Outnation: A Search for the Soul of Japan*. Boston, MA: Harvard Business School Press.

Reece, Richard. 1980. Town and country: The end of Roman Britain. *World Archaeology* 12(1):77-92.

———. 1989. Models of continuity. *Oxford Journal of Archaeology* 8(2): 231-236.

Reed, Sir Edward J. 1880. *Japan: Its History, Traditions and Religions*. London: John Murray.

Refsing, Kirsten. 1986. *The Ainu Language: The Morphology and Syntax of the Shizunai Dialect*. Aarhus, Denmark: Aarhus University Press.

Reischauer, Edwin O., and Albert M. Craig. 1989. *Japan: Tradition and Transformation*. Rev. ed. Sydney: Allen and Unwin.

Renfrew, Colin. 1987. *Archaeology and Language: The Puzzle of Indo-European Origins*. London: Jonathan Cape.

———. 1989. Models of change in language and archaeology. *Transactions of the Philological Society* 87: 103-155.

———. 1991. Before Babel: Speculations on the origins of linguistic diversity. *Cambridge Archaeological Journal* 1: 3-23.

———. 1992a. World languages and human dispersals: A minimalist view. In *Transition to Modernity: Essays on Power, Wealth and Belief*, ed. J. A. Hall and I. C. Jarvie, pp. 11-68. Cambridge: Cambridge University Press.

———. 1992b. Archaeology, genetics and linguistic diversity. *Man* 27: 445-478.

———. 1993. *The Roots of Ethnicity: Archaeology, Genetics and the Origins of Europe*. Rome: Unione Internazionale degli Istituti di Archeologia Storia e Storia dell'Arte in Roma.

Renfrew, Colin, and Paul Bahn. 1991. *Archaeology: Theories, Methods and Practice*. London: Thames and Hudson.

Rhee Song Nai and Choi Mong-Lyong. 1992. Emergence of complex society in prehistoric Korea. *Journal of World Prehistory* 6(1): 51-95.

Ritchie, William A., and Richard S. Macneish. 1949. The pre-Iroquoian pottery of New York State. *American Antiquity* 15(2): 97-124.

Ro Hyuk-Jin 1992. A revised framework for Korean prehistory. In *Pacific Northeast Asia in Prehistory: Hunter-Fisher-Gatherers, Farmers, and Sociopolitical Elites*, ed. C. Melvin Aikens and Song Nai Rhee, pp. 209-213. Pullman: Washington State University Press.

Rodd, Laurel Rasplica. 1980. *Nichiren: Selected Writings*. Honolulu: University of Hawai'i Press.

Roksandic, Zarko, Minagawa Masao, and Akazawa Takeru. 1988. Comparative analysis of dietary habits between Jomon and Ainu hunter-gatherers from stable carbon isotopes of human bone. *JASN* 96(4): 391–404.

Rossabi, Morris. 1982. *The Jurchens in the Yüan and Ming*. Ithaca, NY: Cornell China-Japan Program.

———, ed. 1983. *China Among Equals: The Middle Kingdom and its Neighbors, 10th–14th Centuries*. Berkeley and Los Angeles: University of California Press.

Rouse, Irving. 1958. The inference of migration from anthropological evidence. In *Migrations in New World Culture History*, ed. R. H. Thompson. Tucson: University of Arizona Press.

———. 1965. The place of "peoples" in prehistoric research. *Journal of the Royal Anthropological Institute of Great Britain and Ireland* 95(1): 1–15.

———. 1986. *Migrations in Prehistory: Inferring Population Movement from Cultural Remains*. New Haven, CT: Yale University Press.

Rowlands, Michael. 1987. Centre and periphery: A review of a concept. In *Centre and Periphery in the Ancient World*, ed. M. Rowlands, M. Larsen, and K. Kristiansen, pp. 1–11. Cambridge: Cambridge University Press.

Rowley-Conwy, Peter. 1984. Postglacial foraging and early farming economies in Japan and Korea: A west European perspective. *World Archaeology* 16(1): 28–42.

Ruhlen, Merrit. 1987. *A Guide to the World's Languages*, Vol. 1, *Classification*. Stanford, CA: Stanford University Press.

Sabloff, Jeremy A. 1992. Interpreting the collapse of Classic Maya civilization: A case study of changing archaeological perspectives. In *Metaarchaeology: Reflections by Archaeologists and Philosophers*, ed. Lester Embree, pp. 99–119. Dordrecht, Netherlands: Kluwer Academic.

Sabloff, Jeremy A., and Gordon R. Willey. 1967. The collapse of Maya civilization in the southern lowlands: A consideration of history and process. *Southwestern Journal of Anthropology* 23: 311–336.

Saeki Ariyiko. 1971. *Kenkyūshi Yamataikoku*. Tokyo: Yoshikawa Kōbunkan.

———. 1972. *Kenkyūshi Sengo no Yamataikoku*. Tokyo: Yoshikawa Kōbunkan.

Sahara Makato. 1975. Nōgyō no kaishi to kaikyū shakai no keisei. In *Iwanami Kōza Nihon Rekishi I: Genshi oyobi Kodai 1*, pp. 113–182. Tokyo: Iwanami.

———. 1987a. The Yayoi Culture. In *Recent Archaeological Discoveries in Japan*, ed. Tsuboi Kiyotari, pp. 37–54. Paris and Tokyo: UNESCO and the Centre for East Asian Cultural Studies.

———. 1987b. *Nihonjin no Tanjō*. Shōgakukan.

———. 1987c. Michinoku no Ongagawa. In *Higashi Ajia no Kōko to Rekishi*, Vol. 2, ed. Okazaki Takeshi Sensei Taikan Kinen Jigyōkai, pp. 265–291. Kyoto: Dōhōsha.

———. 1992a. Rice cultivation and the Japanese. *Acta Asiatica* 63: 40–63.

———. 1992b. Yayoi culture in the context of world history. In *Japanese as a Member of the Asian and Pacific Populations,* ed. Hanihara Kazuro, pp. 198-203. Kyoto: Nichibunken.

———. 1993. Nihon no hajimari. In *Nihon Rekishikan,* pp. 41-160. Tokyo: Shōgakukan.

Sahlins, Marshall. 1985. *Islands of History.* Chicago: University of Chicago Press.

Saiki Kazunobu, Wakabe Tetsuaki, and Nagashima Seiji. 1994. Human skeletal remains of the Yayoi period from the Asahikita site, Saga prefecture. *AS* 102(2): 198.

Saitō Naruya. 1994. Mongoroido shoshūdan no identeki kin'en kankei. In *Senshi Mongoroido o Saguru,* ed. Akazawa Takeru, pp. 11-25. Tokyo: Nihon Gakujutsu Shinkōkai.

Saitō Tadashi, ed. 1971. *Nihon Kōkogaku Senshū 2: Tsuboi Shōgorō I.* Tokyo: Tsukuji Shokan.

———. 1974. *Nihon Kōkogakushi.* Tokyo: Yoshikawa Kōbunkan.

Saitō Toshio. 1992. *Hiraizumi: Yomigaeru Chūsei Toshi.* Tokyo: Iwanami.

———. 1993. Ōshū Hiraizumi bunka to wa nani ka. In *Shin Shiten Nihon no Rekishi 3,* ed. Yoshimura Takehiko and Yoshioka Masayuki, pp. 334-341. Tokyo: Shinjinbutsu Ōraisha.

Sakaguchi Yutaka. 1982. Climatic variability during the Holocene epoch in Japan and its causes. *Bulletin of the Department of Geography, University of Tokyo* 14: 1-27.

———. 1983. Warm and cold stages in the past 7600 years in Japan and their global correlation: Especially on climatic impacts to the global sea level changes and the ancient Japanese history. *Bulletin of the Department of Geography, University of Tokyo* 15: 1-31.

Sakai Ryuichi. 1990. Yayoi shakai no shikumi wa dō natte ita no ka. In *Sōten Nihon no Rekishi 1,* ed. Suzuki Kimio, pp. 240-254. Tokyo: Shinjinbutsu Ōraisha.

Sakiyama Osamu. 1989. Nagai rekishi o motsu Nihongo wa "keitōron" de osamaranai kongōgo de aru. *Kikan Yamataikoku* 38: 168-171.

———. 1992. Formation of the Japanese language in connection with Austronesian languages. In *Prehistoric Mongoloid Dispersals,* ed. T. Akazawa and E. Szathmáry, pp. 349-358. Oxford: Oxford University Press.

Sakurai Kiyohiko and Ogata Tamotsu. 1980. Japanese mummies. In *Mummies, Disease, and Ancient Cultures,* ed. Aidan Cockburn and Eve Cockburn, pp. 211-223. Cambridge: Cambridge University Press.

Sanderson, Stephen K. 1991. The evolution of societies and world-systems. In *Core/Periphery Relations in Precapitalist Worlds,* ed. Christopher Chase-Dunn and Thomas D. Hall, pp. 167-192. Boulder, CO: Westview.

———. 1994. The transition from feudalism to capitalism: The theoretical significance of the Japanese case. *Review* 17(1): 15-55.

Sansom, George B. 1973. *Japan: A Short Cultural History,* rev. ed. Rutland, Vermont, and Tokyo: Tuttle.

Sasaki Kōmei. 1971. *Inasaku Izen.* Tokyo: Nihon Hōsō Kyōkai Books 147.

———. 1982. *Shōyōjurin Bunka no Michi.* Tokyo: Nihon Hōsō Kyōkai Books 422.

———. 1987. Jomon culture as an open system. In *The International Congress: Development and Isolation in the Pacific,* pp. 1-6. Osaka: IPPA, Japanese Society for Oceanic Studies and National Museum of Ethnology.

———. 1991a. The Wa people and their culture in ancient Japan: The cultures of swidden cultivation and padi-rice cultivation. *Acta Asiatica* 61: 24-46.

———. 1991b. *Nihonshi Tanjō.* Tokyo: Shūeisha.

———. 1993. Hatasaku bunka to inasaku bunka. In *Iwanami Kōza Nihon Tsūshi 1,* pp. 223-263. Tokyo: Iwanami.

Satō Takao. 1993. "Kuma okuri" no keitō [The tradition of "iwomante" in Ainu culture]. *Kokuritsu Rekishi Minzoku Hakubutsukan Kenkyū Hōkoku* 48: 107-127. (ES)

Satō Yōichirō. 1992. *Ine no Kita Michi.* Tokyo: Shōkabō.

Saunders, Shelly R. 1989. Nonmetric skeletal variation. In *Reconstruction of Life from the Skeleton,* ed. Mehmet Yasar Iscan and Kenneth A. R. Kennedy, pp. 95-108. New York: Alan R. Liss.

Sawada Goichi. 1927. *Narachō Jidai Minsei Keizai no Sūteki Kenkyū.* Tokyo: Fuzanbō.

Schaumann, Werner. 1980. Leistet die Mythe vom Verlorenen Angelhaken (Umisachi-Yamasachi no Shinwa): Einen Beitrag zur Klärung das Problems der Herkunft der japanischen Kultur? *Bonner Zeitschrift für Japanologie* 2: 129-145.

Schermerhorn, R. A. 1970. *Comparative Ethnic Relations: A Framework for Theory and Research.* New York: Random House.

Schneider, Jane. 1977. Was there a precapitalist world-system? *Peasant Studies* 6(1): 20-29. Reprinted in Chase-Dunn and Hall 1991b, pp. 45-66.

Schortman, Edward M., and Patricia A. Urban. 1994. Living on the edge: Core/periphery relations in ancient southeastern Mesoamerica. *CA* 35(4): 401-430.

Schrire, Carmel. 1987. The historical archaeology of colonial-indigenous interactions in South Africa: Proposed research at Oudepost I, Cape. In *Papers in the Prehistory of the Western Cape, South Africa,* Part II, ed. John Pilkington and Martin Hall, pp. 424-461. Oxford: BAR.

———. 1991. The historical archaeology of the impact of colonialism in seventeenth-century South Africa. In *Historical Archaeology in Global Perspective,* ed. Lisa Falk, pp. 69-96. Washington, DC: Smithsonian.

Schrire, Carmel, and Donna Merwick. 1991. Dutch-indigenous relations in New Netherland and the Cape in the seventeenth century. In *Historical Archaeology in Global Perspective,* ed. Lisa Falk, pp. 11-20. Washington, DC: Smithsonian.

Scott, G. Richard, and Christy G. Turner II. 1997. *The Anthropology of Modern Human Teeth: Dental Morphology and Its Variation in Recent Human Populations.* Cambridge: Cambridge University Press.

Segawa Takurō. 1989. Satsumon jidai ni okeru shokuryō seisan, bungyō, kōkan. *Kōkogaku Kenkyū* 36(2): 72–97.

———. 1994. Satsumon jidai no Kamigawa. In *Shin Asahikawa-shi Shi,* Vol. 1, pp. 243–276. Tokyo: Asahikawa City.

Seifert, Wolfgang. 1977. *Nationalismus in Nachkriegs-Japan: Ein Beitrag zur Ideologie der Völkischen Nationalisten.* Hamburg, Germany: Mitteilungendes Instituts für Asienkunde 91.

Senda Minoru. 1980. Territorial possession in ancient Japan: The real and the perceived. In *Geography of Japan,* ed. The Association of Japanese Geographers, pp. 101–120. Tokyo: Teikoku Shoin.

Senda Yoshihiro. 1994. Tosaminato, Fukushimajō no chōsa. In *Chūsei Toshi Tosaminato to Andō-shi,* ed. Kokuritsu Rekishi Minzoku Hakubutsukan, pp. 37–61. Tokyo: Shinjinbutsu Ōraisha.

Serjeantson, Susan W. 1985. Migration and admixture in the Pacific: Insights provided by Human Leucocyte Antigens. In *Out of Asia: Peopling the Americas and the Pacific,* ed. Robert Kirk and Emöke Szathmáry, pp. 105–112. Canberra: The Journal of Pacific History.

Serruys, Henry. 1958. Some types of names adopted by the Mongols during the Yüan and the early Ming periods. *Monumenta Serica* 17: 353–360.

Shannon, Thomas R. 1989. *An Introduction to the World-System Perspective.* Boulder, CO: Westview.

Shennan, Stephen. 1978. Archaeological "cultures": An empirical investigation. In *The Spatial Organization of Culture,* ed. Ian Hodder, pp. 113–139. London: Duckworth.

———. 1989. Introduction: Archaeological approaches to cultural identity. In *Archaeological Approaches to Cultural Identity,* ed. S. J. Shennan, pp. 1–32. London: Unwin Hyman.

Sherrat, Andrew, and Susan Sherratt. 1988. The archaeology of Indo-European: An alternative view. *Antiquity* 62: 584–595.

Shiba Yoshinobu. 1983. Sung foreign trade: Its scope and organization. In *China Among Equals: The Middle Kingdom and Its Neighbors, 10th–14th Centuries,* ed. Morris Rossabi, pp. 89–115. Berkeley and Los Angeles: University of California Press.

Shibatani Masayoshi. 1990. *The Languages of Japan.* Cambridge: Cambridge University Press.

Shibusawa Keizo. 1958. *Japanese Life and Culture in the Meiji Era.* Tokyo: Obunsha.

Shigehara Nobuo, Matsumura Hirofumi, and Nishizawa Toshiaki. 1995. Human skeletal remains of the Yayoi period from Shionoi and Shiozaki sites in Nagano City. *AS* 103(2): 170.

Shih Sheng-Han. 1958. *A Preliminary Survey of the Book* Ch'i Min Yao Shu: *An Agricultural Encyclopedia of the 6th Century.* Beijing: Science Press.

Shillony, Ben-Ami. 1973. *Revolt in Japan: The Young Officers and the February 26, 1936 Incident.* Princeton: Princeton University Press.

———. 1981. *Politics and Culture in Wartime Japan.* Oxford: Clarendon.

Shimizu Yoshihiro. 1987. Hito ga ugoki doki mo ugoku. *Kikan Kōkogaku* 19: 30–33.

Shin Kyung-Cheol. 1993a. Relations between Kaya and Wa in the third to fourth centuries AD. Paper presented at the international conference *Stirrup, Sail and Plough: Continental and Maritime Influences on Japanese Identity.* Canberra, September 20–23.

———. 1993b. Kaya seiritsu zengo no shomondai: Saikin no hakkutsu chōsa seika kara. In *Kaya to Kodai Higashi Ajia,* ed. Oda Fujio et al., pp. 115–160. Tokyo: Shinjinbutsu Ōraisha.

Shinmura Izuru. 1980. Reprint. Kokugo keitō no mondai, in *Nihongo no Keitō,* ed. Ōno Susumu. Special issue of *Gendai no Esupuri,* pp. 35–42. Original edition: 1911. *Taiyō* 17.

Shintaku Nobuhisa. 1992. Fukuoka-ken Kasuya-gun Kasuya-chō Etsuji iseki. *Nihon Kōkogaku Nenpō* 45: 585–589.

Shiraishi Taichirō. 1991. Yamataikoku jidai no Kinai, Tōkai, Kantō. In *Yamataikoku Jidai no Higashi Nihon,* ed. National Museum of Japanese History, pp. 45–71. Tokyo: Rokkō.

Shitara Hiromi. 1991. Kantō chihō no Yayoi bunka. In *Yayoi Bunka: Nihon Bunka no Genryū o Saguru,* ed. Ōsaka Furitsu Yayoi Bunka Hakubutsukan, pp. 196–202. Tokyo: Heibonsha.

———. 1993. Tsubokan saisōbo no kisokuteki kenkyū [Reburial grave with funeral urn in the Yayoi period]. *Kokuritsu Rekishi Minzoku Hakubutsukan Kenkyū Hōkoku* 50: 3–48. (ES)

Sider, Gerald. 1987. When parrots learn to talk, and why they can't: Domination, deception, and self-deception in Indian-White relations. *Comparative Studies in Society and History* 29: 3–23.

Siebold, Henry von. 1879. *Notes on Japanese Archaeology with Especial Reference to the Stone Age.* Tokyo: Yokohama.

Siebold, Philipp Franz von. 1831. Mœurs et usages des Aïnos. *Journal Asiatique* 7: 73–80.

———. 1930. *Nippon. Archiv zur Beschreibung von Japan.* Berlin: Ernst Wasmuth.

Silverberg, Robert. 1968. *Mound Builders of Ancient America: The Archaeology of a Myth.* Athens: Ohio University Press.

Slawik, Alexander. 1955. Austroneische Elemente in der japanischen Reichsgründungssage und das Hayato-Problem. In *Actes du IVe Congrès International des Sciences Anthropologiques et Ethnologiques, Vienne, 1–8 Septembre 1952. Tome II Ethnologica: Première Partie,* pp. 217–223. Vienna: Adolf Holzhausens.

Smith, Anthony D. 1981. *The Ethnic Revival.* Cambridge: Cambridge University Press.

———. 1986. *The Ethnic Origin of Nations.* Oxford: Basil Blackwell.

———. 1991. *National Identity.* Harmondsworth, U.K.: Penguin.

———. 1994. The problem of national identity: Ancient, medieval and modern? *Ethnic and Racial Studies* 17(3): 375-399.

Smith, Philip E. L. 1976. *Food Production and Its Consequences.* Menlo Park, CA: Cummings.

Snow, Dean R. 1990. The incursion hypothesis: Matrilocal residence and Iroquois origins. Paper presented at the annual meeting of the *Conference on Iroquois Research,* Rensselaerville, NY, September.

———. 1991. Population movement during the Woodland periods: The intrusion of Iroquois peoples. Paper presented at the annual meeting of the *New York State Archaeological Association,* Rochester, NY, April.

———. 1992a. L'augmentation de la population chez les groupes Iroquoiens et ses conséquences sur l'étude de leurs origines. *Recherches Amérindiennes au Québec* 22(4): 5-12.

———. 1992b. Paleoecology and the prehistoric incursion of northern Iroquoians into the lower Great Lakes region. In *Great Lakes Archaeology and Paleoecology: Exploring Interdisciplinary Initiatives for the Nineties,* ed. B. Warner and R. MacDonald. Waterloo: University of Waterloo.

———. 1995. Migration in prehistory: The northern Iroquois case. *American Antiquity* 60(1): 59-79.

Solnit, David. 1992. Review of Benedict (1990). *Language* 68: 186-196.

Spielmann, Katherine, and James F. Eder. 1994. Hunters and farmers: Then and now. *ARA* 23: 303-323.

Spriggs, Matthew. 1982. Taro cropping systems in the Southeast Asian-Pacific regions: Archaeological evidence. *Archaeology in Oceania* 17(1): 7-15.

———. 1991. Considering Meacham's considerations on Southeast Asia. *BIPPA* 11: 408-411.

———. 1996. Early agriculture and what went before in Island Melanesia: Continuity or intrusion? In *The Origins and Spread of Agriculture and Pastoralism in Eurasia,* ed. David Harris, pp. 524-537. London: University College London Press.

———, ed. 1984. *Marxist Perspectives in Archaeology.* Cambridge: Cambridge University Press.

Stark, Ken. 1989. *Wealth and Power in Yayoi Period Northern Kyushu.* M.A. thesis, University of British Columbia.

Starostin, S. A. 1986. Problema geneticeskoi obscnosti altaiskikh jazykov. Istoriko-kul'turnye kontakty narodov altaiskoi jazykovoi obscnosti. Tezisy dokladow XXIX sessii Postoiannoi Mezdunaradnoi Altaisticeskoi konferencii [PIAC], 2: 94-112. Moscow.

———. 1991. *Altajsaja Problema i Proisxozhenije Zhaponskogo Jazjka.* Moscow.

Stephan, John J. 1971. *Sakhalin: A History.* Oxford: Clarendon Press.

———. 1974. *The Kuril Islands: Russo-Japanese Frontier in the Pacific.* Oxford: Clarendon Press.

Stieglitz, Robert R. 1993. Migrations in the ancient Near East (3500-500 BC). *Anthropological Science* 101(3): 263-271.

Suda Akiyoshi. 1950. Jinruigaku kara mita Ryūkyūjin. *Minzokugaku Kenkyū* 15: 109–116.

Sugawara Toshiyuki and Yasuda Tadaichi, eds. 1986. *Jizōden B Iseki.* Akita City: Akita Board of Education.

Sugita Mitsuaki. 1992. Ohōtsuku no shuryōmin. In *Shinpan "Kodai no Nihon" 9: Tōhoku, Hokkaidō,* ed. Tsuboi Kiyotari and Hirano Kunio, pp. 475–492. Tokyo: Kadokawa.

Sugiura Yoko. 1987. The Neolithic revolution, a case analysis: A reevaluation of the Childean concept as applied to Jomon Japan. In *Studies in the Neolithic and Urban Revolutions,* ed. Linda Manzanilla, pp. 35–48. Oxford: BAR International Series 349.

Sutō Takashi. 1988. Tōhoku chihō ni okeru Jōmon to Yayoi no sakai. *Kikan Kōkogaku* 23: 23–29.

Suzuki Akira and Takahama Yasuhide. 1992. Tooth crown affinities among five populations from Akita, Tsushima, Tanegashima, Okinawa in Japan, and middle Taiwan. *JASN* 100: 171–182.

Suzuki Akira, Han Byeong-Ju, Takahama Yasuhide, Son Woo-Sung, Ito Kazue, and Matsu'ura Seiko. 1994. Tooth crown affinities among south Korean, central Taiwanese, and certain Japanese populations. *AS* 102(3): 271-283.

Suzuki Hisashi. 1960. Changes in the skull features of the Japanese people from ancient to modern times. In *Men and Cultures,* ed. A. F. C. Wallace, pp. 717–724. Philadelphia: University of Pennsylvania Press.

———. 1963. *Nihonjin no Hone.* Tokyo: Iwanami.

———. 1964. Chiba-ken Tenjinmae iseki shutsudo Yayoi jidai no jinkotsu. *Nihon Kōkogaku Kyōkai Nenpō 30.*

———. 1969. Microevolutionary changes in the Japanese population from the prehistoric age to the present-day. *Journal of the Faculty of Science of Tokyo University, Section V* 3: 279–309.

———. 1981. Racial history of the Japanese. In *Rassengeschichte der Menscheit,* ed. I. Schwidetzky, 8: 7–69. Munich.

Suzuki Juji. 1974. Genshi kodai no nōkō o megutte. *Kodaigaku Kenkyū* 74.

Suzuki Kimio. 1965. "Chashi" no seikaku ni kansuru ichi shiron. *Busshitsu Bunka* 6.

Suzuki Takao. 1991. Paleopathological study on infectious diseases in Japan. In *Human Paleopathology: Current Syntheses and Future Options,* ed. D. J. Ortner and A. C. Aufderheide, 128–139. Washington, DC: Smithsonian.

Suzuki Yasuhiko. 1985. Chūbu, minami Kantō chi'iki ni okeru Jōmon shūraku no henbō [Changes of Jomon settlements in the Chubu and southern Kanto districts]. *Kōkogaku Zasshi* 71(4): 30–53 (ES p. 124)

Tagaya Akira and Ikeda Jiro. 1976. A multivariate analysis of the cranial measurements of the Ryuku Islanders (males). *JASN* 84: 204–220.

Tajima Kazuo. 1994. Seijin T saibō hakketsubyō uirusu to Mongoroido no idō. In *Senshi Mongoroido o Saguru,* ed. Akazawa Takeru, pp. 263-289. Nihon Gakujutsu Shinkōkai.

Tajima Kazuo and Hinuma Yorio. 1992. Epidemiology of HTLV-I/II in Japan and in the world. *Gann Mono* 39: 129–149.

Takada Jun'ichi. 1993. Genshi, kodai no Asahishi-mura. In *Asahishi-mura Shi.* Tokyo: Kumamoto.

Takakura Shinichiro. 1960. The Ainu of northern Japan: A study in conquest and acculturation, trans. John A. Harrison. *Transactions of the American Philosophical Society* 50 (4): 3–88.

Takamiya Hiroe. 1991. *Senshi Kodai no Okinawa.* Tokyo: Daiichi Shobō.

Takamiya Hiroto. 1996a. Kodai minzoku shokubutsugaku kara mita Nazakibaru iseki no seigyō. In *Nazakibaru Iseki Hakkutsu Chōsa Hōkokusho.* Edited and published by Naha City Board of Education.

———. 1996b. Initial colonization, and subsistence adaption processes in the late prehistory of the island of Okinawa. *BIPPA* 15: 143–150.

Takashima Chūhei. 1993. Yoshinogari. In *Iwanami Kōza Nihon Tsūshi 2,* pp. 287–307. Tokyo: Iwanami.

Takasugi Hiroaki. 1982. Satsumon bunka no shūen. *Shigaku* 52(2): 109–131.

Tamburello, Alfredo. 1969. L'etnogenesi Ainu: Posizione di un problema antropologico e culturale. *Il Giappone* 9: 95–110.

———. 1970. Il contributo dell'antropologia al problema dell'etnogenesi giapponese. *Il Giappone* 10: 5–16.

Tanabe Yuichi. 1992. Phylogenetic studies on the Japanese dogs, with emphasis on migration routes of the dogs. In *Japanese as a Member of the Asian and Pacific Populations,* ed. Hanihara Kazuro, pp. 160–173. Kyoto: Nichibunken.

———. 1993. Nihonken no kigen. In *Nihonjin to Nihon Bunka no Keisei,* ed. Hanihara Kazurō, pp. 397–421. Tokyo: Asakura Shoten.

Tanabe, Y., S. Ito, K. Ota, Y. Hashimoto, Y. Y. Sung, J. K. Ryu, and M. O. Faruque. 1991. Biochemical-genetic relationships among Asian and European dogs and the ancestory of the Japanese dog. *Journal of Animal Breeding Genetics* 108: 455–478.

Tanaka Masatake. 1986. Satoimo. In *Encyclopedia Nipponica 2001,* Vol. 10, p. 182. Tokyo: Shōgakukan.

Tanaka Migaku. 1991. *Wajin Sōran.* Tokyo: Shūeisha.

Tanaka, Stefan. 1993. *Japan's Orient: Rendering Pasts into History.* Berkeley and Los Angeles: University of California Press.

Tanaka, T. 1959. A study of the Japanese from the standpoint of the blood groups. *Japanese Journal of Criminology* 25: 37–67.

Tanaka Takeo. 1987. Wakō to higashi Ajia kōtsūken. In *Nihon no Shakaishi 1: Rettō Naigai no Kōtsū to Kokka,* ed. Amino Yoshihiko, pp. 139–181. Tokyo: Iwanami.

Tanaka Yoshiyuki. 1986. Nishi Nihon. In *Yayoi Bunka no Kenkyū,* Vol. 3, ed. Kanaseki Hiroshi and Sahara Makoto, pp. 115–125. Tokyo: Yūzankaku.

———. 1991. Iwayuru toraisetsu no saikentō. In *Yokoyama Kōichi Sensei Taikan Kinen Ronbunshū II: Nihon ni Okeru Shoki Yayoi Bunka no Seiritsu,* ed.

Takakura Hiroaki, pp. 482–505. Fukuoka: Yokoyama Kōichi Taikan Kinen Jigyōkai.

Tao Jing-Shen. 1976. *The Jurchen in Twelfth-Century China: A Study of Sinicization.* Seattle: University of Washington Press.

Terasawa Kaoru and Terasawa Tomoko. 1981. Yayoi jidai shokubutsu shitsu shokuryō no kisoteki kenkyū: Shoki nōkō shakai kenkyū no zentei toshite. *Kōkogaku Ronkō* 5: 1–129.

Teshigawara Akira. 1988. *Nihon Kōkogakushi.* Tokyo: Tokyo University Press.

Thomas, Julian, and Christopher Tilley. 1992. TAG and "post-modernism": A reply to John Bintliff. *Antiquity* 66: 106–111.

Toby, Ronald. P. 1984. *State and Diplomacy in Early Modern Japan: Asia in the Development of the Tokugawa Bakufu.* Princeton, NJ: Princeton University Press.

Tokunaga Katsushi and Juji Takeo. 1992. The migration and dispersal of East Asian populations as viewed from HLA genes and haplotypes. In *The Evolution and Dispersal of Modern Humans in Asia,* ed. T. Akazawa, K. Aoki, and T. Kimura, pp. 599–611. Tokyo: Hokuensha.

Tokyo Board of Education, ed. 1988. *Tōkyō-to Iseki Chizu.* Tokyo: Tōkyō-to Kyōiku Iinkai.

Tōma Seita. 1951. *Nihon Minzoku no Keisei.* Tokyo: Iwanami.

Torao Toshiya. 1993. Nara economic and social institutions. In *The Cambridge History of Japan, Vol. 1,* ed. Delmer Brown, pp. 415–452. Cambridge: Cambridge University Press.

Torii Ryūzō. 1918. *Yūshi Izen no Nihon.* Isobe Kōyōdō.

———. 1919. Études archéologiques et ethnologiques: Les Ainous des Illes Kouriles. *Journal of the College of Science, Imperial University of Tokyo* 42: 1–336.

———. 1920. Musashino no yūshi izen. *Musashino* 3(3). Reprinted in Torii 1974, pp. 12–19.

———. 1923. Wagakuni no dōtaku wa nani minzoku no nokoshita mono ka? *Jinruigaku Zasshi* 38(4). Reprinted in Torii 1974, pp. 57–72.

———. 1924. *Suwa-shi,* Vol. 1. Shinano Kyōikukai Suwa Bukai.

———. 1926. *Kyokutō Minzoku,* Vol. 1. Tokyo: Bunka Seikatsu Kenkyūkai.

———. 1974a. *Nihon Kōkogaku Senshū 6: Torii Ryūzō Shū,* Vol. 1, ed. Saitō Tadashi. Tokyo: Tsukiji Shōkan.

———. 1974b. Reprint. Wagakuni no dōtaku wa nani minzoku no nokoshita mono ka? *Jinruigaku Zasshi* 38(4): 57–72. Original edition, 1923.

Toyama Shūichi. 1992. Chirigaku ni okeru puranto opåru bunseki no ōyō. *Ritsumeikan Chirigaku* 4: 11–25.

Toyama Shūichi and Nakayama Seiji. 1990. Chūbu Nihon ni okeru inasaku nōkō no kigen to sono hakyū. *Teikyō Daigaku Yamanashi Bunkazai Kenkyūjo Kenkyū Hōkoku* 3: 1–43.

———. 1992. Nihon ni okeru inasaku no kaishi to hakyū [The beginning and extension of rice cultivation in Japan]. *Japanese Journal of Historical Botany* 9: 13–22 (ES)

Trewartha, Glenn T. 1965. *Japan: A Geography*. Madison: University of Wisconsin Press.

Trigger, Bruce G. 1968. *Beyond History: The Methods of Prehistory*. New York: Holt, Rinehart and Winston.

———. 1976. *The Children of Aataentsic: A History of the Huron People to 1660*. Kingston and Montreal: McGill-Queen's University Press.

———, ed. 1978a. Introduction to *Handbook of North American Indians*, Vol. 15, *Northeast*, pp. 1-3. Washington, DC: Smithsonian.

———. 1978b. Cultural unity and diversity. In *Handbook of North American Indians*, Vol. 15: *Northeast*, ed. Bruce G. Trigger, pp. 798-804. Washington, DC: Smithsonian.

Trott, Rosemary Gray. 1993. *Japan and the Modern System of States: Constructing a National Identity*. M.A. thesis, Department of International Relations, Research School of Pacific Studies, Australian National University.

———. 1995. The centrality of Edo in the 18th century: A view from Tsugaru. Paper presented at the *9th Biennial conference, Japanese Studies Association of Australia*. Brisbane, July 3-6.

Tsuboi Kiyotari. 1992. Issues in Japanese archaeology. *Acta Asiatica* 63: 1-20.

Tsuboi Shōgorō. 1887. Korobokkuru Hokkaidō ni sumishi narubeshi. *Tōkyō Jinruigakkai Hōkoku* 2(2).

———. Reprint. 1971a. Teikoku daigaku no rinchi ni kaizuka no konseki ari. In Saitō, 1971, pp. 304-311. Original edition, 1889. *Tōyō Gakugei Zasshi* 6(90).

———. 1971b. Reprint. Korobokkuru fūzoku kō. In Saitō, pp. 50-100. Original edition, 1895. *Fūzoku Gahō* 90-108.

Tsude Hiroshi. 1986. Nihon kōkogaku to shakai. In *Iwanami Kōza Nihon Kōkogaku 7: Gendai to Kōkogaku*, ed. Tanaka Migaku, pp. 31-70. Tokyo: Iwanami.

———. 1988. Morimoto Rokuji ron. In *Yayoi Bunka no Kenkyū*, Vol 10, ed. Kanaseki Hiroshi and Sahara Makoto, pp. 133-145. Tokyo: Yūzankaku.

———. 1992. The Kofun period and state formation. *Acta Asiatica* 63: 64-86.

Tsukada Matsuo. 1986. Vegetation in prehistoric Japan: The last 20,000 years. In *Windows on the Japanese Past*, ed. R. Pearson, pp. 11-56. Ann Arbor: Center for Japanese Studies, University of Michigan.

Tsunoda Ryusaku, Wm. Theodore de Bary, and Donald Keene, eds. 1958. *Sources of Japanese Tradition*. New York: Columbia University Press.

Tsunoda Ryusaku and L. C. Goodrich. 1951. *Japan in the Chinese Dynastic Histories*. South Pasadena, CA: PD and Ione Perkins.

Tubielewicz, Jolanta. 1990. Some remarks on the role of the ancient Kibi. *Rocznik Orientalistyczny* 46: 167-172.

Tuck, James. A. 1978. Northern Iroquois prehistory. In *Handbook of North American Indians*, Vol. 15: *Northeast*, ed. Bruce G. Trigger, pp. 322-333. Washington, DC: Smithsonian.

Turner, Christy G. II. 1976. Dental evidence on the origins of the Ainu and Japanese. *Science* 193: 911-913.

———. 1979. Dental anthropological indications of agriculture among the Jomon people of central Japan. *AJPA* 51: 619-636.

———. 1987. Late Pleistocene and Holocene population history of East Asia based on dental variation. *AJPA* 73: 305-321.

———. 1989. Teeth and prehistory in Asia. *Scientific American* 260(2): 70-77.

———. 1990. Major features of Sundadonty and Sinodonty, including suggestions about East Asian microevolution, population history, and late Pleistocene relationships with Australian Aboriginals. *AJPA* 82: 295-317.

———. 1992a. Microevolution of East Asian and European populations: A dental perspective. In *The Evolution and Dispersal of Modern Humans in Asia,* ed. T. Akazawa, K. Aoki, and T. Kimura, pp. 415-438. Tokyo: Hokuensha.

———. 1992b. Sundadonty and Sinodonty in Japan: The dental basis for a dual origin hypothesis for the peopling of the Japanese Islands. In *Japanese as a Member of the Asian and Pacific Populations,* ed. Hanihara Kazuro, pp. 96-112. Kyoto: Nichibunken.

Tyler, Royall. 1994. Korean echoes in the Nō play *Furu. East Asian History* 7: 49-66.

Ueda Masa'aki. 1965. *Kikajin: Kodai Kokka no Seiritsu o Megutte.* Tokyo: Chūō Kōronsha.

———. 1986. A fresh look at ancient history. *Japan Quarterly* 23(4): 403-409.

———, ed. 1993. *Kodai o Kangaeru: Izumo.* Tokyo: Yoshikawa Kōbunkan.

Umehara Takeshi. 1985. Yomigaeru Jōmon. *Chūō Kōron* 11: 140-158.

———. 1987. Watashi wa Yamatoisuto dewa nai. *Chūō Kōron* 8: 242-257.

———. 1990. Nihon to wa nan na no ka: Nihon kenkyū no kokusaika to Nihon bunka no honshitsu. In *Nihon to wa nan na no ka,* ed. Umehara Takeshi, pp. 6-20. Nihon Hōsō Kyōkai Books.

———. 1991. The Japanese view of the "other world": Japanese religion in world perspective. *Japan Review* 2: 161-190.

———. 1993. Kankō ni yosete. In *Nihonjin to Nihon Bunka no Keisei,* ed. Hanihara Kazurō, pp. i-vii. Tokyo: Asakura Shoten.

———. 1994. *Nihon no Shinsō: Jōmon, Ezo Bunka o Saguru.* Tokyo: Shūeisha.

Umehara Takeshi and Hanihara Kazurō. 1993. *Ainu wa Gen-Nihonjin ka.* Tokyo: Shōgakukan.

Umehara Takeshi and Nakagami Kenji. 1984. *Kimi wa Yayoi-jin ka Jōmon-jin ka: Umehara Nihongaku Kōgi.* Tokyo: Asahi.

Umetsu Kazuo and Yuasa Isao. 1990. Mongoroido to ketsueki tanpaku-gata hyōshiki idenshi ni tsuite. *Mongoroido* 8: 17-19.

Umetsu, K., I. Yuasa, T. Yamashita, S. Saito, T. Yamaguchi, S. B. Ellepola, T. Ishida, and T. Suzuki. 1989. Genetic polymorphisms of orosomucoid and alpha-2-HS-glycoprotein in Thai, Sri Lankan and Paraguayan populations. *JJHG* 34: 195-202.

Unger, J. Marshall. 1990a. Summary report of the Altaic panel. In *Trends in Linguistics: Studies and Monographs 45. Linguistic Change and Reconstruction Methodology,* ed. P. Baldi, pp. 479-482. Berlin and New York: Mouton de Gruyter.

———. 1990b. Japanese and what other Altaic languages? In *Trends in Linguistics: Studies and Monographs 45. Linguistic Change and Reconstruction Methodology,* ed. P. Baldi, pp. 547–561. Berlin and New York: Mouton de Gruyter.

Uno Takao. 1991. *Ritsuryō Shakai no Kōkogakuteki Kenkyū: Hokuriku o Butai Toshite* [An Archaeological Study of the Ancient Ritsuryo Society: In the Case of the Hokuriku District, Japan]. Toyama: Katsura Shobō. (ES pp. 1–6)

———. 1994. Nihonkai ni miru chūsei no seisan to ryūtsū. In *Chūsei Toshi Tosaminato to Andō-shi,* ed. Kokuritsu Rekishi Minzoku Hakubutsukan, pp. 97–134. Tokyo: Shinjinbutsu Ōraisha.

Ushiro Hiroshi. 1993a. Ohōtsuku bunka no kakusan to tekiō no haikei. *Chihōshi Kenkyū* 245: 53–59.

———. 1993b. Amūru gawa karyū Karuchōmu III iseki shutsudo no Suzuya-shiki doki. *Kōkogaku Jānaru* 358: 28–32.

Utagawa Hiroshi. 1980. *Ainu Kōkogaku.* Tokyo: Kyōikusha.

———. 1988. *Ainu Bunka Seiritsushi.* Sapporo: Hokkaido Shuppan Kikaku Sentā.

———. 1989. *Iomante no Kōkogaku.* Tokyo: Tokyo University Press.

———. 1992a. The "sending back" rite in Ainu culture. *Japanese Journal of Religious Studies* 19(2–3): 255–270.

———. 1992b. Ezochi to Ainu: Minzoku-kōkogakuteki sokumen kara mite. In *Ajia no Naka no Nihonshi IV: Chi'iki to Minzoku,* ed. Arano Yasunori, Ishii Masatoshi, and Murai Shōsuke, pp. 137–165. Tokyo: Tokyo University Press.

———. 1992c. Chashi to Ainu shakai. In *Shinpan "Kodai no Nihon" 9: Tōhoku, Hokkaidō,* ed. Tsuboi Kiyotari and Hirano Kunio, pp. 515–532. Tokyo: Kadokawa.

Vande Walle, Willy. 1994. Japan: From petty kingdom to Buddha land. *Japan Review* 5: 87–101.

Vaporis, Constantine N. 1994. *Breaking Barriers: Travel and the State in the Early Modern Japan.* Cambridge, MA: Harvard University Press.

———. 1997. To Edo and back: Alternative attendance and Japanese culture in the early modern period. *JJS* 23(1): 25–67.

Vargo, Lars. 1979. The *bemin* system in early Japan. In *European Studies on Japan,* ed. I. Nish and C. Dunn, pp. 10–15. Tenterden, Kent: Paul Norbury.

Varley, H. Paul. 1980. *A Chronicle of Gods and Sovereigns:* Jinno Shotoki *of Kitabatake Chikafusa.* New York: Columbia University Press.

———. 1990. Cultural life in medieval Japan. In *The Cambridge History of Japan,* Vol. 3, ed. Kozo Yamamura, pp. 447–499. Cambridge: Cambridge University Press.

Vasilyevskiy, R. S. 1978. Okhotskaya kultura, ee proiskhosdenie i vzaimootnosheniya s kulturami sosednikh territoriy. *Hoppō Bunka Kenkyū* 12: 1–38.

von Baelz, Erwin. 1885. Die Körperlichen Eigenschaften der Japaner. *Mitteilung der Deutschen Gesellschaft für Natur und Völkerkunde Ostasiens* IV: 35–103.

———. 1908. *Prehistoric Japan*. Washington, DC: Government Printing Office.

———. 1911. Die Riu-kiu-Insulaner, die Aino und andere kaukasierähnliche Reste in Ostasien. *Correspondenzblatt der Deutschen Gesellschaft für Anthropologie, Ethnologie und Urgeschichte* 42: 187-191.

von Wolferen, Karel. 1989. *The Enigma of Japanese Power: People and Politics in a Stateless Nation*. London: Macmillan.

Vos, Frits. 1983. Philipp Franz von Siebold. In *Kodansha Encyclopedia of Japan*, Vol. 7, pp. 192-193. Tokyo: Kodansha.

Vovin, Alexander. 1994a. Is Japanese related to Austronesian? *Oceanic Linguistics* 33(2): 369-390.

———. 1994b. Long-distance relationships, reconstruction methodology, and the origins of Japanese. *Diachronica* 11(1): 95-114.

Wada Atsumu. 1994. Toraijin to Nihon bunka. In *Iwanami Kōza Nihon Tsūshi*, Vol. 3, pp. 231-282. Tokyo: Iwanami.

Wada Sei. 1938. The natives of the lower reaches of the Amur river as represented in Chinese records. *Memoirs of the Research Department, Toyo Bunko* 10: 41-102.

Wada Seigo. 1985. Gyorō. In *Yayoi Bunka no Kenkyū*, Vol. 2, ed. Kanaseki Hiroshi and Sahara Makoto, pp. 153-161. Tokyo: Yūzankaku.

———. 1986. Political interpretations of stone coffin production in protohistoric Japan. In *Windows on the Japanese Past*, ed. R. Pearson, pp. 349-374. Ann Arbor: Center for Japanese Studies, University of Michigan.

Wakabayashi, Bob Tadashi. 1991. In name only: Imperial sovereignty in early modern Japan. *JJS* 17(1): 25-57.

Wakebe Tetsuaki, Saiki Kazunobu, Nagashima Seiji, and Takashima Chuhei. 1994. Human skeletal remains of the Yayoi period from the Yoshinogari site, Saga prefecture (preliminary report). *Anthropological Science* 102(2): 198.

Waley, Arthur, trans. 1938. *The Analects of Confucius*. London: George Allen and Unwin.

Wallerstein, Immanuel. 1960. Ethnicity and national integration in West Africa. *Cahiers d'Études Africaines* 3: 129-139.

———. 1974. *The Modern World-System: Capitalist Agriculture and the Origins of the European World-Economy in the Sixteenth Century*. New York: Academic Press.

———. 1987. World-systems analysis. In *Social Theory Today*, ed. Anthony Giddens and Jonathan Turner, pp. 309-324. Cambridge, U.K.: Polity Press.

Wang Zhongshu 1981. Guan yu Riben Sanjiaoyuan shenshoujing de wunti. *Kaogu* 181(4): 346-358.

Watabe Tadayo. 1993. *Ine no Daichi*. Tokyo: Shōgakukan.

Watanabe Hitoshi. 1972a. The Ainu. In *Hunters and Gatherers Today*, ed. M. G. Bicchieri, pp. 449-484. New York: Holt, Rinehart, and Winston.

———. 1972b. Ainu bunka no seiritsu: Minzoku, rekishi, kōko shogaku no gōryuten [The establishment of Ainu culture: The conflux of ethnographic, historic and archaeological studies]. *Kōkogaku Zasshi* 58(3): 47-64. (ES p. 3)

———. 1974. Ainu bunka no genryū: Toku ni Ohotsuku bunka to no kankei ni tsuite [The source of the Ainu culture: Especially its relationship with the Okhotsk culture]. *Kōkogaku Zasshi* 60(1): 72–82. (ES)

———. 1986. Community habitation and food gathering in prehistoric Japan: An ethnographic interpretation of the archaeological evidence. In *Windows on the Japanese Past*, ed. R. Pearson, pp. 229–254. Ann Arbor: Center for Japanese Studies, University of Michigan.

———. 1989. *Jōmon-shiki Kaisōka Shakai*. Tokyo: Rokkō.

Watanabe Makoto. 1975. *Jōmon Jidai no Shokubutsu Shoku*. Tokyo: Yūzankaku.

Watanabe Minoru. 1964. *Nihon Shokuseikatsu Shi*. Tokyo: Yoshikawa Kōbunkan.

Watanabe, S., S. Kondo, and E. Matsunaga, eds. 1975. *Anthropological and Genetic Studies on the Japanese*. Tokyo: University of Tokyo Press.

Watanabe, S., and Y. Nakagawa. 1975. Morphological status of the Ainu. Section 3.2: Morphology of the external ear. In *Anthropological and Genetic Studies on the Japanese*, ed. S. Watanabe, S. Kondo, and E. Matsunaga, pp. 236–241. Tokyo: University of Tokyo Press.

Watsuji Tetsurō. 1920. *Nihon Kodai Bunka*.

Webb, Herschel F. 1958. *The Thought and Work of the Early Mito School*. Ph.D. dissertation, Columbia University.

Weber, Eugen. 1976. *Peasants into Frenchmen: The Modernization of Rural France, 1870–1914*. Stanford, CA: Stanford University Press.

Weiner, Michael. 1994. *Race and Migration in Imperial Japan*. London: Routledge.

———. 1995. Discources of race, nation and empire in pre-1945 Japan. *Ethnic and Racial Studies* 18(3): 433–456.

Welch, Martin. 1993. *Discovering Anglo-Saxon England*. University Park: Pennsylvania State University Press.

Whalen, Michael E. 1994. Comment on Schortman and Urban (1994). *CA* 35(4): 420–421.

Wheatley, Paul, and Thomas See. 1978. *From Court to Capital: A Tentative Interpretation of the Origins of the Japanese Urban Tradition*. Chicago: University of Chicago Press.

White, James W. 1988. State growth and popular protest in Tokugawa Japan. *JJS* 14(1): 1–25.

White, Joyce C. 1995. Modeling the development of early rice agriculture: Ethnoecological perspectives from northeast Thailand. *AP* 34(1): 37–68.

Whitman, John B. 1985. *The Phonological Basis for the Comparison of Japanese and Korean*. Ph.D. dissertation, Harvard University.

Whymant, A. Neville. J. 1926. The oceanic theory of the origin of the Japanese language and people. *TASJ* 3: 15–81.

Wigen, Kären. 1995. *The Making of a Japanese Periphery, 1750–1920*. Berkeley and Los Angeles: University of California Press.

Wilde, Oscar. 1911. The decay of lying. In *Intentions*, pp. 1–54. 5th ed. London: Methuen.

Willey, Gordon R. and Jeremy A. Sabloff. 1980. *A History of American Archaeology*. 2d ed. San Francisco: W. H. Freeman.

Williams, Gwyn A. 1985. *When was Wales? A History of the Welsh*. London: Black Raven Press.

Wilmsen, Edwin N. 1989. *Land Filled with Flies: A Political Economy of the Kalahari*. Chicago: University of Chicago Press.

———. 1995. Who were the Bushmen? Historical process in the creation of an ethnic construct. In *Articulating Hidden Histories: Exploring the Influence of Eric R. Wolf*, ed. Jane Schneider and Rayna Rapp, pp. 308-321. Berkeley and Los Angeles: University of California Press.

Wissler, Clark. 1923. *Man and Culture*. New York: Thomas Y. Crowell.

Wolf, Eric. 1982. *Europe and the People without History*. Berkeley and Los Angeles: University of California Press.

———. 1994. Perilous ideas: Race, culture, people. *CA* 35(1): 1-12.

Woolf, Greg. 1990. World-systems analysis and the Roman empire. *Journal of Roman Archaeology* 3: 44-58.

Wright, James V. 1972. *Ontario Prehistory: An Eleven-Thousand-Year Archaeological Outline*. Ottawa: National Museums of Canada and National Museum of Man.

———. 1984. The cultural continuity of the northern Iroquoian-speaking peoples. In *Extending the Rafters: Interdisciplinary Approaches to Iroquioan Studies*, ed. M. K. Foster, J. Campisi, and M. Mithun, pp. 283-299. Albany, NY: SUNY Press.

Wu Xinzhi. 1992a. The origin and dispersal of anatomically modern humans in East and Southeast Asia. In *The Evolution and Dispersal of Modern Humans in Asia*, ed. T. Akazawa, K. Aoki, and T. Kimura, pp. 373-378. Tokyo: Hokuensha.

———. 1992b. Origins and affinities of the Stone Age inhabitants of Japan. In *Japanese as a Member of the Asian and Pacific Populations*, ed. K. Hanihara, pp. 1-8. Kyoto: Nichibunken.

Yagi Sōzaburō. 1898. *Nihon Kōkogaku*, Vol. 1. Tokyo: Sūzanbō.

———. 1906. Chūkan doki (Yayoishiki doki) no kaizuka chōsa hōkoku. *Tōkyō Jinruigaku Zasshi* 22.

Yamada Gorō. 1980. Iwate-ken Kitakami-shi Kyūnenbashi iseki no kafun bunseki ni tsuite. In *Kyūnenbashi Iseki, Report No. 6*, ed. Kitakami-shi Kyōiku Iinkai, pp. 63-75. Kitakami: Kitakami Bunkazai Chōsa Hōkoku No.29.

Yamada Hidezō. 1982-1983. *Ainugo Chimei no Kenkyū*, Vols. 1-4. Sōfūkan.

Yamaguchi Bin. 1981. Human skeletal remains in Hokkaido. In *Jinruigaku Kōza 5: Nihonjin I*, ed. Ogata T., pp. 137-156. (In Japanese)

———. 1982. A review of the osteological characteristics of the Jomon population in prehistoric Japan. *JASN* 90 (Suppl.): 77-90.

———. 1987. Metric study of the crania from protohistoric sites in eastern Japan. *Bulletin of the National Science Museum, Tokyo, Series D*, 13: 1-9.

———. 1990. *Nihonjin no Sosen*. Tokyo: Tokuma Bunko.

———. 1992. Skeletal morphology of the Jomon people. In *Japanese as a Member of the Asian and Pacific Populations,* ed. Hanihara Kazuro, pp. 53–63. Kyoto: Nichibunken.

———. 1994. Kojinkotsu ni miru hokubu Nihonjin no keishitsu. In *Kita Nihon no Kōkogaku: Minami to Kita no Chi'ikisei,* ed. Nihon Kōkogaku Kyōkai, pp. 100–123. Tokyo: Yoshikawa Kōbunakan.

Yamaguchi Jōji. 1991. Yayoi bunka seiritsuki no mokki. In *Yokoyama Kōichi Sensei Taikan Kinen Ronbunshū II: Nihon ni Okeru Hakki Yayoi Bunka no Seiritsu,* ed. Takakura Hiroaki, pp. 418–441. Fukuoka: Yokoyama Kōichi Taikan Kinen Jigyōkai.

Yamaguchi Nobuyoshi and Uno Shinkei. 1983. *Osayuki Iseki.* Kitakyushu: Kitakyūshū-shi Kyōiku Iinkai.

Yamamoto Takeo. 1976. *Kikō no Kataru Nihon no Rekishi.*

Yamamura Kozo. 1990. The growth of commerce in medieval Japan. In *The Cambridge History of Japan,* Vol. 3, ed. K. Yamamura, pp. 344–395. Cambridge: Cambridge University Press.

Yamamura Kozo and Kamiki Tetsuo. 1983. Silver mines and Sung coins—a monetary history of medieval and modern Japan in international perspective. In *Precious Metals in the Later Medieval and Early Modern Worlds,* ed. J. F. Richards, pp. 329–362. Durham, NC: Carolina Academic Press.

Yamanaka Shinsuke. 1997. *Ancient Agroecosystem, Cultivars and Crops Based on DNA Polymorphisms Extracted from Plant Remains.* M.Sc. Diss., Shizuoka University, Japan. (In Japanese, with English summary)

Yamanouchi Sugao. 1936a. Nihon kōkogaku no chitsujo. *Minerva* 1(4).

———. 1936b. Nihon kōkogaku no seidō. *Minerva* 1(6).

Yamao Yukihisa. 1990. Sanseiki no Nihon. In *Yamataikoku no Jidai,* ed. Tsude Hiroshi and Yamamoto Saburō, pp. 119–139. Tokyo: Mokujisha.

———. 1991. Yamataikoku to Kunakoku to no sensō. In *Yamataikoku Jidai no Higashi Nihon,* ed. National Museum of Japanese History, pp. 87–123. Tokyo: Rokkō.

Yamauchi Noritsugu. 1987. Yosumi tosshutsubo. *Yayoi Bunka no Kenkyū,* Vol. 8, ed. Kanaseki Hiroshi and Sahara Makoto, pp. 142–147. Tokyo: Yūzankaku.

Yamazaki Sumio. 1978. Jōmon nōkōron no genjō. *Rekishi Kōron* 4(3): 106–112.

———. 1980. Yayaoi bunka seiritsuki ni okeru doki no hennenteki kenkyū. In *Kagamiyama Takeshi Sensei Koki Kinen Kobunka Ronkō,* ed. Kagamiyama Takeshi Sensei Koki Kinen Ronbunshū Kankōkai.

———. 1989. Kyūshū no tottaimon-kei doki yōshiki. In *Jōmon Doki Taikan,* ed. Kobayashi Tatsuo, pp. 348–349. Tokyo: Shōgakkan.

———. 1991. Inasaku no hatsugen. *Kikan Kōkogaku* 37: 17–22.

Yan Wenming. 1991. China's earliest rice agriculture remains. *BIPPA* 10: 118–126.

Yanagita Kunio. 1978. Kaijō no Michi. Tokyo: Iwanami.

Yane Yoshimasa. 1984. Jōmon doki kara Yayoi doki e. In *Jōmon kara Yayoi e.* Nara: Tezukayama Kōkogaku Kenkyūjō.

———. 1987. Yayoi doki no tanjō to henbō. *Kikan Kōkogaku* 19: 18-23.

———. 1993. Ongagawa-shiki doki no seiritsu o megutte. In *Ron'en Kōkogaku,* pp. 267-329. Tokyo: Tensansha.

Yasuda Yoshinori. 1980. *Kankyō Kōkogaku Kotohajime.* Tokyo: Nihon Hōsō Kyōkai Books 365.

Yasumoto Biten. 1990. *Nihongo no Kigen o Saguru.* Tokyo: Tokuma Bunko.

———. 1991. *Shin Chōsengo de Man'yōshū wa Kaidoku Dekinai.* Tokyo: JICC.

Yi Kon-Mu.1991. Kankoku mumon doki no kishu to hennen. In *Nikkan Kōshō: Yayoi Jidai Hen,* ed. Oda Fujio and Han Byong-sam, pp. 26-31. Tokyo: Rokkō.

Yiengpruksawan, Mimi. 1993. The house of gold: Fujiwara Kiyohira's Konjikido. *MN* 48(1): 33-52.

Yokoyama Eisuke. 1990. *Satsumon Bunka.* New Science Press.

Yokoyama Kōichi. 1979. Hakeme gihō no genryū ni kansuru yobiteki kentō. *Kyūshū Bunkashi Kenkyūjō Kiyō* 24.

Yonekawa, H., K. Moriwaki, O. Goto, J. Watanabe, J. Hayashi, N. Miyashita, M. L. Petras, and Y. Tagashira. 1980. Relationship between laboratory mice and three subspecies of *Mus musculus domesticus* based on restriction endonuclease cleavage patterns of mitochondrial DNA. *Japanese Journal of Genetics* 55: 289-296.

Yonekawa, H., K. Moriwaki, O. Goto, J. Hayashi, J. Watanabe, N. Miyashita, M. L. Petras, and Y. Tagashira. 1981. Evolutionary relationships among five subspecies of *Mus musculus* based on restriction enzyme cleavage patterns of mitochondrial DNA. *Genetics* 98: 801-816.

Yonekawa, H., K. Moriwaki, O. Goto, N Miyashita, L. Shi, W. S. Cho, X-L Zhen, and T. Tagashira. 1988. Hybrid origin of Japanese mice *Mus musculus molosinus:* Evidence from restriction analysis of mitochondrial DNA. *Molecular Biology and Evolution* 5: 63-78.

Yoshidome Hidetoshi. 1993. Naka iseki no nijū kangō ikō. *Kōkogaku Kenkyū* 39(4): 132-133.

Yoshie Akio. 1995. Éviter la souillure: Le processus de civilisation dans le Japon ancien. *Annales* 50(2): 283-306.

Yoshikawa Kojiro. 1983. *Jinsai, Sorai, Norinaga: Three Classical Philologists of Mid-Tokugawa Japan.* Tokyo: Toho Gakkai.

Yoshimura Takehiko. 1991. *Kodai Ōken no Tenkai.* Tokyo: Shūeisha.

Yoshino Kosaku. 1992. *Cultural Nationalism in Contemporary Japan: A Sociological Enquiry.* London: Routledge.

Yoshino, M. 1982. Rekishi jidai ni okeru Nihon no kikō. *Kishō* 2614.

Yoshizaki Masakazu. 1963. Prehistoric culture in southern Sakhalin in the light of Japanese research. *AA* 1(2): 131-158.

———. 1986. Hokkaidō ni okeru chi'ikisei. In *Iwanami Kōza Nihon Kōkogaku,* Vol. 5, ed. Tozawa Mitsunori, pp. 289-324. Tokyo: Iwanami.

Young, John. 1958. *The Location of Yamatai: A Case Study in Japanese Historiography, 720-1945.* Baltimore, MD: The Johns Hopkins Press.

Yü Ying-Shih. 1967. *Trade and Expansion in Han China: A Study in the Structure of Sino-Barbarian Economic Relations*. Berkeley and Los Angeles: University of California Press.

Yuasa Isao, Yukio Saneshige, and Kichiro Okada. 1983. Geographical cline of allele frequency of group-specific component (GC) in the Japanese populations: An analysis of data obtained by immunoelectrophoresis. *JJHG* 28: 255–261.

Zvelebil, Marek. 1981. *From Forager to Farmer in the Boreal Zone: Reconstructing economic patterns through catchment analysis in prehistoric Finland*. Oxford: BAR Int. Ser. 115, Part I.

Zvelebil, Marek, and Kamil V. Zvelebil. 1988. Agricultural transition and Indo-European dispersals. *Antiquity* 62: 574–583.

Index

Abakuchi Cave (Iwate), 66
Augustine, St., 165
Aleuts, 36, 225
Andō clan, 219, 221, 223, 231, 242
anthropometric studies, 74-76, 78
Ainu, 5-6, 18-19, 30-40; anthropometric studies, 75-76; archaeology, 45, 207-208, 211-217; ethnicity and ethnogenesis, 3, 11, 12, 14-15, 180, 198, 206-232; genetics, 61, 69-74, 77, 81; Japanese views of, 30-33, 53; Kuril Ainu, 36, 232; language, 4, 90, 92, 97-99, 101-102; origins and usage of term Ainu, 31, 208; place-names, 98, 101; as pre-Japanese people, 34-39, 40; Sakhalin Ainu, 214, 226-227; skeletal biology, 60, 62, 66, 78; teeth, 68-69, 78; trading activities, 5, 207, 209, 212-213, 229
Akazawa Takeru, 50, 135, 143, 250n. 3
Altaic, 46, 88, 89, 251n. 1; doubts over language family, 83, 101; homelands, 85-86, 100; links with Japanese, 82-85
Amino Yoshihiko, 15, 17, 235-236, 241
Anglo-Saxons, 5, 10, 15, 156-159
Anthony, David, 149, 151-152
Aogashima, 78-79
Arai Hakuseki, 23, 26, 30, 53
Australia, 7, 69, 71, 165
Austroasiatic, 46, 84
Austronesian: languages, 82-85, 88-89, 92, 97, 101-102, 197; peoples, 46, 152-154, 159
Awazu (Shiga), 115

Baelz, Erwin von, 40-41, 45-46, 74-75, 78
barley *(Hordeum),* 105, 136, 211
Barnes, Gina, 51, 120, 166, 168, 189, 192
be (occupational groups), 192, 203
Bellwood, Peter, 4, 92, 148, 153-154, 243
broadleaf evergreen culture hypothesis, 104, 114-115
Bronze Age: Japan, 41, 44, 129; Korea, 97, 108, 120
Buddhism, 205, 237-239

cannibalism, 38
capitalism, 177-178
chashi (Ainu forts), 209-210, 216-217, 221, 224
chickens, 117
China: Austronesian expansion, 153-154; East Asian world-system, 183-184; genetics, 71-73, 81; immigration from, 46, 68; lack of lithic parallels with, 125; paleoanthropology in, 67-68; pig ritual, 131; role in Japanese historiography, 25-28,

54; Sinodonty, 69
Christendom, 237-238
Chŭlmun, 119
Chūsonji, 204-205
Confucianism, 24-26, 30, 238
core population, 5, 11-14, 17-19, 233, 236-237, 243
culture: concept in Japanese anthropology, 41-44; Japanese, 2, 13, 17-18, 46, 54, 234-236

Deagan, Kathleen, 165
demography: agricultural colonization, 17-18, 80-82, 91, 100; Jōmon, 104, 106, 138-143; Jōmon/Yayoi admixture, 70, 75-76, 79-81, 135, 145, 163-169; Yayoi, 142-143, 168
Dodo Yukio, 66
dogs, 76-77, 116, 164
Doi, Naomi, 67, 78
Doigahama (Yamaguchi), 62-63, 66, 68, 79, 107
dolmens, 119, 131-132
dōtaku (bronze bells), 169, 250n. 2
dry-field cultivation, 46, 114-115, 117, 241, 245
dual-structure hypothesis, 3, 53, 60-61, 68-69, 73-74, 77-78

Edwards, Walter, 47-48
Egami Namio, 45, 49, 91
Emishi, 33, 223, 242; language, 98; name, 194, 198; Northern Fujiwara as, 10, 204-205; as relict culture, 175; role of Yamato in ethnogenesis of, 179, 197-200, 203, 224
emperor (Japan), 14, 29, 47, 241; imperial ideology, 15-16, 23, 26, 35, 44, 47, 54-55, 235-236, 243. *See also* Jimmu
English: language, 7, 87, 157; people, 2, 12, 14-15, 164. *See also* Anglo-Saxons
Epi-Jōmon, 18, 52, 136, 208, 232; archaeology, 198, 211; skeletal biology, 66
Eskimos, 37, 176, 225
ethnicity and ethnogenesis: archaeology of, 52, 148, 157, 169, 249n. 2; core populations and, 11-14, 233-244; cultural traditions and, 54; definitions of, 6-11, 233; Japanese views of their, 2-3, 23, 52; world-systems theory, 179-182

Frank, A.G., 177, 181

genetic studies: dogs, 76-77; humans, 69-74, 77, 81; mice, 77
glottochronology, 4, 93-94
gourd *(Lagenaria),* 105
"Gurkha syndrome," 195

Hall, J.W., 179
Hanihara Kazurō, 60, 68, 69, 79-81
Harunari Hideji, 131, 132, 133, 136, 166, 250n. 3
Hashiguchi Tatsuya, 134, 147
Hateruma, 241
Hattori Shirō, 88, 93-94, 95-96, 97
Hayashi Razan, 25-26, 29
Hayato, 37, 89, 247, 252n. 6; and Southeast Asia, 175, 197; Yamato state and, 179, 194-197
Hechter, Michael, 5, 178-182, 200, 204, 206, 218
Heian period, 15, 95, 200, 239
Hemudu, 116
Himiko. *See* Pimiko
Hinomoto, 223-224, 242
Hiraizumi, 1-2, 185, 200, 204-205, 220, 248
Horseriders theory, 49, 91-92
horses, 192-193, 199, 200, 227, 241

ikor (Ainu prestige goods), 210, 214, 216
Imamura Keiji, 80, 139-141
iron, vii, 125, 129, 188, 207, 211, 213-214, 220, 223
Iroquois, 98, 154-156, 160, 187, 251n. 1
Itazuke (Fukuoka), 107, 109, 111-113, 119-120, 123, 125, 127, 130, 133

iyomante (bear ceremony), 209, 214, 216-217
Izu islands, 116, 136, 193
Izumo, 187

Japanese language, 2-4, 12, 16, 150; dialects of, 92-96, 100; genetic affiliations, 82-85; as mixed language, 83-84, 88-91
Jimmu, 14, 24-26, 28-32, 34-35, 188
Jinnō Shōtoki, 25, 238
Jōmon, 4-5, 11-12, 34, 44, 49, 53; cultivation, 104-105; DNA, 74; language, 4, 17, 82, 84, 88-90, 92, 99, 101-102; people, 3, 16-19, 69-71, 101, 135, 168, 249n. 1; pottery, 39, 45, 119-123, 137; skeletal biology, 62, 65, 132. *See also* Epi-Jōmon

Kaempfer, Engelbert, 28-29, 59
Kamchatka, 31-32
Kamegaoka pottery, 45, 151, 169
Kanaseki Takeo, 48
Karako-Kagi (Nara), 63-64, 107, 117
Kaya, 188, 202
Kazahari (Aomori), 105, 107-108, 112-113
Kibi, 187-188
Kikajin, 202-203
Kitabatake Chikafusa, 25, 238-239
Kita Sadakichi, 3, 40, 42, 45, 250n. 2
Kiyono Kenji, 40-41, 45, 48
Kobayashi Yukio, 190-191
Kofun: mounds, 184, 186-188, 190, 192; people, 65-68; period, 3, 40, 45-46, 49, 60, 89, 95, 132, 197, 243, 245
Koguryŏ: language, 96-97, 100; state, 201
Kojiki, 23-25, 37-38, 188, 194, 197, 238
Kokugaku (National Learning), 23-24, 26, 49
Korean peninsula, 15, 30, 54, 77, 97, 183, 239; archaeology, 108, 119-121, 123, 125, 128, 129-130, 131; ethnicity, 3, 10; human biology, 68, 69, 73, 75, 81; immigration from, 25-26, 28; language, 83, 86, 91-93, 96-97, 101, 150
Korpokunkur, 36-38, 40
Koryŏ, 15
Kumaso, 194-197, 242, 245-248
Kuril islands, 31-32, 36, 99, 199, 211, 214, 216, 226

language change, 4, 6-7, 86-87, 90-92, 159, 162, 164

Magarita (Fukuoka), 107, 117, 129, 163
Maher, John, 84-85, 89-90
Manchuria, 69, 72, 108, 199, 218, 227-231, 242
Man'yōshū, 94, 202
Marxism, 48-49, 52, 177, 236, 249n. 2
Mashiki Azamabaru (Okinawa), 65
matagi, 98, 251n. 3
Matsuo Bashō, 1-2, 248
Meiji, 32, 34-36, 47, 75-76, 94, 178, 235, 240, 243
Menda (Kumamoto), 245-248
mice, 77
Middle Ages: Europe, 237-238; Japan, 2, 15, 235, 241
migration theory, 5, 50-51, 70, 85, 90, 147-162
Miller, Roy A., 82-83, 85-87, 93, 95, 100, 150, 197, 252n. 3
millet, 104, 110, 136, 211; *Panicum,* 105, 108; *Setaria,* 105, 108
Milne, John, 36, 38, 41
Minami-mizote (Okayama), 107, 109-110, 113
Minatogawa (Okinawa), 67, 69, 251n. 3
Minerva Debate, 24, 44-45
Ming, 15, 178, 226-229
mirrors (bronze), 129, 183-184, 188-192, 245-246
Miura peninsula, 65, 143-145
Miwa (Nara), 107, 135
Mogami Tokunai, 31
mokkan (inscribed wooden tablets), 193

Mongoloids, 45, 60, 67, 73, 76-78, 207
Mongols, 69, 72, 226-228, 239
Moore, John, 6-9, 249n. 2
Morimoto Rokuji, 41-44
Morse, Edward S., 33-34, 37-39, 49
Moto'ori Norinaga, 26-27, 29, 54
Munro, Neil G., 37, 40
Murayama Shichirō, 84, 88, 96-97

Nabatake (Saga), 107, 111-112, 114, 116, 120, 123-125, 130, 133, 163
Nara period, 66, 93-95, 182, 239
nationalism, 10-11; Japan, 2-3, 23-24, 27, 34-35, 41, 44, 47-48, 53-55, 237-244
Native Americans, 38, 69, 71, 164-165, 203, 246, 250n. 4. *See also* Aleuts, Eskimos, Iroquois
Nāzakibaru (Okinawa), 137
Nihon, 238, 241
Nihonjinron, 234-235
Nihon Shoki, 23-24, 37-38, 188, 194-195, 197, 238-239, 252n. 9
Nishikawa Nagao, 41, 55
Nivkh, 67, 225-227
Northern Fujiwara, 1-2, 10, 200, 204-205, 218-220, 231

Ōbayashi Taryō, 46, 88-89, 239
Ohnuki-Tierney, Emiko, 50, 236
Oka Masao, 46, 49, 88-89
Okhotsk: culture, 67, 208, 211, 214, 216, 224, 225-229, 230; people, 67, 211-232
Okinawa, vii-viii, 26, 77, 133, 169-170, 206; ethnic identity, 3, 14, 52-53, 180, 237, 241-242, 243; human biology, 60, 65, 69, 78-79, 81; language (Ryukyuan), 4, 92-95, 100, 251n. 2; Plain Pottery found in, 123; plant cultivation, 115, 136-137; Satsuma conquest of, 178; shell trade, 189, 190, 211
Ōmori (Tokyo), 33-34, 38-39
Ongagawa pottery, 123, 133-135, 151-152, 168
Ōno Susumu, 84, 88, 151

orientalism, 234, 238

paddy fields, 47, 109, 111-112, 114, 136, 142, 168
Paekche, 97, 201-202
Paleolithic (Japan), 11-12, 50, 71, 99, 241
Perilla, 105
phytoliths (rice), 109-110, 112-113, 141, 144, 251n. 2
pigs, 115-117, 130-131
Pimiko, 184, 251n. 2, 252n. 5
Plain Pottery, 108, 119-121, 123-124, 129-131, 169-170
Polynesians, 68-69, 152-154
population. *See* demography
postprocessual archaeology, 148, 235
processual archaeology, 50, 147-148, 161
Puyŏ, 91, 97, 100

racism, 31, 35-36, 85
Renfrew, Colin, 4, 85, 90-92, 99, 101
rice, 107-115, 207; cultivation, vii, 17, 44, 46, 49, 51, 88, 93, 104, 108-115, 118, 133-134, 136, 144, 198; and ideology, 17, 50, 235-236
Ritsuryō: economy, 182, 193, 219; state, 15, 18, 196, 200, 224, 238, 241
Rodrigues, João, 27-28
Romans, 91, 156-159, 162
Rouse, Irving, 149-151, 160-162, 206
Ryukyus. *See* Okinawa

Sahara Makoto, 16, 50, 76, 104, 136
Sakhalin, 32, 67, 99, 178, 199, 211, 214, 216, 225-229, 253n. 3
Sakushu-kotoni River (Hokkaido), 107
Sannai Maruyama (Aomori), 115
Santan trade, 229, 253n. 4
Sasaki Kōmei, 3, 17, 46, 104, 114-115
Satsumon: Ainu culture and, 5, 18, 209, 211, 213-215, 226-227; period, 99, 136, 208, 225
Shimogōri-kuwanae (Oita), 107, 116, 127

Shinmachi (Fukuoka), 63, 107, 127, 132, 163
shiso. See *Perilla*
Siebold, Heinrich Philipp von, 34-35
Siebold, Philipp Franz von, 32-33
Song, 218, 228
Southeast Asia, 3, 18, 67-69, 74, 77, 90, 114, 178, 250n. 2; links with Japan, 61, 82, 84, 197, 201
stone tools, 33, 41, 108, 111, 123, 125-129, 135, 136, 140
Sunazawa (Aomori), 107, 119, 136, 151
Suye mura, 247-248, 254n. 1

Taga castle, 1, 185, 199
Taira no Masakado, 242
Taiwan, 10, 72-73, 77, 79, 153-154
Takamiya Hiroto, 136-137, 211
Tamil, 84, 88, 151
Tanegashima, 63, 65, 67, 79, 189
Tang, 202, 225, 231, 239
Tareyanagi (Aomori), 107, 151
taro *(Colocasia)*, 46, 110, 115-116, 136, 245, 248
teeth: ablation, 132, 164, 250n. 3, 251n. 3; Ainu, 68-69, 78; Jomon, 68-69, 78-79, 115-116; Sinodont & Sundadont, 68-69; Yayoi, 65, 69, 79
Tobinitai culture, 208, 225
Tokugawa: ethnicity, 201, 237, 240-241; historiography and ethnogenesis, 24-27, 29; world-system and, 177-178, 218-219
Torihama (Fukui), 105, 107
Torii Ryūzō, 37, 39-43, 45, 197, 250n. 2
Toro (Shizuoka), 47-48, 107
Tosaminato, 185, 220-221, 223
tottaimon pottery, 118, 121, 134-135, 168
Tsubai Ōtsukayama (Kyoto), 190-191
Tsuboi Shōgorō, 36-37
Tsuchigumo, 37, 40, 201
Tungusic languages, 83, 86, 89, 101
Turner, Christy, 68-69, 115-116
Uehara Nūribaru (Okinawa), 137
Uenoharu (Kumamoto), 105, 107, 112-113
Umehara Takeshi, 5, 18, 24, 52-54, 75, 233
Unger, J.M., 83, 92, 101
Usu 10 (Hokkaido), 63, 66, 185, 211, 232

Wa, 15, 30, 89, 184, 242
wakō, 15, 242-243
Wales, 12, 14
Wallerstein, I., 176-177, 180-182
Watanabe Hitoshi, 5, 50-51, 209
Wei zhi, 166, 183-184, 186-187, 196
Wilde, Oscar, 2
wooden artifacts, 47, 111-112, 123, 125-126, 135-136
world-systems theory, 5, 13, 176-182, 218-219, 228
Wu Taibo, 24-26, 28

yam *(Dioscorea)*, 110, 116, 139-141
Yamanouchi Sugao, 16, 42-46, 52
Yamatai, 88, 186, 252n. 3
Yamato state, 15, 95, 186-203, 246
Yanagita Kunio, 17, 136
Yane Yoshimasa, 121, 123, 164
Yayoi: agriculture, 18, 103, 108-118, 145; archaeological study of, 39-41, 44, 49-51, 52; burials, 131-132; DNA, 74; immigration in, 3-5, 50-51, 84, 89; Japanese core population and, 14; lithics, 123, 125, 127, 128; metallurgy, 129; period in Okinawa, 136-137, 189; pottery, 34, 39-40, 119-123, 165-166, 168-169; settlements, 129-130, 135, 143; skeletal biology, 62, 65, 163-164; transition to in Kanto, 137-145; wooden tools, 125-126. *See also* Pimiko, Yamatai
Yoshinogari (Saga), 62-63, 68, 107, 116-117, 185, 189
Yuan dynasty. *See* Mongols
Yuan shi, 226

About the Author

Mark Hudson, who holds a doctorate in archaeology and anthropology from The Australian National University, is Foreign Professor of Anthropology at the University of Tsukuba, Japan. He is co-editor of *Multicultural Japan: Palaeolithic to Postmodern* (Cambridge University Press, 1996). His current research focuses on skeletal biology and subsistence change in prehistoric Okinawa.